STRANGER THAN FICTION

WEIRD SHIT AND BIZARRE BRITS

Or, the gathering together of many interesting stories from British history for the benefit and help of ladies, gentlemen, and anyone else of an inquisitive disposition. Written with much sauciness and mirth so it may please the reader and satisfy their curiosity to seek out further knowledge.

STRANGER THAN FICTION

WEIRD SHIT AND BIZARRE BRITS

Alan Ferguson

First published in England in 2026 by
Telos Publishing Ltd
139 Whitstable Road, Canterbury, Kent CT2 8EQ, England
www.telos.co.uk

Telos Publishing Ltd values feedback.
Please e-mail us with any comments you may have about this book to:
feedback@telos.co.uk

ISBN: 978-1-84583-260-5

British Library Cataloguing in Publication Data.
A catalogue record for this book is available from the British Library.

For the family

THE BIT AT THE BEGINNING

Britain is a small island in the centre of the world map occupying less than one percent of the Earth's land mass with less than one percent of the Earth's population. It is also a major player in international affairs and an economic and military power with considerable political and cultural influence around the world.

Britain is a unique four-nation state; a global power, cultural superpower and a leading soft power; a G7 member state with the world's sixth largest economy; an NPT designated nuclear weapons state; a permanent member of the UN Security Council; a prominent NATO member and the *de facto* head of the Commonwealth of Nations. Britain is also a country with a big heart and great resilience which promotes its values of democracy, fair play, the rule of law, individual liberty, free speech and tolerance around the world.

No other country relative to its size contributes more to pop culture with its globally recognised brands, music, theatre, cinema, fashion, art, dance, design, architecture and television. Britain also has more famous authors, poets and playwrights than any other country with their work spanning many literary styles and every period of history. Everything from *The Canterbury Tales* to *Fifty Shades of Grey*.

Britain has some of the world's oldest universities. The UK system of higher education consistently performs well in international rankings with the 'Oxbridge' universities considered to be two of the wealthiest, most prestigious and elite learning institutions in the world. Britain has made notable contributions in philosophy, science, economics, technology, politics, religion and medicine, and has the highest number of Nobel Prize winners than any other country apart from the USA.

Britain has an unparalleled sporting history and an unrivalled reputation for being a country noted for the diversity of its sporting interests. It is widely recognised as the birthplace of modern sport with the rules for most games now played throughout the world being invented or codified in Victorian Britain.

The people of Britain are also unique. Britishness is a thing and so is Johnny Foreigner's love of Britain, its people, its history and its culture. The Brits seem to have unwittingly become the world leaders in reclusive, non-conformist, obsessive or exaggerated behaviour. Whilst many cultures prefer to condemn people who think outside the box, Britain seems to embrace them and has become a natural habitat for the individualist. However, eccentricity is also associated with genius and creativity. In fact, the English philosopher John Stuart Mill (1806-1873) once wrote: 'The amount of eccentricity in a society has generally been proportional to the amount of genius, mental vigour and moral courage which it contained.'

London is the capital of the world: one of the most popular tourist destinations, the world's most culturally diverse capital city and one of the world's leading cultural and financial centres. As the English writer Samuel Johnson (1709-1784) famously said: 'When a man is tired of London, he is tired of life; for there is in London all that life can afford.'

English is the most popular and widely spoken language in the world by the number of speakers (after combining native and non-native speakers). It is the most widely taught second language and is either the official language or one of the official languages in over sixty countries. It's the only approved language for aeronautical and maritime communication and the most commonly used language in science, diplomacy and commerce. It is also the most widely published language in the world and the co-official language of the United Nations (UN) and many other international and regional organisations such as the European Union (EU).

Sterling is the world's oldest currency in continuous use, one of the world's most widely traded currencies in the foreign exchange market and one of only five currencies to be included in the IMF's basket of global reserve currencies known as the Special Drawing Rights (SDR). The sign (£) is also one of the world's most recognisable and attractive little squiggles!

Britain was the first industrialised country in the world leading to significant changes in manufacturing techniques, the development of new factory systems and the growth of railway and steamship transportation links. British scientists, explorers, physicians and engineers have all changed the world with their imagination; British writers, artists, actors and musicians have entertained people all over the world; British sportsmen and women have dominated their sports and set world records around the world, and British inventors have invented just about everything that was worth inventing! From Kit-Kats and disposable nappies to television and the postage stamp!

And then there's British history ...

Britain is a country with a fascinating and vibrant past; a history that has impacted the rest of the world like no other, mainly due to the rapid expansion of the British Empire (1497-1997) in the eighteenth and nineteenth centuries. It has generally been acknowledged as the greatest empire the world has ever seen! At its height, between the two World Wars, it covered almost a quarter of the Earth's total land area and ruled over one fifth of its population!

The pages of British history are peppered with so many famous events and colourful characters that are as well known in the far flung corners of the world as they are in Britain; everything from the signing of the Magna Carta (1215), the Gunpowder Plot (1605) and the Battle of Waterloo (1815), and everyone from King Arthur, Robin Hood and Florence Nightingale to Henry VIII, William Shakespeare, and of course, Winston Churchill, who many people consider to be the greatest Briton of them all.

Stranger Than Fiction is a random and slightly irreverent compilation of the best *funny ha-ha* and *funny peculiar* stories about the weird events and the much weirder people that have graced the pages of British history. Everybody likes to laugh at how they did things in the old days and the further back in time you go, the funnier and more peculiar things seem to get. There are some well-known stories, a few anecdotes, a bit of folklore and lots of obscure and very bizarre tales from days gone by. In fact, there are over 250 of them which date from the bloodthirsty Dark Ages right up until modern times. Everything from an exploding William the Conqueror to a woman who gave birth to rabbits!

In this book the focus is on British people and so their dates of birth and death have been included whenever possible. Likewise, the text is peppered with places and organisations and every attempt has been made to provide clarity where it seemed appropriate.

The stories are random and so is the order in which they appear. It just seemed more ridiculous that way.

Enjoy!

Not to know what has been transacted in former times is to be always a child. If no use is made of the labours of past ages, the world must remain always in the infancy of knowledge.

Marcus Tullius Cicero
ROMAN STATESMAN/LAWYER

CONTENTS

CONTENTS

CONTENTS

CONTENTS

the fastest knife in the west end

The pioneering Scottish surgeon Robert Liston (1794-1847) was noted for his speed and skill with a knife. Before anesthetic was used for surgical procedures, haste was of the essence to minimise a patient's pain and suffering and improve the odds of their survival, and it was well-known that Robert could remove a limb in just a matter of seconds!

He began his distinguished medical career at the Edinburgh Royal Infirmary in 1818. He was an abrupt and rather argumentative man known for his brusque manner but he was also unfailingly kind to the poor, frequently tending to the sick in the poorer parts of the city, which in turn led to conflicts with some of his less benevolent colleagues who disapproved of his extra-curricular charitable work. In 1835, to escape his detractors, he moved to London to begin work at the newly founded University College Hospital and it was here in his role as Professor of Clinical Surgery that he perfected his rather unorthodox knife skills ...

The surgeon and anaesthetist Richard Gordon (1921-2017), best known to the public as the author of the popular and long-running *Doctor* series of comic novels beginning with *Doctor in the House* (1952), wrote about Robert in his book *Great Medical Disasters* (1983), describing him as 'the fastest knife in the West End' who 'sprung across the blood-stained boards upon his swooning, sweating, strapped-down patient like a duellist' whilst encouraging his students gathered in the iron-railinged galleries around the operating room to time him with their pocket watches. 'Everyone swore that the first flash of his knife was followed so swiftly by the rasp of saw on bone that sight and sound seemed simultaneous.'

A typical amputation might have taken two or three minutes to perform but Robert was once timed at only 28 seconds. Between 1835 and 1840, he performed a total of 66 amputations and only ten of his patients died, which equated to a mortality rate of less than one in six. Not bad considering the average rate for such operations at the time was about one in four.

But just like everyone else, he wasn't perfect. Even the Victorian Edward Scissorhands was prone to making a few mistakes. On one occasion he amputated a leg but in his haste, he also lopped off the patient's testicles! In a second well-documented case, whilst performing another high-speed leg amputation, he slashed the coat tails of a spectator and amputated his assistant's fingers! The spectator dropped down dead from shock and the assistant died from gangrene a few days later ... as did the patient. This incident is famous for being the only surgical operation ever to have taken place resulting in a 300 percent mortality rate!

Note: On 21 December 1846, Robert performed the first operation in Europe using a modern anaesthetic ...

The patient, Frederick Churchill, underwent a lower limb amputation using diethyl ether, a sweet-smelling and colourless liquid which induces sedation. He was given a rubber tube to hold in his mouth and told to breathe through it for two or three minutes to administer the anesthetic. To the amazement of all the operating room staff, the patient soon became quite still. As always, Robert was ready and waiting with his knife and took only thirty seconds to hack off the infected limb. A few minutes later Frederick awoke and exclaimed: 'When are you going to begin?' much to the amusement of everyone present. When he then seemed to have second thoughts and yelled: 'Take me back. I can't have it done' everyone laughed their little socks off. Only when his amputated leg was held up and dangled in front of his face did he finally accept that the operation had already been carried out.

the posthumous execution of oliver cromwell

The famous English soldier and statesman Oliver Cromwell (1599-1658) died on 3 September 1658.

After wrapping his body in four layers of grave cloth and sealing it inside a lead coffin, which in turn was placed inside a wooden coffin, his corpse was still stinking up the place and the decision was taken to bury him as quickly and as quietly as possible at a private ceremony some two weeks before his state funeral was due to take place. As a result, the body which lay in state at Somerset House in London was just an ornately-dressed wooden mannequin with a wax face mask and the coffin which was then transported through the streets of London to Westminster Abbey during the official public funeral ceremony on 23 November 1658 was most probably empty.

More than two years after his death, Oliver Cromwell was then executed!

After the Restoration (1660), the Indemnity and Oblivion Act 1660 was passed to exonerate anyone who had committed crimes during the English Civil War (1642-1651) and the Interregnum (1649-1660) with the exception of people accused of murder, piracy, buggery, rape, witchcraft and bestiality. Those people specifically named and shamed in the act of being involved in the regicide of Charles I (1600-1649) were also exempt from a pardon.

Charles II (1630-1685) ordered the arrest and trial of everyone who'd played a part in overthrowing his father. Of the 59 men who'd signed his death warrant, many of them were hanged while others were imprisoned for life. Even those who'd died in the interim weren't spared the wrath of the king. Many had their bodies exhumed and reburied in communal pits with three of the worst offenders also being submitted to a very public posthumous execution ...

On 26 January 1661, the bodies of Oliver Cromwell, John Bradshaw (1602-1659) (President of the High Court of Justice) and Henry Ireton (1611-1651) (Oliver Cromwell's son-in-law and a high-ranking official in the Parliamentary Army) were disinterred from their tombs in Westminster Abbey. Then, on the morning of 30 January 1661, exactly twelve years to the day after the execution of Charles I, the three shrouded bodies were placed in open coffins, thrown on the back of a cart and taken to the gallows at Tyburn in London where they were strung up in front of a bemused crowd.

The three heads were later displayed on long wooden poles outside of Westminster Hall and what little remained of their rotting corpses was just dumped in an unmarked pit underneath the Tyburn gallows. The heads then remained on display as a sinister reminder to any other would-be conspirators for over 25 years! The noted diarist Samuel Pepys (1633-1703) recorded seeing them in his diary entry for 5 February 1661: 'My wife and I by water to Westminster. She to her mother's and I to Westminster Hall ... Into the Hall and there saw my Lord Treasurer (who was sworn to-day at the Exchequer, with a great company of Lords and persons of honour to attend him) go up to the Treasury Offices, and take possession thereof; and also saw the heads of Cromwell, Bradshaw and Ireton, set up upon the further end of the Hall.'

OLIVER CROMWELL'S WELL-TRAVELLED HEAD

In 1685, a fierce storm snapped the pole displaying Oliver Cromwell's head and it fell to the ground. It was found by a sentry who took it home with him and hid it in his chimney. On his deathbed, he bequeathed it to his daughter. It's unclear if the poor girl received any money or property or jewellery ... or anything else worth having or just that old rotting head which once belonged to someone famous!

For many years afterwards, the head passed from one private collector or one museum to another ...

Around 1710, it became the property of a collector of curiosities called Mr Claudius Du Puy who put it on display with all the other weird shit he'd collected for his internationally famous *Ripley's Believe It or Not!*-style museum in London. Then, sometime later it came into the possession of the failed comedian and drunkard Samuel Russell. He was a poor man who squandered all his money on drink, so it was inevitable that sooner or later, he'd be forced to sell it. This he did in 1787 to James Cox (c.1723-1800), a prominent jeweller, goldsmith and entrepreneur, who gave him £118 for it.

Twelve years later, James Cox then sold it for £230 to three brothers, who later included it in an exhibition of Cromwell-related memorabilia they organised in 1799. The head remained with the daughters of one of these brothers and in 1814 they sold it to their family physician Dr Josiah Wilkinson, a collector of Cromwellian artefacts. It then stayed in his family for the next 146 years before it was donated to the Sidney Sussex College (University of Cambridge) in 1960.

On 25 March 1960, it was finally interred in a secret location somewhere within the grounds of the university, preserved in the oak box in which the Wilkinson family had kept the head since 1814.

the berners street hoax

The famous hoax was perpetrated by the young playboy prankster Theodore Hook (1788-1841). He'd made a bet with his mate Samuel Beazley (1786-1851) that he could transform any anonymous house into the most talked about address in London within one week. The house he chose for the wager was 54 Berners Street, Westminster (London) belonging to an unassuming widow called Mary Tottingham.

It all began when Theo sent out hundreds of letters in her name requesting various deliveries and the presence of numerous visitors on one particular day, 27 November 1810. As she was a wealthy woman of good social standing and lived in a posh neighbourhood, Theo gambled that all of these requests would be met.

And he wasn't wrong ...

The house was first visited at 5.00am by a succession of chimney sweeps, then a fleet of coal carts, and then a series of other tradesmen, professional folk and dignitaries such as auctioneers, wigmakers, musicians, pastry chefs, doctors, grocers, lawyers, shoemakers, bakers, butchers and fishmongers. There was even a long procession of vicars and priests who'd been summoned to the house to comfort a dying relative! Dignitaries included Prince Frederick Duke of York and Albany (1763-1827), the Governor of the Bank of England and the Lord Mayor of London. At one point, even an undertaker turned up on the doorstep bearing a made-to-measure coffin for poor Mrs T.

The final visitors were a group of young people who arrived at around 5.00pm hoping to be interviewed for a job as a domestic servant.

Berners Street had quickly become congested with all the toing and froing and all the onlookers who'd gathered to watch all that toing and froing unfold. The police were called to the scene but it wasn't until well into the evening when they were able to disperse the large crowds and restore order. Meanwhile, Theo and Sam had been hiding inside a house across the street watching all the commotion and having a right old giggle about it all.

The Berners Street Hoax generated enormous public interest. Newspapers described it at length and it became one of the most notable and talked-about events of the time, and the source for many comic ballads and cartoons.

Although the police began an investigation into the hoax, nobody was ever arrested or prosecuted.

It wasn't until many years later that Theo owned up to being the perpetrator.

the first encyclopedia

The earliest surviving English language encyclopedia *Omne Bonum* (Every Good Thing) (c.1375) was compiled by the government clerk James le Palmer (fl.1327-c.1375) and extends to four-volumes containing 1,100 folia with around 650 illustrations. Entries appeared in a rough alphabetical order (being grouped together by their first letter) for topics such as theology, canon law, geography and natural history. In the book's preface, the writer explained how he'd compiled the book with 'great labour and with unwavering mental striving' for people who 'wish to seek learning and shut out sloth and who desire to occupy themselves with good things.' He also claimed that his fancy new encyclopedia 'would be sufficient for a person of moderate learning without reference to any other book.'

But it was also unfinished, containing only one entry each for the letters N to Z, so it wasn't really much use to anyone!

the gentlemanly art of combat

The English martial art of Bartitsu invented in 1898 by the ex-railway engineer E W Barton-Wright (1860-1951) combined elements of various fighting styles such as boxing, jujitsu, cane-fighting and savate, and was designed as a method of self-defence for young Victorian gentlemen. It was probably the first example of a mixed martial art after deliberately combining numerous skills from both the European and Asian styles of fighting.

After spending three years in Japan where he'd learnt jujitsu, E W returned to Britain, quit his job and started to develop a new self-defence technique, taking all the best bits from the European and Japanese disciplines and incorporating a few of his own using everyday objects such as umbrellas, walking sticks, canes and even raincoats as tools for fighting off ruffians and scoundrels.

The principal aims of Bartitsu were 'to disturb the equilibrium of your assailant, to surprise him before he has time to regain his balance and use his strength, and if necessary to subject the joints of any parts of his body…to strains that they are anatomically and mechanically unable to resist' and E W explained how all this could be achieved by organising demonstrations and exhibitions, writing magazine articles, publishing a manual *The New Art of Self Defence* (1899) and setting up the Bartitsu Academy of Arms and Physical Culture (The Bartitsu Club) in Soho (London) where the best instructors were employed to train the *bartitsukas* (the practitioners of Bartitsu) in the art of his new self-defence discipline.

The popularity of Bartitsu was widespread in Britain amongst politicians, military men and the posh folk of the day. But not for very long. After just a few years everyone seemed to lose interest in it and by 1902 E W was forced to shut his club and change careers again.

But at least he'd managed to gain support for his new way of fighting from one of the most famous men of the age. The great Victorian detective Sherlock Holmes had evidently studied and practiced the martial art, making reference to it in the short story 'The Adventure of the Empty House' (1903): 'I have some knowledge of Baritsu [sic], or the Japanese system of wrestling, which has more than once been very useful to me.' Sherlock might have been a big fan but his assistant John Watson (who was supposedly narrating the story) obviously wasn't. He couldn't even spell it correctly!

It's probably only because Bartitsu was mentioned in this story that it's been remembered at all. The original craze only lasted about four years and despite E W's continual but ill-fated attempts to revive it, Bartitsu never returned to prominence during his lifetime ... or anyone else's lifetime since.

the first dead celebrity

Thomas Becket (c.1119-1170) became the new Archbishop of Canterbury on 3 June 1162. He was in the job for eight years and was known to be one of the most devout and pious clergymen of the twelfth century.

As a young man, his best mate was the future Henry II (1133-1189), so when Henry acceded to the throne in 1154, Thomas was appointed to the role of Lord Chancellor. Everything was hunky-dory for a few years until he took up the archbishop's job and started banging on about the rights and privileges of the church, arguing that it was more powerful than the state and shouldn't be subjected to the same laws of the land as everyone else. Henry was not best pleased. He'd expected his BFF to be more subservient to the crown but as it turned out, he was just as bad, if not worse, than his predecessors. Things got so bad that Thomas was forced to seek sanctuary in France in 1164 after being convicted of showing contempt for royal authority and only returned to England in 1170 after a peace deal between Henry and Thomas was brokered by Pope Alexander III.

But Thomas never changed his ways and continued slagging off the king whenever he got the chance...

On Christmas Day in 1170, he delivered another one of his hysterical, fire-and-brimstone sermons at Canterbury Cathedral; Henry got to hear about it and flew into a rage. At some point during his meltdown, he yelled these fateful words: 'Will no one rid me of this turbulent priest?' Unfortunately, they were misinterpreted as a royal command when overheard by four overly-zealous knights, Hugh de Morville, Reginald Fitzurse, William de Tracy and Richard le Breton. They immediately jumped on their horses and rode off to Canterbury as fast as the wind would carry them to confront the treacherous clergyman ...

On 29 December 1170, the knights stormed into Canterbury Cathedral with their swords drawn and demanded that Thomas accompany them back to Winchester in Hampshire and submit to the king's will. When he refused and announced that he was prepared to die for his faith, the knights killed him there and then. Based on one monk's eyewitness account of the killing, his skull cracked open as he fell with blood and brain matter scattering across the cathedral floor! The assassins then fled north to Hugh de Morville's castle at Knaresborough in North Yorkshire. Although they were never pursued or prosecuted by Henry, they were later excommunicated by the Catholic Church. Seeking forgiveness, the knights then travelled to Rome where they were ordered by the Pope to serve as knights in the Holy Land for fourteen years.

As news of the murder spread, Henry was forced to seek forgiveness from the church and only avoided excommunication by promising to lead a crusade to the Holy Land. But he never actually went anywhere, preferring instead to stay in England to try and exploit the growing cult around the dead clergyman for his own ends.

Thomas was buried in a simple marble tomb in the crypt of Canterbury Cathedral.

The perception of him being the father of the poor and the comforter of the sorrowful was vigorously promoted by the Catholic Church. Since the man was now everybody's favourite martyr, pilgrims arrived from far and wide to pay homage and the cathedral monks weren't slow in exploiting his popularity for their own gain by selling off small flasks of *St Thomas' Water* (mixture of his blood and water) to the gullible pilgrims as a way of earning some extra cash. Images of Thomas became commonplace and manuscripts, wall paintings and stained glass windows were embellished with scenes of his life and death. A type of 'Becketmania' swept across Europe with pictures of him adorning walls from Iceland to Palestine. Even Henry II visited the tomb. Although he took his sweet time about it. He didn't turn up until 1174 and only then because it was supposed to be an act of penance for his involvement in the murder. There's no mention of him stopping off at the gift shop on his way out to by any *St Thomas' Water* either!

In 1220, his remains were moved to a new gold-plated and bejewelled shrine in the cathedral's recently completed Trinity Chapel.

This shrine stood until it was destroyed in 1538 on the orders of Henry VIII (1491-1547) during the Dissolution of the Monasteries (1536-1541). His bones were then scattered 'far and wide' and all mention of his name was prohibited.

The only bit of medieval literature anyone has ever heard of and one of the most important and revered works in the English language was also dedicated to Thomas. *The Canterbury Tales* (1397-1400) by Geoffrey Chaucer (c.1343-1400) contains 24 short stories written mainly in verse which are presented as a story-telling contest by a group of pilgrims travelling from London to Canterbury to visit his shrine.

Thomas has since been venerated as a saint and a martyr by both the Anglican and Catholic churches. The story of his life (but more especially his death) remains popular today with pilgrims and tourists still arriving from all across the world to visit Canterbury Cathedral and see the spot where he was slain.

voyaging through the suez canal

The Suez Canal is a 120-mile (193km) long man-made waterway connecting the Mediterranean Sea and the Indian Ocean via the Red Sea which has provided a direct shipping route between Europe and Asia since it was opened in 1869. Construction began at the northern Port Said [Egypt] end of the canal in early 1859 and took ten years to complete using an estimated workforce of around 1,500,000 men.

It was mainly a French project; planned by them, designed by them and financed by them, so it was only to be expected that the French would lead the opening day celebrations. The French imperial yacht *L'Aigle* with Empress Eugénie de Montijo aboard was supposed to be the first ship to pass through the canal, however, the captain of the British survey ship HMS *Newport* George Nares (1831-1915) had other ideas …

The night before the grand opening on 17 November 1869, under the cover of darkness and without lights, he cleverly manoeuvred his vessel past the mass of waiting ships until it was in front of the moored French yacht. The following morning the French were horrified to discover that the Royal Navy ship was now first in line to travel through the canal. They were even more horrified to discover that it had been positioned in such a way that it couldn't be passed and they'd be forced to let it lead the way.

As a consequence, the French were denied the honour of completing the first transit through the canal.

Although George received an official reprimand from the Admiralty, behind closed doors, where there were no diplomatic niceties to follow, he received nothing but praise for his outstanding seamanship and got a big slap on the back for getting one over on the French!

a day out at bethlem hospital

Bethlem Royal Hospital was founded in 1297 as the Priory of St Mary of Bethlehem by the Italian clergyman Goffredo de Prefetti on land just outside of the London walls in the parish of St Botolph [Bishopsgate] as a charitable institution devoted to healing sick paupers. The original hospital, which was just a single-storey building with twelve small rooms, a chapel and a courtyard, remained at this site until 1676 before relocating to Moorfields (City of London) where the open spaces were thought to be more conducive to a patient's health.

Although the hospital was originally intended for people with physical disabilities, sometime during the fourteenth century, the first patients showing signs of mental illness (which included learning disabilities, falling sickness (epilepsy) and dementia) were also admitted and in the following years, the hospital slowly evolved into the world's first dedicated psychiatric institution. Doctors believed that a patient's 'melancholic humour' was a disease of the body and not the brain and could easily be cured by bleeding from the veins or inducing bouts of vomiting and diarrhoea to rid them of their madness! They would also beat them, shave their heads, dunk them in cold baths or just leave them chained naked to the walls as part of their unique treatment plan!

The hospital came to be known as Bethlehem Hospital, later abbreviated to 'Bethlem' or 'Bedlem'/'Bedlam' [modern spelling] and the word soon entered into everyday language to signify mayhem or madness.

By the mid-eighteenth century the 'crackbrained' patients at Bethlem Hospital had become a must-see tourist attraction, second only in popularity to St Paul's Cathedral. Tens of thousands of Londoners paid just a few pennies for the privilege of being admitted to the cells to taunt and abuse the patients or just stare at them banging their heads against the wall.

By modern standards, this seems cruel and inhumane but the eighteenth century doctors believed that madness robbed the patients of any shame and emotion, so it was perfectly OK to take the piss out of them! Some were verbally abused whilst others were poked with sticks, physically assaulted, sexually harassed or just goaded into doing or saying something ridiculous. Those patients who were incapable of conversation tried to dissuade people from staring at them by spitting or throwing objects. The admission prices and occasional donations raised around £450 a year for the hospital whilst the staff topped up their meagre wages by taking bribes for organising tours around the cells. Many famous people of the day such as the diarist Samuel Pepys (1633-1703), the writers Edward Ward (1667-1731) and Samuel Johnson (1709-1784) and the artist William Hogarth (1697-1764) visited Bethlem Hospital at some time or another and wrote about their experiences.

It wasn't just the tourists who arrived in great numbers at Bethlem Hospital. The place also attracted prostitutes, pickpockets and vendors selling food, drink and trinkets with Edward Ward writing in his diary that it was 'an almshouse for madmen, a showing-room for whores, a sure market for lechers [and] a dry walk for loiterers.'

Bethlem Hospital was so popular, especially during the holiday periods such as Christmas and Easter, that it led to severe overcrowding and riotous behaviour by both patients and visitors alike, and by the end of the 1780s, access became limited to private tours accompanied by the hospital governor or a senior officer.

By the end of the nineteenth century these public visits had stopped altogether.

There was never much chance of anyone ever being cured at Bethlem

Hospital. Instead, the patients were more likely to suffer serious injury, illness or even die from the harsh and unsanitary conditions. There were widespread reports of alcoholism amongst the staff and it wasn't uncommon for the male employees to make improper visits to the cells of female patients whenever they felt the need!

There were no government inspectors to check on the patients or the conditions inside Bethlem Hospital. It wasn't until 1814 when the Quaker philanthropist Edward Wakefield (1774-1854) and a small group of concerned MPs gained admission to the site that the full horrors of Bethlem Hospital became known to the outside world. The building may have looked magnificent from the outside but inside it was dark and cold with no glazed windows and no hot water. The cells were small, dirty and overcrowded with the patients left unattended and chained to their beds. Many were completely naked with just a single blanket to protect them from the cold.

In 1815, the hospital was moved to another site at St George's Fields in Southwark with new doctors and new staff operating under much stricter regulations campaigned for by Edward Wakefield and other social reformers of the day.

The hospital moved to its present site in Beckenham (London) in 1930.

the alexandra limp

Alexandra of Denmark (1844-1925) married the future king Edward VII (1841-1910) on 10 March 1863.

The new princess was very popular with the British public and her fashion sense was greatly admired and copied. It wasn't uncommon for her high-society female fans to mimic her style, even wearing chokers, which the princess only wore to cover a scar on her neck but they wore simply to appear chic and trendy.

But then things got a bit silly after a bout of rheumatic fever left the princess with a pronounced limp …

The fashionable young ladies of the day began imitating her limp by using a walking stick, as the Princess was forced to do on occasions to help her get around, or by wearing odd-sized shoes to make it awkward for them to walk. Then the canny shoemakers cottoned-on to this new bizarre fashion and started selling mismatched shoes, one with a high(ish) heel and the other without a heel, to help their idiotic customers recreate the royal deformity more accurately. One particular Edinburgh shoemaker even advertised the shoes as *The Alexandra.*

The *Dundee Courier and Argus* commented: 'Some remarkably foolish things have been done in imitation of royalty but this is an act which involves a spice of wickedness as well as of folly. There must be a line at which even fashionable folly may be expected to stop short and this line ought to be drawn at the caricaturing of human infirmity.'

Mercifully, it was a short lived fashion, probably because it was just so bloody daft!

It wasn't long before the ladies discarded their odd shoes and started buying normal footwear again. Instead, they started dressing in tight, clingy skirts. In fact, these skirts were so tight and clingy that yet again they were having difficulty in walking properly, seemingly waddling along the pavements of the nation's cities like penguins, as if their feet were tied together with chains!

name calling in the seventeenth century

The Puritans were a religious reform movement within the Church of England which emerged in the mid-sixteenth century.

They were mainly Calvinists and Presbyterians who shared a common dislike of the government and the church. They were dissatisfied with the limited extent of the English Reformation (1527-1590) initiated by Henry VIII (1491-1547) and advocated for much stricter religious reforms, a rigorous enforcement of public morality and the creation of a more disciplined and God fearing society. They eventually seized power in England after the English Civil War (1642-1651) and established the Commonwealth of England (1649-1660) under the leadership of Oliver Cromwell (1599-1658). For over a century, they argued amongst themselves, persecuted Catholics, fought a civil war and still had time to set up a few colonies in the New World.

These guys were such a cheerless bunch of oddballs, it was no surprise to anyone when they quickly stopped people from having a good time by outlawing theatre, sports, drinking, gambling, dancing, popular songs and the wearing of makeup or colourful clothing. They even banned Christmas! Between 1644 and 1659, celebrating the holiday was outlawed by the Puritan-dominated English parliament because it was seen as a Pagan festival and just a poor excuse for 'giving liberty to carnal and sensual delights.' All singing, dancing and merriment was banned with shops and markets forced to stay open on Christmas Day. Soldiers patrolled the streets to enforce the law, churches were locked and everyone had a thoroughly miserable time!

Rather bizarrely, the Puritans liked to demonstrate their faith and devotion to God by lumbering their kids with very long and overly-religious hortatory names. Although a wide variety of Hebrew names had been in common use since *The Great Bible* (1539) became readily accessible, they weren't really humble or pious enough for them, so they invented their own, naming their kids after virtues or religious slogans as a way of ensuring they were constantly reminded of sin and pain and sacrifice. Most children escaped lightly by being baptised as *Hope* or *Prudence* or some other equally innocuous name, others were saddled with *Abstinence* or *Obedience* or *Forsaken*, whilst the unlucky ones got stuck with *Fear-Not* or *Sorry-for-Sin* or *Fight-the-Good-Fight-of-Faith*. But the really, really unlucky ones were the Barebone kids. Their father, Praise-God Barebone (c.1598-1679) was a preacher, Fifth Monarchist and all-round religious nut. He named his eldest son *If-Christ-Had-Not-Died-For-Thee-Thou-Hadst-Been-Damned* (c.1640-c.1698). Which was probably shortened to just *Damned* when his mum called him in for his tea! Not surprisingly, he later changed it to Nicholas. Praise-God's other kids didn't fare much better as they were baptised *Fear-God* and *Jesus-Christ-Came-Into-the-World-to-Save*.

But perhaps the harshest name of them all belonged to a kid baptised in the village of Warbleton, East Sussex on 28 September 1589. His parents were either super cruel or super Puritan because they named him *No-Merit*. Whoever they were, it's probably fair to assume they had a pretty joyless childhood. The non-Puritan kids must have been queuing up to take the piss!

the stuff of legends

BURNING THE CAKES

Alfred the Great (c.849-899) was the King of Wessex [871-899] and the King of the Saxons [886-899] and also the earliest English monarch that everyone has heard of. Alfred was seen as a devout Christian ruler and was reputed to have been a learned and merciful man who encouraged education and enhanced the quality of life for his people; he united all the Saxon kingdoms, improved the country's legal system and military structure, and is one of only two English monarchs afforded the epithet of 'great.'

And yet, despite all this, he's only remembered for burning a few cakes! Which probably weren't cakes but loaves of bread.

After the Vikings launched a surprise attack on the West Saxon stronghold of Chippenham, Wiltshire, in early January 878, Alfred was forced to flee into the Somerset Levels with his family and a few loyal followers, taking refuge on Athelney, a small island in the marshlands. At some point, he sought shelter in the home of an old peasant woman, who apparently asked him to watch her cakes (or loaves) that were baking by the fire. Alfred was naturally preoccupied with the fate of his kingdom. It had just been overrun by a marauding army of Danish thugs and so he was understandably a little distracted and inadvertently let them burn.

However, it's most likely that this story is apocryphal and was intended to show Alfred's humble, man-of-the-people charm during his time in hiding from those nasty Vikings.

THE GREAT CHARTER OF THE LIBERTIES

The *Magna Carta Libertatum* (The Great Charter of the Liberties) is probably one of the most famous documents in the world.

It was drafted by the Archbishop of Canterbury Stephen Langton (c.1150-1228) in an attempt to make peace between an unpopular king and a group of rebellious barons by limiting the powers of the former and protecting the privileges of the latter.

The *Magna Carta* was signed by King John (1166-1216) and various other interested parties at Runnymede, nr Windsor in Berkshire on 15 June 1215. It was the first document to establish the principle that everybody, including the king and his government, were subject to the law. Most of its 63 clauses dealt with regulating feudal customs and particular grievances relating to the king's rule, however, the document's 39th clause stating that all free men have the right to justice and a fair trial is the most famous and certainly the only one that anyone remembers. Many of the *Magna Carta*'s principles were subsequently echoed in the US Bill of Rights (1791) and other constitutional documents in other countries around the world.

That's the bit you learn at school. And it all sounds wonderful except it wasn't quite as simple and clear-cut as all that.

After the document was signed, nobody took a blind bit of notice of it. The despotic king continued throwing his weight around and the rebellious barons became even more rebellious! Both sides had so spectacularly failed to abide by the terms of the *Magna Carta* that it was annulled by Pope Innocent III shortly afterwards, leading to a period of conflict known as the First Barons' War (1215-1217).

HOLDING BACK THE TIDE

Cnut (994-1035) was an influential king and by all accounts he was a popular and effective ruler ... or at least as popular and effective as any Viking king could be in Saxon England. He secured an allegiance with the Scottish kings and forged good relations with the Holy Roman Empire, and his control of the Baltic Sea trade routes greatly benefited England's economy.

Having said all that, he's only remembered as being the king who tried to hold back the tide.

He had ordered his throne to be set down at the seashore. As he sat facing the sea, he then commanded the incoming tide to halt before his feet. According to this anecdotal tale first recorded by Henry of Huntingdon (c.1088-1157) in *Historia Anglorum* (c.1154), the tide then 'dashed over his feet and legs without respect to his royal person.' But the story, as it's told today, has been completely turned on its head. Cnut is made out to be a complete nutter by believing he possessed supernatural powers which could be used to hold back the waves, but in reality, he was only trying to prove his humility by demonstrating to his sycophantic courtiers the futility of his power against the supreme power of God.

After this incident he apparently hung up his gold crown and never wore it again 'to the honour of God the almighty king.'

the great jaffa cake trial

The age old question of whether a Jaffa Cake is a biscuit or a cake was finally settled in 1991.

Biscuits covered with chocolate are considered a luxury item in the UK with the full rate of VAT being applied, whilst chocolate covered cakes, on the other hand, are rather bizarrely considered a staple food and therefore exempt from the tax. In 1991, the snack food company and Jaffa Cakes manufacturer McVitie's was accused by HM Customs & Excise of mislabelling their famous orangey-chocolatey treats as 'cakes' and therefore denying them their VAT money.

The case went to court with the government arguing that Jaffa Cakes looked like biscuits, their packaging was similar to biscuits, they were displayed on the supermarket shelves along with all the other biscuits, and they were eaten just like biscuits. However, the McVitie's defence lawyers argued that their product's ingredients were similar to a cake, the texture was soft just like a cake, and most importantly, it hardened when stale like a cake (unlike biscuits which go soft). They even had a giant Jaffa Cake specially baked and exhibited in court to emphasise their points!

It was a long and costly trial with the judge ruling once and for all that a Jaffa Cake should be recognised as a chocolate covered cake.

Even though it's clearly a bloody biscuit!

book of soyga

The *Book of Soyga* (1500-1550) was an early-sixteenth century treatise on demonology, magic and the dark arts written by an anonymous author. The prominent Anglo-Welsh astronomer and mathematician John Dee (1527-1609) acquired a copy in the early-1580s and then spent the rest of his life trying to decipher its secrets.

He understood the descriptions for the various magical rituals and incantations, all the astrological guff and the passages relating to angels and demons but what he didn't understand were the last eighteen pages of the book containing 36 tables (each with 36 rows and 36 columns) of what appeared to be random letters set out in a random order. John was convinced that it was some kind of coded message because the letters and the layout didn't correspond to any logical or linguistic pattern. Despite his best efforts, however, he was unable to decipher it, so he turned to his friend, the occultist, alchemist and scryer Edward Kelley (1555-1598) for help.

Not only did Edward claim to possess the secret of alchemy, he could also communicate with angels, so he was a pretty useful friend to have in this sort of situation! Without further ado, he summoned the angel of wisdom, illumination and light, the Archangel Uriel. Fortunately for them, Uriel seemed only too happy to meet up for a chat and recount the story of how the *Book of Soyga* was given to Adam in the Garden of Eden and could only be interpreted by the protector and leader of God's army himself, the Archangel Michael. He also mentioned that the book was cursed and warned them that anyone correctly interpreting the coded tables would die soon after! So, best not to try! There doesn't seem to be a record of what happened after that, so either the two men heeded Uriel's warning, Edward's magical powers suddenly deserted him or the Archangel Michael wasn't quite so forthcoming in divulging the book's secrets as they'd hoped.

The *Book of Soyga* disappeared after John Dee's death in 1609. Many historians and occultists feared that it had been lost forever but in 1994 a copy was discovered buried under a pile of other books somewhere in the bowels of the British Library (London) by the American scholar and novelist Deborah Harkness. Unbelievably, she then uncovered another copy of the book that nobody knew about at the University of Oxford's Bodleian Library a couple of months later.

Although the American cryptographer and historian Jim Reeds later deciphered the construction algorithm and the code words used in forming the tables, their actual contents and their significance remain a mystery, with many historians and cryptographers still convinced that the last eighteen pages continue to hide some forbidden knowledge.

the absent-minded conductor

Thomas Beecham (1879-1961) was an English conductor and impresario best known for establishing the London Philharmonic Orchestra (1932) and the Royal Philharmonic Orchestra (1946). It's been said that he once attended a function and met a very distinguished looking woman whose face was familiar to him but whose name he couldn't quite recall. After making polite conversation for a few minutes, he then asked her if she was keeping well …

'Oh, very well, but my brother has been rather ill lately,' she said.

'Ah, yes, your brother. I'm sorry to hear that. And, what is your brother doing at the moment?'

'Well … he's still king!' she replied.

The woman he'd failed to recognise was the very recognisable Mary, Princess Royal and Countess of Harewood (1897-1965) and the brother of George VI (1895-1952).

the curious disappearance of agatha christie

On the evening of 3 December 1926, Agatha Christie (1890-1976) kissed her daughter goodnight, left the house, climbed into her car and drove off into the night. She wasn't seen again until eleven days later!

Agatha Christie was (and still is) one of the world's most celebrated authors; the world's bestselling fiction writer of all time and the world's most translated author. Her books are the third most widely published work after the Bible and the plays of William Shakespeare (1564-1616). *And Then There Were None* (1939) remains the world's bestselling crime-thriller and *The Mousetrap* (1952) holds the record for being the world's longest running stage play. She is probably best known for the novels and short stories featuring her two most famous and instantly recognisable characters, Hercule Poirot and Jane Marple, who made their respective debuts in *The Mysterious Affair at Styles* (1920) and *The Thirteen Problems* (1932).

Even in 1926, at the beginning of her career, Agatha Christie had published six novels and was already a very famous writer. So when she suddenly disappeared without a trace, an unprecedented manhunt involving 1,000 police officers and about 15,000 civilian volunteers was launched to try and find her. They discovered her abandoned car as quickly as the next day, partially hidden in bushes by the side of a road near Guildford in Surrey. The headlights were still switched on and a suitcase and a coat had been left on the back seat but there was no sign of Miss Christie. It was a mystery worthy of one of the writer's own novels!

The police initially suspected her husband Archibald Christie (1889-1962) and his lover Nancy Neele (1899-1958) of being involved in her disappearance as he'd been the last person to see her on the night she'd gone missing. Although he admitted to quarrelling with his wife, he also claimed to have left the house to spend the weekend with Nancy and a group of friends in the country before she'd disappeared. The general public, on the other hand, mostly believed that her disappearance was nothing more than just a cynical publicity stunt by the author. Another popular theory at the time was suicide. Her beloved mother had died earlier in the year and she had never really recovered from the loss. She was still feeling depressed about it all and her philanderer husband who'd recently asked her for a divorce wasn't making things any easier, so perhaps she'd just decided to end it all. It was certainly a line of inquiry that the police were pursuing too.

A few famous names tried to help in the search. The novelists Arthur Conan Doyle (1859-1930) and Dorothy L Sayers (1893-1957) were both invited to lend a hand because of their experience in writing puzzle-solving mystery novels. Arthur was also a keen occultist and so he jumped at the chance to take the missing writer's gloves to a clairvoyant in the hope that all that mystic, supernatural mumbo-jumbo he was so keen on might provide a few answers. Needless to say he was none the wiser after their meeting! Next up was Dotty, who visited the scene of Agatha's disappearance to look for clues but she too hit a brick wall and failed to provide any new leads.

By the second week, the story had spread around the world. It even made the front page of the *New York Times.*

Then, the headwaiter of a hotel in Harrogate (North Yorkshire) contacted the police on 14 December 1926 claiming that their lively and vivacious South African guest registered under the name of Mrs Tressa Neele could well be the missing author.

Archie and the boys in blue travelled north to the hotel. Archie took a seat in the corner of the hotel's dining room and waited for his estranged wife to arrive. He watched her walk in, take a seat at a table and begin reading a newspaper. Witnesses later said that when Archie had approached her, she seemed a little puzzled, appearing not to recognise him as the man she'd been married to for nearly twelve years. But even stranger is why she'd chosen the alias of 'Neele', the same name as her husband's lover!

Agatha was unable to say what had happened to her. She remembered nothing and Archie later informed the media that she'd suffered a total memory loss as a result of a car crash.

Ever since then everyone has speculated as to the real reason for her disappearance. It could have been depression, a clever publicity stunt, out-of-body amnesia, or maybe just an elaborate hoax to embarrass her unfaithful husband.

Agatha and Archie went their separate ways shortly afterwards. He later married Nancy and she married the prominent archaeologist Max Mallowan (1904-1978). Nobody ever spoke of the incident again and even in her autobiography *Agatha Christie: An Autobiography* (1977) it was never mentioned.

The most intriguing of all her mysteries still remains unresolved to this day.

someone wicked this way comes

Matthew Hopkins (c.1620-1647) was the feared English witch hunter active in East Anglia between 1644 and 1647.

Little is known of his life until he took up his witch finding duties. Sometime in the early-1640s he'd moved to Manningtree in Essex and used a recently acquired inheritance to buy a tavern and pass himself off as a gentleman. It's often assumed that he trained as a lawyer, although there is no real evidence to support this.

In 1644, after supposedly overhearing a group of women discussing their meetings with the Devil, he took it upon himself to bring them to trial. Of those 23 women he named and shamed, four died in prison and nineteen were later convicted and hanged for acts of witchery. A year later, he appointed himself to the role of Witch-Finder General, after claiming to have been commissioned by Parliament to uncover and prosecute more witches, and then set off with his assistant John Stearne (c.1610-1670) and a group of militant followers around East Anglia looking for them …

In his pamphlet *The Discovery of Witches* (1647) Matthew stated that he took 'twenty shillings in a town' for his work. Such was the high cost to the local communities that many towns and villages were forced to levy a special tax just to pay for his witch finding services!

Matthew would travel through the villages of Essex, Suffolk and Norfolk asking the residents to hand over any suspected witches, then he'd question them or torture them to extract a confession. One of his favourite torture methods was the *swimming test* whereby a woman was tied to a chair and thrown into the village pond. If she sank and drowned, then she was probably innocent of the charges (but at least she would be received into Heaven) but if she floated and survived, then she would be branded a witch and sent for trial.

Back then, any old crone who mixed a few herbs together to make potions or medicines and who was known as a bit of a healer would be accused of witchcraft sooner or later, so there was never any shortage of potential victims. But just to make sure he didn't miss anyone, his followers, who were known as 'prickers' were employed to jab the arms of all the village women with a needle, pin or knife. If they didn't bleed then they were assumed to be a witch. But as there was a very good living to be made from hunting down these poor women, many of the more unscrupulous prickers would use blunt or retractable blades to increase their chances of success!

It's estimated that Matthew was responsible for the executions of over 300 alleged witches between 1644 and 1646.

Who'd have thought there would have been so many of them?

Accounts of Matthew's own death are a little vague. He may have died at home of tuberculosis or he may have been drowned undergoing his own *swimming test* after being accused of witchcraft himself.

the first evil stepmother

The Saxon king Edgar the Peaceful (c.943-975) was looking for a new queen and he'd been told about a young lass called Ælfthryth (Elfrida) (c.945-c.1001). She was the daughter of Ealdorman Ordgar, a wealthy West Country landowner, and would make a perfect second or third wife (nobody is quite sure) but only if she was as pretty as everyone said.

According to *Gesta Regum Anglorum* (1125) written by the historian William of Malmesbury (c.1095-1143), the king dispatched his most trusted and favoured noblemen Æthelwald to check her out and 'offer her marriage [to Edgar] if her beauty were really equal to report.' When she turned out to be even prettier than everyone said, Æthelwald married her himself and then told Edgar that her beauty had been greatly exaggerated and that she was merely 'a girl of vulgar and common place appearance' and by no means worthy of a king.

Edgar initially accepted his word but then learnt of the deception and swore vengeance against Æthelwald.

He decided to pay the happy couple a visit. News of his arrival sent Æthelwald into a spin and he confessed to Ælfthryth how he'd effectively stolen her from the king and then begged her to play along and wear the plainest clothes and make herself look as unattractive as possible for when he arrived. However, Ælfthryth was an ambitious little cow and the realisation that she'd missed out on becoming queen didn't go down too well with her. Instead of complying with her husband's wishes, she did the exact opposite and Edgar immediately fell for her good looks and charm. In fact, he became quite besotted with the lovely Ælfthryth and wished for nothing more than to take her as his bride. But that was only going to happen if Æthelwald was out of the picture ...

Rather conveniently, Æthelwald was then killed on a hunting expedition organised by Edgar in Harewood Forest, Hampshire. It was officially recorded as an accident but some later accounts of his death just flat-out accused Edgar of running him through with his sword.

With the traitor Æthelwald out of the way, the king was now free to marry Ælfthryth. Although he took his time about it because they didn't actually tie the knot until two years later in 964.

Ælfthryth later gave birth to a son, Æthelred (c.966-1016). He was Edgar's third child, having previously fathered Edward (c.962-978) and Eadgifu (c.963-c.986) (later known as St Edith of Wilton) by wives (or mistresses) number one and two – Æthelflæd and Wulfthryth.

Despite being the king since 959, Edgar wasn't actually crowned until fourteen years later at a ceremony on 11 May 973 at Bath Abbey. He was originally only King of Mercia and Northumbria but after the death of his brother King Eadwig of the West Saxons (c.940-959), he inherited that part of England too and united the country under his rule. Ælfthryth was now a proper queen and she probably thought this would give her son Æthelred seniority over Edgar's oldest son Edward (whose mother was never queen) when it was time to choose the heir to the throne.

That time came only two years later in 975.

Predictably, Queen Ælfthryth supported her own son to accede Edgar but Edward had the support of the clergy, particularly the all-powerful Archbishop of Canterbury, Dunstan (c.909-988), and was crowned King of England on 8 July 975. However, his reign was fairly short lived. Less than three years later, on the evening of 18 March 978, he was murdered whilst visiting his stepmum Ælfthryth and his half-brother Æthelred at Corfe Castle in Dorset.

According to an account of his death written in *Vita Oswaldi* (c.1000) by the monk and historian Byrhtferth (c.970-c.1020) the 'nobles and chief men, who stayed with the queen' came out to meet him in the courtyard when he arrived. The young king was still sitting on his horse when he was offered a drink, and as he reached down to take the flask, one man pulled his right arm towards him whilst another then roughly seized his left arm and repeatedly stabbed him. The horse panicked and bolted; Edward's foot got trapped in the stirrup as he fell, and he was dragged around the courtyard.

Stabbed and scraped to death!

Æthelred was only 10 years-old and too young to be suspected of any involvement in the murder. Although Ælfthryth wasn't specifically implicated either, many people thought it was just a little too convenient that her stepson's murder was committed on her estate and by her followers. At the very least, they suspected her of plotting to have him killed beforehand and allowing the killers to go free.

However, by the mid-eleventh century, a greater role in the king's mysterious death had been afforded to Ælfthryth and she was being portrayed in the chronicles of the time as an evil stepmother and a stereotypical bad queen. Some reports even placed her in the courtyard, offering Edward the drink herself and signalling to her attendants to stab him. The monks of Ely Abbey who composed *Liber Eliensis* (Book of Ely) (c.1131-c.1174) had no doubt as to her guilt. They even accused her of being a witch!

Æthelred was crowned king on 14 April 979 when he was only 12 years-old and reigned on-and-off until 1016. But until he came of age in 984, during the early part of his reign, it was Ælfthryth who called the shots and for a brief few years, she was the most powerful person in the whole of England.

After 984, when Æthelred turned eighteen, however, she quickly faded into the background; spending her days at court or just looking after the grandkids. Around 999, she retired to a nunnery (as all the powerful women seemed to do back then) passing her final days in religious seclusion.

putting on the top hat

The origins of the top hat are a little vague. It was definitely invented in England, most probably in 1793 by a hatter from Middlesex called George Dunnage. However, a much funnier anecdote involves the haberdasher John Hetherington who is sometimes erroneously credited with inventing the ridiculous headwear. It was once reported in the *London Evening News* that he'd 'appeared on the public highway' on 15 January 1797 wearing a top hat like some kind of eighteenth-century Mr Monopoly and was immediately arrested for causing a breach of the peace and inciting a riot!

The court heard how he'd been 'wearing upon his head what he called a silk hat ... a tall structure having a shiny lustre, and calculated to frighten timid people.' His appearance soon attracted a large and hysterical crowd, 'several women fainted, children screamed and dogs yelped' and the younger son of Cordwainer Thomas (whoever he was?) 'was thrown down ... and had his right arm broken.'

Who would have thought that wearing an oversized hat could have caused so much fuss?

the phantom battle of edgehill

The Battle of Edgehill took place on 23 October 1642 and was the first major battle of the English Civil War (1642-1651). Royalist troops commanded by Prince Rupert of the Rhine, Duke of Cumberland (1619-

1682) were marching from Shrewsbury towards London when they were ambushed by Parliamentarian troops led by Robert Devereux, 3rd Earl of Essex (1591-1646). Around 30,000 soldiers then battled it out in a field near the village of Edgehill in Warwickshire for a couple of hours with both sides suffering heavy casualties before withdrawing their armies and calling it a draw.

On Christmas Eve 1642, shepherds and local farm workers witnessed a ghostly re-enactment of the battle. As they walked across the fields, they began hearing the distant sounds of war: cannon fire, the cries of dying soldiers, the clash of armour and the screams of terrified horses. The sounds got closer and closer until eventually it seemed like the battle was on top of them ...

Then, when they all looked up, they saw the two phantom armies fighting it out in the night sky above them!

There were so many sightings of these ghostly soldiers over the next few days that a pamphlet, *A Great Wonder in Heaven* (1643) detailing the spooky goings-on at Edgehill was published in January 1643. News of the sightings soon reached Charles I (1600-1649) who was sufficiently intrigued to set up a Royal Commission and appoint some of his most trusted officers to visit the site of the battle and investigate the matter further. They too witnessed the grisly spectacle being re-played in the sky above them. They even recognised some of the combatants, many of whom were men they'd fought alongside in the real battle just a few months earlier!

As a result of that investigation, the Battle of Edgehill soldiers are the only ghosts officially recognised by The National Archives.

attack on whitehaven

In 1775, John Paul Jones (1747-1792) was commanding the armed British merchant ship *Betsy* when he stabbed and killed a mutinous crew member over a dispute about unpaid wages. He then fled England to avoid being arrested and ended up in the Colony of Virginia where he joined the fledgling Continental Navy to fight in the American Revolutionary War (1775-1783). Although he was a fairly disagreeable chap, his temperament didn't seem to hinder his rise through the ranks and on 14 June 1777 he was given command of the newly built sloop-of-war USS *Ranger* with orders to sail away and assist the American cause in whatever way possible.

After some early successes against British merchant shipping in the Irish Sea, J P hatched a plan to invade England.

He'd decided to attack the small coastal town of Whitehaven in Cumbria but the unfavourable winds soon forced him to abandon that idea as his ship was blown in the opposite direction towards Ireland. Not to worry because the British warship HMS *Drake* was anchored in the harbour at Carrickfergus in Co Antrim and they could pass their time attacking that instead. The assault was due to take place just after midnight on 20 April 1778 but the crewman responsible for dropping the anchor to bring the USS *Ranger* alongside the *Drake* was drunk and he ballsed it up, misjudging the timing in the dark, so they had to abandon that idea too! But not to worry, the winds were blowing in the opposite direction now, so they all sailed back across the Irish Sea towards Whitehaven again.

The invasion of England was suddenly back on the agenda …

Two boats with thirty men aboard armed with pistols and cutlasses were launched from the USS *Ranger* at 3.00am on 23 April 1778. They rowed against the tide and landed in the town's harbour some three hours later. One group of men led by J P attacked the fort, disabled the cannons and took a few prisoners, whilst the other group approached the dock. They'd planned to set light to the hundreds of ships which were packed tightly together and stranded in the low water but starting fires proved impossible because their lanterns had no fuel. You'd think someone might have checked that before they left the ship! Some of the men were then dispatched to a quayside pub to fetch the necessary fuel … and then just stayed there and got drunk. They didn't return until dawn and J P and his men were only able to set fire to one small coal boat before the townsfolk streamed out of their houses and chased them away.

Their invasion of England had been a complete farce from start to finish … but not to worry because J P had another cunning plan …

The USS *Ranger* sailed northwards to Kirkcudbright in Scotland where he intended to abduct Dunbar Douglas, 4th Earl of Selkirk (1722-1799) and hold him hostage in exchange for the release of US sailors who'd been press-ganged into service with the Royal Navy. But this idea turned out to be a bit naff too! The Earl wasn't at home when they arrived, so his wife entertained the officers while they waited and even made them a cup of tea! So, there they all were, sipping tea in the drawing room and waiting patiently for the Earl to return … but the Earl never returned and they couldn't wait forever, so they just said their goodbyes and wandered back to the ship. But not before helping themselves to some of the family silver, other valuables and even her ladyship's teapot from which she'd served them their tea! However, they didn't get away with much, having been outsmarted by the family butler, who'd filled up their sacks with coal before laying just a few valuables on the top.

Despite these three hastily-planned and foolhardy attacks in Carrickfergus, Whitehaven and Kirkcudbright, J P wasn't quite as crap at his job as you might think. He went on to establish himself as one of history's great naval commanders and became famous for his victory against the British at the Battle of Flamborough Head (1779), the first major success of the new Continental Navy.

He just got off to a bad start.

the man from the ministry

The inventor, author and one-time missionary Charles Fraser-Smith (1904-1992) has been widely credited as the real-life inspiration for the Q (Quartermaster) character in the *James Bond* books by Ian Fleming (1908-1964).

He was employed by the Ministry of Supply during World War II (1939-1945) to develop gadgets and equipment nicknamed 'Q-devices' for British Special Operations Executive operatives working behind enemy lines in occupied Europe. Classic espionage accessories such as fountain pens containing compasses, cigarette lighters fitted with hidden miniature cameras, pencils containing rolled-up maps and steel shoelaces made of surgical saw-wire (doubling as garrottes) were all designed by him. He also developed a garlic flavoured chocolate which was distributed to the spies in case they were captured by the Nazis and they needed to make their breath smell a little more French!

the tomb of king arthur

Glastonbury Abbey in Somerset was founded in 712 by King Ine of Wessex (c.670-c.726) and rapidly became the wealthiest monastery in England. The abbey was famous for its beauty and its glassworks and attracted pilgrims from far and wide. But then tragedy struck in 1184 when a massive fire destroyed nearly all of the buildings.

Then, in 1191, the monks reportedly discovered a grave containing an oak coffin holding the remains of a gigantic man who'd been severely wounded in the head. Buried alongside him was a woman with a tress of golden hair.

The Cambro-Norman priest Gerald of Wales (c.1146-c.1223) described their spectacular find in *De Principis Instructione* (c.1193):

'Although legends had fabricated something fantastical about his demise (that he had not suffered death, and was conveyed, as if by a spirit, to a distant place), his body was discovered at Glastonbury, in our own times, hidden very deep in the earth in an oak-hollow, between two stone pyramids that were erected long ago in that holy place. The tomb was sealed up with astonishing tokens, like some sort of miracle. The body was then conveyed into the church with honour, and properly committed to a marble tomb. A lead cross was placed under the stone, not above as is usual in our times, but instead fastened to the underside. I have seen this cross, and have traced the engraved letters - not visible and facing outward, but rather turned inwardly toward the stone. It read: Here lies entombed King Arthur, with Guenevere his second wife on the Isle of Avalon.'

On 19 April 1278, the remains of Arthur and Guinevere were removed and Edward I (1239-1307) had them placed in a black marble tomb where they remained until the English Reformation (1527-1590) and the dissolution of Glastonbury Abbey in 1539.

Despite the esteemed cleric's detailed account of the tomb's discovery and his own assertion to have seen the cross, most historians take a more cynical view of what actually happened, believing that it was all just an elaborate PR stunt perpetrated by the monks to raise some much needed funds for the reconstruction of the abbey after the great fire of 1184. They also needed a gimmick to make the abbey seem more relevant because they had to compete with Canterbury Cathedral for pilgrims and the Kent boys had the tomb of Britain's first dead celebrity Thomas Becket (c.1119-1170) to pull in the crowds. By inventing a link between their abbey and the legendary King of the Britons Arthur Pendragon however, it wasn't long before the pilgrims started arriving from all over the country again and they were only too keen to make a donation to the rebuilding costs.

It was a clever ploy by the monks. A few decades earlier, the Catholic cleric/scholar Geoffrey of Monmouth (c.1095-c.1155) had popularised the legends of the early British kings after writing his most famous work, the pseudohistorical account of British history, *Historia Regum Britanniae* (c.1136) in which he introduced many of the themes, events and characters of the Arthurian legend we're all familiar with today. Of course, it was all complete bollocks from start to finish but the people were a bit dim back then and believed every word of it; the monks jumped on the King Arthur bandwagon because of Glastonbury's close links to the legend; the people bought into the idea of them finding the great man's grave, and the abbey soon became a must-see tourist attraction again.

The abbey remained popular well into the sixteenth century and those crafty monks continued cashing in on the legend for all that time. Right up until 1539 when it was disestablished by Henry VIII (1491-1547). The fact that the remains of King Arthur and Queen Guinevere were then conveniently lost at this time just adds weight to the belief that the monks were taking the piss out of everyone to line their own pockets!

THE HOLY GRAIL

According to all four of the canonical gospels in the Bible, Joseph of Arimathea was the man who assumed responsibility for the burial of Jesus Christ after his crucifixion. Medieval legend states that he became a missionary soon afterwards and eventually travelled to England to preach the word of God, bringing with him the Holy Grail.

Some legends have Joseph visiting England years before the crucifixion to pursue his interests in the tin trade. He may (or may not) have been accompanied at that time by a young Jesus Christ. There was a strong Jewish presence in the west of England and many of the tin miners were believed to have been Jewish settlers. The story of Jesus accompanying Joseph when he was a young man was the inspiration for the famous poem, *And Did Those Feet in Ancient Time* (1804) by William Blake (1757-1827).

After the crucifixion, Joseph apparently headed westwards again …

He was granted land on which to build a church after he and his followers arrived in England. The church was founded around 63BE on the site that was to become Glastonbury Abbey. It's been said that he brought with him the Holy Grail. Different accounts describe it as a cup, dish or a stone with miraculous powers providing happiness, eternal youth or sustenance in infinite abundance. According to the French poet Robert de Boron who wrote *Joseph d'Arimathie* (c.1200), the Holy Grail was the vessel used by Jesus during the Last Supper, which Joseph later used to catch his blood at the crucifixion. He maintained that the chalice was taken to England for safekeeping by the followers of Joseph (and not Joseph himself) although in various other subsequent medieval accounts of the story, it was Joseph who came to England bringing with him the Holy Grail and other precious relics.

He may have kept the Holy Grail at the church or he may have buried it at the foot of Glastonbury Tor, possibly at a site now known as the Chalice Well. Legend states that when Joseph placed the Holy Grail beneath its waters they immediately flowed red.

bicycle face

There was a time when cyclists were more concerned about contracting Bicycle Face than being mowed down by a car!

When cycling became popular with the middle classes at the end of the nineteenth century, many physicians warned of a dangerous medical condition associated with the new pastime which was particularly prevalent amongst young women.

On 7 September 1895, it was reported in *The Literary Digest* that 'over-exertion, the upright position on the wheel and the unconscious effort to maintain one's balance produces a wearied and exhausted bicycle face. The main symptoms are a hard, clenched jaw and bulging eyes, as well as being flushed and wearing a haggard, anxious expression.' Other symptoms of this terrifying new disease might include a tan and even a bit of sunburn! As a pale complexion was considered desirable in the nineteenth-century, women tended to avoid exposure to the sun by using a parasol or a broad-brimmed hat to block out all that nasty vitamin D. Not only did cycling make it difficult for a young lady to maintain her sickly, white demeanour but it could even coarsen her appearance and make her seem suspiciously exhilarated, leading everyone to assume that she'd just been masturbating!

Many physicians argued that ruddy cheeks and strained face muscles could eventually lead to more serious medical conditions. In 1896, the *British Medical Journal* reported that cycling could exacerbate chest problems, inflame the urethra and should be avoided by women suffering from pelvic mischief. Other side effects might include exhaustion, insomnia, depression, heart palpitations and dementia!

Inevitably, there were also the fanatical preachers who felt that riding around on bicycles on the Sabbath was to blame for the disease and would ultimately lead to womanhood being destroyed forever and even the end of civilisation!

The so-called experts of the day all agreed on the causes and the symptoms of the disease but seemed divided on its long term effects. Some believed it was a permanent condition whilst others maintained that it was curable with the effects likely to subside after a prolonged spell out of the saddle.

Of course, it's highly possible that this disease was just dreamed up to curb the rise of the feminist movement. Women were embracing their first tastes of freedom, and many prominent suffragettes liked nothing better than toodling around town on their fancy new bicycles, so trying to dissuade them from taking up the new hobby may have just been a thinly disguised plot to curb their liberty by some of the less enlightened doctors of the time. A woman's place was in the home, barefoot and pregnant, pandering to her husband's every whim, not pratting about on a bike!

By the turn of the century, however, nobody really believed that Bicycle Face was a thing anymore. People riding horses or driving cars didn't suffer with any lasting effects or injuries, so why should it be any different for people riding a bike?

touring australia

The Prince and Princess of Wales were travelling around Australia in 1983 on their first overseas tour together. During one particular outing in South

Australia, Princess Diana (1961-1997) approached a crowd of young children. After walking up to one little boy and giving him a pat on the head she asked him why he wasn't in school that day …

'I was sent home,' he replied, 'because I've got head lice!'

the covent garden ladies

Although similar publications such as *The Wandering Whore* (1660-1661) and *A Catalogue of Jilts, Cracks & Prostitutes, Night-Walkers, Whores, She-Friends, Kind Women, and Others of the Linnen-Lifting Tribe* (1691) had been published listing the location of London's many brothels and the small army of prostitutes that plied their trade on the city's streets, *Harris's List of Covent Garden Ladies* (1757-1795) was the best known, the first to be published annually, the first bestseller (shifting around 8,000 copies a year) and the first to become essential reading for any well-to-do young gentleman visiting London who might fancy a bit of hanky-panky!

This popular little guidebook published annually between 1757 and 1795 listed the details of around 120-150 prostitutes working in and around the Covent Garden area of London. Everyone from the 'low-born errant drabs' to the famous courtesans of the day like Kitty Fisher (1741-1767) and Fanny Murray (c.1729-1778). The detailed reviews included their names, ages and prices, a physical description (including the size of their breasts), any particular bedroom talents (often depicted in quite lurid detail) and, most importantly, the address where a gentleman might find these nice young ladies. Whether they sang, danced or conversed well might also have been noted.

A typical review was the 1761 entry for the lovely Miss Nelson of St Martin's Lane: 'A jolly smart wench, a good companion at table; but particularly joyous in bed; there are few whores to be found so generous as she is, often restoring the money when she likes her man; but she drinks damnably, and is then too apt to be saucy' and the 1788 entry for a Miss Clicamp of York Street who was described in an unintentional tongue-twister as being 'one of the finest, fattest figures as fully finished for fun and frolic as fertile fancy ever formed …'

The 1793 edition described a Mrs Pierce of 19 St George's Row as being '… still in her teens, with fine dark eyes and hair, her mouth opens to display a regular set of teeth. In bed she will twine and twist, sigh and murmur, pant and glow with unfeigned emotions, and never be tired of love's game …' and a Mrs Brooks, who lived next door to the pawnbroker in Newman Street, as 'a genteel lady, about 23 … with well-formed projecting bubbies that defy the result of any manual pressure, panting and glowing with unfeigned desire, and soon inviting the gratification of senses.'

The descriptions weren't always so complementary. A Miss Berry was once described as being 'almost rotten, and her breath cadaverous' (1773) and a Miss Montague was labelled as being 'too fat to be genteel, too short to be elegant, too brown to be handsome' with her entire appearance dismissed as 'too plain for any gentleman to risk more than a guinea for a nocturnal exhibition' (1789).

The little pocketbook sold for 2s.6d and the original author was probably the Irish poet Samuel Derrick (1724-1769). It's believed that the book was based on a list of over 400 women compiled and provided to him by the self-proclaimed Pimp-General of All England, Jack Harris who worked at the Shakespear's Head Tavern in Covent Garden.

the lloyds bank coprolite

Coprolite is the proper scientific name for a fossilised human turd!

And the world's largest coprolite is currently on display at the JORVIK Viking Centre in York.

In 1972, during construction work for a new Lloyds Bank branch in Pavement Street, various artefacts from the city's Viking period were unearthed. Amongst all the usual bits of broken pottery, metalwork and old bones they might have expected to find, archaeologists also stumbled across an 8 x 2 inch (20 x 5cm) lump of perfectly preserved human excrement!

Coprolites are extremely rare and only tend to be found in very dry or frozen environments, but it seems the oxygen-deprived wet clay underneath Pavement Street turned out to be the perfect conditions for preserving one particular piece of Viking crap for prosperity. After being carefully analysed, the scientists reached the conclusion that whoever it belonged to had eaten large quantities of meat, bread and grain before visiting the toilet. They also discovered the presence of several hundred whipworm and maw-worm eggs in the stool, suggesting that their body was riddled with intestinal parasites. Judging by the size of the thing, they probably hadn't gone for a few days either!

An even bigger discovery of Viking artefacts was discovered in 1976, in nearby Coppergate Street during the construction of a new shopping centre. In fact, there was so much of it that they were able to open a museum. In 1984, the JORVIK Viking Centre opened its doors to the public and it has since become one of Britain's most popular tourist attractions. But despite all the Coppergate Street stuff filling the majority of the exhibit cases, the most popular and talked about artefact is still that big lump of shit they found under Pavement Street. They've even guessed at what it must have smelt like and then re-created that same odour around the area where it's on display!

henry's extraordinary marital merry-go-round

Divorced, beheaded, died. Divorced, beheaded, survived.

Henry VIII (1491-1547) ruled over England for 36 years from 1509 until his death in 1547, initiating the English Reformation (1527-1590), presiding over the early years of the English Renaissance (1485-1660) and overseeing the legal and political union of England and Wales. But he's probably best remembered for his wild lifestyle, his tumultuous love life, his extraordinary marital merry-go-round and his unwavering desire for a son to secure the Tudor dynasty.

The first of his six wives was the diminutive auburn-haired beauty Catherine of Aragon (1485-1536). She was the daughter of Ferdinand II of Spain and the widow of Henry's late brother Arthur, Prince of Wales (1486-1502). They were married on 11 June 1509, thirteen days before Henry was crowned king. After many pregnancies and several births, the only child to survive was a girl, Mary – the future Mary I (1516-1558). Frustrated by the queen's apparent unwillingness to give him what he wanted, Henry's eyes began to wander. As the queen grew older, her looks faded and she turned to study whilst Henry's attention turned to finding himself a mistress. He was the king and the queen wasn't doing it for him anymore, so he started enticing some of the more ready-and-willing servants into his bedchamber at night for a bit of hanky-panky.

It's unclear just how many flings he actually had as they were generally short lived and unacknowledged. His most famous mistress was the queen's lady-in-waiting Elizabeth Blount (c.1500-c.1539). Their affair began in 1516 and she gave birth to a son Henry FitzRoy, Duke of Richmond & Somerset (1519-1536), the only one of his many illegitimate children the king ever actually acknowledged. Possibly because it proved that he was more than capable of fathering healthy baby boys! Soon after the birth, he dumped her and started banging another lady-in-waiting, Mary Boleyn (c.1499-1543). She was also rumoured to have been a mistress of Henry's great rival, Francis I of France so dating kings was obviously her thing.

By 1525, however, he'd become infatuated with Mary's sister, Anne Boleyn (c.1501-1536). But she was playing hard to get, refusing to become his mistress and insisting that he had to marry her if he wanted to bed her.

The queen was getting too old to have kids but Henry still needed a male heir. By 1527, he'd convinced himself that their marriage was blighted in the eyes of God because of some obscure bible passage: 'If a man shall take his brother's wife, it is an impurity; he hath uncovered his brother's nakedness; they shall be childless' (Leviticus 20:21) so he instructed the Lord High Chancellor of England, Cardinal Thomas Wolsey (1473-1530) to approach Pope Clement VII and ask for an annulment.

The pope then politely declined his request but Henry refused to take no for an answer.

The German and French theologians Martin Luther and John Calvin had already started challenging papal authority in Europe and now it was Henry's turn to do the same thing in England. But whereas the first two gentlemen questioned the Catholic Church's ability to define Christian practices and led a religious, political and cultural change in their countries, Henry wasn't really all that interested in the theological side of things, he just wanted to move Anne into his bedchamber! She was a bit of a party girl and he was going crazy watching her swanning about court every day, flirting with him and dropping subtle hints about wanting to be queen.

By now, Henry was thinking with his dick. He was the king and should be able to do whatever the hell he liked. So he secretly married Anne in defiance of the Catholic Church and finally got his wicked way with her. The couple were later married again in a formal ceremony on 25 January 1533. To cover all the bases, the newly installed Archbishop of Canterbury, Thomas Cranmer (1489-1556) then declared that Henry and Catherine's marriage had been illegal. Meanwhile, Catherine was banished from court and formally stripped of her title as queen consort. She refused to enter a nunnery and lived out her days at Kimbolton Castle in Cambridgeshire. In a last letter to Henry she wrote: 'For my part I pardon you everything and I wish devoutly to pray God that He will pardon you also.'

Soon afterwards, Anne fell pregnant and on 7 September 1533, the new queen gave birth to a daughter, Elizabeth – the future Elizabeth I (1533-1603). Meanwhile, Henry was now busy setting up his own church …

The Church of England's break from the practices and laws of the Catholic Church in Rome was effected by a series of acts of parliament passed between 1532 and 1534, including the Act of Supremacy 1534 which declared Henry to be the Supreme Head of the Church of England, allowing him the final say in all doctrinal and legal disputes and depriving the papacy of valuable revenue. Shrines were destroyed and monasteries were dissolved; church land was confiscated and many clergymen were expelled from parliament.

Henry had obviously been hugely disappointed by the birth of another daughter and hoped a son would come along soon. But after three miscarriages, things weren't looking too good and he was beginning to lose patience. By March 1536, he'd moved on and was busy shagging another lady-in-waiting, Jane Seymour (c.1508-1537). But in order to marry her, he had to find a reason to end his marriage to Anne …

On 2 May 1536, Anne was arrested and imprisoned in the Tower of London charged with adultery, incest and treason. Her brother George Boleyn, 2nd Viscount Rochford (c.1503-1536) and another four other courtiers, including the king's Groom of the Stool, Henry Norris (c.1482-1536), had all been found guilty of having sexual relations with the queen behind the king's back and were executed on 17 May 1536. As an act of mercy, Henry commuted Anne's sentence from burning to beheading, and rather than have her executed by an axeman like a commoner, he employed the services of an expert swordsman from France to do the job. She was beheaded on the morning of 19 May 1536 in front of an invited crowd of royal officials and VIPs, which included aldermen, sheriffs, the Lord Mayor of London and representatives of the various craft guilds. After a brief farewell to her servants, a quick speech and an even quicker prayer, her head was lopped off.

With Anne out of the way, Henry then married Jane on 30 May 1536. Whereas Anne had been a bit of a party girl, Jane was very strict and conservative. All the extravagance and lavish entertainment that her predecessor had enjoyed at court was replaced by more demur and sombre activities.

By Christmas of 1536, Jane was pregnant but lost the child. But it wasn't long before she was pregnant again and on 12 October 1537, Henry finally had his son! Edward – the future Edward VI (1537-1553) was born at Hampton Court Palace. However, Jane had suffered terribly during a difficult labour lasting two days and three nights; she soon fell seriously ill and died on 24 October 1537. Poor Henry was distraught with grief.

The German princess, Anne of Cleves (1515-1557) became wife number four on 6 January 1540. But the marriage only lasted six months! It had only gone ahead because Henry's chief minister Thomas Cromwell (c.1485-1540) had recommended cosying up to her brother, the Protestant leader William, Duke of Jülich-Cleves-Berg in case England needed an ally to fend off any attacks from Catholic France and the Holy Roman Empire. The morning after his wedding night Henry confessed to him: 'I liked her before not well, but now I like her much worse.' Eventually, Henry grew tired of her and she was commanded to leave the palace on 24 June 1540. The marriage was annulled on 9 July 1540, on the grounds of non-consummation and Thomas Cromwell was executed for treason on 28 July 1540. After all, it had been his idea to marry her in the first place! Because Anne had so readily agreed to the annulment, saving Henry a lot of grief and embarrassment, he awarded her a generous financial settlement. They even became good friends; she continued to maintain a close relationship with his children and was known affectionately as 'the king's sister' at court.

With the disastrous marriage to Anne of Cleves behind him, Henry decided to find his next wife himself, and once again turned his attention to the enormous pool of ladies-in-waiting at his disposal. Luckily, 17 year-old Catherine Howard (c.1523-1542) had just arrived at court and her youth, good looks and vivacity immediately caught his eye. Suddenly, the king was head-over-heels in love again. He acted like a lovesick teenager, indulging her every whim and bestowing her with gifts, new clothes and jewels. They were married on 28 July 1540, the same day as Thomas Cromwell was executed.

By now, Henry was nearly 50 years-old, a cantankerous old git with an ulcerous leg, prone to violent mood swings and the size of a small house! Understandably, poor Catherine looked around for someone a bit younger and a bit fitter to share her bed and settled on Henry's favourite courtier Thomas Culpeper (c.1514-1541). At the same time, she also employed Francis Dereham (c.1506-1541) as her private secretary, with whom she'd previously had a little fling before her marriage to the king. As it turned out, it wasn't a particularly bright idea to hire an ex-boyfriend. To cut a long story short, the Archbishop of Canterbury Thomas Cranmer came to hear about her pre-marital love life and told the king, Frances admitted it and then told him about Catherine's affair with Thomas. The king was mortified. It seemed like everyone at court had banged his wife at one time or another.

Both men were immediately executed and Catherine herself was beheaded on 13 February 1542 for treason and adultery.

Last, but by no means least, there was the merry widow Catherine Parr (1512-1548) – Henry's sixth and final wife, the one that outlived him and the one who brought a bit of stability to court after so many years of scandal and turmoil. She helped reconcile Henry with his daughters, Mary and Elizabeth, and ensured that the Royal Family was presented to the world as a close-knit household. She also persuaded Henry to pass the Third Succession Act 1543 which re-instated his daughters to the line of succession. Henry might have been a bit long in the tooth for chasing the ladies-in-waiting around his bedchamber but not so for fighting on the battlefield. Such was Henry's trust in Catherine that he chose her to rule over England while he was away in Europe fighting the Italian War (1542-1546), and in the event of his death, she was also to act as queen regnant to his successor, the young King Edward VI.

Later in life, Henry became so obese that he had to be moved around with the help of mechanical machines! There is no doubt that his obesity hastened his death. On 28 January 1547, aged 55 years-old, Henry died at the Palace of Whitehall and was succeeded to the throne by Edward with Catherine at his side.

the moustache law

Between 1860 and 1916 every soldier in the British Army was obliged to grow a moustache!

Soldiers of the East India Company (1600-1874) first adopted the policy in 1854 because the Indians believed that bare faces were juvenile or unmanly. Then, six years later in 1860, the British Army embraced the idea of everyone in their ranks sporting a well-groomed moustache when they issued Command No. 1,695 of the King's Regulations: 'The hair of the head will be kept short. The chin and the under-lip will be shaved, but not the upper-lip. Whiskers, if worn, will be of moderate length.'

Everything from a bit of bum fluff to a bloody great Edward Elgar-style moustache was permissible just as long as there was something fuzzy and hairy decorating their stiff-upper-lips! However, during World War I (1914-1918) many of the soldiers began ignoring the regulation despite the risk of being disciplined, as the moustaches were preventing them from fitting their gas masks properly. All of a sudden, marching into battle with immaculately groomed facial hair didn't seem all that important anymore! It was alright for the generals sitting behind a desk somewhere back in London; they could afford to grow more and more outrageous moustaches because they weren't the ones being gassed.

Eventually, in 1916, the regulation was dropped and the troops were officially allowed to be clean-shaven again. The order to abolish the ridiculous law was finally signed on 6 October 1916 by General Sir Nevil Macready (1862-1946). He hated moustaches as much as the next man and popped into a barbershop on his way home from the office that very same evening to have the damn thing shaved off.

operation tamarisk

One of the most successful spying operations of the Cold War (1945-1991).

Through a reciprocal arrangement between France/UK/USA and the Soviet Union, each side was allowed to deploy a small number of military intelligence officers in each other's territory in East and West Germany. Although the scheme was originally intended as a way of improving relations between the two opposing sides, it soon evolved into a convenient way for them to spy on one another.

Operation Tamarisk (1979-1990) involved Allied spies sifting through rubbish left behind by the Soviets in litterbins, skips and dumpsters outside their homes, offices, barracks, and sometimes even in fields previously used for military exercises. It was easy enough to do because both the East Germans and the Soviets were so shockingly bad at organising their refuse collection services. There was literally rubbish lying around everywhere!

It seems that the Soviet troops weren't issued with toilet paper in the field which meant making do with whatever came to hand. Although it was mostly pages torn from notebooks or old letters from home, sometimes they foolishly used top secret military documents to wipe their arses! As these shit-stained pieces of paper weren't soluble and would clog up the sewer pipes if flushed down the toilet, they were just chucked away with all the other rubbish and then the Allied agents had the unenviable task of rummaging through them all looking for secrets. They were sometimes incredibly valuable, providing vital intelligence on ciphers, weapons specifications, morale, equipment deliveries, training exercises and even troop movements. One particularly useful dumpster-diving exercise in the town of Neustrelitz by the British Military Liaison Mission (BRIXMIS) revealed top-secret data about the strengths and weaknesses of a new Russian tank. The intel caused such a stir back in London, an urgent R&D programme for a new anti-tank missile was immediately put in place!

It's perfectly reasonable to assume that the Soviets were completely unaware that all their secrets were being whisked out of the bins and sent to London and Washington for analysis, since the quantity and quality of information recovered never seemed to diminish over all the years Operation Tamarisk was active, and even more telling, the Soviets never thought to issue their troops with loo rolls in all that time either!

As if poking through bins full of food scraps, old files, shitty documents, dead rats and goodness knows what other hazardous materials wasn't bad enough, when they were rummaging through the dumpsters outside military hospitals they had to wade through medical waste and even discarded body parts too!

It was all so far removed from the glamorous lifestyles of their literary counterparts.

the pig war

The only war in history triggered by the death of a pig!

Even though it wasn't actually a war ... just a lot of posturing, a few harsh words and a bit of sabre rattling.

The Oregon Treaty (1846) signed on 5 June 1846 in Washington DC between Britain and USA sought to settle the longstanding border dispute between the two countries relating to the land between the Rocky Mountains and the Pacific coastline. With regards to the waters south of Vancouver, it was agreed that the border should run through 'the middle of the channel separating the continent from Vancouver's Island.' Which was all very well and good, except this area of sea was full of little islands, notably San Juan Island and drawing a straight line through this channel meant drawing a straight line through this area of land too.

The island was of equal strategic importance to both countries with British and American settlers making their home there. Both communities were getting along just fine until one fateful day in June 1859 when an American farmer Lyman Cutlar found a large black pig wandering around in his garden, happily stuffing its face with his potatoes! Needless to say, he wasn't best pleased. In fact, he was really pissed off about it and shot the pig dead. Unfortunately, the animal belonged to a British farmer Charles Griffin, who confronted his trigger happy neighbour and demanded £100 compensation. One anecdotal account of their meeting had Lyman saying to Charles, 'It was eating my potatoes', and Charles replying, 'It is up to you to keep your potatoes out of my pig!' It goes without saying that Lyman refused to pay the £100 and when the British authorities threatened to arrest him, he appealed to the US military for protection.

The Commander of the Department of Oregon, General William S Harney, who was well-known for his anti-British views, couldn't wait to lend a hand and dispatched a company of troops from the 9th Infantry Regiment to San Juan Island on 27 July 1859. Then, as a show of force, the Governor of British Columbia, James Douglas (1803-1877) ordered three warships to the area. Over the next month, both sides continued to increase their military presence on the island. By early August 1859, 460 American troops and 14 cannons had been moved into the south of the island and an ever increasing number of warships and 2,140 British soldiers had been sent to the north. Despite being heavily outnumbered, the Americans refused to budge and hunkered down for a fight. However, the commanding officers on both sides, appear to have received the same orders: defend yourselves but whatever you do ... don't fire the first shot.

When the British Commander-in-Chief (Pacific Station) Robert L Baynes (1796-1869) arrived on the island, he was ordered by James Douglas to engage the Americans in battle to resolve the stalemate. At which point, Robert famously refused the order stating that he would not 'involve two great nations in a war over a squabble about a pig.'

When news of the standoff finally reached London and Washington DC, both governments were shocked to learn that they were almost at war with one another because of a bloody pig! A truce was quickly negotiated and it was agreed that the two sides should maintain no more than 100 troops on the island. The Brits in the north and the Yanks in the south.

Aside from the death of one poor pig, there were no other casualties reported.

Note: Ownership of the island wasn't decided until 1872 when an international commission led by Kaiser Wilhelm I of Germany ruled that the maritime border should pass through the Haro Strait to the west of San Juan Island and not to the east through the Rosario Strait as the British had wanted, meaning that from now on San Juan Island belonged to the USA.

the gin craze

Between 1689 and 1697, the British government passed legislation aimed at restricting the import of foreign liquors (especially brandy and cognac from France) and encouraging British distillers to produce more gin by reducing taxes and abolishing the need for licences.

Around the same time, food prices decreased, incomes increased and those people lucky enough to be in work suddenly had a few more pennies to spend on some of life's little luxuries, like getting pissed on gin which was suddenly very available and very cheap. Not to be left out, the jobless and the homeless also felt compelled to spend whatever money they could beg, borrow or steal on gin too. For most of them, drinking themselves unconscious was a cheap and very convenient way of escaping the hardships and struggles they faced in their everyday lives.

Gin was for sale everywhere for just a few pennies, at street stalls, shops and taverns, and at the many dingy basement drinking dens which had opened up. By 1730, there were an estimated 7,000 gin shops in London leading to much drunkenness, social deprivation and violence amongst the poor … and much moral panic amongst the ruling classes and the filthy rich! In 1736, the courtier/political writer, John Hervey, 2nd Baron Hervey (1696-1743) commented, 'The drunkenness of the common people was so universal … the whole town of London swarmed with drunken people from morning till night.'

The home-brewed gin was much stronger than the gin sold today and was often mixed with turpentine spirit and sulphuric acid to give it a little extra oomph! By the early-eighteenth century gin had become cheaper than beer and everyone was addicted to the stuff. Poor people were begging, thieving and whoring to get their gin money; they were going insane and a lot of them were just dropping down dead at the bar from alcoholic poisoning!

Things went from bad to worse when the case of Judith Dufour (c.1704-1734) became public knowledge. She had the habit of leaving her two year-old child Mary at the workhouse whenever she ran out of money. On one particular occasion in 1734 she'd entrusted Mary into their care and then reclaimed her a couple of days later, after forging a note from the church authorising the child's release. She then went out boozing with a friend called Sukey who was later described as 'one of the most vilest creatures in or about the town.' The workhouse had dressed Mary in new clothes, so when the couple ran out of gin money, he persuaded Judith to sell them to earn a few more shillings. They took the little girl into a field, strangled her, left her naked body in a ditch and then sold her clothes before returning to the gin shops to carry on drinking! On 8 March 1734, Judith was hanged for her heinous crime and her body anatomised (a detailed dissection, examination, and analysis). The *Ordinary of Newgate's Account* (1734) which contained the biographies and statements of prisoners who were due to be executed, later reported her confession. 'She said, she was very sorry for what was done, that she never was at Peace since it happened, that she scarce desired to live; and therefore she made a voluntary Confession she had been always of a very surly Disposition, and untractable Creature, a Despiser of Religion, negligent in her Duty to God and Man, and would take no good Advice of her Friends, nor of any god or sober People. She drank and swore much, and was averse to Virtue and Sobriety, delighting in the vilest Companies, and ready to Practice the worst of Actions. She acknowledged the Justice of her Sentence, and died in Peace with all

Mankind.'

The beginning of the end came when the government passed a series of laws to try and curb London's unquenchable thirst for gin, most notably the Spirit Duties Act 1735 (Gin Act 1736) which introduced a retail tax and the need for gin sellers to purchase annual licences. But whereas reputable sellers were forced out of business, the bootleggers survived and distilled even more potent and impure gin than before. The Sale of Spirts Act 1750 (Gin Act 1751) was a little more successful; restricting retail licences to substantial property holders, prohibiting distillers from selling to unlicensed premises and even encouraging people to start drinking beer again!

The artist and social commentator William Hogarth (1697-1764) drew his famous satirical prints 'Gin Lane' (1751) and 'Beer Street' (1751) in support of the Gin Act 1751. The two prints, which were designed to be viewed alongside each other, depicted the squalor and despair of the 'Gin Lane' community with scenes of drunkenness, debauchery and crime, whilst the 'Beer Street' community were portrayed as cheerful, happy-go-lucky and positively sparkling with good health because they'd had the good sense to drink good old-fashioned English ale!

the blockade of porto bello

The Anglo-Spanish War (1727-1729) wasn't a very exciting war. It was short and achieved very little with the highlights being a failed Spanish blockade of Gibraltar (1727) and an equally unsuccessful British blockade of Porto Bello in Panama (1726-1729). Both sides seemed to get bored fairly quickly with a truce being declared in February 1728 and the whole thing being wrapped up a year later after the signing of the *Treaty of Seville* on 9 November 1729.

Britain had been worried that Spain was trying to form an alliance with Austria as a prelude to declaring war. In an attempt to weaken their resolve and discourage them from pursuing such a reckless coalition, the British sent a fleet of twenty warships under the command of Rear-Admiral Francis Hosier (c.1673-1727) to the Spanish West Indies, with orders to blockade the town of Porto Bello and to stop and seize the Spanish treasure ships if any of them tried to leave port.

The fleet arrived off the coast of Panama on 16 June 1726 and just sat out at sea for six months, allowing no ships to pass in or out of the port without first being boarded and subjected to a strict search.

However, after six months, most of the British sailors were dead or dying from yellow fever and Francis Hosier was forced to sail to Jamaica to recruit new men to crew his ships, leaving Porto Bello unguarded. Of course, as soon as the British turned their backs, the Spanish treasure ships just left the port and sailed off towards Spain!

Two months later, after their stopover in Jamaica, the British fleet was again at sea and ready to resume their blockade. But they were still losing men to the fever; Francis himself died of it on 23 August 1727, and then both of his replacements, Edward Hopson (1671-1728) and Edward St Lo (c.1682-1729) died of it too! For two years, the British fleet sailed back and forth between Panama and Jamaica and the Spanish ships just bided their time and made a break for it whenever they weren't being watched. In all that time, the British never seized any treasure and in the process, they lost 3,000 to 4,000 men to yellow fever!

Back in Blighty, Francis Hosier was blamed for the mission's failure, even though he'd just been following orders by waiting it out at sea and not attacking the port. But somebody had to be the fall guy and who better than a dead man who couldn't defend himself?

Note: In 1739, at the start of yet another war between Britain and Spain, Vice-Admiral Edward Vernon (1684-1757) led a small fleet of six ships to Panama with the intention of attacking Porto Bello in revenge for the earlier failed mission. After a fairly quick and relatively bloodless assault, the British took the fort and then hung around for another three weeks ransacking the town, destroying buildings and drinking themselves silly.

death photography

One of the most unsettling practices in Victorian Britain was post-mortem photography.

Portraits of infants and young children were particularly popular as it was the last chance a family had to remember the deceased.

The earliest form of death portraiture were simple shots of the dead child lying in an open casket which were usually taken in the home before family and friends came to pay their respects. But then things got a bit weird. Parents would often pose alongside their dead children; babies would be held in their mother's arms and the bigger kids would be propped up on chairs or held upright by specially designed stands covered by curtains. The child's favourite toys or even the family pet might also appear in the photo. The dead kids would often appear asleep but as the technology improved, photographers began painting open eyes and rosy cheeks onto the negatives to make them seem a little more alive!

It wasn't only the parents who posed for the photos. Sometimes the brothers and sisters would be pictured alongside their deceased siblings. These portraits would often be displayed in the home or sent to other family members or friends as a memento.

Towards the end of the Victorian era, as healthcare improved and the cost of photography decreased, a lot of people could suddenly afford to have photos taken of family members when they were still alive and the fashion for death photography fell away.

the celebrity centenarian

Most of what historians have learnt about the life and times of the agricultural labourer and celebrity pensioner Tom Parr (1483-1635) has been derived from the pamphlet *The Old, Old, Very Old Man: or, The Age and Very Long Life of Thomas Parr* (1635) written by the poet John Taylor (1578-1653). He was supposedly knocking about for 152 years and 9 months having lived through the reigns of ten monarchs from Edward IV (1442-1483) to Charles I (1600-1649).

Of course, there was no actual proof that Old Tom was born in 1483 because nobody thought to keep any records of such things back then and everyone from his own generation who could have supported or disputed his claim had long since died off, but that's what Tom believed and that's what he told everyone.

Although he joined the army when he was 17 years-old, Tom spent most of his life working as a farm labourer in his home county of

Shropshire. He married his first wife Jane Taylor when he was already 80 years-old and they had two children, both of whom died in infancy; he then had an affair and an illegitimate child with Katherine Milton when he was 100 years-old (and was forced to do penance for adultery by wearing a 'sheet of bastardy' (a single white sheet worn during acts of religious penance) when attending his parish church) and then ten years after the death of his first wife, he married Jane Lloyd when he was purportedly 122 years-old.

Stories about the man known as 'Old Parr' with the withered face and the grey beard who was half blind and unable to walk unaided reached the courtier Thomas Howard, 14th Earl of Arundel (1585-1646) who tracked him down in Shropshire and invited him back to London to meet the king. During his audience with Charles I he was asked about his secret for living a long life, to which he replied, 'Keep your head cool by temperance and your feet warm by exercise. Rise early, go soon to bed, and if you want to grow fat [prosperous] keep your eyes open and your mouth shut.' He was known to be a non-smoker and a strict vegetarian (living on a diet of green cheese, onions, coarse bread, buttermilk and ale or cider) but that was probably because he couldn't afford tobacco or anything better to eat as he was so poor!

Old Tom became an overnight celebrity in London and was treated with great kindness by the crowds who came to see him at his many public appearances around town; he had his portrait painted by the two leading Flemish artists Peter Paul Rubens and Anthony van Dyck; he was wined and dined by London's nobility ... and then he dropped down dead.

After his demise on 13 November 1635, the king directed his personal physician William Harvey (1578-1657) to conduct an autopsy. His records from the examination were first published in *De Ortu et Natura Sanguinis* (1669) by John Betts (c.1623-1695) in a section entitled *Anatomical Examination of the Body of Thomas Parr, aged 152 Years* and concluded that the old man had died from a sudden change 'in the non-naturals, the chief mischief being connected with the change of air.' It seems that after breathing in the cool, pure air of Shropshire for all of his life, his lungs couldn't cope with the foul stench of the London air.

THE SECRET TO LONG LIFE

According to the eccentric English writer Philip Thicknesse (1719-1792) it was inhaling the breath of young virgins!

He was adamant that it would ensure a long and happy life and justified his controversial and very creepy theory in *The Valetudinarians Bath Guide, or the Means of Obtaining Long Life and Health* (1780) by citing several examples of men who'd all lived to a considerable age just by being around young people, most notably a 115-year old ex-schoolmaster called Claudius Hermippus who'd been the 'director of a college of young virgins' for many years.

catching leeches

Using leeches to suck out infections and cure the body of disease had been a popular practice for centuries but it wasn't until the early-nineteenth century after the man with too many first names, the French physician, Francois-Joseph-Victor Broussais claimed that most diseases could be treated by bloodletting that the craze for hirudotherapy or medicinal leech therapy really took off.

The Leech Catchers were the poor bastards who earned their living standing around knee deep in dirty water trying to capture as many of the bloodsucking parasites as possible to sell on to the gentlemen physicians. They would happily wade into ponds, bogs and rivers and just stand there using their own bare legs as bait to attract the little suckers.

They would usually have to let them suck away at them for at least twenty minutes or so as it was easier to dislodge fat leeches full of blood than the thinner and much hungrier ones. Their wounds might continue to bleed for hours afterwards, which was good for attracting even more leeches, but not so good for their overall health. Inevitably, many suffered from a dangerous loss of blood or contracted some nasty infection after a hard day's work paddling around in the polluted water. If they were really unlucky, a leech might regurgitate its stomach contents into an open wound which could then turn septic. And if that happened, they'd fall ill and most probably die!

And you thought your job was bad.

the mowing devil

The Mowing-Devil: or, Strange News Out of Hartford-shire (1678) was a pamphlet that told the story of a 'rich industrious farmer' who needed his field of oats harvested. He approached a local labourer, who'd undertaken such work for him in the past, but was taken aback by the extortionate amount of money the man was now demanding to do the job. The two men argued, with the labourer eventually relenting and agreeing to do the work for whatever price the farmer thought fair. But the farmer had changed his mind and refused to discuss the matter any further, telling him 'that the Devil himself should mow his oats before he should have anything to do with them.'

That night many people reported seeing the field on fire. It seemed to burn all night much 'to the great consternation of those that beheld it.' The following morning, the farmer feared that his crops had been ruined but instead, he found them so perfectly mowed in a way 'that no mortal man was able to do the like.' Unusually, the crops had been mowed 'in round circles' (are there any other kind?) and with such a degree of exactness 'that it would have taken up above an age for any man to perform' such a labour in one night.

The pamphlet seemed to suggest that the Devil himself had taken the farmer at his word and spent the night cutting his crops for him! It's certainly what the farmer believed because it was also reported that he was too scared to actually gather them up and so they were just left to rot in the field. Maybe he shouldn't have been such a stingy old git in the first place!

Despite the fact that nobody knows who wrote the pamphlet or the identity of the farmer and the labourer or the mysterious mower, cerealogists and other like-minded weirdos still believe that the pamphlet recounts the story of the world's first recorded crop circle!

mr dodd's holiday camp

Dodd's Socialist Holiday Camp was launched by the political activist and strict teetotaller John Fletcher Dodd (1862-1952) in 1906 with just three bell tents set up in the back garden of his house in Caister, Norfolk. It was one of Britain's first holiday camps and was intended to offer the poor folk from the slums of London's East End the chance to sample the delights of a seaside holiday.

The happy campers slept on straw beds and shared one cold water standpipe; loud talking was banned after 11.00pm and lights-out was at 11.30pm; there was a strict no alcohol and no gambling policy, and on top of all that, everyone was expected to help out with the cooking and the cleaning! Entertainment included sing-songs and storytelling around a camp fire, but the highlight of the week, was the Sunday night political lecture from John banging on about the labour movement, trade unions and his socialist ideals!

the battle of maldon

In the summer of 991, a fleet of Viking ships, possibly commanded by the future King of Norway himself Olaf Tryggvason sailed through the mist along the River Blackwater near Maldon in Essex and dropped anchor at Northey Island after mistaking it for the mainland. Alerted to a possible invasion, a small militia of Saxon villagers and farmers led by the local warlord Byrhtnoth (c.931-991) assembled by the shoreline ready to repel their unwanted visitors.

As the mist cleared, the Vikings realised their mistake and found themselves trapped on the island. An envoy was quickly dispatched across the water by Olaf to inform Byrhtnoth that they would quite happily sail away again and leave the Saxons in peace if they agreed to pay them off with a large amount of gold. But the Saxons were having none of it, preferring instead to stand their ground and fight, with Byrhtnoth sending the envoy back with a message of his own: 'We will pay you with spear tips and sword blades.'

Both sides then waited patiently for the tide to go out ...

The Vikings began an assault across the small causeway which separated the two armies but were surprised by how easily the Saxons could repel their attacks. The extreme narrowness of the land bridge allowed for only a small number of them to cross at any one time and they were easily being picked off and killed by the waiting Saxons. According to the epic poem *The Battle of Maldon* (c.995) only three of their militiamen were employed to hold them off.

Olaf soon grew tired of watching his men running across the causeway and being hacked to bits. It was no way to fight a battle and so he complained to Byrhtnoth that it was all a little unfair. Unbelievably, Byrhtnoth agreed with him and allowed the Vikings to leave the island and reassemble in a nearby field where they could all meet up again and continue the fight!

Olaf hadn't forgotten his manners. He thanked Byrhtnoth for his sportsmanship and then promptly ordered his 3,000-strong army to slaughter every last one of the Saxon militiamen! Unfortunately, Byrhtnoth had completely overlooked the fact that his band of merry men were completely 'outgunned' and outnumbered by a murderous bunch of bloodthirsty Pagan thugs hell-bent on turning the field red with their blood. Almost to a man, they were slain by the Norse invaders with Byrhtnoth being killed early on in the battle, having been speared by an arrow and then chopped into tiny pieces!

If only Byrhtnoth hadn't been quite so chivalrous. There's a fair chance that if he'd played the waiting game, reinforcements would have arrived or the Vikings might have got bored and just sailed away. Instead, his misplaced sportsmanship indirectly led to more battles and more massacres, the *Danegeld* taxes and eventually a Viking being crowned King of England in 1013.

Well done, Byrhtnoth!

the exeter book

The *Codex Exoniensis* (The Exeter Book) (c.970) is the oldest existing anthology of Anglo-Saxon poetry and the earliest collection of Old English literature. The original 131-page book contained forty religious and secular poems and 96 riddles and was donated to Exeter Cathedral by the first Bishop of Exeter Leofric (fl.1016-1072) in 1072. *The Exeter Book* is the most varied and the best preserved of the four surviving major poetic manuscripts written in the Old English vernacular, and in 2016, UNESCO recognised it as one of the world's principal cultural artefacts by placing it on the *Memory of the World* register.

Some of the riddles were written using double entendres and were clearly intended to shock the reader:

'A curiosity hangs by the thigh of a man, under its master's cloak. It is pierced through in the front; it is stiff and hard and it has a good standing-place. When the man pulls up his own robe above his knee, he means to poke with the head of his hanging thing that familiar hole of matching length which he has often filled before!'

What is it?

A key.

the murder of bridget cleary

Bridget Boland (c.1869-1895) married Michael Cleary in 1887. She was a dressmaker and he was a cooper, and they shared a cottage in the village of Ballyvadlea [Ireland] with her elderly father Patrick Boland. By all accounts they were quite a prosperous young couple and lived in the best house in the village. For the time and the place, they seemed to live a fairly comfortable life.

On 4 March 1895, Bridget went to deliver some eggs to her father's cousin Jack Dunne who lived about 2 miles (3.2km) away near the site of a Bronze Age ringfort at Kylenagranagh Hill. Unfortunately, Jack wasn't at home when she arrived, so Bridget decided to hang around and wait for him to return and it's highly likely that she spent some of that time at the ringfort. In Irish folklore, these sites were thought of as fairy forts, places imbued with magic and best avoided but Bridget didn't seem to worry about that! Bridget had always been fascinated by the stories she'd been told by Jack about the fairies. He was a charismatic man, well versed in fairy mythology and known to be a bit of a *seanchai* (storyteller) and so she liked to visit the fort as often as possible.

It was only when it started to rain that she began the long walk home back to her cottage.

The next day, Bridget was confined to her bed with a fever and was visited by the local doctor who diagnosed her with bronchitis. Hardly surprising after all that gallivanting around in the cold and the rain! Just to be on the safe side, a priest was also called to the cottage to give her the last rites!

Her illness continued throughout the week and on Friday 8 March 1895, Jack Dunne visited the house. As he approached Bridget, he suddenly exclaimed: 'That's not Bridget Boland!' and then pointed out that one of her legs now seemed shorter than the other, implying that the real Bridget had been abducted by the fairies and a changeling left in her place. It was well known that when a human was abducted, the changeling would often have some illness or physical disability and Bridget's sudden lopsided appearance seemed to confirm his assertion. It's unsure whether the daft old bugger was really convinced that the fairies had taken her or he'd just meant it as a joke, but whatever his motives, it sowed a seed of doubt in her husband's mind, so he went to seek out the local fairy doctor.

These so-called doctors were supposedly very knowledgeable about fairies and their realms. They usually held an esteemed position in the rural communities of Ireland, particularly amongst the poor and uneducated folk, who really believed that these mischievous little creatures lived at the bottom of their gardens. They were usually people who claimed to have had family members 'touched by the fairies' or had them returned from the fairy realm after being abducted. Their primary role was to prescribe remedies and advise people on how to force the fairies into returning their victims to the human realm. For the most part their services were free of charge although there were also a few unscrupulous fairy doctors who liked to hand out mountains of pills and potions and then charge a whopping big fee for them!

Michael Cleary returned from the fairy doctor clutching a bag full of mixed herbs which were to be boiled in new milk – the nutrient-rich milk first produced by a cow after calving. That night, as three of his cousins held her down, he force-fed his wife the bitter concoction of herb-flavoured milk then everyone shook her and yelled 'Away with you! Come back Bridget Boland, in the name of God!' The men then dragged her to the fireplace as the heat from the flames was supposed to drive out the evil fairy within her. By the end of her ordeal, Michael seemed satisfied that she'd been cured and the following day the priest arrived at the house again to banish any evil spirits that may have still been lingering around. The priest was certainly kept busy by this family!

On 15 March 1895, Bridget got out of bed for the first time in eleven days. Later that afternoon, several family members arrived at their cottage for tea. That was when Bridget made the fatal mistake of asking her husband for some milk. Apparently, fairies were known to love drinking fresh milk and even though Bridget may have always drunk milk, Michael became suspicious. When he confronted her, she taunted him by saying, 'Your mother used to go with the fairies and that is why you think I am going with them.'

One thing led to another ... and Bridget ended up being burnt to death!

Michael had stripped her naked, threatened her with a hot poker from the fire and then poured paraffin oil all over her before setting poor Bridget alight. As her body burned, his family begged him to put out the fire but he refused, claiming, 'She's not my wife. She's an old deceiver sent in place of my wife.' According to him, killing off the fake Bridget was the only way of ensuring the safe return of the real one!

He then wrapped her body in a sheet and buried her in a shallow grave near to the cottage.

Rumours soon circulated around the village that Bridget was missing. As the police began a search for her, Michael retreated to the fairy fort at Kylenagranagh Hill where he spent the next few days and nights waiting for his real wife to be returned to him. On 20 March 1895, arrest warrants were issued for Michael, Jack, Patrick Boland and other family members as well as the fairy doctor Denis Ganey. Two days later police found Bridget's body.

Michael was found guilty of manslaughter on 5 July 1895 after a two day trial and sentenced to twenty years of penal servitude. The judge ruled out a verdict of murder because he was convinced that Michael had acted out of a genuine belief that the fairies had taken his wife. The trial was closely followed by the newspapers in both Ireland and Britain and the story was reported around the world. Obviously, there was plenty of speculation about the family and their motives for the killing. Some people were convinced that Michael really believed in fairies whilst others were a little more sceptical. Bridget had always been a strong independent woman and was rumoured to have been unfaithful to him, so all that gobbledygook about fairies might have just been a convenient excuse for him to bump her off and save face in the village.

the forgotten craze of seaweed collecting

Whilst the gentlemen naturalists and botanists travelled the world drawing, describing and collecting plants, the little women stayed at home and collected seaweed! Tracking down different varieties of the marine algae from around Britain's coasts became a popular pursuit in Victorian Britain and it was viewed as a gentle and uncontroversial way for the women folk to show their appreciation and understanding of the natural world.

They studied it; they lovingly kept scrapbooks to preserve it, and some of the more enthusiastic ladies even gave lectures about it or wrote books about it. One of the best known and most dedicated of these *seaweeders* was the children's book author Margaret Gatty (1809-1873) who took up the pastime when she was visiting Hastings in 1848 and later wrote the fully illustrated encyclopaedia *British Sea-Weeds* (1863) to assist other like-minded hobbyists in their relentless pursuit of the much-coveted flowers of the sea.

Days out and family holidays at the seaside became more and more popular during the late-nineteenth century and what better way to pass the time than strolling along the beaches, climbing over rocks and foraging around at the shoreline, ankle-deep in water and filling up buckets with seaweed. Scrapbooking was already a craze and seaweed with all its various shapes and bright colours made a particularly attractive addition to the pages, and because of its gummy jellylike structure, it stuck itself to the paper, so there was no need to buy any glue!

It's believed that Queen Victoria (1819-1901) was an avid collector. The novelist George Eliot (Mary Ann Evans) (1819-1880) was also thought to have dabbled with the hobby after writing in her journal that the tide pools at Ilfracombe in Devon 'made me quite in love with seaweeds.'

Although the popularity of collecting seaweed was fairly short lived, it had an enormous impact on the environment with some of the most popular and over-collected species almost disappearing from Britain's coastlines altogether!

It might seem a little strange that the Victorians got such a kick out of collecting something so bland as seaweed but the modern trend of eating the stuff would seem even stranger to them!

Note: The world's first ever book illustrated with photographic images was a book about seaweed!

Instead of including drawings of the seaweeds in her three-volume book *Photographs of British Algae: Cyanotype Impressions* (1843-1853), the author Anna Atkins (1799-1871) took advantage of the newly devised blueprinting process invented by John Herschel (1792-1871) and included over 400 very elegant and imaginative photograms of them instead.

circumnavigating the world

In 1580, the English explorer/privateer Francis Drake (c.1540-1596) completed the second known circumnavigation of the world.

He sailed from Plymouth on 13 December 1577 in a squadron of five ships and then spent the next three years attacking Spanish ports, capturing Spanish treasure ships and seizing Spanish land, most notably all the territories north of Mexico including what is now California. He returned to England a hero on 26 September 1580 and a year later he was knighted by Elizabeth I (1533-1603) aboard his ship at Deptford in London.

But there was no great public celebration because nobody wanted to upset the Spanish!

the suspicious death of william rufus

William II (c.1056-1100), more commonly known as William Rufus ('The Red') because of his ruddy complexion but more likely because of the red hair he had as a child, was the third son of William I (William the Conqueror) (c.1028-1087) and acceded to the throne of England in 1087. He wasn't a very popular king with the *Anglo-Saxon Chronicle* describing him as being 'hateful to almost all his people and odious to God.' He was particularly loathed by the clergy. Unlike his father, who donated large amounts of money and land to the Catholic Church, William seemed to go out of his way to do the opposite by raiding the monasteries whenever he ran out of money. He also upset England's powerful noblemen by imposing higher taxes and helping himself to their properties and land as punishment for disloyalty or rebellion.

On 2 August 1100, William was out hunting in the New Forest. He and the Anglo-Norman nobleman Walter Tirel (1065-1136) had become separated from the rest of the hunting party, and at some point during their time alone together, it's been said that Walter fired a wild shot at a passing stag but struck the king in the chest with his arrow instead.

The most extensive near-contemporary account of the incident was recorded in *De Gestis Regum Anglorum* (c.1125) written by the twelfth century's foremost historian William of Malmesbury (c.1095-1143):

'The day before the king died he dreamt that he went to hell and the Devil said to him "I can't wait for tomorrow because we can finally meet in person!" He suddenly awoke. He commanded a light to be brought, and forbade his attendants to leave him. The next day he went into the forest ... He was attended by a few persons ... Walter Thurold [Walter Tirel] remained with him, while the others were on the chase. The sun was now declining, when the king, drawing his bow and letting fly an arrow, slightly wounded a stag which passed before him … The stag was still running … The king, followed it a long time with his eyes, holding up his hand to keep off the power of the sun's rays. At this instant Walter decided to kill another stag. Oh, gracious God! The arrow pierced the king's breast. On receiving the wound the king uttered not a word; but breaking off the shaft of the arrow where it projected from his body … This accelerated his death … Walter immediately ran up, but as he found him senseless, he leapt upon his horse, and escaped with the utmost speed. Indeed there were none to pursue him: some helped his flight; others felt sorry for him …'

Fearful of reprisals, Walter had made his escape to France where he sought sanctuary in a monastery with his old pal, the French monk and historian Suger and was never seen or heard of again. Everyone else in the hunting party had also left the forest just as quickly as Walter, as they too were scared of being implicated in the king's death, and it was left to some passing peasant to do the decent thing and transport his body into the nearest town of Winchester on the back of his cart.

William of Malmesbury might have pinned the blame for the king's death on poor old Walter but nobody really knows for sure if it was him or someone else, and whether it was murder or just an unfortunate accident. None of the other huntsmen reportedly saw the arrow being fired and Walter was known to have been a skilful bowman, so it's unlikely that he would have taken such an impetuous shot. Abbot Suger later said of his friend, 'I have often heard him, when he had nothing to fear nor to hope, solemnly swear that on the day in question he was not in the part of the forest where the king was hunting, nor ever saw him in the forest at all.'

The king had plenty of enemies and it's easy to assume that one of them might have been lurking behind a tree somewhere eager to exact their revenge but it was actually his younger brother Henry (c.1068-1135) who had most to gain from his death. He was present in the forest that day too and could have just as easily fired that fatal shot. Their eldest brother Robert Curthose (c.1051-1134) and the rightful heir to the throne was conveniently out of the country, still making his way home from the Holy Land after doing his bit in the First Crusade (1095-1099), so with William lying dead in the forest, the throne was there for the taking. Rather than go to William's aid, shed a tear or two and organise a funeral as most grieving siblings might have done, young Henry left William where he'd fallen, made a mad dash to London, grabbed the nearest bishop he could find and had himself crowned king at Westminster Abbey only three days later on 5 August 1100.

spring-heeled jack

In the early nineteenth century, a devilish, fire-breathing creature nicknamed Spring-Heeled Jack terrorised the streets of London!

He was first sighted in 1837 by a young servant girl called Mary Stevens when she was out walking in Lavender Hill after the mysterious, cloaked figure suddenly leapt out in front of her and began scratching at her clothes with his claws! Although her screams drew the attention of passers-by, by the time they'd reached the scene her assailant had disappeared back into the shadows. Following this incident, several other young women came forward to report sightings of him around suburban London with every one of them describing their aggressor as a shape-shifting figure, ghostly in appearance with eyes like red fireballs and wearing gloves with claws.

Stories about this strange creature quickly spread around London with the newspapers nicknaming him Spring-Heeled Jack due to his extraordinary ability to leap through the air.

Two of the most famous assaults occurred in February 1838. A young woman called Jane Alsop was attacked on the doorstep of her house after Jack had knocked on the door. He breathed flames in her face and tore at her clothes with metal claws until her sister, who was also in the house at the time, ran to her aid and scared him away. Days later, another attack took place in a different part of the city. This time a man jumped in front of two young women who were out walking and allegedly blew flames at them. The testimonies in both cases seemed to strengthen the popular belief that Jack was some kind of devilish fire-breathing phantom. A man named Thomas Millbank was later arrested for the first attack. However, due to Jane Alsop's insistence that her attacker had breathed out fire and the accused man was clearly incapable of doing so, the case against him was dropped!

It wasn't long before Spring-Heeled Jack was being spotted all over England, although many of the reported attacks were obviously being perpetrated by copycat assailants eager to take advantage of all the hysteria surrounding the real Jack.

By now he was appearing regularly in novels, plays and *Penny Dreadful* storybooks of the time and many unsolved crimes were also being attributed to him by lazy policemen and unscrupulous reporters eager to sell more newspapers.

Although sightings of Jack continued to be reported from all over the country, by the end of the decade they were becoming more and more infrequent. He supposedly made his last appearance in Liverpool in 1904, where he was seen leaping up and down before jumping across the rooftops and running away forever.

the snarky comeback

The incompetent Tory politician John Montagu, 4th Earl of Sandwich (1718-1792) held many offices of state during his rather long and undistinguished political career, including Postmaster General, First Lord of the Admiralty and Secretary of State for the Northern Department. However, he's probably best remembered as the unwitting inventor of the sandwich!

His long-time adversary John Wilkes (1725-1797) was a radical Whig politician and journalist known for his charm and quick wit. He was also a famously ugly man, having a protruding jaw and a rather unsightly squint. Nevertheless, he often boasted that it 'took him only half an hour to talk away his face' due to his amiable personality, although the duration of his efforts seemed to change every time he told the story!

The relationship between the two men had always been strained, not least because of their opposing political views, and they appear to have sustained a long and bitter feud that occasionally flared up into an open confrontation. In one particularly fiery exchange of words, the Earl exclaimed, 'Sir, I do not know whether you will die on the gallows or of the pox!' to which Johnny Boy reportedly quipped, 'That will depend my Lord, on whether I embrace your principles or your mistress!'

knocking-up the workers

Back in the days before people had alarm clocks, they had to hire someone to wake them up in the morning! They were the poor folks like the mill workers, miners, dockers, factory workers and manual labourers, who worked the early shift and needed to be out of their beds long before everyone else.

The people they hired were called knocker-uppers. At first, they used to just bang on the door but that soon proved impractical as they'd wake up the entire household, but even more significantly, they'd usually wake up the people in the houses next door who either didn't want to be woken up or hadn't paid for their services. Then they started tapping lightly on the bedroom windows using a long pole. Some knocker-uppers were a little more inventive with one famous Londoner, Mary Smith using a pea-shooter! It was certainly a lot more practical than traipsing around the streets with a bloody great long pole under your arm. She'd just stand outside the houses and shoot dried peas at the window until her customer was awake. It probably cost her a bit in dried peas though!

In return for being woken up every morning, the customers paid a weekly fee based on how far the knocker-upper had to travel and/or the time they wanted knocking-up. And if the customer didn't settle their bill ... well, they didn't get woken up anymore and they'd be late for work.

The clients would chalk the time they'd want knocking-up on their doorsteps or on a blackboard hanging by their front door. The job was usually carried out by elderly men and women but often police constables might supplement their incomes by knocking-up people on their beat. Although, it was sometimes the case that their knocking-up duties took precedence over their crime-fighting duties …

Robert Paul was the man who stumbled across the body of Jack the Ripper's first victim Mary Ann Nichols (1845-1888). He informed a policeman of his grisly find but it was obvious that he didn't want to be distracted from his knocking-upper duties. He later testified at an inquest, 'I saw a policeman in Church-row, just at the top of Buck's-row, who was going round calling people up and I told him what I had seen, and I asked him to come, but he did not say whether he should come or not. He continued calling the people up, which I thought was a great shame, after I told him the woman was dead.'

the naughty nuns of littlemore

The Benedictine priory at Littlemore in Oxfordshire was founded in 1110 during the reign of King Stephen (1092-1154).

By the mid-fifteenth century there were already reports that abstinence, chastity and prayer were playing very little part in the lives of the prioress and her nuns. In 1445, John Darby, a commissary of William Alnwick, Bishop of Lincoln (fl.1413-1449) had visited the priory only to discover that some of the nuns shared a bed at night, they admitted women boarders and didn't seem particularly keen on all that religious stuff they were supposed to be keen on. The distinctly unholy affairs of the prioress, Alice Wakeley were also exposed. Apparently, she'd regularly entertain various gentlemen in her room after dark and they'd get drunk together! Although the Bishop later instructed the nuns to sleep in separate beds and prohibited any secular persons from visiting the priory, which presumably included any of those amorous gentleman callers, it seems that the prioress and the naughty nuns just continued with their alternative lifestyle as before.

The unconventional behaviour carried on well into the next century with a different set of nuns …

On 17 June 1517, Edmund Horde, a commissary of Bishop William Atwater of Lincoln (1440-1521) arrived at Littlemore Priory. The bishop had heard of all the irregular goings-on and had sent his trusted servant to investigate.

His subsequent *comperta* [report] was very detailed but was effectively nothing more than just a long list of accusations made by the nuns against their prioress Katherine Wells. She'd apparently instructed the nuns to lie to him in order to create a better impression of life at Littlemore Priory but luckily for Edmund, they'd ignored her wishes and couldn't wait to dish the dirt …

It seems that the prioress had given birth to an illegitimate daughter after carrying-on with a chaplain from Kent by the name of Richard Hewes. This had clearly happened some years earlier but had been concealed from the church. The chaplain continued to visit the priory two or three times a year and whilst he was there, he and the prioress lived as a couple and shared the same bed! The nuns told the commissary that they'd pleaded with her to end the affair but she'd refused after claiming they were in love with one another. It was also noted in the *comperta* how she'd intended for her daughter to have a good marriage and had already sold off some of the priory's precious artefacts to raise money for the girl's dowry. The nuns also complained about her strict disciplinarian ways as she would often withhold food, clothing and pay, or have them placed in the stocks for a minor infraction of the rules. Furthermore, they accused her of passing too much time walking around unaccompanied outside of the priory rather than passing it in contemplation and prayer or attending to the priory's administrative duties.

Edmund Horde's report also made reference to Littlemore Priory's shocking state of disrepair. No effort had been made to maintain the buildings, the roofs and walls were damaged and they all leaked water. Some of the outbuildings had even been leased out and the prioress was apparently keeping the rent for herself.

The bishop was understandably upset when he received the report and summoned the prioress to appear before him. She eventually admitted to all the wrong-doings and was sacked on the spot. But realising he had nobody else to fill the post, the bishop then had to let her continue in the job until a suitable replacement could be found. Although any decisions she made, especially those involving disciplinary issues, now had to be approved by Edmund first.

Around nine months later, on 2 September 1518, the bishop visited the priory himself and was appalled to discover that the behaviour of both the prioress and the nuns hadn't improved one little bit since that meeting …

According to the prioress, the nuns were running wild; they romped with boys from the nearby village and refused to be corrected for their wickedness. When she'd placed one of them in the stocks, the others rescued her and burnt the stocks! Before help from neighbours and servants arrived, the nuns had broken a window and made their escape to the nearby village, where they'd abandoned their religion and taken refuge with some sympathetic villagers. She accused them of persistently being disrespectful during mass, playing games, joking around, and chatting and laughing loudly. The prioress also complained about one particular nun, Juliana Wynter, who'd given birth to a child two years earlier, but obviously hadn't learnt the error of her ways, as she was still seeking the company of men!

The nuns, for their part, explained how they'd been punished by the prioress after the commissary's visit for speaking the truth; she'd placed one of them, Anne Wilye in the stocks for a month, seemingly without any provocation, and she'd hit another, Elizabeth Wynter 'on the head with fists and feet, correcting her in an immoderate way.' They also snitched on the prioress about Richard Hewes. Despite all her promises, the randy chaplain had continued to visit the priory and the happy couple had continued to share a bed. Another nun, Juliana Bechamp told the bishop that she was 'ashamed to [be] here [under] the evil ruele [of] my ladye.'

By now, the scandalous behaviour at Littlemore Priory was public knowledge in the surrounding towns. Any potential benefactors donated their money elsewhere and the young women thinking of devoting their lives to the church were travelling longer distances to join other nunneries. The place was falling apart, the prioress was a bully and the nuns were some kind of medieval girl-gang, pissing it up and shagging their way through all the boys in the village!

In 1525, the priory was finally shut down by Cardinal Thomas Wolsey (1473-1530) who then sold off the land to raise funds for a new school, Cardinal College (University of Oxford). The sole remaining monastic building at Littlemore Priory became a pub but closed in 2015 allowing an archaeological dig to take place at the site which uncovered a medieval burial ground containing 92 skeletons. Most of these skeletons were female but many were unidentifiable; one was buried in a stone coffin and she was probably a prioress, and some had been buried face downwards, possibly as a penitential act to atone for their sins.

the man who didn't shoot george washington

The American Revolutionary War (1775-1783) had been raging for two years …

On 11 September 1777, an army of 12,500 British troops were marching through the Pennsylvania countryside towards the patriot capital of Philadelphia. Guarding their flank was a detachment of marksmen led by the 33 year-old Scotsman Patrick Ferguson (1744-1780) who was reputed to be the best shot in the British Army.

Suddenly, an enemy cavalry officer dressed in a flamboyant hussar uniform and another officer wearing a large cocked hat rode into view. Despite first ordering three of his best riflemen to creep forward and pick them off, Patrick then changed his mind and told them to stand down because the enemy soldiers had their backs to them and shooting them in the back just wasn't a very sporting thing to do!

But at least it was still possible to take them captive. Stepping out of the bushes, Patrick then called out to the officers to dismount. The men turned around to see the British soldier pointing his rifle at them but then turned away and rode off. Within a few moments both men had disappeared from view. Patrick later recounted how he could have easily shot them both dead 'but it was not pleasant to fire at the back of an unoffending individual who was acquitting himself coolly of his duty' and so he'd just let them make their escape!

That same day, at the Battle of Brandywine (1772), Patrick was wounded and transferred to a field hospital. It was whilst he was convalescing from his injuries that someone told him the identity of the two enemy soldiers. The hussar was some unknown French officer but the other guy just happened to be the Commander-in-Chief of the Continental Army and the future first President of the United States of America George Washington (1732-1799).

Imagine how differently things might have turned out if only Patrick had taken that shot?

the biggest failure in the history of british motoring

The English inventor/entrepreneur Clive Sinclair (1940-2021) was famous for founding several companies specialising in manufacturing consumer electronics. He probably had his greatest success with the Sinclair Executive (1972) (the world's first slimline electronic pocket calculator) and the Sinclair ZX80 (1980) (Britain's first cheaply-priced, mass-produced home computer).

But then he went and spoilt it all by inventing the Sinclair C5 …

It was a disastrous attempt to produce a mass-market electric vehicle long before such things became fashionable. The C5 was a small, one-person, electric tricycle selling for a whopping £399. But unfortunately for him there weren't a lot of people willing to splash that kind of cash on such a preposterous machine. It wasn't a car and it wasn't a motorcycle or a scooter, just a strange capsule-shaped box on three tiny wheels! The power came from a 0.34hp electric motor allowing for a range of just twenty miles and a top speed of 15mph (24 km/h). Drivers looked uncomfortable and just a little bit ridiculous as they trundled around town, but they looked even more uncomfortable and ridiculous when the battery died and they had to pedal home!

It was too small, too low, too unreliable and far too slow and dangerous for Britain's overcrowded roads. Basically it was just crap!

Sir Clive had projected to sell around 200,000 vehicles a year but of the 14,000 C5s that made it off the production line, only 5,000 were ever sold before the manufacturer, Sinclair Vehicles Ltd, was forced into receivership.

THE SALOON SCOOTER

Britain has a long tradition of producing quirky little cars with unconventional designs and absolutely no mass-market appeal. Everything from Mr Bean's three-wheeled Reliant Robin (which could topple over in anything stronger than a light breeze) to the old-fashioned, wooden framed Morgan sports cars and the luxury Bristol saloons with their bizarre styling and idiosyncratic engineering. Or the DeLorean DMC-12, the ill-fated Belfast-built sports car which was more successful as a time machine than it ever was as a sports car.

One of the quirkiest was the world's smallest production car manufactured by the Peel Engineering Company (Isle of Man) between 1962 and 1965. The Peel P50 Saloon Scooter was a three-wheeled microcar available in just three colours (red, white and blue) with a top speed of 37mph (60km/h) which was advertised as seating just 'one adult and a shopping bag'. It had one door, one headlamp and one tiny windscreen wiper ... but no reverse gear! Because of the car's lightweight fibreglass body, the driver was just expected to get out, lift it up and turn it around before getting back in again and driving forward.

painting the town red

There are several possible origins of the phrase 'painting the town red' but the one involving Henry Beresford, 3rd Marquess of Waterford (1811-1859) is the most often repeated.

Henry was one of those idle, upper-class, mischief-making types. If he'd been poor he'd have been described as a ruffian or a hooligan, but he wasn't, so he was just thought of as a bit eccentric.

In the early hours of 6 April 1837, he and his aristocratic pals were returning home to Melton Mowbray in Leicestershire after a day at the Croxton Park racetrack. They'd obviously had a great day out because they were all pissed out of their heads! On arriving at a tollgate on the road back into town they found a ladder, a few tools and some pots of red paint left behind by workmen ... and decided to have some fun! Henry and his chums grabbed the paint and started splashing it all over the gate, the tollhouse ... and, by all accounts, all over the tollgate keeper too (who'd had the audacity to refuse them entry because of their boisterous drunken state) before continuing into town where they rampaged through the streets knocking over flower pots, smashing windows, trampling gardens, vandalising buildings and chucking red paint everywhere.

At the Red Lion pub they pulled down the sign and threw it into the canal and at the Old Swan Inn Henry was hoisted onto a friend's shoulders so he could splash red paint onto their sign. Occasionally, a policeman would try to intervene but they were beaten up and doused with red paint too!

Eventually more police arrived on the scene. One of the other drunken toffs, Edward Raynard was arrested and thrown in jail but his pals rescued him easily enough by breaking the locks and beating up a few more policemen, some of whom were presumably doused with red paint in keeping with the theme of the evening!

The following day, when Henry had sobered up, he paid for all the damages and apologised to the townsfolk for his unruly behaviour. But he and his drunken pals were still charged with common assault and fined the hefty sum of £100 each.

doing things the easy way

In the early-nineteenth century, the Edinburgh hospitals were the leading centres for anatomical study in Europe but with Scottish law only allowing for medical research on suicide victims and the corpses arriving from prisons and orphanages, this inevitably led to a shortage of cadavers on which the surgeons and physicians of the city could practice their trade.

In the seventeenth century there were no end of dead bodies. Many hundreds of people were executed each year, often for quite trivial offences, so the medics had their pick of the bunch. But a century later all that had changed. Executions had dropped to around fifty a year (as most criminals were now being transported abroad to penal colonies) but the medical staff still needed around 500 bodies a year to continue their studies.

The chronic shortage of cadavers inevitably led to some of the city's more enterprising criminals coming up with a scheme to ensure that supply continued to keep up with demand. They started robbing graves, snatching the dead bodies and selling them on to the hospitals for anatomical research. The crime of bodysnatching was only classed as a misdemeanour, not a felony, and therefore only punishable by a fine or imprisonment rather than execution or transportation to a penal colony. Body snatching soon became a lucrative business for Edinburgh's lowlife criminals; the surgeons paid well and didn't ask too many questions, and the authorities tended to turn a blind eye most of the time. It became so prevalent that relatives would often bury the dearly departed in iron coffins or mount night time vigils at the graveyards. Sometimes the graves were protected by *mortsafes*, a complex and heavy framework of iron bars held in place by rods and padlocks. They were usually laid over the graves for about six weeks then removed when the body inside the coffin was thought to be sufficiently decomposed.

The infamous Edinburgh criminals William Burke (1792-1829) and William Hare (c.1807-fl.1829) are often thought of as being grave robbers but they never actually went anywhere near a grave! These guys didn't wait until the bodies were in the ground, preferring instead to seek out their victims before they were actually dead! It was a lot more convenient than skulking around graveyards in the dead of night and dragging decomposing corpses out of the ground.

They took up their murderous trade on 29 November 1827 when a lodger died in William Hare's boarding house and the two men decided to sell his body for the handsome sum of £7.10s to the prominent surgeon Robert Knox (1793-1862) to use for dissection in his anatomy classes. Two months later another lodger was suffering from a fever and William Hare was concerned that his sickly state would deter other guests from boarding at his house, so the lads just bumped him off too and sold his body to Robert Knox. They continued their killing spree for the rest of 1828, racking up a total of sixteen murders and were only caught after some lodgers discovered the body of their latest victim and contacted the police.

William Hare was offered a deal. He was granted immunity from prosecution if he provided details of the murder and all the others they suspected him and his pal of committing. With the help of the police, he was escorted out of the city and was last seen heading towards the English border. However, William Burke wasn't quite so lucky. He was tried for all the murders, found guilty and sentenced to death. He was hanged on 28 January 1829 and then, through a rather macabre twist of fate, his body was sent to the University of Edinburgh to be used in an anatomy class!

the king who rode to his death

Alexander III of Scotland (1241-1286) was regarded as one of Scotland's greatest monarchs with his long reign marking a period of peace and prosperity in the country. On 18 March 1286, he'd spent the evening at Edinburgh Castle overseeing a meeting with his advisors. When his business was concluded, he decided to proceed straight to Kinghorn in Fife so he could be with his wife Yolande de Dreux (1263-1330) to celebrate her birthday the following day. Despite the late hour, the numerous goblets of wine consumed and the treacherous weather, and against the advice of everyone else present at the meeting, he set off on the long ride home. The ferrymen also tried to dissuade him from continuing his journey but he just waived off their protests and ordered them to take him across the Firth of Forth. Having made it to the other side, further efforts were made to stop him with many of the local people offering to put him up for the night. But yet again, the king refused to listen to reason and continued on his way …

He became separated from his two companions in the dark but blundered on regardless, riding through the fields and the forests without having the faintest idea where the hell he was going. Then he suddenly ran out of all those fields and forests and galloped straight off a cliff edge!

The following morning the bodies of both the king and his horse were found dead at the foot of the cliff.

Alexander had two sons and a daughter who had all predeceased him. However, his daughter Margaret (1261-1283) had been married to King Eric II of Norway and their daughter, who was also called Margaret became the rightful heir to the throne of Scotland. She was only a kid when granddad had died but four years later in 1290 she finally made the trip from Norway to Scotland to be crowned queen … but then rather inconveniently fell ill and died on the way. Keeling over from a bout of food poisoning in Orkney!

So now there was literally no one to take on the job of ruling Scotland.

With the country threatening to descend into chaos, the six noblemen known as the 'Guardians of Scotland' who had been looking after things for all this time in the absence of a monarch had the daft idea of asking the English tyrant Edward I (1239-1307) to decide which of them should be crowned king. This was the guy who'd ruthlessly conquered Wales, expelled the Jews from England and was making plans to go crusading around the Holy Land and start another war with France! He hated the

Scots just as much as he hated the Welsh, the Jews, the Muslims and the French, so it seemed strange that he was considered the best man to decide the future of Scotland.

Nevertheless, it was him they asked and by 1292 he'd made his decision, ruling in favour of John Balliol (c.1249-1314), a weak and unpopular man who he believed would be totally subservient to him. But, a couple of years later, when Edward asked for his support in a military campaign against France, John suddenly grew a pair and refused to comply with his request. In fact, he did the complete opposite and formed a military alliance with Philip IV of France. Edward then ordered his army to attack Berwick-upon-Tweed, Scotland's most important trading port, which was second only to London in economic importance in medieval Britain. *The Scotichronicon*, a fifteenth-century chronicle of Scottish history compiled by the clergyman Walter Bower (c.1385-1449) described the horrific events that took place there: 'When the town had been taken in this way and its citizens had submitted, Edward spared no one, whatever the age or sex, and for two days, streams of blood flowed from the bodies of the slain, for in his tyrannous rage, he ordered 7,500 souls of both sexes to be massacred.' The English army then continued their advance into southern Scotland, beginning the First War of Scottish Independence (1296-1328) ... which was swiftly followed by the Second War of Scottish Independence (1332-1357).

And all because some ancient, pissed-up Scottish king was so bloody insistent on getting back home for some birthday sex!

the combat of the thirty

The little-known War of the Breton Succession (1341-1365) was just one of the many spin-off conflicts in the more famous Hundred Years' War (1337-1453) and involved a fight between the House of Montfort supported by England and Edward III (1312-1377) and the House of Blois supported by France and Philip VI [FRA] for control of the Duchy of Brittany.

And it was during this little-known war, on 26 March 1351, that two groups of thirty opposing English and French knights met-up in a field somewhere in Brittany to do battle ...

According to the medieval French chronicler Jean Froissart, the leader of the French forces Jean de Beaumanoir had challenged his opposing number Robert Bemborough to a fight. At the time, both sides were stuck in their own little enclaves (having failed to make any significant advances for a very long time) and were reduced to just making the occasional, half-hearted sorties into enemy territory now and again for a little bit of fisticuffs. With the real fighting seemingly at a standstill, it's quite possible that the Frenchman issued the challenge just because he was getting bored! Robert Bemborough then increased the stakes by suggesting a tournament involving their best knights and the challenge was duly accepted by Jean …

On the day of the battle, a large crowd gathered to watch the knights slug it out …

They set about their task with relish. Both sides fought bravely and for a very long time. Eventually someone called a time-out and the knights who were still standing sought medical attention and helped themselves to some refreshments! It seems that the crowd had brought along some snacks for the half-time break and the knights took full advantage of their hospitality. England were winning at the interval having killed off four French knights with the loss of only two of their own men.

But things changed in the second-half. As soon as the fighting resumed Robert Bemborough got himself killed and the Englishmen were forced to form a tight defensive formation in an attempt to fend off the repeated French attacks. The French nobleman, Guillaume de Montauban later became the star of the show when he mounted his horse and charged into the enemy line, slaying seven of the English knights and forcing them to surrender.

The French team had emerged victorious with a final score of England - 9 dead, France - 6 dead.

Then, the survivors all shook hands and the crowd packed up their picnics and returned home.

The English prisoners were later released on payment of a small ransom and the War of the Breton Succession continued as before …

the timely death of george v

George V (1865-1936) was an old-fashioned, no-nonsense type of guy with a keen sense of duty, perfectly suited to ruling over Britain and the Empire during the difficult inter-war years. He was much mourned by the public when he passed away on 20 January 1936.

His last words were always assumed to be 'Bugger Bognor!' after he'd been informed that the little seaside town of Bognor in West Sussex was to be renamed Bognor Regis in his honour but after the private diaries of his physician Bertrand Dawson, 1st Viscount Dawson of Penn (1864-1945) were made public in 1986, it seems that his last words were actually 'God damn you!' which were aimed at some poor nurse who was trying to give him a sedative.

Lord Dawson also wrote that he'd hastened the king's death by injecting him with lethal doses of morphine and cocaine!

At around 11.00pm he administered ¾ of a grain of morphine followed shortly afterwards by a grain of coke … and 55 minutes later at 11.55pm the king was pronounced dead. He claimed that he'd acted to preserve the king's dignity and to prevent further distress to his family, but more importantly, he knew that if the king hung around much longer it would be too late to have his death announced in the morning edition of *The Times*. If he didn't expedite matters then his death would end up being reported first by the 'less appropriate evening journals'. And that would never do!

Neither the queen consort, Mary of Teck (Queen Mary) (1867-1953), who was a deeply religious woman, nor the Prince of Wales (Edward VIII) (1894-1972) would have sanctioned euthanasia, so the good doctor took matters into his own hands, secretly administered the lethal cocktail of drugs and then telephoned his wife and told her to ask *The Times* to hold the front page as an important announcement from Buckingham Palace was imminent.

the work of the devil

The Scottish engineer James Blyth (1839-1906) was a pioneer in the field of generating electricity through the use of wind power. In 1887, he installed a cloth-sailed wind turbine in the garden of his holiday cottage at Marykirk in Aberdeenshire. The turbine had a 33-foot (10m) windshaft and stored enough generated electricity in its accumulators (batteries) to power the lights in his cottage, making it the first house in the world to have a wind-powered electricity supply.

He tinkered about with the design of his 'wind engine' for the next few years and in 1891 he was awarded a patent. By now his newly improved wind turbines could generate so much electricity that he had too much of the stuff for his own use and so he offered to light the nearby town's High Street. But the superstitious residents refused his proposal, believing that the mysterious electric light was the work of the Devil!

the hanging of margaret dickson

Margaret Dickson (c.1702-c.1765) lived in Musselburgh in East Lothian with her fisherman husband. Life was tough with Maggie forced to sell fish in the marketplace to make ends meet. Then, in 1722, her husband mysteriously disappeared (most probably after being press-ganged into the Royal Navy) and life suddenly got a lot tougher. There was no more fish to sell, so Maggie went travelling around the country looking for work …

She found it a year later at a tavern in Kelso, Roxburghshire. After beginning an affair with the innkeeper's son, she soon fell pregnant but became fearful of losing her job, so she decided to keep her condition a secret. Tragically, the baby was born prematurely and died a few days later. Still hiding the baby's existence, she'd planned to dispose of the body in the River Tweed but when push came to shove, she couldn't bring herself to do it and just left the body on the riverbank instead.

That same day, the baby was discovered and an investigation by the local authorities led them to Maggie.

She was charged under the Concealment of Pregnancy Act, taken to Edinburgh for trial and hanged on 2 September 1724.

After Maggie was left swinging on the end of a rope, a group of medical students rushed forward to claim the fresh, dissection-ready cadaver for use in class but they were fought off by Maggie's family and friends who wanted her body for a Christian burial. Maggie was soon sealed in a wooden coffin and placed on the back of a cart for transportation back to her home town of Musselburgh. Then, at some point during the journey, the driver heard banging and scratching sounds coming from inside the coffin. He tentatively lifted the lid and was shocked to find Maggie staring back at him, seemingly a lot more alive than she was dead!

The authorities were convinced that the jostling of the cart had literally shaken her back to life and it must have been God's will that Maggie should survive. As a consequence she was immediately pardoned and allowed to live as a free woman.

Her wayward husband then returned and they resumed their life together.

Maggie became a local celebrity around the streets of Edinburgh with the locals nicknaming her 'Half Hangit Maggie'.

the horwood book

The Horwood Book (1821) is one of the most famous examples of anthropodermic bibliopegy, the macabre practice of using human skin to bind books which was common in the eighteenth and nineteenth centuries.

John Horwood (1803-1821) was a miner's son from Hanham near Bristol who was convicted of the murder of Eliza Balsom in 1821. He'd become infatuated with her but after she'd rejected his clumsy advances he started harassing her. A note in the Horwood Book states: 'It appears that Horwood for some time past, teased the girl with proposals, which she had uniformly and indignantly refused: and having latterly endeavoured to intimidate her with his threats, she became alarmed at his conduct, and took every means of avoiding him.'

Then, on 25 January 1821, he saw Eliza talking with another boy and threw a stone at her. Although her injuries were fairly superficial, the wound became infected and she died four days later. John's name was passed on to the police and they went to arrest him for her murder: 'The villain guessed their errand, and tried to jump out from a bedroom window in his shirt ... he seized a quarryman's hammer, and placing himself on the top of the stairs, threatened, with horrid oaths, the destruction of all who approached ... The villain made a great many blows with his hammer ... The Officers closed upon him, knocked him down and after a desperate conflict, at last handcuffed him and dragged him to the carriage.'

His trial began on 11 April 1821 and two days later he was hanged for the murder of Eliza Balsom.

The court case was unusual because some of the key evidence against John Horwood included a detailed phrenological report from Mary Anne Schimmelpenninck (1778-1856), the phrenologist and author of *Theory on the Classification of Beauty and Deformity* (1815). (Phrenology is a pseudoscience involving the detection and measurement of bumps on the skull to predict mental traits). Although she admitted that the 'bump of murder' (which was supposedly a cranial characteristic of all killers) was not present, it was still her conclusion that the shape of John Horwood's skull was proof enough of his inherent wickedness!

His body was handed over to Richard Smith, a doctor at the Bristol Royal Infirmary for dissection in a public lecture. As part of the anatomisation process Horwood's skin had to be removed. Normally, human skin would have been incinerated as medical waste, but Dr Smith had other ideas. Being a keen antiquarian, he decided to make a book out of it. The skin was tanned and then used to bind all the papers and press cuttings he'd written and collected documenting the trial, execution and dissection of John Horwood. The book's front cover was embossed with a skull and crossbones and the words *Cutis Vera Johannis Horwood* (The True Skin of John Horwood).

The Horwood Book is now on permanent display at the M Shed Museum in Bristol.

the explosion of william the conqueror

William I (c.1028-1087), also known as William the Conqueror (to his face) and William the Bastard (behind his back), was a heartless and brutal ruler with his reign of terror over England marked by oppression, massacres, famine and the complete suppression of all Saxon culture. He was a man with a fierce temper and an even fiercer appetite! In later life he piled on the pounds which prompted King Philip I of France to once compare him to a pregnant woman, although it's unclear if he ever became known as William the Fat Bastard!

Early accounts of his death suggested that he'd collapsed from heat exhaustion during the Siege of Mantes (1087) but then the historian William of Malmesbury (c.1095-1143) reported that it was actually the nasty injures he'd sustained after being thrown forward on his horse and squashing his fat belly against the pommel of his saddle which eventually led to his death.

William was carted away from the battlefield to the Priory of Saint Gervase, Rouen in Normandy but his medical staff were powerless to help him and so he just lay there for six weeks before finally popping his clogs on 9 September 1087. Nobody in attendance stood around looking sad and mournful for very long. Instead, they looted the room and ran away with whatever they could carry, leaving William sprawled naked on the floor, having literally robbed him of the clothes off his back. It was only sometime later that a passing knight appears to have taken pity on William and arranged for his decomposed body to be embalmed before being taken to the Benedictine monastery at L'Abbaye-aux-Hommes (Abbey of Saint-Étienne), Caen in Normandy for burial.

The funeral service was delayed by a fire in the town … and then delayed again when one of the townsfolk declared that the king had robbed his father of the land now occupied by the abbey and how unfair it would be if he was laid to rest on stolen ground. His claim was later found to have some merit and after a few weeks of negotiation, the matter was settled. No doubt after a big pile of money had changed hands.

By the time they actually got around to burying poor William, his body was bloated beyond all recognition. In fact, it was so large that it wouldn't fit into the stone sarcophagus that had been specially made for him. As everyone tried pushing and shoving it into place, the corpse suddenly exploded! According to the chronicler/monk Orderic Vitalis (1075-c.1142) 'the swollen bowels burst and an intolerable stench assailed the nostrils of the by-standers and the whole crowd.' Everyone was gagging from the stink and no amount of incense could mask their discomfort. Many people were so traumatised by the experience, they fell ill or ran screaming from the church. But the really unlucky ones were those people standing closest to William who suddenly found themselves covered in big chunks of his rotting flesh!

the chain-smoking, shipyard crane-operator from barrow-in-furness

Britain sweltered in record-high temperatures in the summer of 1976. It was a time of melting roads, shrubland fires, hosepipe bans and 'Phew! What a Scorcher!' newspaper headlines. It was so hot that the gentlemen attending the Henley Royal Regatta were allowed to take off their jackets for the first time in 137 years! Meanwhile, in Barrow-in-Furness a shipyard crane-operator by the name of Maurice Flitcroft (1929-2007) was preparing for his first summer as a professional golfer …

Over the years, he'd worked a series of dead-end jobs and tried his luck at song writing, painting and mountain climbing with varying degrees of success but after watching the 1974 World Match Play Championship on TV, he'd fallen in love with the game of golf. He'd taught himself how to play by reading a manual written by the former pro-golfer and TV commentator Peter Alliss (1931-2020), ordered himself a set of clubs out of a mail order catalogue, and then practiced his putting in the back garden and his bunker shots in a long jump pit at a local athletics field in readiness for his first proper competitive round of golf.

And that first round just happened to be an 18-hole, qualifying game for the British Open Championship, the sport's oldest and grandest competition. He'd filled in the form (declaring himself to be a professional golfer) paid the entrance fee and then simply turned up on the day allocated to him by the tournament organisers.

He arrived late at Formby Golf Club (Merseyside) having got lost on the way and never had the opportunity to have a little knockabout first. As soon as he'd parked his car, he ran into the club shop to buy a few balls and then sprinted across to the first tee where his opponent was waiting for him …

His first tee shot on the first hole set the scene for a truly unremarkable round of golf. He skied the ball straight up in the air and it came back down again with a loud thud just 40 yards (36.6m) further along the fairway from where he was standing. What followed was an unenviable succession of triple and quadruple bogey shots resulting in him carding a round of 121 which was 49 over-par and the worst score in the championship's history! Maurice blamed his shocking performance on nerves. He'd also left his 4-wood club in the car and claimed that his forgetfulness had hampered his style. He didn't bother to play his second-round game after calculating that he'd have to shoot 23 (including 13 holes-in-one) to have any chance of qualifying for the 105th staging of the British Open Championship at Royal Birkdale later that year. Even if he remembered to take his 4-wood with him next time, it was still never going to happen, so he just made his excuses and left.

The previous day, Maurice had played a couple of practice holes with his niece Sandra acting as his caddy and had then retired to the nineteenth hole for a well-earned drink. Unfortunately, he upset the golf club's hierarchy by strolling into the men-only clubhouse bar with Sandra at his side and still wearing his cap (which was a big no-no apparently). The next day, he'd then made headline news with his quite dreadful exhibition on the golf course. His bad behaviour on and off the course hadn't gone down well with the Secretary of the Royal & Ancient Golf Club, Keith Mackenzie, who then banned him from playing at all R&A courses and from entering the tournament ever again!

But what followed became a fanatical 14-year cat-and-mouse game between the two men. A little thing like a lifetime ban wasn't going to get in the way of a man like Maurice from realising his dream. He continued to enter the tournament every year using more and more ludicrous pseudonyms in an attempt to fool Keith, and Keith continued to do his darndest to stop him ever reaching the first tee. He even employed handwriting experts to scrutinise the application forms in an attempt to catch him out.

In 1978, Maurice rolled up to the course as the American Gene Pacecki but was stopped by an official after playing two holes. According to Maurice, he was only caught out because he couldn't do the accent! In 1983, Maurice entered as the Swiss professional golfer Gerald Hoppy and got to play nine holes before he was rumbled and escorted off the course, and in 1990, he turned up as the Frenchman James Beau Jolly who could only speak a few words of English! As well as all the fake names he gave himself, he sometimes appeared in disguise wearing a false moustache, dark glasses or an unusual hat to try and thwart Keith's goons who were on the lookout for him.

The *Daily Telegraph* later described Maurice in his obituary as a 'chain-smoking, shipyard crane-operator from Barrow-in-Furness whose persistent attempts to gate-crash the British Open golf championship produced a sense of humour failure among the members of the golfing establishment.'

the first prince of wales

After suppressing a couple of minor rebellions, Edward I (1239-1307) launched a full-scale military invasion of Wales in 1277. Although the country wouldn't officially become part of the Kingdom of England until the Laws in Wales Acts (1535/1542), the conquests of 1277 and 1282 effectively marked the end of Welsh independence.

The tradition of conferring the title of 'Prince of Wales' on the heir apparent to the English throne began in 1301 when Edward invested his son, Edward of Caernarfon (Edward II) (1284-1327). In an effort to appease the rebellious Welshmen, he'd promised to name 'a prince born in Wales who did not speak a word of English' and then proceeded to present them with his young son who'd been born in Caernarfon (Gwynedd) and only spoke Norman-French!

Not only was he a ruthless bastard, he was a cunning one too!

the last swordsman

In 1926, Jack 'Mad Dog' Churchill (1906-1996) graduated from the Royal Military College, Sandhurst and was commissioned into the 2nd Battalion Manchester Regiment stationed in Rangoon, Burma. But a life in the military during peacetime wasn't particularly exciting for a man like Jack and ten years later he left the army to pursue a career as an actor and entertainer. He'd already had an uncredited role in the film *The Thief of Baghdad* (1924) in which he'd played the part of an archer and after his discharge he immediately resumed his movie career by portraying a bagpipe-playing Scottish soldier in *The Drum* (1938).

He also represented Britain at the World Archery Championships in Oslo in 1939.

Then war broke out and Jack was more than willing and able to serve his country again. He immediately re-enlisted and was shipped off to France as part of the British Expeditionary Force where he led his men into battle wielding a large claymore sword, firmly believing that 'any officer who goes into action without [it] is improperly dressed.' He also took his longbow with him to France. After shooting the officer in charge of a German patrol near the town of L'Épinette with a perfectly aimed arrow, he then raised his sword and led a full scale attack. More kills followed and the sight of this extraordinary soldier rampaging through the French countryside swinging his sword and shooting his arrows like Robin Hood inspired his own men and drew great admiration from other British squaddies in other regiments too.

In 1941, he was the second-in-command of No.3 Commando for a raid on a German garrison at Vågsøy in Norway. As the first landing craft's ramp was lowered into the water, Jack leapt forward playing 'March of the Cameron Men' on his bagpipes before lobbing a few grenades and charging into battle! The whole operation took less than ten minutes with all the enemy soldiers killed or captured.

In 1943, as commanding officer of No.2 Commando, he landed at Catania in Italy before leading his troops through Sicily. Later, during the Salerno Landings, he was ordered to capture a German observation post just outside the town of Molina which overlooked a pass leading down to the beachhead at Salerno. Armed only with his trusty claymore sword, he and another soldier sneaked into the town at night, Jack stuck his sword into the back of the first German soldier they found and then marched him to a sentry post, where they captured more German soldiers ... and so on and so on until they'd rounded up all 42 of them and secured the town! Jack later admitted that the whole mission was 'a bit Errol Flynn-ish'.

In 1944, Jack found himself in Yugoslavia. After storming a hilltop, with six other men who were all killed or wounded in a mortar attack, Jack defiantly played his bagpipes before being knocked unconscious by an exploding grenade. He was later taken prisoner and shipped off to Berlin for interrogation as the Nazis mistakenly believed that he was in some way related to Winston (1874-1965). When they discovered that he wasn't, they transferred him to a POW camp near Oranienburg in Germany. Later that same year, he and an RAF officer Bertram James (1915-2008) crawled under the camp's fence through an abandoned drain and then attempted to walk to the Baltic coast. But they were captured near Rostock just a few miles from the sea, and Jack was sent to another POW camp, this time in Austria. Unsurprisingly, he managed to escape again and walked across the Brenner Pass into Italy where he met up with an advancing column of American troops.

With the war in Europe at its end, Jack was sent to Burma where the fighting was still raging. But by the time he arrived, the war was over there too. Peace was very disappointing for Jack; he'd thoroughly enjoyed the war and was just a little bit upset when all the fighting stopped, prompting him to famously remark: 'If it hadn't been for those damn Yanks, we could have kept the war going for another ten years!'

After the war, he was off to Palestine, where he served with the 1st Battalion, Highland Light Infantry.

In 1952, he reprised his acting career with a role as a castle guard in the big-budget Hollywood film *Ivanhoe* (1952) where he was seen briefly firing his arrows from the battlements of Warwick Castle and then in 1959, he retired from the army altogether and took a desk job at the Ministry of Defence. It was a far cry from storming beaches and blowing shit up ... and it was all rather boring. He was only really 'Mad Jack' now on the commute home from London, when he'd sometimes throw his briefcase out of the train window much to the bemusement of the other passengers. His house backed onto the railway line and the briefcase would always land in his garden ... but they didn't know that.

sabrina island

On 12 June 1811, the sloop-of-war HMS *Sabrina* was patrolling the waters around São Miguel Island in the Azores [Portugal] during the ongoing Peninsular War (1807-1814) when the crew detected seismic activity and then observed an underwater volcanic eruption. Despite various attempts to approach the area again over the next few days to investigate further, poor weather conditions, most notably the weak winds, prevented them from travelling far from their base at Ponta Delgada.

It wasn't until six days later on 18 June 1811 when the ship was finally able to draw close again. This time they saw rock formations just below the surface and witnessed violent emissions of ash and steam rising from underneath the sea. After three hours, the growing volcanic landmass had reached an estimated height of some 22 feet (10m) above sea level.

The ship's captain James Tillard named the new island *Sabrina* after his ship, and on 4 July 1811, when it was safe enough for him and his crew to go ashore, he planted a Union Jack and formally claimed the territory for Great Britain and George III (1738-1820).

A diplomatic row ensued with Portugal but then the island sunk back into the sea again … and nobody really cared anymore!

the darien scheme

The Scottish trader and banker William Paterson (1658-1719) is better known for co-founding the Bank of England in 1694 but he was also the principal architect behind Scotland's ill-fated attempt to establish a colony at Darien on the Isthmus of Panama – the narrow strip of land that lies between the Caribbean Sea/Atlantic Ocean and the Pacific Ocean linking North and South America. Scotland wanted an empire just like England and setting up shop in an area of the world where they could control the foreign trade passing through the world's two great oceans seemed like a jolly good idea at the time.

He established the Company of Scotland (1695-1707) to finance the scheme. Half of the investment capital was meant to be put up by the English government but after pressure from the East India Company (1600-1874), who were afraid of losing their monopoly on trade in the area, they pulled out of the deal, leaving the Scots as the sole stakeholders. Nevertheless, anyone in Scotland with a few pennies to spare invested in the scheme and many more volunteered to become colonists.

Five ships carrying 1,200 settlers set sail with much fanfare from Leith on 12 July 1698.

A few months later, on 2 November 1698, they landed on an

inhospitable, mosquito-infested scrap of land, renamed it Caledonia and set about erecting a fort and the settlement of New Edinburgh. However, their first task was to bury everyone who'd died on the voyage!

The whole expedition was beset by quarrelling, drunkenness and poor leadership; agriculture proved difficult and a lack of food soon took its toll with many of the colonists falling ill from dysentery or the fever; the Spaniards attacked them and the English organised a blockade of the area. William III (1650-1702) also instructed the English and Dutch colonies in North America not to send any supplies to the settlement so as not to upset the Spanish Empire, who were the dominant European power of the time. Only the local tribes seemed willing to offer the Scots any aid by bringing them gifts of fruit and fish.

After only eight months, the settlement was abandoned. When they'd discovered that the Spanish were about to launch an all-out attack, the colonists had called it quits and returned home to Scotland. Only 300 of the original 1,200 made it back alive.

Unfortunately, word of the disastrous expedition didn't reach Scotland in time to prevent a second fleet of six ships carrying another 1,300 colonists from setting sail to Caledonia. They arrived on 30 November 1699 and set about rebuilding the ruined settlement. But the second lot turned out to be just as hopeless as the first. They were completely unprepared for the harshness of the terrain; morale was low, drunkenness and ill-discipline was rife and everyone was dropping like flies from various hideous diseases! One of the three Presbyterian ministers who had accompanied them, Archibald Stobo (1670-1737) was scandalised by their behaviour and claimed the sickness which had blighted their colony was a judgement of God.

It wasn't until the young, swashbuckling nobleman Alexander Campbell (c.1663-c.1729) was sent by the Company of Scotland to take charge that their fortunes started to change. Fearing an imminent Spanish attack, he soon installed some discipline and organised the men into rebuilding the fort. He even led a successful pre-emptive strike against a nearby Spanish stockade in January 1700 … but was wounded in the battle and fell sick with the fever. So he was no bloody use to anyone after that. The colonists then seemed to revert back to their old incompetent and undisciplined ways.

By now, the Spanish were getting really pissed off. This was their part of the world and they didn't take kindly to the Scots setting up a home from home in their territory. And now they'd suffered the ultimate humiliation of having their stockade overrun by these disorganised drunken intruders. So, they gathered together a massive army and attacked New Edinburgh. After laying siege to the fort for a month, the Spanish commander ordered the Scots to surrender, warning them that no quarter would be given if they were forced to make a final assault. After negotiating their surrender, the Scots were allowed to leave unharmed and Caledonia was abandoned forever.

The Darien Scheme had been a complete disaster from start to finish. All the investors had lost their money, the colonists lucky enough to have survived their misadventures in Panama suddenly became the victims of a hate campaign and Scotland was left bankrupt. The scheme's failure was an important factor in Scotland accepting the terms of the Act of Union 1707 and becoming a junior partner in the newly formed Kingdom of Great Britain (1707-1800). As part of the deal, England paid off Scotland's debts with most of that money being diverted to covering the losses incurred by the Company of Scotland.

the german wish list

The Spitfire (1938-1948) was the iconic single-seat World War II fighter plane cherished by its pilots and adored by the public; a symbol of national defiance that helped the RAF turn Britain's darkest hour into its finest during the Battle of Britain (1940).

The swashbuckling, darkly romantic young Luftwaffe pilot Adolf Galland was also a big fan ...

He was a hugely popular figure with his fellow pilots and the German public alike but his aggressive individualism had brought him into conflict on more than one occasion with his commander-in-chief, Reichsmarschall Hermann Göring.

On 3 September 1940, the Reichsmarschall paid a visit to the Pas de Calais airfield in France where Adolf was stationed during the Battle of Britain and started berating him and the other pilots for their lack of success in defeating the RAF. After sarcastically asking Adolf what more he needed to secure a victory, the young flying ace bluntly replied: 'A squadron of spitfires!'

Herr Göring was apparently left speechless with rage!

sunday trading

The Sunday Trading Act 1994 which came into effect on 26 August 1994 allowed for shops in England and Wales to open on a Sunday but for some inexplicable reason, it restricted the times for larger stores over 3,000 sq. ft (280m^2) to a maximum of six hours between 10.00am and 4.00pm.

Which explains why the local Sainsbury's shuts early but the Sainsbury's Local doesn't.

TILL-FREE INCONVENIENCE

The Sainsbury's Local in Holborn, London, was Britain's first till-free convenience store when it opened for business on 30 April 2019. Using the store's own SmartShop app, shoppers could scan the groceries as they went around the mini-supermarket and then use a QR code before leaving to confirm payment instead of standing in a long queue at the checkout. The supermarket thought that time-poor shoppers would welcome the self-scan, till-free experience but they couldn't have been more wrong …

Five months later, they were forced to install two self-scan tills and a checkout (manned by a human) because most of the customers had been using the store's helpdesk (manned by a human) to pay for their goods, resulting in long queues and completely defeating the entre 'shopper in a hurry' principle of the store!

the man in the iron mask

The Story Goes Something Like This …

Harry Bensley (1876-1956) purportedly earned a good annual income from his investments and business activities in Russia and had plenty of cash left over for gambling, drinking and womanising.

He was also a member of the prestigious National Sporting Club in London and it was after dinner one night in 1907 that he became embroiled in an extraordinary wager between two of the club's more prominent members, the American financier and banker J P Morgan and the English peer Hugh Lowther, 5th Earl of Lonsdale (1857-1944). The two men had been arguing if it was possible to walk around the world without ever being identified. On overhearing their conversation, Harry stepped forward and offered to prove it for them one way or another. The two men accepted his offer and agreed to pay him the extravagant sum of $100,000 if he pulled it off. (Another version of this story has Harry losing heavily at cards and unable to pay off his debts. He'd then pleaded with the other two men to accept a forfeit as a means of payment and they'd come up with the idea of having him walk around the world. Judging by the complicated set of rules he was expected to follow this alternative version of events seems a little more plausible).

He was never to be identified; he had to finance the journey himself; he was only allowed to take a change of underwear with him; he had to push a perambulator (pram) all the way, he had to wear a bloody great iron mask on his head … and find himself a wife along the way without letting her know who he was! Harry would also have to pass through 169 British towns and cities followed by 125 others in 18 different countries and J P Morgan would pay for a minder to accompany him at all times just to make sure he didn't cheat and followed the exact route they'd planned out for him.

On 1 January 1908, Harry set off from Trafalgar Square with his assistant, a man known only as Mr Allen, and supposedly spent the next 6½ years on the road …

He was only allowed £1 spending money but his pram was full of photos, pamphlets and postcards advertising his epic journey which he was allowed to sell to earn some more money along the way. At some stops he sold as many as 600-800 mementos, sometimes for as little as a penny, but he still earned enough for food and lodgings.

At Newmarket Races he met Edward VII (1841-1910) and sold him a postcard for £5. It's alleged that the king then asked him for his autograph but Harry politely refused as signing his name would have revealed his identity. Later, in Bexleyheath, he was arrested by an over-zealous policeman for selling his merchandise without a licence. After arriving in court still dressed like some medieval knight, the angry judge ordered him to remove his mask, but after explaining about the wager, Harry was allowed to keep it on and was tried under the name of 'The Man in the Iron Mask'. He was eventually fined 2s.6d (12½p) and then allowed to continue on his journey.

There were huge crowds everywhere Harry stopped and many newspapers reported on his progress around the country. One unnamed newspaper apparently offered a £1,000 reward to anyone who could identity him, prompting an enterprising hotel chambermaid to hide under his bed one night in the hope of seeing his face and claiming the money. But she was discovered just before he pulled off his mask.

By the end of 1908, Harry had walked 2,400 miles (3,862km) around England, averaging 10 miles (16.09km) per day, and was last seen heading towards Scotland. Incredibly, he'd also found himself a wife by this time too!

But the Reality is More Like This …

According to an article, *The Great Masked Man Hoax: The True Story of an Astounding Fraud* which appeared in *Answers* magazine on 19 December 1908, an unidentified author described how he'd duped the public and the newspapers into believing that he was walking around the world with a 4lb 5oz (1.9kg) helmet on his head. He'd had the idea sitting in a jail cell after reading the novel *The Man in the Iron Mask* (1850) by Alexandre Dumas and kept up the ruse for about ten months until headaches, fainting fits and his wife's nagging forced him to call it a day. The author might have been anonymous but there's a fair chance it was Harry … unless there was some other nutter wandering around the country that year with a bloody great helmet on his head!

Then, five years later, Harry popped up again with another version of events ...

He now claimed to have continued travelling for all this time. On 14 August 1914 he'd been in Genoa, after completing 30,000 miles (48,280km) of his journey and having only seven countries left on his to-do list, when war broke out in Europe making it impossible for him to continue. Furthermore, he believed it was his patriotic duty to return to Britain and enlist. He also claimed that J P Morgan called off the bet at the outbreak of World War I (1914-1918) and gave him £4,000 as some sort of consolation prize, which Harry had then donated to charity. It's a nice little end to the story, except Harry was a rake and a scoundrel and the last person you'd expect to make such a heart-warming gesture ... and besides, J P had died over a year earlier!

Perhaps he thought nobody had read that magazine article or enough time had elapsed for them to have forgotten all about it.

He did at least fight for king and country but was invalided out of the army after a year. He never had any business interests in Russia but then claimed to have lost everything in the Russian Revolution (1917) forcing him to spend the rest of his life working dead-end jobs and living in poverty.

mutiny on the *margaret*

The British merchant ship *Margaret* was *en route* from Durban in South Africa to Boston in the USA in 1890 with a cargo of live animals for the city's zoo.

Things were going well until the rats on the ship gobbled up all the grain that was meant for the 400 cockatoos and the cockatoos all died. Then the ship ran into a storm, the snakes and the crocodiles broke free of their cages, and the terrified crew understandably went to hide in their cabins. At this point, it's unclear who was actually steering the ship! The crocodiles and the snakes started fighting each other, one crocodile was killed, and all the snakes were eaten leaving one crocodile to roam the ship at will. Luckily, he didn't have much time to explore as he was crushed to death under falling cargo crates a short time later. After the crew had reclaimed their ship, the monkeys broke free from their cages and started climbing the rigging. The crew tried to dislodge them and shoo them back into the hold but with little success. Then a huge wave crashed over the ship, destroying the masts and sweeping most of the monkeys out to sea.

Then the gorilla forced the lid off his crate and clambered out. 'Having obtained possession of an iron bar, he commanded all objects within 10 feet [3m] of where he was chained,' reported *The Devizes and Wiltshire Gazette*. 'With this formidable truncheon he threatened to brain every sailor who came within range. The cook one day unwarily approaching heard the bar whistling through the air and ducked, but not in time to save his head, which was half scalped.' The cook was then seized by the gorilla after being stunned by the blow and 'would doubtless have throttled him had not a sailor come up with a hatchet and stunned the monster.'

After the ship arrived in Boston and the staff of the zoo arrived at the port to collect their cargo, all that was left to hand over were three monkeys, four parrots and one slightly dazed gorilla!

The Lloyd's Weekly Newspaper reported that it had been 'the most remarkable voyage that has been chronicled outside the realms of fiction for a long time' whilst the ship's captain, who was a master of understatement, merely commented that it was an experience he didn't wish to repeat.

seemed like a good idea at the time

THE WOMEN'S PERIODICAL

The Ladies' Mercury published by John Dunton (1659-1733) was the earliest known periodical designed specifically for women readers. The single-sheet, double-sided paper promised to respond to 'all the most nice and curious questions concerning love, marriage, behaviour, dress and humour of the female sex, whether virgins, wives, or widows' when it first hit the newsstands on 27 February 1693. Unfortunately, the virgins, wives and widows of Britain couldn't have been all that impressed because *The Ladies' Mercury* folded after only four weeks!

LOST IN THE DARK

The origin of cross-country running derives from the older games of Paper Chase and Hare & Hounds played at the English public schools.

The earliest known cross-country club, Thames Hare & Hounds was founded by members of the Thames Rowing Club because they were looking for something to keep themselves fit during the long winter months and unbelievably they decided it should be the lonely, dirty and under-appreciated sport of cross-country running!

They also organised the world's first open cross-country race which was held on Wimbledon Common on 7 December 1867. But it wasn't a particularly well-planned event. The course was 3½ miles (5.63km) long and much of it was over boggy and hilly terrain with few markers to guide the runners. It also started at 5.00pm when it was already dark! Unsurprisingly, many of the competitors got lost and never completed the race.

THE TIN CAN

In 1810, the English merchant Peter Durand (1766-1822) invented the tin can for preserving animal food, vegetables and other perishable goods. It's just a pity that the actual can opener wasn't invented until another thirty years later! The first cans were so heavy and robust, they weighed more than the foodstuff inside and people had to try and open them with whatever tools they had to hand. The instructions on the side of a can usually suggested using a hammer and chisel!

revenge porn

Could revenge porn really have been invented in the fourteenth century?

In medieval law, a person accused of a serious crime would be called to court three times, then on the fourth occasion, if they still hadn't turned up to answer the charges against them, they would be outlawed and executed without trial if caught. As part of this judicial process, one of the earliest written mentions of the f-word was recorded in the Chester County Court Plea Rolls of 3 November 1310 when a man called Roger Fuckebythenavele was included in a long list of outlaws ordered to appear before the magistrates.

It's doubtful if this was his real name. In 2015, the historian Paul Booth (1946-) theorised that it definitely had sexual connotations and that poor Roger may have been saddled with his unflattering nickname, having tried through ignorance or clumsiness to have sexual intercourse via his partner's naval. Or he really believed that was the way things were done! It's quite likely that he would have been called the name by someone who obviously couldn't wait to start blabbing about his naivety in the bedroom. So it's entirely possible that this could have been the first recorded case of revenge porn.

JOHN LE FUCKER

John was mentioned in the Close Rolls of the Chancery of England in an entry dated 26 April 1278 and according to many etymologists it was the first written record of the f-word. However, according to others, his name might have been just another spelling or misspelling for another popular medieval name. The most likely is *Fulcher* meaning soldier which was similar to other variations such as *Foucher, Foucar, Fouchia, Foker, Fucher* and *Fuker.* Of course it wasn't uncommon back then to have a name that described a particular quality, occupation or characteristic, like John the Simple or John the Pious, so why not John the Fucker if that was his particular talent?

the cobra effect

The Cobra Effect occurs when an attempted solution to a problem makes the problem worse and originated from this little anecdotal story set at the time of British colonial rule in India.

To put an end to the deadly menace of snakes crawling around New Delhi in India, more specifically the venomous cobra, the British tried to enlist the help of the local population by offering them a reward for each snake that was killed. The British authorities were soon inundated with dead cobras. Even after many months there was still no let-up in the number of dead snakes being handed in.

Who would have thought there'd be so many of the slimy little critters in one city?

Eventually, someone somewhere became suspicious of all those dead snakes and an investigation started. As it turned out, the Delhiites were a lot more cunning than anyone had imagined. Once they'd discovered how lucrative this source of income could be for them, they'd set up special farms to start breeding the snakes. It was a lot more convenient than searching for them around the city and the Brits were still foolish enough to pay out the big bucks for them!

But not for very long. Once the true reason for the city's never-ending snake problem was discovered, the payments were stopped with immediate effect, causing the cobra breeders to set the now-worthless snakes free. And as a result, there were now more cobras slithering around the streets of New Delhi than ever before!

the greatest curiosity in the world

Daniel Lambert (1770-1809) had been a pretty decent athlete and a keen swimmer in his youth. He'd had a particular interest in field sports and enjoyed hunting, shooting and fishing. His father was a gaol keeper and after working for a short time in a factory, Daniel had then served as his assistant before taking over the position when he retired.

By his own account, he didn't eat and drink a lot and regularly exercised, but despite his fairly healthy lifestyle, he somehow managed to gain an enormous amount of weight and by 1801 when he was only 33 years-old he'd ballooned to around 40 stone (250kg).

In 1805, the gaol closed and Daniel found himself out of work. By now he'd gained another few pounds and had become something of a local celebrity in his home town of Leicester after apparently outweighing Britain's chubbiest person Edward Bright (1721-1750) known as 'The Fat Man of Maldon'. But he was also unemployable now, people were beginning to point at him in the street and so he locked himself away in his home and refused to meet anyone. But this new reclusive lifestyle wouldn't pay the bills. Despite his shyness, he badly needed to earn some money and saw no alternative but to become a professional fat man by exhibiting himself and charging people for the privilege! On 2 April 1806, he placed an advertisement in *The Times* and then set off for London in a specially built, reinforced carriage to make his fortune …

> EXHIBITION – Mr DANIEL LAMBERT of Leicester, the greatest Curiosity in the World, who at the age of 36, weighs upwards of FIFTY STONE … Mr Lambert will see Company at his house, No. 53 Piccadilly, opposite St James's Church, from 12 to 5 o'clock. Admittance 1s.

In the early nineteenth-century there weren't that many chunky people around and even less morbidly obese people like Daniel, so he was viewed as a bit of a curiosity by everyone who came to see him. For five hours each day, he welcomed visitors into his rented home. They were ushered into the parlour, three to five people at a time just to gawp at him and have a little chat. Some customers visited him more than once and many travelled great distances across the country to see him. As well as being impressed by his size, many of his more well-to-do, upper class customers were also impressed by his wit and intellect, possibly due to their shared interest in field sports and his knowledge of dogs and animal breeding. His house at 53 Piccadilly was described as having the air of a fashionable resort and it was noted how happy he appeared when his customers treated him with courtesy and respect. It soon became very cool and very trendy to visit the 'celebrated human mammoth' with some people even counting him as a friend. At one point, he was seeing around 400 people a day!

Of course, not everyone was quite so kind to him. Some visitors saw him more as a freak and would come along just to poke fun at him and ask stupid questions about his diet or the size of his clothes.

Daniel soon grew disillusioned with his new career but luckily for him he didn't need to stick it out for very long. His little business venture had been so successful that he gave it all up after only four months and returned home as a rich man to pursue his passions of cock fighting and breeding hunting dogs. However, he didn't give up his showbiz life altogether. Every now and again, when he was running short of money, he'd embark on a little fundraising tour around the country.

Unfortunately, it was during one of these tours when Daniel collapsed and died. He was staying at a tavern in Stamford and on the morning of 21 June 1808, he'd woken up at his usual time and seemed in good health, but as soon as he began shaving, he had difficulty breathing and started having chest pains. Ten minutes later he was dead!

Because of the obvious logistical problems of transporting his corpse back to Leicester, the authorities made the decision there and then to bury him locally. His body was loaded into a hastily built extra-large coffin and carted off to the nearest cemetery. A suitable XXL sized grave was dug with a sloping approach to avoid having to lower the coffin in from above ... but it still took twenty men half-an-hour to slide it into the grave!

After his death, Daniel became a bit of a cult figure. His biography was published in 1809; pubs were named after him; his clothes and possessions were sold at auction and many are still preserved in libraries and museums to this day, and the term 'Daniel Lambert' entered common usage to mean any grossly overweight or obese person. He is still a popular character in Leicester, where the local newspaper, the *Leicester Mercury* recently described him as 'one of the city's most cherished icons'.

the dunce's hat

The Scottish Catholic priest John Duns Scotus (c.1266-1308) was one of the leading Christian philosophers and theologians of the Middle Ages. He founded the school of scholastic thought known as Scotism and wrote many important works on metaphysics, ethics and theology which later earned him the papal accolade of *Doctor Subtilis* (Subtle Teacher).

He was also a great proponent of wearing pointed hats, strongly believing that wisdom would flow into the hat's tip and then spread into the brain below. If only it was that simple! These hats became popular amongst his students known as the Dunsmen who presumably wore them in the hope of acquiring as much wisdom as their teacher.

John's theories continued to be viewed favourably by ecclesiastical scholars for a long time after his death and the Dunsmen continued to follow his teachings and wear their pointy hats. However, by the seventeenth century, after the Protestant Reformation (1527-1590) and the Renaissance (1485-1660), many of his ideas and philosophies were considered outdated, overly complicated and far too analytical by the reformers and humanist scholars of the time. The Dunsmen were thought to be hopelessly out-of-touch with modern thinking and the term 'dunsman' or 'dunce' was now being used as a derogatory term for anyone daft enough to still follow the teachings of John Duns Scotus. As a consequence their pointy hats were now seen as symbols of foolishness rather than wisdom and eventually became known as the Dunce's Hat.

So, now you know!

brothel tokens

After the Romans occupied Britain they built forts, public baths, shops, taverns and theatres; constructed fresh water systems, canals and long straight roads, and introduced the concepts of education, medicine, sanitation and public order.

They also built a lot of brothels!

There doesn't seem to be any evidence of organised prostitution in Britain until the Romans turned up and established their first *lupanarium* [brothel] in the area of London which is now Southwark. Prostitutes were shipped in from the far corners of the Roman Empire and would literally spend the rest of their short lives performing sexual acts and submitting to whatever indignities were forced upon them.

Southwark's busy brothels soon attracted other low-life businesses to the area such as taverns, race tracks, bath houses and clandestine gambling dens, which in turn attracted thieves, conmen and killers ... and even more prostitutes.

Southwark quickly became a large and ever-expanding red light district, although it was kept quite separate from the more respectable neighbourhoods in the walled city of Londinium (London) on the northern side of the River Thames, with the prostitutes plying their trade in the whorehouses, bath houses, public gardens, graveyards and even shops, where special rooms were set aside for them in the back.

The Romans were one of the biggest sex traffickers in history and prostitution in London during their occupation of the city was just as well organised as all their other activities. The brothels used coins known as *spintriae* (brothel tokens). These little brass coins had a number from I to XVI on one side and a motif illustrating a particular sexual act on the other. It's believed they were used as order slips to avoid any confusion between the buyers and sellers, who rarely came from the same corner of the Empire and/or spoke the same language. By explaining their needs at reception and paying the appropriate fee, the customer would then be handed a specific token graphically portraying their choice of sex act, eliminating any confusion when they finally met up with a young lady in the back room.

THE HOUSE OF PAYNE

Something similar to the Roman brothel token in late-1970s Britain appears to have been the luncheon voucher!

The party hostess and brothel keeper Cynthia Payne (1932-2015) made the headlines in 1978 when her home in a leafy, tree-lined avenue in Streatham, a suburb of London, was raided by police whilst one of her infamous sex parties was in full swing. Fifty-three men including company directors, solicitors, several MPs, a peer of the realm and even a few vicars were discovered in various states of undress frolicking with the young ladies of the house!

When the case came to trial in 1980 it was incorrectly reported in the press that Madame Cyn (as she was known to her clientele) gladly accepted luncheon vouchers as a means of payment but that wasn't the case. The clients would pay her the entry fee and receive the voucher in return; the voucher would then be passed on to the girl upstairs, and the girls would later redeem them for cash from Madame Cyn as proof of services rendered. Originally she used little plastic badges bought from a well-known high street stationery store but the girls weren't daft and started buying their own badges from the same shop, in the hope of earning a little extra money for services very much unrendered.

the gun that fired square bullets

The Puckle Gun was a manually-operated, tripod-mounted machine gun invented by the English lawyer/writer James Puckle (1667-1724) in 1718 and advertised as an anti-boarding gun for use on warships. But it was a fairly clumsy and unreliable device, prone to mechanical problems and difficult to mass produce because of all its many intricate and custom-made parts. Despite the gun's many obvious flaws and the British military's complete lack of interest in buying it, James began selling shares in his company to the public in 1720 to finance the R&D of a newer, more advanced, second-generation version of his machine gun.

One writer of the time rather unkindly remarked that the gun was so bad it 'only wounded [those] who have shares therein'.

To sell his venture to potential investors and sell himself as a stalwart defender of the Christian faith, he demonstrated two different configurations of the gun - one that fired conventional round bullets and one that fired square-shaped bullets! Apparently, they were far more lethal than the round ones and, according to James, they could be used exclusively against the Muslim Turks to 'convince [them] of the benefits of Christian civilisation'.

But James died a few years later and, much to the relief of Muslim Turks everywhere, his new gun was never fired in anger.

the king's mistress

After all those killjoy Puritans were ousted from government and the monarchy was restored in 1660, the people of England resorted to their old ways of drunkenness and debauchery with Charles II (1630-1685) seemingly leading the way by shagging his way around London like a man possessed! Although he'd married the Portuguese beauty Catherine of Braganza in 1662 that didn't stop him from seeing other women.

Nell Gwyn (1650-1687) was just one of the thirteen women who are thought to have shared his bed during his 25 year reign.

She was one of the many new actresses on the English stage; a famous celebrity, the Meryl Streep of her day, and the only royal mistress in history beloved as much by the general public as the king himself. The diarist Samuel Pepys (1633-1703) called her 'pretty, witty Nell' and the poet/playwright John Dryden (1631-1700) wrote plays especially for her to exploit her talents as a comic actress.

Nell's love affair with the king began in April 1668. They were both attending a performance of *She Would If She Could* (1668) by George Etherege (c.1636-1692) at the Lincoln's Inn Fields Theatre. From all accounts, the king spent more time gauping at Nell sitting in an adjacent box than he did watching the play! Having previously been the mistress of the actor Charles Hart (1625-1683) and the poet and courtier Charles Sackville, 6th Earl of Dorset (1643-1706), Nell jokingly referred to him as 'Charles the third'.

During the first couple of years of their affair, there were no rivals for the king's affection but then Louise de Kérouaille arrived from France to serve as a maid-of-honour to Queen Catherine. Obviously, it wasn't long before the king noticed his wife's new servant girl and she was whisked into his bed and made a duchess.

The two women were very different. Louise was French and Catholic whilst Nell was English and Protestant; Louise was despised by the people and Nell was loved by them; Louise was an aristocrat and Nell was a spirited, ex-orange seller, actress and former prostitute! Although the two women were rivals in love and they spent a lot of their time publicly insulting each other, they were also known to take tea together!

Nell had a tongue on her. But she was also very clever and quite droll with her criticism. Unsurprisingly, she is best remembered for one particular witticism involving her rival, which was first recounted by the French nobleman/courtier Philibert de Gramont in his autobiography *Mémoires* (1713). She'd been travelling by coach through Oxford when a mob mistook her for Louise de Kérouaille and began yelling abuse at her, calling her a Catholic whore and 'hooting and loading her with every opprobrious epithet'. Sticking her head out of the window, she called back to them: 'Pray good people be civil. You are mistaken; I am the *Protestant* whore.'

bitten to death by a dead man

Sigurd Eysteinsson of Norway was the ruler of the island of Orkney; a typical man of his time and a typical Viking. He spent most of his life fighting battles in the conquest of Northern Scotland and his fearsome ways soon earned him the nickname of Sigurd the Mighty.

According to the *Orkneyinga Saga,* a history of the Orkney and Shetland Islands thought to have been written between 1192 and 1206, Sigurd met his end after a battle with one of the native Pictish warlords Máel Brigte the Buck-Toothed, who'd obviously gained his less than complimentary moniker because he had a mouthful of pretty impressive teeth!

Sigurd had challenged Máel Brigte to a forty-a-side battle to settle their differences. Máel willingly accepted the challenge and turned up at the agreed battlefield rendezvous point with his 39 best men, only to discover that Sigurd had betrayed him having arrived with eighty men! Needless to say, Máel Brigte and his army were quickly defeated with the Vikings cutting off their heads to take home as souvenirs. Sigurd obviously claimed the head of Máel Brigte and strapped it to his saddle for the long journey back to Orkney.

But Máel Brigte got his revenge. As his severed head bounced around on the horse, those big buck teeth of his continually scratched Sigurd's leg. The leg became inflamed, infection set in and Sigurd was dead before arriving home!

the beggar's benison

The Most Ancient and Most Puissant Order of the Beggar's Benison and Merryland or *Beggar's Benison* [Beggar's Blessing] was founded in 1732 in the picturesque little fishing village of Anstruther in Fife and was devoted to celebrating male sexuality! The secret society's 500-odd membership of prominent merchants, magistrates, aristocrats, landowners, churchmen and businessmen were all dedicated to the 'convivial celebration of male sexuality' and met regularly for an evening of drinking, whoring and masturbating! They dined together, drunk themselves stupid, sung bawdy songs, recited erotic poetry, looked at racy literature, discussed sex, admired naked models, shagged prostitutes and jerked themselves off a lot.

The initiation ceremony for any new member was quite unique. The inductee would sit alone in a room until he got an erection, then someone would blow a penis-shaped horn before leading him into the main chamber where the other society members had gathered. After flopping down his penis on a pewter, everyone else would inspect it and rub their own genitalia up against it. If all went well, although it's unclear what could have gone wrong, the new guy would be welcomed into the fraternity with a toast: 'May prick nor purse ne'er fail you' and then everyone would jerk off together! Finally ... presumably after they'd all finished, the second and final toast was offered: 'Firm erection, fine insertion. Excellent distillation, no contamination' before swigging down a celebratory glass of port.

One of the club's most prized possessions was a wig. But not just any old wig. This one was supposedly made from the pubic hairs of all the mistresses of Charles II (1630-1685). Unfortunately, it was stolen in 1775 after two members quarrelled and one of them ran off to Edinburgh with it and set up his own similarly-themed venture *The Wig Club*. Members would kiss the wig and add a pubic hair from one of their own lady friends to replace the fading ones! George IV (1762-1830) was an honorary member of the *Beggar's Benison* and tried to make amends for the theft by very kindly gifting the club a silver snuff box containing a lock of his own mistress's pubic hairs to replace the stolen wig.

The *Beggar's Benison* was dissolved in 1836 when the fun-filled Georgian era of decadence, sex and debauchery came to an end and was suddenly replaced by the more sombre Victorian era of abstinence and morality.

the curious case of the campden wonder

On 16 August, 1660, 70 year-old William Harrison left his home in Chipping Campden in Gloucestershire to walk the 2 miles (3.2km) to the nearby village of Charingworth to collect some rent payments for his employer. When he failed to return home that evening, his wife sent their servant John Perry to look for him. But then he disappeared too! Neither of the two men had returned by the following morning, so William's son Edward was then sent out to look for them both …

He found the servant, who informed him that he'd been unable to locate his master. Together, they walked to the village of Ebrington, where a few people confirmed having seen William the previous evening, then on to the nearby village of Paxford, where nobody claimed to have seen him. Somehow, he'd managed to disappear between the two villages! Whilst the two men were travelling back home again, they found William's hat, shirt and blood-stained neckband lying by the side of the road. But there was still no sign of William.

Suspicion soon fell on the servant. It was rumoured that he'd murdered his master and that's why he'd stayed out all night. But during questioning, when he was accounting for his movements, he only admitted to being afraid of the dark! There'd been no Moon that night and he'd just hidden in a hen house when first sent out to look for William. He'd only began his search much later around midnight when the clouds had lifted and the Moon had suddenly appeared in the sky but then a mist had descended and he'd got lost, so he decided to sleep under a bush and resume his search in the morning, which is when he'd run into Edward Harrison. But the local magistrate didn't believe a word of it and remanded him in custody for further questioning.

During a subsequent interrogation he then changed his story. Twice! First, he said that a travelling tinker had murdered William Harrison then he claimed that a servant of a local gentleman had robbed and killed him. But it was a fourth and final version of events that the magistrate chose to believe. Having been interrogated further, John Perry then maintained that his mother Joan and his brother Richard had murdered him. They'd waited until he'd finished collecting the rents, robbed him and then dumped his lifeless body in a pond. He also admitted being involved in the get-rich-quick murder plot himself by tipping them off about his master's movements that fateful night. It was also him who'd planted the blood-stained clothing along the roadside, hoping to fool everyone into thinking that William had been murdered at that spot.

Now it was Joan and Richard's turn to be questioned but they denied everything. Although the pond was dredged and no body found, Joan and the boys were still arrested for William's murder. They didn't have an alibi for the night of his disappearance and that was as good as a confession in the seventeenth-century! However, rather unusually, the judge Christopher Turnor (1607-1675) refused to preside over a trial until a body had been found and so Joan and Richard were released from custody.

During his time behind bars, John Perry had also been questioned about a robbery at the Harrison house a year earlier in which £140 was stolen. He admitted telling his brother Richard where the old man kept his money but he himself hadn't actually been involved in the robbery. Afterwards, they'd buried the loot in their garden, only planning to spend it much later when all the fuss had died down and people had forgotten all about the robbery. The stolen money should have still been there but when their garden was dug up, no money was found. Apart from John's confession, there was no real evidence that his family had committed the crime but nonetheless his mother, his brother and him all decided to plead guilty to the robbery charges! Under the Indemnity and Oblivion Act 1660 (pardoning anyone committing a crime during the English Civil War (1642-1651) and the Interregnum (1649-1660) so long as it wasn't for murder, piracy, buggery, rape, witchcraft or bestiality), a first offence was 'on the house' and they knew perfectly well that they'd be pardoned. The family were obviously convinced that pleading guilty to this little misdemeanour was a lot easier than trying to prove their innocence but their willingness to exploit the law and accept their get-out-of-jail-free card would also prove to be their undoing …

By the following year, William Harrison still hadn't turned up, and the new judge in town Robert Hyde (1595-1665) wasn't at all concerned about the lack of evidence or the lack of a body, so Joan and the boys were arrested again and finally put on trial for William's murder. The three defendants were now classed as convicted criminals, having foolishly confessed to that robbery, and in the minds of the judge and the jury this meant that they were far more likely to have committed a murder! Despite continuing to protest their innocence, they were duly convicted of killing William and marched off to the gallows. Being the seventeenth century, it was also assumed that Joan was most probably a witch, so she was hanged first, just in case she'd cast a spell over her sons which had prevented them from confessing. But when she was swinging at the end of a rope, the boys were still claiming that it had all been a terrible misunderstanding, so they were hanged too.

End of story. But not quite …

William Harrison turned up alive and well a year later! As right as rain and eager to start work and return to his old life. He was completely unaware that he was supposed to be dead and that three innocent people had been executed for his murder. He claimed to have been robbed and kidnapped by two men on horseback, then whisked away from England on a ship having been sold for £7 to a group of slave traders. The ship had been attacked somewhere off the North African coast by Turkish pirates, who eventually re-sold him to an elderly doctor in Smyrna, Turkey. Luckily for him, the doctor had died a year or so later and he was able to escape captivity after stowing away on a boat to Portugal where he'd then met an Englishman who took pity on him, gave him some food and money and arranged for his safe passage back to England.

It was an interesting little story but also totally unbelievable! Why would pirates want a 70 year-old man? He was worth nothing to them and the costs and risks of transporting him half way around the world would have far outweighed his £7 value and even the rent money he was supposed to be carrying. However, William Harrison was a well-respected man, reasonably well off and seemingly content with his lot, so the notion that he would have faked his own death and skipped town seems just as unlikely as his convoluted story about the pirates.

Nobody will ever know what really happened to him ...

Or why John Perry had been so keen to implicate himself and his family in a non-existent murder.

the book of the civilised man

The first English Book of Manners or Courtesy Book, *Urbanus Magnus* (Book of the Civilised Man) (c.1270) was most likely written by a medieval nobleman called Daniel of Beccles and was actually a 3,000-line, Latin-verse poem offering advice on etiquette, behaviour and morals.

There were three major recurrent themes to the poem – social hierarchy, self-control and sexual morality. The text was written for well-to-do gentlemen and covered a wide range of day-to-day topics, offering useful advice on how to behave correctly in church, how to conduct yourself at the dinner table and how to entertain guests of a higher or lower order. Daniel's handy little tips included pearls of wisdom such as: 'Do not attack your enemy while he is squatting to defecate' and 'If there is something you do not want people to know, do not tell it to your wife.'

Just in case you weren't up to speed on privy etiquette, Daniel filled in a few of the blanks. Only the host was allowed to go for a piss up against the wall in the dining hall, with all the guests and the servants expected to step outside! 'Clearing the bowels' should always be done outdoors too, preferably in a secluded place with your arse facing 'into the wind' (even though it must have been safer and much more practical to face the other way). If you were unlucky enough to be sharing a communal toilet then it was considered good manners to hang around until the other guy had finished: 'If two together are sitting on a privy, one should not rise while the other is still emptying himself.'

Daniel also imparted his wisdom about picking up working girls too: 'If you are overcome with erotic desire when you are young and your penis drives you to go to a prostitute, do not go to a common whore; empty your testicles quickly and depart quickly.'

He went on to say that a wife should be chosen carefully and only after examining the value of her property. Daniel clearly didn't like women very much, especially the married kind, describing them as lustful, untrustworthy and likely to be screwing around: 'The lascivious woman throws herself around the neck of her lover, her fingers give him those secret touches that she denies to her husband in bed; one wicked act with her lover pleases the lascivious adulteress more than a hundred with her husband; women's minds always burn for the forbidden.' He further states that a wife is always ready and eager to start an affair with 'a cook or a half-wit, a peasant or a ploughman or a chaplain ...' and what she longs for is a 'thick, leaping, robust piece of equipment, long, smooth and stiff ...'

the burning of honoretta

Honoretta Brooks Pratt (1676-1769) was the first recorded European in modern times to be cremated after her corpse was burned in an open grave at a burial ground in Hanover Square in London on 26 September 1769. She firmly believed that vapours rising from the graves in a churchyard harmed the living and was insistent that her own vapours shouldn't be added to the mix!

Which was nice of her.

shooting pigeons

The Games of the II Olympiad held in Paris, France, between 14 May and 28 October 1900 featured live pigeon shooting! It was the first and only time in the history of the Olympic Games when animals were killed for sport.

There were two competitions: the *Grand Prix du Centenaire* (Centenary Grand Prize) held between 19/20 June 1900, attracting 166 competitors; and the main event, the *Grand Prix de l'Exposition Universelle de 1900* (World Expo Grand Prize 1900) held between 25/27 June 1900, attracting 54 competitors. Both events were held in a public park and the only difference between them seems to have been a slight variation in the entry fee that each competitor was expected to pay.

The birds were released into the air about 90 feet (27m) away from the shooters. The rules were simple enough: whoever shot down the most pigeons was the winner with competitors being eliminated after missing a bird. Around 300 pigeons were released altogether but only a few escaped with their lives! Things started to get messy very quickly with dead and injured birds littering the ground. There was blood and feathers all over the park and the women in the audience shrieked with horror at the carnage.

As Australia wasn't yet an independent country in 1900, Australian Donald Mackintosh blasted away with his shotgun in both events for the Great Britain team. He picked up a gold medal after shooting down 22 pigeons in the *Grand Prix du Centenaire* and shared third place for his 18 dead bird tally in the main event, three behind the eventual winner Léon de Lunden of Belgium.

Donald and his fellow pigeon-shooters didn't really regard themselves as Olympians and their achievements were initially omitted from the official records. In 1956, the historian Ferenc Mező was commissioned by the International Olympic Committee to compile a comprehensive record of Olympic champions and he included Donald and his pals as medallists in his final list … but incorrectly listed them as having competed in an archery contest. Although this error was finally brought to light in 1987, it wasn't corrected until 1992 when the Committee updated their records … but then by 2012, all the pigeon-shooters had mysteriously disappeared from the record books again. It's doubtful they'll ever return either.

LONG JUMPING HORSES & OTHER WEIRD OLYMPIC SPORTS

Apart from gunning down innocent pigeons, Olympic athletes could also compete in a few other rather unusual events at the 1900 Paris Olympic Games..

A men's underwater swimming contest was held on 12 August 1900 with fourteen competitors from four nations taking part. Points were awarded for the distance and the time spent underwater; two points for every metre and one point for every second. Although the Frenchman Charles Devendeville picked up the gold medal with 188.4 points, it was reported at the time that the third-place finisher Peder Lykkeberg was the better swimmer and probably swam further than Charlie's winning 60 metres, but for some inexplicable reason, instead of swimming off in a straight line, the Danish champion chose to swim around in circles! The event seems to have been discontinued after these Games, presumably when the organisers realised that it wasn't much of a spectator sport!

Another one-off swimming event was the Men's 200-Metre Obstacle Race which took place on 11/12 August 1900 along the River Seine. Twelve swimmers from five nations competed in the two-day event with Frederick Lane of Australia representing Great Britain and winning the gold medal. Not only did the competitors have to swim the 200-metre course in the quickest time, they also had to shimmy up and down a long pole sticking out of the water, clamber over a line of boats and then swim underneath another line of boats, whilst all the time battling against the river's strong current and the big lumps of raw sewage floating about in the water!

Normally, horses are asked to run around a racetrack or jump over things but at the 1900 Paris Games, they were expected to jump long distances too. The Equestrian Long Jump event was won by the strikingly named Belgian, Constant Octave van Langhendonck on Extra-Dry after jumping a rather unimpressive distance of just over 20 feet (6.32m), which was less than the human gold medal winning long jumper, the American Alvin Kraenzlein, who managed 23½ feet (7.185m).

Bizarrely, the French had also insisted on holding a cricket tournament. Belgium and Holland pulled out, so that only left one game to play between Great Britain and France on 19/20 August 1900. Neither team was nationally selected; the British were represented by a club side The Devon & Somerset Wanderers and the French team was cobbled together from British ex-pats living in Paris, British Embassy staff and a few random Frenchmen brave enough to give it a go! Predictably, the British team triumphed with a 158-run victory after two innings and picked up the gold medal. Neither side seemed particularly aware that they'd even competed in the Olympic Games, as the match was originally a separate competition arranged as part of the *Exposition Universelle* (1900 Paris Exposition) held in the same period between 14 April and 12 November 1900. It was only much later that the tournament was actually included in the official records.

For the first time in Olympic history, women were also allowed to compete in a few events, one of which was a croquet competition. Not that unconventional but maybe a little unconventional for the time because only one person bought a ticket to watch it ... and croquet has never featured at an Olympic Games since! Likewise, hot air ballooning, which was included as a demonstration sport, with competitors being judged by the longest distance and the highest altitude travelled ... and for the best photograph taken from their balloon!

OLYMPIC ART

Art once formed part of the Olympic Games between 1912 and 1948 with medals being awarded for work inspired by sport in five different categories - Architecture, Literature, Music, Painting and Sculpture.

It was the founder of the modern Olympic Games, Baron Pierre de Coubertin who had campaigned for the competitions to be included in the itinerary, believing that a true Olympian should be skilled in art, music and literature as well as being able to run and jump around. He eventually got his way at the Games of the V Olympiad in Stockholm in 1912. But the number of entrants was somewhat disappointing with only 35 artists submitting their work for consideration … and one of them was the Baron himself! In an effort to support his fledgling idea, he'd submitted a poem 'Ode to Sport' (1912) under a pseudonym and then rather fortuitously picked up a gold medal in the literature category.

In 1920, at the Games of the VII Olympiad in Antwerp, the art competitions were little more than just an amusing sideshow to the sporting events, but four years later in Paris, they appeared to have been taken seriously for the first time, with 193 artists submitting their work to the juries. The popularity of these artistic competitions continued right up until 1948 at the Games of the XIV Olympiad in London, even though the competition's format was still fairly chaotic and attracted a lot of submissions sadly lacking in any imagination. Sometimes, the juries were so disappointed by the submissions they didn't bother actually awarding any medals!

The British artist John Copley (1875-1950) is noted for being the world's oldest recipient of any Olympic medal having been awarded a silver medal at the London Games for his engraving 'Polo Players' (1948) in the 'Mixed Painting, Engravings & Etchings' arts event when he was 73 years-old.

Believe it or not, Town Planning was included as a discipline in the Architecture category and medals were awarded four times between 1928 (Amsterdam) and 1948 (London) to the guys with the T-squares and the 2H pencils who'd submitted plans for public parks, stadiums and recreation centres!

In 1949, a report from the International Olympic Committee highlighted the fact that the artists were nearly all professional and this didn't really fit with their ideology of rewarding amateurism, so the competition was dropped. Sadly, the 151 medals that had been awarded between 1912 and 1948 were all officially stricken from the records and no longer count towards a country's overall medal count.

the league of extraordinary communities

In 2012, the little Scottish town of Dull unofficially twinned with Boring in the USA as a means of promoting tourism and encouraging travel between the two rather uninspiring places, and in 2013, the equally as dreary-sounding town of Bland, Australia also joined the partnership to form *The*

League of Extraordinary Communities.

Note: The world's first twinned towns were Keighley in West Yorkshire and Poix-du-Nord in France. A group of soldiers from Keighley, who'd been stationed in the French town during World War I (1914-1918), petitioned their local council on their return to Blighty to set up the scheme as a gesture of solidarity and goodwill between the two communities. It was finally made official in 1920 which led to a fundraising campaign being launched to build the Keighley Hall Community Centre in Poix-du-Nord. The little red-brick building, which is still in use today, was opened in 1922 to cries of 'Vive Keighley! Vive l'Angleterre!'

Note: As yet there is still no word on the towns of Fucking in Austria and Twatt in Orkney pairing up.

Shame.

the resistance fighter

Caratacus (c.10-fl.50) was the leader of the Catuvellauni tribe occupying the town of Verlamion (near modern day St Albans) and a large area of land north of the River Thames.

When the Romans turned up in 43 BE and tried to take his land away from him, he was determined to put up a fight to keep it. This he did successfully for almost a decade after the invasion until the Battle of Caer Caradoc (50) when his army was defeated by the forces of Publius Ostorius Scapula. It was his final battle against the Roman aggressors and led to them securing control of southern *Britannia*. His wife, son and daughter were all captured and his brother surrendered during the fighting, but Caratacus escaped, and fled north to seek refuge amongst the Brigantes, a Celtic tribe controlling most of Northern England. Unfortunately for him, their queen, Cartimandua was loyal to Rome and immediately handed him over to the pursuing Roman soldiers.

Caratacus was then shipped off to Rome and paraded in front of Emperor Claudius. Notwithstanding his dire predicament, he was then allowed to address the Roman senate. He was obviously a very clever man because he managed to convince his captors that his stubborn resistance to their army's occupation of his homeland somehow made Rome's glory in defeating him all the greater: 'I am as nobly born as you. I had men and horses, lands and great riches. Was it wonderful that I wished to keep them? You fight to gain possession of the whole world and make all men your slaves, but I fought for my own land and for freedom. Kill me now and people will think little of you; but if you grant me my life, all men will know that you are not only powerful but merciful.'

The Romans fell for his spiel, he was immediately pardoned and then allowed to live out the rest of his life in peace in Rome.

This guy has to be the greatest bullshitter in history!

the twickenham streaker

Britain's first streaker was actually an Australian called Michael O'Brien who ran stark-bollock naked across the pitch during an England-France Rugby Union game at Twickenham on 20 April 1974. He was apprehended by PC Bruce Perry who famously placed his helmet over the man's dangly bits to spare all our blushes! Later, when being interviewed about the incident, the constable very matter-of-factly commented: 'It was an extremely cold day and Michael had nothing to be proud of.'

the st scholastica day riot

Relations between the townsfolk and the students at Oxford University weren't always as peaceful as they are today …

One of the more infamous events in the history of Oxford and the most serious of the many town vs gown confrontations occurred on 10 February 1355.

It all kicked-off after a rowdy bunch of priests and students drinking in The Swindlestock Tavern complained about the quality of the wine they were being served. The landlord appeared unsympathetic to their grievance and was reported to have responded with 'stubborn and saucy language' and so one of the students threw a quart pot at his head! One thing led to another and before very long, church bells were being rung all across the town to summon both sides to arms!

Both the townsfolk and the students armed themselves with cudgels, staves, bows and arrows, and anything else they could lay their hands on, and were soon battling it out on the streets. The Chancellor of the University, Humphrey de Cherlton, tried to calm the situation but then someone fired an arrow at his head, and he ran away like a big girl.

They fought until nightfall … and then they all went home.

The following morning, the Chancellor issued a proclamation forbidding anyone from disturbing the peace, bearing arms or assaulting anyone else. But everyone just ignored him again and followed the advice of the town's bailiffs instead, who were actively encouraging everyone to pick up their weapons and carry on from where they'd left off the night before!

About eighty townsfolk stormed into St Giles' Church where they knew some of the students were hiding. They chased them to a nearby priory, killing at least one of them and badly injuring a few others on the way, and then shooting and injuring a university professor when he tried to make his escape. Later that day, a 2,000-strong mob arrived from the surrounding villages in support of the townsfolk, waving banners, ransacking taverns and hostels, pissing it up and attacking any students they found cowering in their dorms.

Edward III (1312-1377) issued an urgent decree forbidding any more violence and the following day he summoned the chancellor and other senior university members to a meeting in Woodstock in Oxfordshire. Meanwhile, the townsfolk had gathered for a third day of looting and killing and happily went about their task, even in the full knowledge that they were disobeying a direct order from their king. By the end of that day's rioting much of the town had been burnt to the ground and most of the scholars had fled; the university halls had been vandalised and plundered of any valuables, and around 63 students and perhaps as many as thirty townsfolk lay dead in the cesspits and ditches around Oxford.

The king ordered an immediate investigation into the incident which later found in favour of the university. He then pardoned all of the scholars for their part in the violence, fined the town council and sent the mayor and bailiffs to jail. In addition, he also decreed that all future mayors of Oxford were to march through the streets to the University Church of St Mary the Virgin, on the anniversary of the riots every year for all time, to beg forgiveness from the chancellor and then pay a fine of one penny for every student killed in the violence. This tradition continued for almost five centuries until 1858 when the then Mayor of Oxford Isaac Grubb (1807-1885) just decided not to bother doing it anymore!

the second best whore in the city

Priss Fotheringham (c.1615-c.1668) was one of seventeenth-century London's most famous prostitutes and brothel madams.

The young Priss was reportedly a 'cat-eyed gypsy [and] pleasing to the eye' although her looks quickly faded in later life due to illness and years of knocking back the gin.

She'd left Scotland as a young girl to pursue her whoring career in London but little is known of her early life until the first of her many court appearances in 1652. After Parish Officers had entered an establishment believed to be a house of ill repute and found her 'sitting between two Dutchmen with her breasts naked to the waist and without stockings, drinking and singing in a very uncivil manner' she was hauled into court, found guilty of being a bit of an old prozzy and banged up for a couple of years in the notorious Newgate Prison.

In 1656, she married a loser called Edmund Fotheringham who bullied her, beat her and acted as her pimp. She eventually left him, stole his money and shacked up with another man, but when the money ran out, he abandoned her and she returned to Edmund who promptly had her arrested for theft. She was branded 'a notorious strumpet, a common field walker and one that hath undone several men by giving them the foul disease' at her trial and sentenced to be hanged. However, the Lord Protector, Richard Cromwell (1626-1712) seemingly took pity on her and later commuted the sentence to a bit more jail time in Newgate.

In later life, as her looks faded, Priss bought the Six Windmills tavern and set herself up as a madam. References to her brothel appeared in the pamphlet *The Wandering Whore* (1660) (which described her as the 'second best whore in the city') and many other like-minded publications of the time. What set Priss apart from the other more celebrated prostitutes/madams of the day such as Damaris Page (c.1610-1669) and Elizabeth Cresswell (c.1625-1698) was her celebrated 'chucking' novelty sex act which she continued to perform for her appreciative clientele at the Six Windmills. According to *The Wandering Whore*, Priss would stand on her head naked with her legs apart and have her clients throw coins into her 'commodity' (a common metaphor at the time for the vagina). Her 'chucking' trick proved very lucrative and her 'commodity' would be filled with 'French dollars, Spanish pistols and English half-crowns' several times a day. The money was described as being 'as plentifully poured in as Rhenish wine' and according to legend she could fit sixteen half-crowns in there!

All her girls were taught how to perform the trick and her tavern, which was nicknamed Priscilla Fotheringham's Chuck Office soon became one of the most talked about brothels in all of London.

the last invasion of britain

In 1797, the newly formed French revolutionary government devised a plan to invade Britain.

It would be a three-pronged attack with the main invasion force of 15,000 troops landing at Bantry Bay in Ireland with two smaller diversionary attacks taking place in northern England and Wales. However, the first two invasions never went ahead due to bad weather with the order given just to sail back to France again. That only left the lot heading towards Wales ...

And what a disaster they turned out to be ...

On the night of 22 February 1797, around 1400 French soldiers of the *Légion Noire* led by the Irish-American William Tate disembarked from their ships and landed on British soil near Fishguard. They were nothing more than just a hastily assembled, ill-disciplined mix of regular troops, deserters, convicts and Royalist prisoners mainly because the leader of France, Napoleon Bonaparte, who was busy rampaging his way through Europe at the time, had kept all the best troops for his own military campaigns.

Despite outnumbering the local militia led by John Campbell, 1st Baron Cawdor (c.1753-1821), they quickly lost their enthusiasm for the invasion, many of them deserted the ranks and those who remained descended into a drunken rabble. Very little fighting was done and casualties were light on both sides …

And then after only two days, the invaders were forced into an unconditional surrender!

The surrender document prepared by William Tate referred to the British attacking them with 'troops of the line to the number of several thousand.' But no such numbers were present in the region at that time and it's since been hypothesised that the French forces were probably tricked into believing that the ranks of the British militia had been swelled by the arrival of reinforcements after they'd spotted local women standing high on the clifftop dressed in the traditional Welsh costumes of scarlet tunics and tall black hats. From a distance they would have looked exactly like British soldiers!

A special mention goes to a 47-year old spinster called Jemima Nicholas (c.1750-1832), known locally as Jemima Fawr (Jemima the Great), who single-handedly rounded-up a dozen French soldiers armed only with her pitchfork and marched them away to a makeshift jail in the local church!

After a brief spell in prison, William Tate and most of his soldiers were returned to France in a prisoner swap a year later.

the foggy commentary

The War Emergency League (Eastern Division) football match between Hibernian FC and Hearts FC took place at Easter Road in Edinburgh on 1 January 1940 and was broadcast live on the radio by the BBC.

Unfortunately, the city was shrouded in fog with the players and the estimated 12,000 crowd unable to see anything further than the end of their own noses! Under normal circumstances the match would have been postponed but it was wartime; the game was being broadcast to British soldiers fighting overseas, and cancelling the match might have alerted the Germans to the weather conditions in Edinburgh. The nearby dockyards at Leith and the Forth Railway Bridge were both major targets for the Luftwaffe and the low clouds would have provided perfect cover for a bombing raid.

The game went ahead with the BBC's match reporter Bob Kingsley being instructed not to mention the fog and provide a commentary as if it was a bright sunny day. Although he employed runners to go back and forth between the pitch and his commentary position to tell him what was happening, the messages he received were often muddled and only added to the confusion, so for the most part he just made things up as he went along! Luckily, he had a vivid imagination and described a game packed with exciting play, loads of goals, crunching tackles, goalmouth scrambles and near misses.

He didn't know it at the time but his adlibbing wasn't all that far from the truth ...

Hibs went into the break winning 3-2 but then the referee realised that he'd blown his whistle after only 43 minutes and so the teams were led back onto the field again to play out the remaining two minutes ... during which time Hearts scored another two goals! In the second half, Hibs went 5-3 down but managed to pull it back to 5-5 before the Hearts striker Tommy Walker (1915-1993) scored the winner in the last minute of the game.

Of course everyone at the stadium had no idea what was happening and the people listening to the match on the radio were following a completely different game! As darkness descended late in the game, many in the crowd drifted away but there were just as many fans who didn't even know the game had finished and remained on the terraces for ten minutes or more after the final whistle! Bob himself continued his commentary for fifteen minutes after the game had ended!

It was reported afterwards that Bob Kingsley was a little disappointed to discover that the real game had turned out to be just as exciting as his imaginary commentary.

the wicked bible

The *King James Bible* was the third English translation of the Bible. Conceived in 1604 by James I (1566-1625) and representatives from the Church of England, and first published in 1611. The Bible contained all 39 books of the Old Testament, the 14 books of the Apocrypha and the 27 books of the New Testament. It was noted for its majesty of style and is considered to be one of the most important literary accomplishments of early-modern England.

However, the 1631 re-print undertaken by the royal printers, Robert Barker and Martin Lucas contained the worst typographical error in history! They'd accidentally omitted the word 'not' from the seventh commandment (Exodus 20:14) resulting in the text proudly proclaiming: 'Thou shall commit adultery'. Charles I (1600-1649) was outraged when he learnt of the blunder and the Archbishop of Canterbury George Abbot (1562-1633) wasn't too pleased either! The clumsy printers were immediately hauled into court to answer for their crime, fined £300 and deprived of their printing licence, which effectively ended their careers.

Considering the time and the crime it could be argued they got off rather lightly.

the missionary man

In 563, the Irish missionary Columba (521-597) and twelve of his followers arrived on the white sandy beaches of Iona, a small island in the Ulster kingdom of Dál Riata, to establish a monastic community and convert the northern Pictish tribes to Christianity.

Columba was the grandson of the legendary Irish king Niall Noigíallach. He studied at the Irish monastic school of Clonard Abbey and became one of the twelve students and monastic saints tutored by St Finnian (470-549) known as the 'Twelve Apostles of Ireland'.

Sometime around 560, Columba is rumoured to have had a bit of a falling-out with another monk Finnian of Movilla (c.495-589) after he'd secretly copied his psalter and decided to keep it for his own use. Columba argued that he owned the duplicate manuscript because he'd done all the copying but Finnian contended that he owned it because he owned the original. The conflict between the two clergymen might be described as the world's first copyright dispute! Both men then took their grievances to the High King of Ireland, Diarmait mac Cerbaill (c.486-c.565) who ruled in favour of Finnian, famously summing up his verdict by announcing: 'To every cow belongs her calf, therefore to every book belongs its copy.' In other words, every copy of a book belonged to the owner of the original book. Columba was not best pleased by the king's ruling, the two men continued squabbling ... one thing led to another ... and before long clans were fighting other clans at the Battle of Cúl Dreimhne (561) with the loss of 3,000 lives.

Columba and his supporters might have won that battle but afterwards he was full of remorse and fled Ireland with the intention of converting as many souls to Christianity as had been lost on the battlefield. He didn't travel very far though, settling on the first place he found where it was impossible to see his homeland of Ireland.

He set about building an abbey and then went wandering around mainland Scotland preaching the word of God, performing the odd miracle or two, building churches and hobnobbing with the local kings. As well as being a scholar, monk, missionary, poet, politician and diplomat he was also a bit of a nutter! As soon as he arrived on Iona, he immediately banished all women and cows from the island claiming: 'Where there is a cow there is a woman, and where there is a woman there is mischief.' Why were people so fixated with cows back then? The workers who built his abbey were therefore forced to leave their wives and daughters on the nearby island of Eilean nam Ban (Woman's Island). Stranger still, Columba then banished all frogs and snakes from Iona too. Although it remains unclear how he actually achieved this!

The voices in his head had persuaded Columba that he couldn't complete his abbey unless someone was buried alive in the building's foundations! His BFF, Odran of Iona, promptly volunteered for the job and Columba continued building his abbey around him. But that wasn't the last anyone saw of good old Odran. Apparently, he later lifted his head out of the ground and bellowed: 'There is no Hell as you suppose, nor Heaven that people talk about,' at which point, Columba ordered more earth to be shovelled on top of him to stop his blaspheming. Another version of the story has Columba wanting to see his old mate one last time and ordering the pit where he lay to be uncovered. To his horror, Odran was still alive and he then tried to climb out of his grave. Maybe he'd changed his mind? But Columba was having none of it and ordered more earth thrown into the pit to make him stay put.

As soon as the abbey was built, all the monks set about their various tasks. They loved nothing better than scribbling manuscripts and their 'bestselling work' was the illuminated manuscript *The Book of Kells* (c.800) containing the first four Gospels of the New Testament, which is now considered to be Ireland's finest national treasure.

THE FIRST SIGHTING OF NESSIE

The Highlands of Scotland are the wildest, remotest and the most beautiful part of the British Isles. Mountains, lochs, fairytale castles, white sandy beaches, moorland tinged with the purple hues of heather and even a big scary monster called Nessie!

The first sighting of the Loch Ness Monster was recorded by the great man himself in 565BE. He and his followers were roaming around the Highlands one day when they stumbled across a burial party by the banks of the River Ness. The deceased man had apparently been attacked by a huge 'water beast' whilst swimming in the river. Columba then sent a follower into the river to entice the creature out of hiding. As it suddenly appeared from the water, Columba made the sign of the cross and yelled: 'Go no further! Do not touch the man! Go back at once!' The beast stopped dead in its tracks before swimming away and Columba and his followers then gave thanks to God for what they believed to be a miracle.

ALAN FERGUSON

the surgeon's photograph

The Loch Ness Monster is believed to be a *Plesiosaurus Dolichodeirus,* a type of marine dinosaur which roamed the earth some 205 million years ago. She was nicknamed Nessie sometime in the 1940s and the famous naturalist Peter Scott (1909-1989) awarded her the scientific name of *Nessiteras Rhombopteryx* in 1975.

The first full scientific survey of Loch Ness was carried out in 1901. Since then, Nessie hunters have used underwater cameras, sonar, fish bait, submarines and even big chunks of bacon to try and lure the creature out of the water! The most expensive Nessie hunt to date occurred in 1987 but their findings only showed a creature 'larger than a shark but smaller than a whale' present somewhere in the loch.

The most famous sighting of the Loch Ness Monster occurred in 1934 and was captured in a photograph by the gynaecologist/surgeon Robert Kenneth Wilson (1899-1969). The grainy black-and-white image, which later became known as the 'Surgeon's Photograph' showed Nessie emerging from the rippling waters of the loch and was first published in the *Daily Mail* on 21 April 1934. Although there were plenty of doubts about its authenticity at the time and for many years afterwards, it wasn't until the mid-1990s when it was finally proven to be a fake.

In 1933, the actor, film director and big-game hunter Marmaduke Wetherell (1883-1939) had been hired by the *Daily Mail* to find proof of

Nessie's existence. He claimed to have found gigantic footprints by the shores of the loch, however, when casts were taken and sent to the boffins at the Natural History Museum (London) for analysis they turned out to have been made by a hippopotamus ... or more accurately, by one of those tasteless hippopotamus-foot umbrella stands that were so popular at the time!

Marmaduke had been fooled by the hoax or had perpetrated the hoax. It's a little unclear. Either way it wasn't a good look for him and he was ridiculed by the *Daily Mail*. He might have retreated from public view but he wanted revenge on the newspaper who'd made him look so stupid. A year later, he enlisted the help of his stepson Christian Spurling (1904-1993) and together they constructed a model of Nessie from some wood putty and a toy submarine and took a photograph of it bobbing around on the surface of Loch Ness. The submarine was later sunk and is presumably still lying at the bottom of the loch somewhere! Then, they recruited their good friend, the esteemed gynaecologist Robert Kenneth Wilson, who enjoyed a practical joke, to act as their 'front man' because his trusted reputation as a doctor would lend some credibility to their little prank.

Luckily, the *Daily Mail* was still obsessed with finding Nessie and jumped at the chance to publish the photo along with an interview with Robert. He described the creature as having a small head with a swan-like neck protruding 3 feet (0.9m) above the water's surface and went on to explain how he'd just been standing by the edge of the loch when he saw it, grabbed his camera, and took the shot!

For sixty years people thought that photo was the real thing but then Christian Spurling confessed to the hoax on his deathbed.

The legend of this strange, notoriously shy water beast living in Loch Ness continues to feature in books, films and TV shows and is kept alive by the canny locals making money out of it, the gullible tourists and the ever-hopeful army of scientists and amateur Nessie hunters who regularly descend on the loch searching for her.

the cleveland street scandal

On 4 July 1889, a 15 year-old GPO telegraph messenger boy, Charles Swinscow was detained by the police and found to have fourteen shillings in his pocket, a considerable amount of money and the equivalent of several weeks' wages. During questioning he admitted to being a prostitute and working for a man called Charles Hammond in a brothel at 19 Cleveland Street in London, where for the sum of four shillings, he would permit his clients to 'have a go between [his] legs' and 'put their persons into [him].' He then went on to identify a few other GPO colleagues supplementing their wages doing the same thing.

Victorian London's most famous policeman Frederick Abberline (1843-1929) was assigned to the case and immediately set off with a team of officers to search the brothel and arrest Charles Hammond for 'the abominable crime of buggery'. But when they arrived at the north London address, their man had already fled.

The police staked out the premises and observed that someone they knew only as 'Mr Brown' came and went with alarming regularity. After the messenger boy identified the mysterious man as one of their more frequent customers, the police followed him back to an army barracks in Knightsbridge and were shocked to discover that Mr Brown was none other than Lord Arthur Somerset (1851-1926), a pillar of late-Victorian London aristocratic society, a Major in the Royal Horse Guards regiment and equerry to Edward, Prince of Wales (Edward VII) (1841-1910). The Prince of Wales was flabbergasted when he was told of the news: 'I won't believe it, any more than I should if they accused the Archbishop of Canterbury!'

Despite the Prince's support, Lord Somerset wasted no time in hiring a lawyer, who warned the authorities that if the case ever came to court, he might be forced to reveal the name of the brothel's most distinguished client currently known only by the initials PAV. Everyone assumed that PAV was Queen Victoria's grandson, Prince Albert Victor, Duke of Clarence and Avondale (1864-1892) and started to panic. The police then seemed to conveniently drag their heels, prolonging the investigation and delaying the court case just long enough for Lord Somerset to flee the country! So now there was nobody to prosecute apart from the poor messenger boys. Four of them were found guilty of gross indecency and sentenced to between four and nine months hard labour.

That might have been the end of it, if it hadn't been for a journalist by the name of Ernest Parke, the founder of *The North London Press*. In an article published on 16 November 1889, he named three men, Lord Somerset, Henry FitzRoy, Earl of Euston (1848-1912) and a mysterious 'more distinguished and more highly placed' gentleman (who everyone just assumed was Prince Albert Victor again) as being clients of the brothel. Ernest mistakenly believed that the two aristocrats he'd named and shamed were abroad and unlikely to return to England, but the Earl of Euston was still in London and felt obliged to take him to court for libel. The trial began on 19 January 1890 with his Lordship claiming his appearance at 19 Cleveland Street was all just a terrible misunderstanding. It was true ... he had visited the brothel but only because he thought there were women inside. Once he'd realised his mistake, he'd made his excuses and left. Yeah, right! Despite Ernest Parke summoning a witness called John Saul, who'd worked at the brothel, and who then went on to describe in great detail the kind of 'services' he'd provided to his Lordship, the judge rejected his evidence because John Saul was a self-confessed prostitute and therefore unlikely to be a reliable and trustworthy witness! Ernest Parke was later found guilty of libel and sentenced to one year in prison!

At the end of it all, the messenger boys were imprisoned, and the toffs ... the real villains of the piece, just carried on with their lives as if nothing had happened. The Earl of Euston was absolved from any wrongdoing and the mysterious Lord Somerset never returned to Britain to face charges choosing instead to spend the rest of his life living it up in the south of France with a companion called Andrew. Presumably things turned out as they did because the queen's grandson was most probably involved and a massive damage limitation exercise had been put in place by the government to protect him.

lost in translation

Notwithstanding only one percent of the UK population (and about twenty percent of the population of Wales) speaking Welsh (Cymraeg), the Welsh government, the local authorities and all businesses and shops in the country are still expected to produce any literature, signs and public notices in both English and Welsh.

But things don't always go to plan ...

Back in 2008, there was a famous incident involving Swansea Council. The Highways department had sent an e-mail to their in-house translation office asking for the phrase: 'No entry for heavy goods vehicles. Residential site only' to be translated into Welsh for a proposed new road sign and received an immediate reply reading: 'Nid wyf yn y swyddfa ar hyn o bryd. Anfonwch unrhyw waith I'w gyfieithu.' It was only after the sign had been erected in Llansamlet that their mistake came to light as the translated message actually read: 'I am not in the office at the moment. Please send any work to be translated.'

TOO GOOD TO BE TRUE

In 2019, it was the supermarket chain ASDA who got it so spectacularly wrong! When shoppers at their store in Cwmbran noticed the free booze offer it seemed too good to be true. And it was ... because it was just another dodgy translation. They'd inadvertently hung up a sign advertising 'alcohol am ddim' instead of 'di-alcohol' ('free alcohol' instead of 'alcohol free').

the anglo-zanzibar war

Germany signed over the little African state of Zanzibar to Britain in exchange for control of Tanzania in the Heligoland-Zanzibar Treaty (1890). The British government declared that the island was now their protectorate and in 1893 they installed the puppet-leader Sultan Hamad bin Thuwaini who'd always been a keen supporter of British rule in the region.

He ruled Zanzibar for three years. Then, on 25 August 1896, he suddenly dropped dead! It's generally believed that his cousin, Khalid bin Barghash had him poisoned; a belief strengthened by the fact that he was already moving his stuff into the palace when Hamad's body was still warm! He must have seemed pretty pleased with himself strutting about his new palace like some kind of African Billy Big Bollocks but he'd carried out his dastardly plan without the approval of the British and the British weren't too happy about it.

The British Consul to the island, Basil Cave (1865-1931) ordered him to leave the palace immediately but he ignored the demand and began gathering his army around him. As more and more ultimatums were issued and then ignored and more and more British warships started arriving in the harbour, Basil sent a telegram to the Foreign Office in London: 'Are we authorised in the event of all attempts at a peaceful solution proving useless, to fire on the palace from the men-of-war?' A fairly candid and forthright reply arrived shortly afterwards: 'You are authorised to adopt whatever measures you may consider necessary, and will be supported in your action by Her Majesty's Government.'

A final warning was issued to Khalid bin Barghash on 26 August 1896 demanding that he leave the palace immediately. The following morning on 27 August 1896 at 8.00am, the Sultan finally replied to the ultimatum: 'We have no intention of hauling down our flag and we do not believe you would open fire on us.' He couldn't have been more wrong …

The bombardment began just an hour later at 9.02am. As soon as the first high explosive shells fell, Khalid bin Barghash high-tailed it out the back door of the palace, leaving the staff and about 3,000 soldiers standing around wondering what to do next. The assault stopped at 9.40am, by which time the Sultan's artillery positions had been silenced and the palace and the attached harem were in flames.

Over 500 Zanzibari soldiers were killed or wounded in those 38 minutes of warfare with only one British casualty reported. A naval officer aboard HMS *Thrush* anchored in the harbour was wounded but later recovered from his injuries in hospital.

Meanwhile, Khalid bin Barghash and a few of his cronies had taken refuge inside the German consulate. Despite the British authorities requesting his extradition, the Germans refused to give him up because the

Heligoland-Zanzibar Treaty specifically excluded any clauses about the exchange of political prisoners. Instead, they whisked him out of the country. For fear of arrest, the evacuation was organised in such a way that the Sultan never actually set foot on Zanzibar soil. On 2 October 1896, an Imperial German Navy boat drew alongside the consulate's garden gate and the Sultan stepped directly from the grounds onto the boat before being transferred to the warship SMS *Seeadier* waiting out at sea.

The British installed Hamoud bin Mohammed Al-Said as the new Sultan of Zanzibar. He was pro-British and wouldn't cause them any problems. They also forced the followers of the rebel Sultan to pay for the shells they'd used during the bombardment and to cover the costs of repairing the damage caused by all the looting and rioting which had followed their attack!

Khalid bin Barghash escaped justice until 1916 when he was captured in Dar-Es-Salaam in Tanzania by British forces during the East African Campaign of World War I (1914-1918) and exiled to the Seychelles. Which wasn't the worst place to live out your days in exile!

The Anglo-Zanzibar War (1896) still holds the record of being the shortest war in history having lasted only 38 minutes!

the trial of lady chatterley

In 1960, Penguin Books announced their intention to publish the full unexpurgated edition of *Lady Chatterley's Lover* (1928).

The book was written by the famous English poet and novelist D H Lawrence (1885-1930) and had previously been banned in Britain because of its explicit language and lurid, uninhibited descriptions of sex. Their controversial decision to publish such a novel immediately incurred the wrath of the British establishment and a court case *R v Penguin Books Ltd* began at the Old Bailey in London on 20 October 1960 in an effort to try and stop them.

Penguin Books was being prosecuted under the Obscene Publications Act 1959 with the jury being asked to decide whether the novel would 'deprave and corrupt persons likely to read it' (contravening section 2 of the act). If that was the case, should it still be exempt from any ban because of its literary merit and 'public good' (as outlined in section 4 of the same act).

The prosecutor, Mervyn Griffith-Jones (1909-1979), began the trial by informing the jury that the book contained eighty obscene words. Although he conceded that D H Lawrence was indeed a writer of stature, he still argued that the book should not be exempt from the law due to its liberal use of lewd and explicit language (especially the f-word) and its promotion of extra-marital promiscuity. According to him the plot was just padding for numerous graphic descriptions of sexual intercourse and was definitely obscene and definitely contrary to the public good. He was later ridiculed for being out of touch with changing social values when he asked the jury members to consider if it was the kind of book 'you would wish your wife or servants to read.'

Gerald Gardiner (1900-1990), as counsel for the defence, argued that the book was definitely not obscene under section 2 of the act as it wouldn't deprave or corrupt anyone, and because of the author's artistic reputation, publication was justified under section 4 because it was in the interests of science, literature, art or learning. The defence called a number of academics, literary critics, and writers, including the eminent novelist E M Forster (1879-1970) to testify as to the artistic, sociological and moral value of the book. Perhaps the most surprising witness, however, was John Robinson, Bishop of Woolwich (1919-1983) who gave the thumbs-up to Christians everywhere that it was OK to read it. If a man of God wasn't offended by all that bonking and smutty language then nobody else should be either!

After only three hours of deliberation the jury found for the defendant, highlighting how detached the establishment had become from popular opinion and the rapidly changing public attitudes towards sexuality and the British class system.

Lady Chatterley's Lover was published a month later with all 200,000 copies sold on the first day!

The second edition of the book contained a publisher's declaration: 'For having published this book, Penguin Books was prosecuted under the Obscene Publications Act 1959 at the Old Bailey in London from 20 October to 2 November 1960. This edition is therefore dedicated to the twelve jurors, three women and nine men, who returned a verdict of "not guilty" and thus made D H Lawrence's last novel available for the first time to the public in the United Kingdom.'

The trial resulted in the liberalisation of the publishing laws in Britain. It was suddenly perfectly acceptable to start printing and selling X-rated material and the trial is often cited as being the start of the permissive society in Britain.

MEMOIRS OF A WOMAN OF PLEASURE

Fanny Hill: or, the Memoirs of a Woman of Pleasure (1748-1749) by John Cleland (1709-1789) is considered to be the first original English prose pornography and the first published erotic novel. The two-volume book was written when the author was languishing in a debtors' prison and tells the story of a teenage orphan girl from Lancashire who travels to London to work as a prostitute. It was considered scandalous at the time for depicting a woman enjoying and even revelling in performing sexual acts with no dire moral or physical consequences, even though the author used many different euphemisms for the act itself and all the human body's naughty bits! He used fifty different euphemisms just for the penis alone!

In November 1749, John was arrested and charged with corrupting the king's subjects. In court, he renounced the book stating that it should be 'buried and forgot'. It was later withdrawn from sale and wasn't legally published again until over a hundred years later!

the discovery of america

According to folklore, the Welsh prince Madoc ab Owain Gwynedd (c.1150-fl.1171) landed in the Americas in 1170, around 300 years before the famous Italian explorer Cristoforo Colombo (Christopher Columbus).

The Welsh cleric Caradoc of Llancarfan, who compiled *Historie of Cambrai* (1584) described how he and his brother set sail in two ships from Aber-Kerrick-Gwynan [Rhos-on-Sea] on the North Wales coast to explore the western oceans and landed somewhere in what is now modern day Alabama. Although, if that's the case, they must have taken the scenic route! A few months later he then returned to Wales, recounting his adventures in a newly-discovered pleasant and fertile land. After convincing many more of his countrymen to accompany him westwards on a second voyage, he set sail in a fleet of ten ships from Lundy Island in 1171 ... and was never seen again.

The earliest pioneers and explorers of the New World found evidence of Welsh colonies along the Alabama River. Several stone forts said by the Cherokee tribes to have been constructed by 'white people' and similar in design to Dolwyddelan Castle in Wales have since been dated to a few hundred years before Christopher Columbus even set foot in the New World. There were also reports of people speaking in a language similar to Welsh, using coracles (rounded, lightweight boats traditional to Wales) instead of canoes and building small European style villages with streets laid out in grid patterns.

The story of Madoc was later used by Elizabeth I (1533-1603) as an assertion of prior discovery and legal possession of North America during England's territorial spats with Spain in the late-sixteenth century.

the duelling prime minister

The Anglo-Irish politician George Tierney (1761-1830) challenged the Prime Minister William Pitt the Younger (1759-1806) to a duel.

During a House of Commons debate on 25 May 1798, the PM had proposed increasing the manpower of the Royal Navy due to the ongoing French Revolutionary Wars (1792-1802) but the MP objected to his plan, claiming more time was needed to debate it. The PM wasn't best pleased and lashed out at his opponent's antipathy, claiming that it was a blatant attempt to obstruct the defence of the country. The MP didn't take kindly to having his patriotism questioned and demanded that the PM retract his remarks. He refused and so the MP wrote to the PM challenging him to a duel.

The two men met on Putney Common on the morning of 27 May 1798 with their pistols drawn …

It was noted at the time that the duel slightly favoured the PM as he was very slim, whilst the MP was a bit of a fat bastard and presented a much larger target! However, as it turned out, both men were pretty lousy shots so it didn't really matter who was fatter or thinner than who. Both of them missed … and then everyone just went home again!

THE SECOND DUELLING PRIME MINISTER

On 13 April 1829, the Roman Catholic Relief Act 1829 was passed by Parliament. The act was promoted by the Tory government led by the Prime Minister Arthur Wellesley, 1st Duke of Wellington (1769-1852) and was the culmination of the Catholic emancipation process which involved reducing or removing altogether many of the outdated restrictions placed on Catholics living in Britain. As part of this legislation Catholic MPs would also be permitted to take their seats in Parliament.

George Finch-Hatton, 10th Earl of Winchilsea, 5th Earl of Nottingham (1791-1858) was a staunch Protestant and vehemently opposed the new legislation, accusing the PM of 'an insidious design for the infringement of our liberties and the introduction of popery into every department of the State.'

Feeling deeply insulted, the PM sent his political opponent a letter challenging him to a duel: 'Since the insult, unprovoked on my part, and not denied by your Lordship, I have done everything in my power to induce your Lordship to make me reparation, but in vain. Instead of apologising for your own conduct your Lordship has called upon me to explain mine … I now call upon your Lordship to give me that satisfaction for your conduct which a gentleman has a right to require and which a gentleman never refuses to give.'

The two men met at 8.00am on Saturday, 21 March 1829 at Battersea Field in South London. The duke and his second Henry Hardinge, 1st Viscount Hardinge (1785-1856), arrived at the scene on horseback whilst the Earl of Winchilsea and his second Edward Boscawen, 1st Earl of Falmouth (1787-1841), arrived by coach. The physician John Hume (c.1781-

1857) was also in attendance in case of injury.

Both men held the pistols by their sides and the two seconds stepped back a few paces. Viscount Hardinge issued the final instructions to the two duellists: 'Gentlemen, I shall ask you if you are ready and give the word fire, without any further signal or preparation.' A few moments later he did just that.

'Gentlemen, are you ready … Fire!'

The duke raised his pistol first. But noticing that the Earl had not immediately raised his pistol on the command, he seemed to hesitate before firing … and then missed. The Earl was obviously unscathed and instantly discharged his pistol into the air. No harm done and the honour of both men had been satisfied.

The duke then rode off straight to Downing Street as if duelling was just another prime ministerial chore to be completed in the day! Although some people were shocked by his reckless behaviour, the duel generally enhanced his reputation and he was praised in various accounts of the incident for his 'manly forbearance'.

the sinking of the *lusitania*

On 7 May 1915, a German U-boat torpedoed the British passenger ship RMS *Lusitania*. The vessel sank within eighteen minutes of being attacked 11 miles (18km) off the south-west coast of Ireland with the loss of 1,198 lives. The sinking turned public opinion in many countries against Germany, including in the USA and indirectly led to them entering the war … albeit two years later than everyone else and when it was almost

finished!

The Germans claimed that the ship had been carrying large quantities of wartime supplies and had been fitted with guns so they were perfectly justified in sinking her. And anyway, their embassy in Washington DC had placed advertisements in fifty US newspapers on 22 April 1915 warning people not to travel on the liner as they were likely to get blown up.

Oh well, that's alright then!

the unfortunate death of mr huskisson

The Liverpool and Manchester Railway (L&MR) was built by the English civil engineer George Stephenson (1781-1848).

The 35-mile (56km) line between the two cities was principally designed to provide a much needed faster transport link for shifting raw materials, goods and passengers from the mills and factories in Manchester to the docks in Liverpool. The L&MR was the world's first railway to rely entirely on steam-powered locomotives, the first double-tracked railway line and the first fully timetabled railway. It probably wasn't long before the first commuters, the first 'wrong type of snow' and the first rail replacement horse and cart appeared too!

The L&MR line also passed through the Wapping Tunnel in Liverpool. The 1¼ mile (2m) long tunnel running from Edge Hill in the east of the city to Wapping Dock in the west was constructed between 1826 and 1829 and was the world's first underground railway tunnel bored under the streets of a city.

The owners of the L&MR were understandably keen to put on a good show for their opening day on 15 September 1830. Unfortunately, their plans were somewhat marred by the tragic and untimely death of a certain Mr Huskisson …

Eight trains were scheduled to travel along the line; seven on the northbound track and one special train reserved for VIPs drawn by the L&MR's newest and most advanced locomotive the *Northumbrian* on the southbound track. Behind the locomotive was a flatbed wagon carrying a band and then three passenger carriages, including one reserved for the Prime Minister Arthur Wellesley, 1st Duke of Wellington (1769-1852), and his guests.

Shortly before 10.00am as the duke arrived at Crown Street Station in Liverpool, the band struck up 'See, the Conquering Hero Comes' in his honour, a gun was fired to mark the railway's official opening and the VIP train set off along the track, waved off by a large and excitable crowd. The other seven trains followed at 11.00am, and it was intended that every now and again, the *Northumbrian* would slow down, allowing the VIPs to watch the northbound trains as they passed.

At the midpoint of their journey, the VIP train stopped near Newton-le-Willows on Merseyside to take on more water. All the VIPs were warned not to alight from the train but nobody took a blind bit of notice and around fifty very fidgety gentlemen climbed down from their carriages to stretch their legs along the track with the financier and politician William Huskisson (1770-1830) being one of them.

He was happily chatting away to the Duke of Wellington when one of those northbound trains was spotted coming their way and a shout went up: 'An engine is approaching! Take care, Gentlemen!' The oncoming train was being pulled by the *Rocket* driven by the engineer Joseph Locke (1805-1860). It has since become George Stephenson's most famous locomotive, but it was only a prototype, it didn't have any brakes, and so the only way of slowing it down was to throw it into reverse! By the time, it drew close to the *Northumbrian* it was still travelling at a fairly high speed …

Everyone managed to get out of the way of the approaching train either by climbing back into their carriages or scrambling up the embankment. Everyone, except the politician William Holmes (1779-1851) and William Huskisson …

There was a 4-foot (1.2m) gap between the trains but the carriages overhung the tracks by about 2 feet (0.6m). Nevertheless, it was still a big enough gap to fill and escape injury by standing perfectly still. Mr Holmes pressed himself up against the stationary train and took a sharp intake of breath, urging Mr Huskisson to do the same: 'For God's sake, Mr Huskisson, be firm!' But Mr Huskisson was doing everything but staying firm. He'd already made two attempts to cross the tracks to reach the embankment but had changed his mind and darted back towards the *Northumbrian* again. By now, he was starting to panic. Then he grabbed hold of a carriage door and dragged it open in an ill-judged attempt to try and re-board the train. Unfortunately for him, the door swung open too far, he was unable to gain a foothold and was left dangling in the path of the *Rocket* …

SPLAT!

In the words of the diarist Harriet Arbuthnot (1793-1834) who was sitting in the duke's carriage, he was 'thrown down and the engine passed over his leg and thigh, crushing it in a most frightful way.'

The other passengers noted that he didn't appear to be in much pain. He was more dazed and confused than anything else, staring at his mangled leg, calling for his wife and shouting: 'This is the death of me!' over and over again. He was eventually loaded onto the flatbed wagon of the *Northumbrian*, the other three carriages were decoupled and the locomotive sped off towards Manchester with the great man George Stephenson at the wheel. The crowds lining the route, unaware of the tragedy, cheered and waved as it rushed past them at a world record speed of 40mph (64km/h).

The L&MR's opening day had been completely ruined by the clumsy Mr Huskisson.

Later that evening he then went and died too! Talk about spoiling the party!

the first national lottery

Due to many years of underfunding and mismanagement, the harbours and ports of England had fallen into a perilous state of disrepair and urgently needed some money spent on them. Luckily, the Secretary of State William Cecil, 1st Baron Burghley (1520-1598), who was the chief flatterer and manipulator of Elizabeth I (1533-1603) for most of her reign, was also a genius at thinking up innovative money making schemes to bolster the royal coffers! Instead of introducing another unpopular tax to finance the work needed to improve the ports or authorising more government borrowing at exorbitant rates of interest, he persuaded a sceptical queen to hold a national lottery.

A royal proclamation was issued on 23 August 1567 heralding: 'A very Rich Lotterie Generall without Any Blanckes' and posters were displayed all around the country advertising the ticket prices, prizes and the date of the draw, and explaining that the proceeds were all to be used for 'the reparation of the havens [harbours] and the strength of the realme and towards such other publique good workes.'

The tickets cost 10 shillings each and were available to buy from 24 August 1567. They were specially printed slips on which the punter was asked to write their name, address and a short message (biographical note or bible quote) that was unique to them so they could easily be identified if they won a prize. Essentially, it was the Tudor equivalent of the modern password reset security question! First prize was £5,000 (£3,000 in cash, £700 in gold and silver plate and £1,300 worth of tapestries and high quality linens). Other monetary rewards included a second prize of £3,000 down to the many 14 shilling consolation prizes. Numerous other smaller and/or more unusual prizes were also on offer such as silver wine goblets, free admission to libraries and Monopoly-style get-out-of-jail-free cards giving the holder immunity from arrest for any crimes committed (excluding murder, treason or piracy).

The draw was originally due to take place on 25 June 1568.

Instructions were sent to the Sheriffs and the Justices of the Peace around the country asking them to establish a system for managing the lottery. They were required to employ a team of collectors, with the promise that for every pound collected in ticket sales, the chief collector would be awarded sixpence to be split between them and his assistants.

Despite the impressive publicity campaign and the dazzling array of prizes on offer, however, the lottery failed to capture the public's imagination. Ticket sales were poor, mainly because very few people actually trusted the government to honour their commitments, and so the draw had to be postponed in the hope of eventually selling enough tickets to cover the set-up costs. Despite another hastily arranged attempt to whip up a bit of enthusiasm for the lottery with more publicity campaigns and more exhibitions, it continued to be viewed by the public with great suspicion. It didn't help that the tickets cost 10 shillings either. This was well beyond the reach of ordinary people and so it was only ever going to be the rich folks who bought one. And there weren't really that many rich folks around.

The draw did eventually take place but almost two years later on 11 January 1569 near the west door of St Paul's Cathedral in London. It was a laborious and ridiculously long-drawn out affair, continuing 'daie and night' for four months until 6 May 1569, with blindfolded kids being employed to pick the winning tickets and the prizes.

Because only one twelfth of the expected £400,000 revenue had been collected, the available prize money also had to be reduced by a similar amount. Bad news for the first prize ticket holder who only picked up £416 13s and 4d instead of the £5,000 windfall they'd been expecting!

Some of the personal messages were read out to jeers and cheers from the crowd in an attempt to liven up the lengthy proceedings. One ticket which belonged to a Mr William Seintleger of Canterbury (Kent) gleefully proclaimed: 'In God I hope and a fart for the Pope!' Another ticket which has survived all this time read: 'God send a good lot for my children and me, which have had twenty by one wife truly.' It's probably fair to assume that he might have needed the money more than most!

The lottery had proved to be a complete disaster from start to finish! Fewer than 34,000 tickets had been sold (instead of the expected 400,000), less than £5,000 was raised (instead of the expected £100,000) and the ports were only repaired after the government was forced to negotiate an emergency 12 month loan from a coalition of London merchants.

the birdman of malmesbury

The English Benedictine monk Eilmer of Malmesbury (c.980-c.1069) became famous after his attempt to fly like a bird using mechanical wings! According to *Gesta Regum Anglorum* (1125) compiled by one of his fellow monks and England's foremost historian of the twelfth century William of Malmesbury (c.1095-1143), Eilmer fixed some wings to his hands and feet and then threw himself off the tower at Malmesbury Abbey, Malmesbury: 'Collecting the breeze upon the summit of a tower, [he] flew for more than a furlong. But agitated by the violence of the wind and the swirling of air, as well as by the awareness of his rash attempt, he fell, broke both his legs and was lame ever after. He used to relate the cause of his failure, his forgetting to provide himself a tail.'

If only it was that simple!

the pretty song book

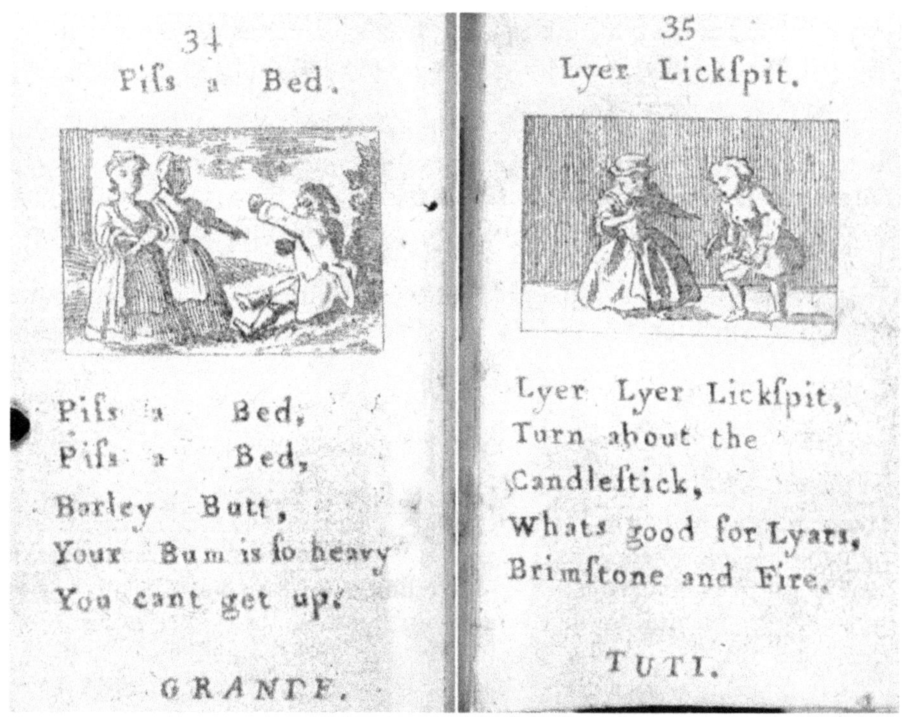

34

Piſs a Bed.

Piſs a Bed,
Piſs a Bed,
Barley Butt,
Your Bum is ſo heavy
You cant get up.

GRANDF.

35

Lyer Lickſpit.

Lyer Lyer Lickſpit,
Turn about the
Candleſtick,
Whats good for Lyars,
Brimſtone and Fire.

TUTI.

Tommy Thumb's Pretty Song-Book (1744) is the oldest surviving printed collection of British nursery rhymes.

The book was designed to appeal especially to young children. It was very small and all the pages were illustrated. Although the author's name appeared as 'Nurse Lovechild' it's likely to have been the

London-based publisher/bookseller Mary Cooper (fl.1744-1761) who compiled the rhymes. The book was originally published in two volumes but unfortunately no copies of Volume I have survived. Many of the forty rhymes included in Volume II are still familiar today such as *Baa, Baa Black Sheep* and *Hickory Dickory Dock* but others such as the one about bed wetting called *Piss a Bed* have understandably fallen out of favour!

when giants roamed the earth

In June 1674, the English naturalist Robert Plot (1640-1696) began collecting and studying various artefacts he found lying around the Oxfordshire countryside and published his findings three years later in *The Natural History of Oxford-Shire* (1677). The essay described and illustrated various plants, animals, and geological formations, including many fossils, rocks and minerals, and was a huge success with all the learned folk of the day, earning him membership of the Royal Society on 8 December 1677.

The book also contained a description of a bone which he was unable to identify: 'If then they are neither the Bones of Horses, Oxen, nor Elephants, as I am strongly persuaded they are not ... It remains, that (notwithstanding their extravagant Magnitude) they must have been the bones of Men or Women.'

It seems that the learned Dr Plot wasn't quite such a smarty-pants after all. According to him, he'd just discovered the bones of a gigantic human!

the wycliffe bible

Many people believed that the Black Death (1346-1353) was God's punishment for their sins because that's what they'd been told to believe by their clergymen. But since the church had been powerless to stop the plague and an abnormally high number of priests and monks had died off, the people begun to question their beliefs and the doctrines and practices of the Catholic Church.

It wasn't a great time for the church ... and then along came John Wycliffe (c.1320-1384) to make things worse ...

The English theologian and philosopher believed that Joe Public wanted to learn and understand more about the Bible but didn't want to be preached to by what he called unworthy and corrupt priests. He often attacked the privileged status of the Catholic Church and maintained that all Christians should only heed the words of the Bible and not the words of the church's clerics. But at that time the Bible was only available to anyone who could read Latin. The poor folk were totally reliant on oral versions of the scriptures or watching mystery plays and just had to accept that what they were being told was the true word of God. John Wycliffe insisted that 'it helpeth Christian men to study the Gospel in that tongue in which they know best Christ's sentence' and so he and his followers set about the task of translating the Bible from the Latin Vulgate into English (Middle English). Most historians accept that he personally translated the four gospels of Matthew, Mark, Luke and John, and probably most if not all of the New Testament. The first manuscripts were completed in 1382, with further updated versions being re-written by his disciple John Purvey (c.1354-c.1414) in 1388 and 1395. Although what updates he found to add to the Bible is unclear!

The *Wycliffe Bible* (1382) as it is now known was the first complete English language Bible ever produced.

The Catholic Church wasn't best pleased. Joe Public could now read the Bible for themselves, and more importantly, they could see just how far the established church had strayed from the teachings of the scriptures. Although they shouldn't have been too concerned because the *Wycliffe Bible* had a very limited appeal. Not only couldn't people read Latin, they couldn't read English either! Or at least very few of them could. So, it didn't really matter what language his fancy bible was written in, they remained just as ignorant as they were before! Nevertheless, the Catholic Church made a point of seizing and destroying the new Bibles whenever and wherever they could get hold of them. Despite their best efforts, however, around 250 partial and complete copies have still survived to this day.

The English monarchy and the Catholic Church held a grudge against poor John Wycliffe for a very long time after his death. In 1413, he was declared a heretic and a law was passed stating that anyone caught reading the scriptures in English would 'forfeit land, cattle, goods, body and life from themselves and their heirs forever' and in 1427, Pope Martin V had his corpse exhumed and burnt, and his ashes cast into a river!

The *Wycliffe Bible* laid the groundwork for many further translations of the Bible into English, most notably the *King James Bible* in 1611 which retained much of the original wording. John Wycliffe died believing that everyone should have access to the Bible in a language they could understand and he has now been credited as one of the founders of the sixteenth century Protestant Reformation in Europe.

the gong farmers

In medieval Britain the rich folk took a crap in a chamber pot and the poor folk just went wherever the hell they liked! Either way, it all ended up in the street. If you were lucky enough to live at the top of a hill, the rain would flush it all away and the air would suddenly smell fresher and sweeter again. That wasn't the case if you lived at the bottom of the hill though!

By the late-Middle Ages, however, many local authorities had installed public toilets known as Houses of Easement and some people had built their own cesspits under cellar floors or in the backyard of their houses. These cesspits were just holes in the ground so they weren't watertight and over time the liquid waste would drain away leaving only the solid stuff behind. It was only a matter of time before they filled up and that's when the householder called upon the services of a Gong Farmer.

It was their job to empty the cesspit; shovelling out all the crap, loading it onto a cart and then selling it on to the local farmers or just dumping it somewhere outside of the city. They were only allowed to work at night between 9.00pm and 5.00am so the sight and smell of cartloads of human excrement being wheeled through the streets didn't offend people. As a result of these restrictive working hours their cargo was known as 'night soil' and they were sometimes called 'Nightmen'. They normally worked in gangs of three; one inside the cesspit doing all the shovelling, one pulling the bucket out of the hole by rope, and another carrying the load to the cart. It wasn't unusual for small boys to be employed in the cesspit because they could manoeuvre around more easily.

The Gong Farmer's lot was not a happy one. After all, working waist deep in a big pile of shit in the dead of night was nobody's idea of a dream job! It was often dangerous work; they could easily lose their footing and drown or dig into pockets of deadly poisonous gasses and be overcome by the noxious fumes; rotting pit ceilings could collapse on top of them, and many contracted some very serious diseases. But at least it was well paid with most Nightmen earning an average weekly wage in just one shift.

Gong farming continued well into the eighteenth century but as fewer cesspits were needed after the introduction of more modern sewage disposal systems during the nineteenth century, the need for the Nightmen obviously fell away too.

the man who didn't invent the toilet

Contrary to popular belief the English plumber and self-styled sanitary engineer Thomas Crapper (1836-1910) didn't invent the flushing toilet. That honour goes to John Harington (1560-1612) way back in 1596. Thomas, on the other hand, improved the S-bend (1775) by inventing the U-bend (1880), and prior to that in 1866, he opened the world's first bathroom fittings store in Chelsea. His name soon become synonymous with the products he sold after American servicemen who were stationed in Britain during World War I (1914-1918) referred to the toilet as a 'crapper' because of the company's name that was emblazoned on the cisterns.

Note: John Harington was a poet but is remembered more for his fancy bathroom fittings than his fancy words after engineering the world's first modern flushing toilet with a raised cistern and a small downpipe through which water ran to flush away anything nasty into a cesspit outside. 'If water be plenty, the oftener it is used and opened, the sweeter [it will be]' he wrote of his invention.

John was one of the many godchildren of Elizabeth I (1533-1603) and was known as the 'saucy godson' due to his love for writing rather risqué poetry. During one particular visit to his manor house at Kelston in Somerset, the queen couldn't wait to try out his swanky new toilet for herself, and was so impressed that she immediately ordered something similar to be installed at Richmond Palace.

Just so you know.

the love chair

The future Edward VII (1841-1910) also known as 'Dirty Bertie' or 'Edward the Caresser' was a man with a big sexual appetite who scoured the brothels of Europe looking for cheap thrills and shagged his way through most of the available (and some of the unavailable) Victorian high society ladyfolk like a crazed tomcat! He might have been quickly married off to Princess Alexandra of Denmark (1844-1925) in 1863 but that didn't stop him from pursuing other women.

Bertie was caught up in his first sex scandal when he was only 19 years-old. Prince Albert (1819-1861) then popped his clogs shortly afterwards and Queen Victoria (1819-1901) blamed Bertie, claiming that he'd been so upset by his son's inappropriate behaviour that he'd died of a broken heart. It's rumoured that she only reigned for as long as she did to keep him off the throne!

During his decades-long wait to become king, Bertie bedded a string of women. One of his most famous lovers was the actress and socialite Lillie Langtry (1853-1929). They were together between 1877 and 1880. It's been said that Bertie once complained that he had spent enough on her to 'build a battleship' and she had retorted 'and you've spent enough in me to float one!'

During the 1880s and 1890s, Bertie would often trot off to France to visit the famous Paris brothel *Le Chabanais*. And he wasn't alone either. The bordello had many rich and famous clients and the French government often included a stopover at *Le Chabanais* as part of a programme of events for visiting foreign dignitaries! Bertie was such a frequent visitor that he had his own room decorated with the royal coat of arms and furnished to his specific tastes.

Because he loved his food as much as he loved screwing around, in later life, he'd become a bit of an old fatty. Years of fine dining had taken its toll on poor Bertie's waistline and his obesity was threatening to spoil his fun at the brothel. In order to overcome any potential performance difficulties, a special chair known as the *siège d'amour* (love chair) was constructed by a local French cabinetmaker Louis Soubrier which allowed him to indulge in his sexual fantasies with minimal exertion and contortions on his part and without the girls being crushed to death underneath his enormous girth! The chair is said to have allowed Bertie to pleasure two partners at once, although nobody is quite sure how that was possible! It's pretty clear that he stood with his feet planted on the two sturdy footpads and gripped hold of the handles as his partner reclined on the elevated chaise lounge bit, which was positioned at just the right height for royal access, but what is less clear is how the other girl, lying on another padded bit of the chair underneath the first girl, was supposed to derive any satisfaction!

the lost days

On 22 May 1751, the Calendar (New Style) Act 1750 received royal assent from George II (1683-1760).

The act replaced the outdated Julian Calendar (devised by the Roman Emperor, Julius Caesar and introduced into Britain by Augustine of Canterbury in 597) with the Gregorian Calendar (established by Pope Gregory XIII in 1582) which meant New Year's Day now fell on 1 January (instead of 25 March) bringing the whole of Great Britain and Ireland into line with most other European countries.

Aligning the calendars in this way also meant losing eleven days somewhere!

The act stipulated that Wednesday, 2 September 1752 would be immediately followed by Thursday, 14 September 1752. The lost days were 3 September until 13 September 1752 when nobody was born and nobody died. The introduction of the new legislation also meant that 1751 only had 282 days (from 25 March 1751 until 31 December 1751) and the new leap year of 1752 (which began on 1 January 1752) only had 355 days. Understandably, Joe Public was a little confused with all this messing around; many people objected to the imposition of a 'popish calendar' and the really dim ones genuinely believed that their lives were being shortened by eleven days!

the optimistic coroner

Bridget Driscoll (c.1851-1896) became Britain's first road fatality when she was hit by a car being used for rides around the park at Crystal Palace on 17 August 1896. At the inquest which followed, one witness claimed that the car was travelling at a 'tremendous pace, like a fire engine – as fast as a good horse could gallop' but the driver Arthur James Edsall (1857-1941) maintained that he was only doing about 4mph (6.4km/h) before the collision and had repeatedly rung his bell and shouted 'stand back' before trying to swerve out of the way. The jury returned a verdict of accidental death with the coroner Percy Morrison remarking that he hoped 'such a thing would never happen again.'

Definitely a half-glass-full kind of guy!

the english armada

The English Armada followed the Spanish one but nobody has ever heard of it because it resulted in a defeat!

Most of the ships lost by Spain a year earlier during their ill-fated attempt to invade England had been merchantmen (armed merchant ships), whilst the core of their fleet – the galleons of the Squadron of Portugal of the Armada del Mar Oceano (Atlantic Fleet) – survived the battle and had docked in the ports at Santander and San Sebastian in Spain where they were due to lay for months undergoing refits.

The English Armada had three main objectives: destroy the Atlantic Fleet, intercept the Spanish treasure ships re-entering port from the Americas, and invade Lisbon and the Azores to encourage an uprising against Phillip II of Spain and restore António, Prior of Crato to the throne of Portugal.

On 17 April 1589, an English fleet of six galleons, sixty armed merchantmen, sixty Dutch flyboats and twenty pinnaces (small boats) commanded by the famous seafarer, privateer and avid bowls player Francis Drake (c.1540-1596) sailed from Plymouth straight for Lisbon with 23,000 sailors, professional soldiers and gentlemen adventurers aboard.

But before the fleet had even reached Portugal, they'd run out of food, forcing them to attack the largely undefended Spanish city of Corunna to seize provisions. Whilst procuring these supplies, fighting off Spanish soldiers and generally making a nuisance of themselves, they stumbled across a large stash of wine casks and then spent most of their remaining time ashore lying around in the hot sun getting drunk.

In the meantime, the Spanish caught wind of the drunken Englishmen marauding around Corunna, shored up their defences and quickly executed any supporters of António.

Eventually, the fleet left Corunna and moved on down the coast towards Portugal to rendezvous with the ship bringing one of Queen Elizabeth I's favourite noblemen to join the fight, the flamboyant and hot-headed Robert Devereux, 2nd Earl of Essex (1565-1601). He was determined to have some fun and play a big part in the defeat of Spain but after the fleet arrived at the port of Peniche in Portugal, he made a bit of an arse of himself. In a foolhardy show of bravado, he leapt off the ship far too early and landed in deep water! Not only did he look rather ridiculous swimming onto Spanish soil instead of marching onto it, his actions compelled many of his followers to do the same and some of them drowned!

Sir Francis and the commander of the land forces John Norreys (c.1547-1597) then decided to abandon their mission's most important objective of destroying the Spanish fleet and concentrate all their efforts on attacking Lisbon instead. Sir Francis would lead the fleet further down the coast to Cascais and then head up the River Tagus to Lisbon while John Norreys was to journey overland with the army.

Their 40-mile (64km) march was across hostile terrain and a large number of soldiers died from starvation and heat exhaustion. When they finally reached Lisbon on 3 June 1589, the expected uprising from the supporters of António failed to happen (because they'd all been killed off earlier) and the English fleet was nowhere to be seen. Apparently, Sir Francis had resorted to his old privateering ways on the voyage and was apparently too busy attacking treasure ships along the coast to lend his support. More worryingly, they couldn't breech the city wall. They didn't have any artillery to blast through it and they didn't have any scaling ladders to climb over it either!

With no attack from the English, the Spanish took the initiative and started doing the attacking themselves.

The English were outnumbered and quickly became more and more outnumbered as the death toll rose. Those not killed by the Spanish continued dropping dead from hunger and exhaustion; they soon ran out of supplies and that bloody Sir Francis Drake was still nowhere to be seen! During the night of 4 June 1589, the English decided to make a run for it back to Cascais.

The Spanish pursued them, inflicting many more casualties along the way. They were ready to do battle in Cascais too but were forced to retreat themselves this time when they were met by cannon fire from the English fleet. Guess who'd finally turned up to the fight?

The Earl of Essex made an arse of himself again. He was angry at their mission's lack of success and still champing at the bit for a fight so he sent a letter via messenger to the commander of the Spanish forces on 8 June 1589 challenging them to a winner-takes-all battle. But the letter was sent back to him unopened … which presumably angered him even more!

The Spanish were convinced that the English would remount an attack at any time and continued building up their forces outside of Cascais. But that wasn't the case. The English had decided to cut their losses and sail back to Blighty!

The English Armada had been a complete failure with none of the campaign's objectives being achieved. The English had been chased out of Portugal and had lost forty ships and 15,000 men without inflicting any substantiable damage on the weakened Spanish fleet.

the decca audition

The Beatles (1960-1970) were the most influential and commercially successful band in the history of popular music!

Their famous audition for Decca Records which took place on 1 January 1962 followed an invitation from one of the company's A&R men Mike Smith (1935-2011) to play at their studios in West Hampstead. He'd seen them in concert on 13 December 1961 at the Cavern Club in Liverpool and wanted to offer them the chance to secure a record deal. The band played fifteen songs which were most likely recorded in a single take without overdubs and the entire session, which began at 11.00am, only took an hour to complete.

Unfortunately for The Beatles, Brian Poole and the Tremeloes were also auditioning that day and the record company were forced to choose which act they wanted to sign. Dick Rowe (1921-1986) who was Head of A&R (Singles) at Decca later commented: 'I told Mike [Mike Smith] he'd have to decide between them. It was up to him – The Beatles or Brian Poole and the Tremeloes. He said, "They're both good, but one's a local group, the other comes from Liverpool …"' It was therefore decided to sign The Tremeloes from Dagenham because they'd be a lot easier to manage than a group based all that distance away in Liverpool.

To add insult to injury the band's manager Brian Epstein (1934-1967) was then informed that 'guitar groups are on the way out' and 'The Beatles have no future in show business!'

After that, Mike Smith was forever known as the man who turned down The Beatles.

the north bank mural

The government inquiry into the Hillsborough Stadium Disaster (1989) resulted in the *Taylor Report* (1990) which recommended that all football league grounds should be converted into all-seater stadiums to ensure greater spectator safety. As part of their plans to modernise Highbury, Arsenal FC decided to knock down their old Northbank stand and replace it with a brand spanking new all-seater version. However, the club vice-chairman David Dein (1943-) didn't want their home games in the first season of the newly-launched Premier League to be played against a backdrop of cranes, cement trucks and scaffolding, so he commissioned a fancy mural to conceal all the building work.

A huge, hand-painted vinyl mural depicting excited little Arsenal fans wearing red and white shirts and waving scarves was eventually erected across the entire width of the pitch at the Northbank end behind the goal.

However, a day before the team's opening game of the season against Norwich, the players had been training on the pitch when it was pointed out by their striker Kevin Campbell (1970-2024) that there were no black faces in the crowd. The artist was immediately summoned back to Highbury and overnight he added a bit of colour to some of the faces to better represent the team's diverse fanbase. But despite the mural's emergency overnight makeover, the club continued to receive complaints that black people were still underrepresented.

And then things get a bit apocryphal from here …

There were no women and children or disabled people either so they were all painted in too. But because of all this fiddling around, it was now apparent that some of the children were sitting alone or next to adults who didn't appear to be with their parents prompting criticism from children's charities and adoption agencies. All the kids were subsequently painted the same colour as the nearest adult and another 1,000 portraits were changed into women including several hundred in saris, burkas and traditional African headgear to cover all their bases. Just for the hell of it, some nuns were painted in too! Fifty Sikhs were also added, some brandishing ceremonial swords, which then brought a complaint from the police! It was also rumoured that a gay rights group had complained because there weren't enough homosexuals in the crowd and that a bunch of heterosexuals had then complained that the few homosexuals that were already present in the mural had been painted dangerously near to women and children. The mural wasn't altered but the club were forced to issue a statement saying that homosexuals looked no different from anyone else and posed no threat to women or children at football grounds or anywhere else!

A backdrop of cranes, cement trucks and scaffolding might have been more appealing after all.

Much to everyone's relief the mural was taken down a year later.

the gentleman flasher

John Villiers Shelley (1808-1867) was a Tory politician, landowner, sportsman, and by all accounts, a bit of a ladies' man. In 1861, when he was the MP for Westminster, he appeared in court charged with gross indecency. Several witnesses testified that they'd seen him fondling himself standing by the window of his apartment:'I distinctly saw him expose his person. He looked directly [into my house] and used his hands incidentally, and then kissed his hands towards our house. There were ladies and servants at our windows.

'He appeared to have some loose gown on and drawers but his legs were bare ... He exposed his person and did it again several times in the course of the afternoon.

'I saw him put his hands down and open his drawers and I turned away ... I had seen him that day do it two or three times. I have seen him frequently since do it ... On those occasions I saw his private parts naked.'

So, fairly damning evidence ...

Except his lawyer argued that poor Sir John had only been disrobed and prancing about in front of his window because he was too hot and the witnesses had accidentally seen him through very thin curtains. The judge accepted this defence, completely dismissing all the eyewitness testimony and adding that Sir John would never do such a thing anyway because he was a gentleman!

that after dinner speech

Gerald Ratner (1949-) was the CEO of the Ratner Group PLC which operated a chain of popular high street jewellery stores. He'd inherited his father's modest business in 1984 and within a few short years had turned it into a thriving multimillion-pound industry. Every British high street appeared to have one of his shops selling cheap and cheerful jewellery and people flocked to spend their hard earned cash on heavily discounted rings, bracelets, earrings and all the other little trinkets they were flogging.

The business was going great and life for Gerald couldn't have been sweeter ...

But then he made that infamous speech at an Institute of Directors

Conference held at the Royal Albert Hall on 23 April 1991. He referred to a cut-glass sherry decanter, six glasses and a silver-plated tray which was available to buy in his stores for only £4.95 and said: 'People say, "How can you sell this for such a low price?" [and] I say, "Because it's total crap!"' Just to make things worse, he then went on to remark that his earrings were 'cheaper than an M&S prawn sandwich but probably wouldn't last as long!'

His reckless comments led to a dramatic loss of customer confidence and within a few weeks £500m had been wiped off the company's stock market value. By the following year the name Ratners had disappeared from the British high street altogether!

Way to go, Gerry!

the oxford martyrs

Mary I (Mary Tudor) (1516-1558) was crowned as the first Queen of England on 1 October 1553. She's best remembered for her violent and brutal attempts to reverse the English Reformation (1527-1590) and restore Roman Catholicism to the country. During her short, five-year reign from 1553 until 1558 over 280 religious dissenters were burnt at the stake, earning her the nickname of 'Bloody Mary'.

A detailed account of each and every martyr who died for their faith was reported by the English historian John Foxe (c.1516-1587) in *Actes and Monuments* (1563) which was more popularly known as *Foxe's Book of Martyrs*. Most famously, he included the crimes and punishments of the three great clergymen Hugh Latimer, the Bishop of Worcester (c.1487-1555), Nicholas Ridley, the Bishop of London (c.1500-1555) and Thomas Cranmer, the Archbishop of Canterbury (1489-1556) who were later known as the 'Oxford Martyrs'.

After disposing of her political opponents and the supporters of the English noblewoman and *de facto* Queen of England, Lady Jane Grey (c.1537-1554), Mary had then turned her attention to the religious leaders of the Reformation. On 8 March 1554, the Privy Council ordered the three clergymen to be detained and stand trial for heresy. Although Thomas Cranmer's trial began first the other two men who'd been held at Bocardo Prison in Oxford were first to be executed. They were burnt at the stake just outside the city walls on 16 October 1555 with Thomas granted a day-release from the Tower of London to go and watch the show! Hugh Latimer is believed to have said to Nicholas Ridley: 'Be of good comfort, and play the man, Master Ridley; we shall this day light such a candle, by God's grace, in England, as I trust shall never be put out.' It was alright for him; he lost consciousness almost immediately and died from suffocation. Poor Nicholas wasn't quite so lucky. It was reported by John Foxe that the fire burnt very slowly and he suffered greatly throughout the ordeal, despite the best efforts of his brother-in-law who tried to expedite his death by furiously adding more tinder to the pyre, which only had the effect of strengthening the flames around his feet! Writhing in agony he repeatedly cried out: 'Lord have mercy upon me!'

Thomas had held the office of Archbishop of Canterbury from 1533 until 1555; he was one of the architects of the English Reformation and established the first doctrinal structure of the newly reformed Church of England; he published the first officially authorised vernacular service *Exhortation and Litany* (1544) and he wrote and compiled the first two editions of the *Book of Common Prayer* (1549-1552). You couldn't have found a bigger Protestant than this guy! But after spending all that time in prison and watching how unrepentant heretics were dealt with by the authorities, he wisely decided to recant his faith, despite being the most important and most committed Protestant in the land. In fact, he recanted it four times, just to make sure his message was heard! But Edmund Bonner (c.1500-1569), the Bishop of London and Mary's chief prosecutor known as 'Bloody Bonner' was unimpressed with his change of heart, claiming that it didn't go far enough, and a date for his execution was pencilled into everyone's diary.

A short time later, Thomas issued a fifth recantation, submitting to papal supremacy and fully accepting Catholic theology. Despite the law stipulating that recanting heretics should be reprieved, Mary was a belligerent old woman and was determined to make an example of him, arguing that 'his iniquity and obstinacy was so great against God' that any mercy would be misplaced, and confirmed the date for his execution as 21 March 1556.

On the big day, Thomas was expected to recant again. But towards the end of his farewell speech he completely ignored his pre-authorised script and recanted his previous recantations by yelling: 'And as for the Pope, I refuse him, as Christ's enemy and Antichrist with all his false doctrine.' Needless to say, the fire was lit pretty sharply after that and Thomas was soon burning away nicely in the flames.

the last postmaster

The role of Postmaster General was created by Oliver Cromwell (1599-1658) in 1657.

The last person to hold the job before the position was abolished was John Stonehouse (1925-1988) between 1 July 1968 and 1 October 1969. As well as being a prominent politician he also thought of himself as a bit of a businessman and entrepreneur. He'd set up a number of companies in the late-Sixties and early-Seventies in an attempt to secure a little more financial independence for himself and his family but by 1974 they were all near to collapse and he'd resorted to a little creative accountancy to cover the cracks and plug the holes.

Then, on 20 November 1974, a pile of his clothes was found on a beach in Miami, Florida, giving the impression that he'd gone into the sea for a swim and never returned. Everyone assumed he'd either drowned or had been killed by a shark. In reality, he'd staged his own death, after the cracks and the holes in all those failed and fraudulent business schemes became too big to manage, and was on his way to Australia, hoping to start a new life with his mistress and former secretary Sheila Buckley (1941-2025).

He turned up in Melbourne five weeks later. Whilst he was busy shifting money around the local banks using various fake identities, one bank clerk became suspicious and informed the police, who then kept him under surveillance because they thought he may have been that other famous British fugitive of the time John Bingham, 7th Earl of Lucan (1934-1999), better known as just Lord Lucan, the playboy aristocrat who was wanted for the murder of his children's nanny.

The Aussie police contacted Scotland Yard requesting a photograph of both men. They didn't look anything like each other but that didn't stop them from asking John Stonehouse to drop his trousers when they arrested him on 24 December 1974. They were completely obsessed with Lord Lucan and were only convinced that the man they had in custody wasn't him because he didn't have a 6-inch (15cm) scar on the inside of his right leg as his Lordship was known to have. Still, they'd caught the next best thing ... the ex-politician who'd faked his own death and was wanted back in Blighty on charges of fraud, deception, theft, forgery and even wasting police time!

Johnny Boy tried to claim asylum in Sweden and Mauritius but was eventually deported back to Britain where he was remanded in Brixton Prison before being released on bail in August 1975. Then he took up his day job as a Labour MP again!

He was arrogant enough to conduct his own defence when his trial began but his lawyering skills turned out to be just as crap as his business skills because he was convicted and sentenced to seven years in prison on 6 August 1975.

He then seems to have passed a lot of his time inside playing chess with Moors Murderer Ian Brady (1938-2017). So he wasn't at all fussy about the company he kept! He also did a lot of moaning about the prison workshop radios always being tuned to stations playing pop music! Not surprising, considering he was the Postmaster General who oversaw that idiotic policy of jamming the signals from pirate radio stations in the late-1960s.

In 1976, he finally resigned as an MP and a Privy Councillor and joined the English National Party (1966-1981). After suffering three heart attacks, he was released early from prison on 14 August 1979 and then spent the rest of his life cashing-in on his faked death with book deals, radio broadcasts and TV appearances.

John Stonehouse was a philanderer, a fraudster and a chancer. It turns out that he was also a traitor to his country too!

More than twenty years after his death, it was publicly revealed that he had been spying for Czechoslovakia.

In 1969, Josef Frolik, an ex-Czech spy who had defected to the USA, outed Johnny Boy to the security services. Of course, he denied everything and was never formally charged with spying because there was no real evidence against him. Then, in the mid-1990s, the newly formed Czech intelligence service, the Office for Foreign Relations & Information acknowledged that John Stonehouse had worked for their predecessor, State Security as a spy from 1962. Apparently, they'd been a bit disappointed in the quality of intelligence he was able to pass on to them. So, he was just as crap at the spying game as he was at being a politician and a businessman!

calculating pi and eating pie

Pi (π) is the ratio of a circle's circumference to its diameter which is approximately 3.14159 and Pi Day is the worldwide annual celebration of this mathematical constant which was first observed by the American physicist Larry Shaw on 14 March 1988. Typically, a lot of geeky types sit around reciting Pi, talking about maths and eating a lot of fruit pies!

The English amateur mathematician William Shanks (1812-1882) was just as obsessed with this mathematical ratio as his modern counterparts, after manually calculating its value to 707 places (of which the first 527 places turned out to be correct). This was the longest expansion of Pi until the advent of the computer. He also published a table of prime numbers up to 60,000 places and played around with logarithms and the Euler-Mascheroni Constant, spending his mornings doing all the calculations and his afternoons checking them!

And you thought your life was dull.

In 2019, to celebrate Pi Day, Google successfully calculated Pi to 31.4 trillion decimal places.

Poor William must have been spinning in his grave!

mary toft's rabbits

Mary Toft (c.1701-1763) was a short, stocky young woman of 'sullen temper' who lived with her husband and three children in Godalming (Surrey). On 27 September 1726, she went into premature labour with her fourth child and a physician called John Howard was summoned to her house. But to his amazement, he watched her give birth to dismembered animals! First, it was something resembling a pig's bladder and a cat's paw and then a succession of bits and pieces which once belonged to a rabbit!

And over the next few days she continued giving birth to even more body parts!

John Howard then reported this extraordinary occurrence to some of his peers in London. However, they just assumed he was some kind of weirdo from the Shires and ignored his preposterous claims but then George I (1660-1727) got to hear about the woman in Surrey giving birth to rabbits and ordered his Swiss-born personal physician Nathaniel St André to investigate the matter further. He travelled to her house and arrived just in time to witness Mary giving birth to a rabbit's torso! He noted that her abdomen quivered as though the animals were crawling through her body searching for an escape route and then concluded that it was the pressure of being expelled from her uterus which resulted in them being born crushed and mutilated. Later that day, she gave birth to another bit of rabbit and in the evening some rabbit skin too!

Convinced that this woman was some kind of medical phenomenon, he took a few bits of newly-born rabbit back to London to show the king and then arranged for her to be studied by all the greatest scientists of the age. He also wrote a paper, *A Short Narrative of an Extraordinary Delivery of Rabbets* (1726) about the poor woman's extraordinary births, which now seemed to occur with a frightening regularity for anyone wanting to witness them.

By now Mary was a bit of a celebrity. The courtier and political writer John Hervey, 2nd Baron Hervey (1696-1743) wrote at the time: 'Every creature in town, both men and women, have been to see and feel her: the perpetual emotions, noises and rumblings in her Belly are something prodigious; all the eminent physicians, surgeons and man-midwives in London are there Day and Night to watch her next production.'

One of those other eminent physicians who'd examined her was John Maubray (1700-1732). He was a keen proponent of Maternal Impression, a widely held belief at the time that conception and pregnancy could be influenced by what a mother dreamt of or saw around her. He'd previously reported on another mother's over-familiarity with a household pet which had evidently caused her child to resemble that particular animal. Since Mary had admitted to having a craving for rabbit stew during her pregnancy, giving birth to rabbit body parts seemed to support his theory and he too was happy to lend his name to the ever-growing list of doctors and physicians supporting the validity of these strange births.

But not everyone was quite so convinced …

The king's surgeon Cyriacus Ahlers was the first to have doubts. He'd visited Mary around 21 November 1726 to witness the births for himself and had then been allowed to take some of the newly-born bits of rabbit back to London with him for analysis. He soon discovered that they'd been cut-up with man-made instruments and the animal's stomach contained undigested vegetable matter which meant it had been fed normally. There were also droppings in amongst the body parts which contained straw and grain! All this rather damning new information seemed to dispel any notion that they'd all just popped out of the woman's vagina as she'd claimed!

The hoax finally began to unravel in December 1726 …

By now, Mary must have guessed that she'd been rumbled because every time she pretended to go into labour, she never gave birth, at least, never in the presence of the ever-growing number of suspicious doctors camped out at the bottom of her bed.

The prominent physician/anatomist James Douglas (1675-1742) then questioned her on three or four occasions over several days in order to expose her as a fraud, but it wasn't until 7 December 1726, when another sceptic, the man-midwife Richard Manningham (1690-1759), who'd previously witnessed her giving birth to a hog's bladder, threatened to perform a very painful exploratory surgery on her to discover the truth about her strange condition, that she broke down in tears and confessed that her abnormal pregnancies had all been an elaborate hoax.

She claimed that a travelling woman had given her the moneymaking idea after demonstrating how to insert the animal parts into her body. How this came up in conversation is anyone's guess! Then, her husband Joshua Toft had bought all the rabbits and bribed the porter at their lodgings to turn a blind eye as he smuggled them into the building.

On 7 January 1727, Mary was accused of 'being an abominable cheat and imposter in pretending to be delivered of several monstrous births' and carted off to jail to await trial. But on 8 April 1727, she was released again because nobody was quite sure what crime she'd actually committed, and she returned home to Godalming. A year later, in February 1728, she gave birth to a daughter, Elizabeth, which was recorded in the parish register as 'her first child after her pretended Rabett-breeding.'

The satirists and journalists of the day had a great time mocking all those famous doctors who'd believed her story. And the guy that got it in the neck the most was the opportunistic fop, Nathaniel St André. Initially, he was suspected of being involved in the hoax but he was soon cleared of any wrong-doing. However, his gullibility cost him his job as the king's physician. Mary, on the other hand, was generally pitied as a simple fool who'd been manipulated by her scheming husband into perpetrating the scam in the hope of making some extra cash. She was generally believed to have been a confused and impressionable young woman who was probably just craving a little attention and a few extra shillings to help feed her family.

the china drink

Life – Making it from one cup of tea to the next.

The seventeenth century Portuguese noblewoman Catherine of Braganza has been credited with introducing the British to the joys of tea-drinking. It was very popular amongst the Portuguese nobility at the time, and when the future wife of Charles II (1630-1685) arrived in England on 14 May 1662, one of the first things she did was ask for a cup of tea.

Her unconventional use of tea as a thirst-quenching beverage and not as a pick-me-up medicinal drink (previously prescribed by physicians and pharmacists as a remedy for a wide array of minor ailments) soon made tea drinking a very fashionable pastime with the aristocracy and the well-mannered classes. Before long it had become everyone's favourite temperance drink.

The first person who seems to have written about enjoying a cup of tea socially rather than medicinally was the famous English diarist Samuel Pepys (1633-1703). As part of his diary entry for 25 September 1660, he wrote about a high-level meeting between various naval officials at which he was present. When it had finished, he was obviously in need of a little refreshment because he signed off by saying: 'And afterwards, I did send for a cup of tee (a China drink) of which I never had drank before.' But he never actually said if he'd enjoyed it or not. Possibly not because he only ever mentioned it again in a brief diary entry on 28 June 1667 after his wife had been prescribed tea as a cure for her cold: 'I went away and by coach home, and there find my wife making of tea, a drink which Mr Pelling, the Potticary, tells her is good for her cold and defluxions.'

The British imported more and more tea throughout the eighteenth and nineteenth centuries. An increase in its availability and a slump in its price soon transformed tea drinking from a respectable pastime amongst the upper classes into an absolute necessity for the lower classes too. It was cheaper than ale; it was particularly appealing in Britain's cold and wet climate, and the leaves (and later the bags) could be used more than once if necessary. The government actively encouraged tea drinking; it was suddenly inherently British and everyone's patriotic duty to drink gallons of the stuff … but only because the raw materials came from a British colony instead of some other country's colony!

The Brits started adding milk to their tea sometime in the early eighteenth century. And ever since then, a debate has raged as to whether the milk or the tea should be poured first. *A Nice Cup of Tea* (1946) was an essay written by the famous novelist George Orwell (1903-1950) outlining the dos and don'ts for making a perfect cup of tea which was first published in the *Evening Standard* on 12 January 1946. The author maintained that the tea should always be poured first because 'one can exactly regulate the amount of milk whereas one is liable to put in too much milk if one does it the other way round.'

It's unclear when tea and sympathy became a thing. It's a peculiarly British belief that putting the kettle on can resolve all of life's problems. It doesn't matter if you've just broken a nail or escaped the clutches of a serial killer, a nice cup of tea will somehow help you feel better!

christmas greetings

The custom of sending Christmas cards began in Britain in 1843.

The first commercially produced card was just a simple hand-painted picture printed onto a piece of stiff cardboard commissioned by Henry Cole (1808-1882) and designed by the painter/illustrator John Callcott Horsley (1817-1903).

The design consisted of three panels. The two outer panels depicted scenes of charity with food and clothing being handed out to the poor, and the centre panel featured three generations of a stereotypical rosy-cheeked Victorian family (including a very young girl) sitting around a table supping wine along with the traditional yuletide greeting: *A Merry Christmas and a Happy New Year to You*. There was also a 'To___' and 'From___' space at the top and bottom for inserting names.

One thousand cards were printed and they were sold for a shilling apiece.

The benefit of mass-producing the card eliminated the need for people to handwrite dozens of letters and at the same time added to the profits of the newly-formed Uniform Penny Post (1840) which by pure coincidence Henry himself had set-up a few years earlier.

However, the fancy new greetings card wasn't welcomed by everyone. The puritanical British Temperance Movement objected to what they described as the scandalous image of a little girl drinking wine and organised a campaign to censor and suppress the cards.

They kicked up such a fuss that nobody dared produce any more Christmas cards for another three years!

the curious case of captain robert campbell

Robert Campbell (1885-1966) joined the British Army in 1903. A few weeks after war broke out in 1914, he was leading the 1st Battalion East Surrey Regiment in north-west France when they came under attack from German forces. During the fighting Robert was seriously injured and captured. Afterwards, he was taken to a German military hospital in Cologne before being shipped off to a POW camp in Magdeburg where he remained incarcerated for the next two years.

In 1916, he received a letter from home informing him that his mother was dying of cancer. With nothing to lose, he wrote to Kaiser Wilhelm II asking for compassionate leave to visit her before she died. Astonishingly, the Kaiser agreed to his request and granted him two weeks leave provided he gave his word as a British Army officer that he would return after concluding his affairs in Britain. Robert immediately accepted his terms and was released from the camp. He then set off for Blighty and reached his mother's bedside on 7 November 1916.

He spent a week in his hometown of Gravesend with his mother and then returned to Germany! No one, not even the Kaiser himself had expected him to return, but as an officer and a gentleman, he felt obliged to keep his word.

However, as soon as he returned to the camp, he set about trying to escape. Just as he'd been honour bound to keep his word as a gentleman, he was also honour bound as a British Army officer to try and escape from captivity. He and a group of other prisoners spent the next nine months digging a tunnel out of the camp. They got as far as the Dutch border before being recaptured and sent back.

After the war Captain Campbell was released and remained in the army until he retired in 1925.

Note: The Germans probably believed that their extraordinary act of kindness and good faith would be reciprocated by the British government when Peter Gastreich, a German POW held at a camp on the Isle of Man, requested a similar concession after learning that his father was dying. But that wasn't the case. The British government denied the request after claiming that Captain Campbell's temporary release shouldn't be considered a precedent for such behaviour. They'd never been consulted before his two-weeks leave was agreed and wouldn't have consented to such a proposal even if they had! So, there was no way some bloody German was getting a free pass home!

the travels of sir john mandeville

The Travels of Sir John Mandeville (1357) was one of the most popular books of the late-Middle Ages.

It was purportedly written by the English knight John Mandeville and described his journeys through Egypt, Ethiopia, India, Persia and Turkey and his encounters with the fantastical people of these lands; the pygmies whose mouths were so small that they had to suck up their food through reeds, the race of one-eyed giants who ate only raw fish and raw meat, wild men with horns and hooves, the poor souls with eyes in their shoulders, men that were half human and half dog, and the folk that spent all their lives hopping around because they only had one leg! It was absolute bollocks from start to finish but because the author's fanciful portrayals of Johnny Foreigner were so expertly interwoven with accurate geographical descriptions of the lands he'd supposedly explored, it all seemed perfectly believable!

The character of Sir John Mandeville was almost certainly fictitious, despite the esteemed English polymath Thomas Browne (1605-1682) once describing him as 'the greatest liar of all time.' Clearly, he didn't believe a word he wrote but was still willing to accept that Sir John was a real person.

Although the manuscript was written in French, there's still some debate as to whether the original author was English or French, or whether medieval scholars really took the book seriously or not. One person who definitely did take it seriously was the Italian explorer Christopher Columbus who considered it to be an invaluable work of reference when he was travelling around the world.

Even though he normally travelled in the opposite direction from those lands described in the book!

the brahan seer

The prophet Kenneth the Sallow, also known as Coinneach Odhar or 'The Brahan Seer' was born at Baile-na-Cille in the parish of Uig, Isle of Lewis sometime in the early-seventeenth century.

It was whilst working as a labourer for the aristocrat Kenneth Mackenzie, 3rd Earl of Seaforth (1635-1678) at his estate near Dingwall that he apparently acquired his supernatural powers. According to legend, his mother had encountered the ghost of a Danish princess in a cemetery one night and then prevented her from returning to her grave unless she granted her son the gift of second sight. Later that same day, Kenny found a stone in his pocket and this stone had a hole in it through which he was suddenly able to see the future …

Whereas other famous prophets such as Nostradamus would speak in riddles about future world-changing events, possibly so their predictions could be interpreted in a thousand different ways and could never be proved right or wrong, Kenny spoke plainly, mainly about local events, and his visions were often a lot more mundane, like the ones he had about a collapsing church roof or the birth of a two-headed calf.

But that's not to say that he didn't tackle the big stuff too. He prophesised about future events such as the Battle of Culloden (1746), the Highland Clearances (1750-1860), the building of the Caledonian Canal (1822) and the discovery of North Sea oil (1969) as well as future inventions such as 'a chariot without horse or bridle' (railways, automobiles), 'hills strewn with ribbons' (powerlines) and streams of fire and water running beneath the streets into houses (gas and water pipes).

At the height of his fame, Kenny made his most famous prediction which would ultimately cost him his life …

He was asked by the Earl's wife, Isabella about her husband's welfare, as he'd recently travelled to Paris in France and she was worried about him. Kenny reported that he was in good health and left it at that. But Isabella wasn't satisfied with this rather vague answer; she wanted more details and pressed him to elaborate or she'd have him killed. So he did elaborate and she had him killed anyway! He'd told her that her husband was screwing around with another woman, fairer than herself (which wasn't all that surprising considering Isabella was reputed to be one of the ugliest women in Scotland) and that her family line would end with the last male heir being deaf and dumb. Isabella was so incensed by his scandalous prophecies that she had him thrown head first into a barrel of boiling tar!

Unsurprisingly, Kenny's final prophecies both turned out to be true. The Earl had indeed been busy poking a fair French maiden and the family line did come to an end. Francis Mackenzie, 1st Baron Seaforth (1754-1815), contracted scarlet fever in 1766 when he was about 12 years-old, leaving him deaf and dumb, and when he died in 1815, he left no heirs after his four sons had all predeceased him.

Before Kenny's death, Isabella had claimed that his soul would not enter Heaven because he'd dabbled in witchcraft. He counterclaimed that upon his death, a dove and a raven would meet in the air and rest on his ashes. If the raven landed first then Isabella would be proved right but if the dove landed first then his soul would enter Heaven and hers would enter Hell. According to legend, the two birds did appear in the air just as he'd predicted and the dove landed first.

The life and times of Coinneach Odhar were originally documented in *The Prophecies of the Brahan Seer* (1888) by the eminent Scottish folklorist

Alexander Mackenzie (1838-1898). There are no contemporary accounts or other historical documents with known provenance corroborating the man's existence or a record of his prophecies but this shouldn't be too surprising judging by the scarcity of written sources from Scotland during that period. Most probably, the prophecies were passed down through the generations by word of mouth and slightly embellished with each telling, and it was these stories which eventually became accepted as fact and made it into the book.

Nonetheless, that doesn't mean to say that people don't take Kenny's prophecies seriously …

There's a small Pictish monument located on a hillside near the village of Strathpeffer in Ross & Cromarty called *Clach an Tiompain* (Sounding Stone) which supposedly marks the site of a 1411 battle between the Munro clan and the MacDonald clan. Kenny had predicted that if the stone fell over three times, then Loch Ussie would burst its banks and flood the valley below. To date the stone has fallen over twice and just to be on the safe side, it's now set in concrete!

the london monster

The man the newspapers called the London Monster got his jollies from pricking, poking or stabbing young women on the streets of late-eighteenth century London. It's believed that he claimed more than fifty victims during his two-year reign of terror!

The women were all from wealthy families and most reported being attacked by a man who shouted obscenities and then tried to stab them. Some of his victims claimed that he'd had a small knife strapped to his knee whilst others reported that he'd invited them to smell a fake nosegay before poking them in the face with a spike hidden in the flowers. The women were often left distraught with torn clothes and serious wounds and their attacker always managed to flee the scene long before help arrived.

Things got so bad that the young ladies began wearing pots and pans underneath their clothes for protection! One wealthy businessman John Julius Angerstein (1735-1823) offered a £100 reward to anyone who apprehended the madman, and some men organised themselves into vigilante groups to patrol the streets or joined clubs entitling them to wear special badges reassuring women that they weren't the Monster and it was perfectly safe to approach them. Yeah, because the real Monster would never think just to wear a badge himself!

It has since been speculated that the London Monster may have only attacked a few women with all the other victims inflicting their own wounds just to make it look like they'd been attacked. It was obvious that he only assaulted the most beautiful women and so the butt-ugly ones may have started faking attacks to gain a little attention!

In 1790, a 23 year-old florist, Rhynwick Williams was arrested on suspicion of being the Monster. He'd been spotted in St James's Park by Anne Porter, one of his alleged victims, whilst she was out walking with her boyfriend. She identified him as the man who'd pricked her and they followed him back to his house. Upon seeing the man close up and personal again, Anne Porter fainted and the police were summoned.

Mr Williams protested his innocence but was arrested and sent for trial.

Some of the prosecution witness statements were obviously contradictory; his co-workers provided him with an alibi for many of the attacks and his defence lawyer, the Irish poet/writer Theophilus Swift (1746-1815) argued that Anne Porter had only accused his client of being her assailant because she'd wanted to collect the £100 reward money. Despite the overwhelming evidence proving his innocence, Mr Williams was still convicted of the crimes and jailed for six years.

However, having said all that, reports of further attacks tailed off dramatically after he was marched off to prison. Maybe that was just an unfortunate coincidence. Or maybe not.

the southwark miser

John Overs was definitely a real person and definitely a miserly Southwark ferryman in Saxon London but the popular stories about him and the manner of his death, as reported in the pamphlet *The True History of the Life and Sudden Death of Old John Overs* (1744) might have been exaggerated a little by the anonymous author.

John's business was very successful and he'd soon accumulated a great wealth, acquiring a considerable estate on the south bank of the River Thames, and employing many servants and apprentices. Notwithstanding his great fortune, however, he remained miserly in his ways; dressing like a poor man and scouring the markets for bargains and the cheapest food, buying the stalest bread and the coarsest cuts of meat. He even begrudged his own staff their meals. He bought black puddings and the cheapest meat, and as he handed them their meagre allowance, he would often remark: 'There, you hungry dogs, you will undo me with eating!'

John was always looking for some convoluted way to save money. One day he came up with a plan to fake his own death, believing that his family and servants would then mourn him and observe a strict fast out of respect, allowing him to save on provisions. At the end of the day, he then intended to delight everyone with his miraculous recovery.

He compelled his daughter Mary to assist him in his cunning plan by laying him out, covering him with a sheet and then informing the servants of his sad demise.

And that's when things started to go wrong …

Instead of being distraught with grief, the servants were overcome with joy at his death. They sang and danced around his miserable corpse to celebrate their release from servitude and feasted on bread, cheese and ale … and then sang and danced a bit more. John just lay there motionless listening to their merriment, seething with anger at the disrespect … and the abhorrent waste of good food! Eventually he could contain himself no more and started to sit up. One of the servants spotted him struggling under the sheet; he thought it was a ghost or even the Devil himself, so he grabbed an oar (which just happened to be lying around the house) and smashed the miserly old bastard over the head with it … killing him for real this time!

tumbling toast

Toast is a British superfood. Consumed at any time of the day or night as a snack or as part of a main meal. The British put more 'on toast' than any other nation: jam; marmalade; potted meats; Marmite; tinned tomatoes; scrambled eggs; fried eggs (and any other type of egg); beans; sardines; cheese; and even spaghetti hoops! Because of our love for burnt bread, it was inevitable that sooner or later someone would conduct a survey to prove (or disprove) the theory that buttered toast always lands butter-side down after falling on the floor.

The English novelist James Payn (1830-1898) first described the phenomenon in his 1884 poem:

I never had a slice of bread,
Particularly large and wide,
That did not fall upon the floor,
And always on the buttered side.

The Lurpak Tumbling Toast Test in 2001 was the biggest study of the phenomenon ever undertaken with over 1,000 school children from all across Britain letting a piece of toast fall off their plate more than 21,000 times. The results conclusively proved what everyone already knew, that the law really was a thing, with 62 percent of the toast slices falling butter-side down!

the speeding motorist

The world's first speeding motorist was a guy called Walter Arnold. He was spotted doing 8mph (13km/h) in a 2mph (3.2km/h) zone in Paddock Wood, Kent, on 28 January 1896 but was easily apprehended by a policeman giving chase on his bike!

Walter was later fined a shilling for his reckless behaviour.

the stale bread act

Britain had been at war with France since 1793 which impeded the importation of grain into the country. Harvests since the mid-1790s had been poor and much of the home grown grain was being bought by the government for use by the armed forces. This inevitably led to a shortage of bread in the shops and by 1795 the country was on the brink of famine.

Bread was the staple diet of the poor. It was the main component of every meal and without it the population would starve. The bread shortages, the inevitable price hikes and the blatant profiteering by the millers, who were accused of hoarding grain or withholding it from the local markets and sending it to the big cities where it fetched a higher price, soon led to civil unrest around the country.

The government feared a revolution and took swift action against the radical groups coordinating the disorder. Meetings were banned and the group leaders arrested. Although the threat of a revolution quickly diminished, the violent protests which had started the unrest continued. But the government had a cunning plan ...

They passed the 'Stale Bread Act' which stopped people from buying fresh bread! Under the terms of the act, bakers were forced to keep bread 24 hours before being allowed to sell it. Why would this solve the bread shortage? Because stale bread fills you up more than fresh bread. Up to 20 percent more in fact, so people would need less of it to eat than before.

Bakers were slapped with a heavy fine if caught selling fresh bread and people were encouraged to snitch on anyone offering them fresh bread, entitling them to half the 5 shilling fine as a reward. Many career criminals actually supplemented their income by tricking bakers into selling them a few fresh loaves and then informing the authorities.

It was such a daft idea that the act was repealed less than a year later!

lord nelson's coffin

Benjamin Hallowell Carew (1761-1834) was the captain of HMS *Swiftsure* at the Battle of the Nile (1798) during the French Revolutionary Wars (1792-1802). He was one of the favoured captains known as the 'Band of Brothers' who served under one of Britain's greatest military leaders, Vice-Admiral Horatio Nelson, 1st Viscount Nelson, 1st Duke of Bronte (1758-1805).

However, he was probably best known for his macabre gift of a coffin to his boss!

During the battle, HMS *Swiftsure* had engaged the French flagship *L'Orient* and had played a major part in her destruction. He then ordered a coffin to be made from the salvaged bits of *L'Orient's* main mast and had it delivered to Lord Nelson with an accompanying note: 'Sir, I have taken the liberty of presenting you a coffin made from the main mast of *L'Orient*, that when you have finished your military career in this world you may be buried in one of your trophies. But may that period be far distant is the earnest wish of your sincere friend, Benjamin Hallowell.'

Rather surprisingly, Lord Nelson loved his gift and kept it nearby until he had a use for it.

That day came on 9 August 1805 when he was interred in the crypt of St Paul's Cathedral (London).

the queen's executioner

In 1558, the staunchly Catholic Mary I (1516-1558) was succeeded to the English throne by her half-sister Elizabeth I (1533-1603) who immediately restored Protestantism.

The Jesuits Act 1584 decreed that all Catholic priests were to be banned from entering the country and the ones that were already here had to leave within forty days or be tried for treason. Similarly, anyone who harboured these priests or knew of their whereabouts but failed to notify the authorities would also be charged with treason. Despite this new law, however, many of the priests stayed put and the even more committed ones actually travelled from the Continent to England to support the wealthy Catholic families who felt threatened by all the anti-Catholic feeling in the country at the time. They pretended to be members of the family and would often live with them in their houses. Hiding places or 'priest holes' were concealed in fireplaces, attics and staircases, hidden behind panelling or built inside walls just in case the householders had an unexpected visit from the Priest Hunters and they needed a place to hide.

The Priest Hunters were the volunteers, soldiers and spies employed by the government who travelled around the country raiding homes, snooping on families, meeting with informants and making arrests. It was also common practice for them to pose as Catholics and trick other people into making incriminating statements. This technique was most famously used to arrest the English priest Richard Simpson (c.1553-1588). In January 1588, he'd been travelling through the Peak District and met a stranger along the road who pretended to be a Catholic. He was so convincing that the unsuspecting priest revealed his true identity and was arrested on the spot. It goes without saying that he was then imprisoned, tortured and put to death.

The most infamous Priest Hunter was the politician Richard Topcliffe (1531-1604).

He entered the service of Queen Elizabeth in 1557, a year before her accession to the throne, and soon became a tireless agent of her government's resolve to eradicate Catholicism from England, working closely with her Principal Secretary and Chief Spymaster Francis Walsingham (c.1532-1590). He hunted down, arrested, interrogated and tortured hundreds of priests with the publisher/humourist Richard Rowlands (c.1550-1640) commenting that his 'inhuman cruelty is so great ... he will not spare to extend any torture whatsoever.' As well as using all the traditional ways of inflicting pain, Richard was ahead of his time and liked to use rape, sleep deprivation and other inventive torture methods to extract a confession. He was so enthusiastic about his work that he would often attend the executions himself acting as the Master of Ceremonies!

His most famous victims were probably the Jesuit priests Robert

Southwell (c.1561-1595) and Henry Walpole (1558-1595) who were both charged with treason, tortured and then executed.

But it wasn't just priests who fell victim to his relentless campaign of persecution. Anyone who was just suspected of being a Catholic could have been picked up and interrogated by the man often described as the cruellest tyrant in all of England. He had torture chambers built in all the prisons but sometimes he preferred to work from home! His house in Westminster was also kitted out with all the latest devices so he didn't have to travel into the 'office' every day!

the rendlesham forest incident

A series of reported sightings of unexplained lights in the sky above Rendlesham Forest (Suffolk) just outside the perimeter gates of RAF Woodbridge (which was being used at the time by the US Air Force) became one of the world's best known reported UFO sightings and has often been referred to as 'Britain's Roswell'.

The Ministry of Defence announced that these strange lights posed no threat to national security: 'No evidence was found of any threat to the defence of the United Kingdom, and no further investigations were carried out. No further information has come to light which alters our view that the sightings of these lights was of no defence significance.' The incident has since been explained away by sceptics as just nocturnal lights, fireballs, extra bright stars or even a prank played by the SAS on their US counterparts.

In the early hours of 26 December 1980, US military personnel spotted strange lights above Rendlesham Forest and left their base to investigate. One of the men, Jim Penniston later claimed to have encountered a spacecraft with no apparent landing gear covered in what appeared to be hieroglyphic characters which he estimated to have been about 10 feet (3m) tall and 10 feet (3m) wide at its base. Indentations in the ground as well as damage to the trees in the area where the lights had been spotted were found the following morning and radiation levels recorded at the site were also unusually high.

On 28 December 1980, things got even weirder …

Larry Warren, Adrian Bustinza and other personnel were sent out on patrol towards the forest where they encountered a team of officers with Geiger counters moving around and appearing to examine something on the ground. Shortly afterwards a small red light appeared in the sky. It moved in a downward arc before stopping and hovering around 20 feet (6m) off the ground. Then it suddenly exploded and a spacecraft appeared. It had no markings and Larry Warren said that its true shape was only visible to him through his peripheral vision. At this stage, the officers asked them to leave the area but from a distance they claimed to have witnessed another man, Gordon Williams approach the craft and encounter an alien with 'what looked like eyes, facial features [and] bright clothing.' Larry Warren claimed there was then a silent stand-off between them rather than any communication.

Gordon Williams has never gone on record about this incident.

After Larry Warren returned to base, Adrian Bustinza said he watched the spacecraft depart from the forest: 'When it took off, it was hovering. It went up and took off at about a 45-degree angle, and if you would have blinked, you would have missed it ... And we got a cold draft of air that lasted about a good 10 seconds. You know, like when you get a good blow of dust or wind. No noise though. I do remember that.'

the phantom island of hy-brasil

Hy-Brasil was the name of a mystical island surrounded by mist and hidden from the eyes of the outside world which was said to lie somewhere west of Ireland in the North Atlantic Ocean. Stories about this earthly paradise inhabited by fairies and magicians had been circulating around Europe for many years and the cartographers of the Middle Ages were so confident of its existence that they began including it on their maps and nautical charts.

It was first noted on a chart as *Bracile* compiled in 1325 by the famous Genoese cartographer Angelino Dulcert.

The earliest known accounts of the island's existence came from the Irish saints St Brendan (c.484-c.578) and St Barrind (c.550-623) who both claimed to have seen Hy-Brasil. Since that time there have been many unsuccessful expeditions to find the island including those of the legendary Italian and Portuguese explorers John Cabot in 1497 and Pedro Álvares Cabral in 1500.

Perhaps the most famous story about Hy-Brasil was actually a piece of literary invention by the unfortunately named Irish writer and bookseller Richard Head (c.1637-1686). He recounted the story of Captain John Nesbitt who stumbled across the mysterious island in 1674 whilst travelling home from France to Ireland. He'd been lost in a thick fog and his ship had drifted into shallow waters near to a beach. When the fog lifted, he and his crew disembarked and began exploring the island only to discover that it was home to giant black rabbits and a wise old magician who lived all alone in a castle. He invited them into his home, explained that the spell he'd cast on the island to prevent it from being seen from the outside world had been broken and then plied them with gold and silver before sending them on their merry way!

One person who read about Captain Nesbitt's adventures was the real-life seventeenth-century sea captain Alexander Johnson. He obviously believed every word of Dick Head's fanciful story and was inspired to try and find Hy-Brasil for himself. Even more surprisingly, he returned shortly afterwards telling tales of landing on the island and encountering the same magician and the same black rabbits!

A couple of centuries later, in 1872, the Irish antiquarian/folklorist T J Westropp (1860-1922) claimed to have seen the island appear and disappear through the mist and in 1878, according to the US writer D R McAnally, the residents of Ballycotton in Ireland also noticed an island 'where none was known to exist' in the exact spot where their fishermen 'knew the sea as well as they knew the land' and where 'the day before, they had been out in their boats and sailed where the strange island now appeared.'

The island continued to be marked on maps up until the mid-nineteenth century but by then it was being labelled as the Brasil Rock.

Note: During his reported close encounter of the third kind at Rendlesham Forest in 1980, the US airman Jim Penniston claimed to have telepathically received a binary code message. One particular line of this decoded message read 'origin 52.0942532N 13.131269W' which might have been the coordinates for Hy-Brasil, as it seemed to refer to a totally innocuous spot in the Atlantic Ocean, south-west of Galway where many maps and nautical charts of the Middle Ages had shown the island to be. Although the message apparently listed six other locations in Greece, Peru, Egypt, USA, China and Belize, the coordinates which might have referred to Hy-Brasil were the only ones seemingly indicating a spot in the middle of nowhere! Is it possible that the island is a secret alien base using some kind of cloaking device to keep its location a secret? Or is the whole thing just a load of old medieval nonsense?

the pressing of john weekes

Pressing or Crushing was a barbaric form of torture practiced in numerous places around the world. The techniques would often vary from country to country but always involved placing heavy weights on top of a person with the intent of injuring or killing them. In Asia they liked to use elephants to sit on people but in England they were forced to use something a little less exotic like stones and heavy rocks!

John Weekes of Fittleworth in West Sussex was arrested for highway robbery and murder in 1735. According to court records, he had been caught red-handed with 'several spots of blood and part of the [stolen] goods … found upon him.' So, he looked good for it! At his trial, however, he attempted to avoid justice after refusing to enter a plea by feigning stupidity and an inability to speak. The judge was not amused and accused him of 'standing mute through malice' before sentencing him to *peine forte et dure* (hard and forceful punishment) in order to help him regain his power of speech. It was a common practice at the time, with prisoners literally being pressed to death under a big pile of heavy rocks unless they relented to the demands of the court and entered a plea.

This particularly unpleasant and inventive punishment was usually carried out behind closed doors in some dingy prison dungeon somewhere, but poor John was ordered to endure his penance in full view of everyone in the marketplace at Horsham.

On 11 August 1735, he was stripped naked and laid on his back and then had a series of boulders placed on top of his body one at a time every few minutes. Within an hour he was lying under 400lbs (181kg) but he was still breathing and still refusing to enter a plea … and they'd ran out of boulders! However, the guy doing the pressing was a big lad, weighing about 17 stone (108kg), so he just sat on him and bounced up and down a couple of times … and killed him off that way!

the lost sport of pedestrianism

Pedestrianism was the sport of competitive walking funded by betting from which the modern sport of race walking has developed.

Captain Robert Barclay Allardice (1779-1854) was a notable Scottish walker who has been credited with starting it all after completing his much celebrated 1,000 mile (1,609km) walk in 1,000 successive hours to win a bet of 1,000 guineas. He was already a committed and much experienced walker long before accepting the bet from his pal and fellow British Army officer James Webster-Wedderburn (1788-1840) and so it seemed like easy money.

A straight-line, ½-mile (0.8m) course was laid out on open land near Newmarket with tents set up at each end for use by his assistants and the race officials, and gas lamps mounted on poles 100 yards (91m) apart along the path for his night time strolls. He began the walk just after midnight on 1 June 1809, starting each mile about fifteen minutes before the end of each hour and then doing the next mile at the start of the second hour, allowing himself ninety minutes of rest before heading out again for the next two miles. He was always dressed in casual gentleman's attire of a jacket, breeches and woollen stockings, and would normally have two men walking alongside him day and night as witnesses. The first day went well and at 5.00am, he stopped for a big breakfast of roast fowl with bread and butter, washed down with two cups of tea and a pint of strong ale! For the first few days he didn't even go to bed. Instead, he just napped on a sofa or went for another stroll outside of the course!

The weather was fairly consistent and very British for the first twenty days of the walk. Sunny, cloudy and occasionally a bit wet. But then it turned rather hot, hardening the course and making the walk more difficult. The much warmer weather also brought out the crowds. They'd come along to watch him and often had picnics along the edge of the course as they cheered him on. Supporting Captain Barclay walking his 1,000 miles had suddenly become a very popular way to pass an afternoon. But not everyone was rooting for him. Some people had bet against him and so he was forced to carry a pistol and hire a bodyguard just in case they decided to try and stop him from reaching the finish line.

He normally ate four meals a day every six hours. His daily diet always included meat, vegetables and two bottles of port!

For every mile walked, he also added a few extra yards, just to avoid any disputes that might arise.

His walk wasn't by any means easy. He suffered from fatigue, muscle aches, spasms, sleep deprivation and even toothache! On day twenty-three he had a fever and on day thirty-two he needed help getting to his feet. His times soon slowed to around 30 minutes for each mile, making it harder for him to get any proper rest, and at one stage, he was in so much pain that he stopped walking and started shuffling along the course like an old man! But there was no way he was going to give up. He'd rather die on the road and so he just kept on walking ...

During the last few days of his walk, his health had improved and he appeared cheerful and optimistic, completing the miles in much shorter times. On the afternoon of the forty-second day, 12 July 1809, he finished his last mile 'with perfect ease and great spirits, amidst an immense concourse of spectators' having spent twelve days and eight hours on the course.

THE COPYCATS

After Captain Barclay's amazing achievement, other likeminded folk were queueing up to copy what became known as The Barclay Match by walking their own 1,000 mile courses. Attempts to walk hundreds of miles against the clock had suddenly become a major sporting attraction, drawing huge crowds and attracting big prize money. Not only did they try to equal The Barclay Match, sometimes they tried to go one better. The first successful copycat was Thomas Standen in 1811 who walked 1,100 miles (1,770km) in 1,100 hours. But nobody seemed to care as his walk didn't receive much public attention.

On 10 November 1815, Josiah Eaton, a baker from Woodford in Northamptonshire began a similar 1,100-mile walk ... not realising that Thomas Standen had already beaten him to it. He may have successfully completed the walk on 26 December 1815 but he'd failed to secure any financial reward for his endeavours (which was the whole bloody point!) and had been running up debts after neglecting his bakery business, resulting in bankruptcy and a spell in prison! He emerged from jail undaunted a few months later and immediately organised another 1,100 x 1,100 walk starting on 10 June 1816. This time he began each mile at the top of the hour, which was much harder as he'd only receive 45 minutes rest. He was doing fine with 75 miles (120km) to go, then an ankle injury forced him to use a walking stick. But he still managed to hobble over the line to complete the challenge on 20 July 1816.

Later that same year, he began another challenge. This time he wanted to walk 2,000 half-miles in 2,000 half hours, meaning he'd only manage about 22 minutes of rest each half hour! He had no problems completing the task but deliberately chose not to. He'd been promised money from several businessmen but as he neared the finish line, he discovered that they weren't going to pay him a penny. One of them had died in the meantime and so the rest of them had decided that meant all bets were off. There was never going to be any big payoff and so Josiah issued a statement: 'I feel myself fully competent to complete the task I have undertaken, of walking 2,000 half miles in 2,000 successive half hours, which would have been finished on 5 December at noon; but being deceived by the gentlemen who should have supported me, I am determined not to complete the task. I therefore hereby give notice, I shall walk only until 11:00 on Thursday, 5 December 1816, being only 1,998 half miles, and recommend all parties to consider their bets to be null and void.' True to his word he stopped walking with one mile to go.

But this guy was like some kind of nineteenth century Forrest Gump. He just couldn't stop walking and it wasn't long before he was at it again with a 4,032 quarter-mile walk in 4,032 quarter-hours beginning on 11 May 1818. God only knows when the man slept! After a walk that nobody cared about which ended in a prison sentence and a walk that he deliberately didn't complete after being diddled out of his money, it was third time lucky for Josiah when he walked across the finish line on 30 June 1818 like a true sporting hero and was finally afforded the recognition he deserved.

There were many other walks during The Barclay Match craze, some more successful than others, but the race lengths and timings had quickly become a lot more complicated and certainly a lot more ridiculous. In 1816, someone called N B Barnet successfully walked 1,000 miles in 667 hours (1½ miles per hour) and in 1822, Robert Skipper managed 1,200 miles in 1,200 hours (1 mile per hour) ... and then celebrated his sporting triumph by walking another 6 miles (9.6km) just for the fun of it! A few months later, he was at it again, successfully completing a walk of 1,000 miles in 1,000 half hours (2 miles per hour). In 1838, J E Molloy walked 1,250 miles in 1,000 hours (1¼ miles per hour) and in the same year, Charles Harris walked 1,750 miles in 1,000 hours (1¾ miles per hour). In 1852, James Searles completed 2,000 miles in 2000 half hours (2 miles per hour) and in 1877, William Gale finished two walks - an easy 1,500 miles in 1,000 hours and then the much more difficult and quite stupid 4,000 quarter-miles in 4,000 periods of 10 minutes!

THE WARWICKSHIRE ANTELOPE

Perhaps the most elaborate of all these races occurred in 1851 at the Barrack Tavern Grounds in Sheffield when the ex-bricklayer Richard Manks (1818-1862) known as 'The Warwickshire Antelope' completed a truly extraordinary three-part walk - 1,000 quarter-miles in 1,000 quarter-hours, 1,000 half-miles in 1,000 half-hours, and then 1,000 miles in 1,000 hours (1,750 miles in 1,750 hours).

He completed his first 1,000 quarter-miles, rested for just twelve minutes and was off walking again on the next 1,000 half-miles. The walk was the most extraordinary exercise in sleep deprivation ever seen; sometimes he needed a couple of helpers to hold him upright and steer him around the course, with many of the spectators believing that he was walking himself into an early grave! At one stage he was so delirious that he walked into a wall and ended up with a bruised face! But he somehow managed to finish the half-mile challenge too and against all the odds, he immediately set off on the final 1000-mile stage. It has been estimated that around 160,000 people came out to watch him on the last few days of his walk as he neared his target of 1,750 miles in 1,750 hours. Seemingly recovered from his earlier near exhaustion, he began averaging 12-minute miles during the day and 16-minute miles at night. He was even strong enough to entertain the crowds, often racing against other pedestrians who'd come to see him.

Later that same year, he became the first pedestrian to complete a 1,000 miles in 500 hours walk. But his first attempt in September 1851 ended in disaster when he succumbed to a particularly nasty bout of diarrhoea after only 129 miles (207.6km) and the world record attempt had to be postponed until early October. After only two weeks R&R, he set off again around the outfield of The Oval in London on the afternoon of 10 October 1851. He passed the first 100 miles (160km) after only 43 hours and his second 100 miles after a further 44 hours, averaging 14 minutes-per-mile, allowing himself only 16 minutes every half hour to eat, sleep, wash, change his clothes, have a pee or do whatever else he needed to do! He ate ten times a day, mainly game and poultry dishes, roast beef and steaks, mutton and chops, all washed down with endless cups of strong beef tea, brandy and ale. Is it any wonder he had the shits the first time around?

Even in the early stages of his walk, it was rumoured that he was on the verge of achieving something quite special and large crowds gathered at the cricket ground to watch him. A few lamps were set up around the course, so he could be seen in the dark, making this walk the world's very first floodlit sporting event! The weather had been kind to him up until this point but then with less than 150 miles (241km) to go, the heavens opened. the *Illustrated London News* reported: 'Still onward Manks went, against the most fearful odds and obstacles although his feet were severely blistered, his limbs in great pain and he altogether showed the frightful effects of his incessant labour.'

At 11.37am on 31 October 1851 he finally crossed the finishing line. After completing his walk, the route around The Oval outfield was measured again ... although the reason why anyone would want to do this is unclear. It was found to be 21 yards (19.2m) longer than it needed to be. Some silly arse had measured it wrong and this meant that Richard Manks had not only walked 1,000 miles (1,609km) he'd also walked another 12 miles (19km) more than he should have!

THE FIRST FEMALE PEDESTRIAN

On 29 October 1864, Emma Sharp (1832-1920) became the first woman pedestrian. Wisely, she had just decided to do the original Barclay Match 1,000 miles x 1,000 hours walk. She took her first tentative steps on 17 September 1864, walking day and night around a roped off 120-yard (109.7m) course set up at the Quarry Gap Hotel in Laisterdyke, Bradford, for 30 minutes at a time and then enjoying a 90-minute break ... in the pub across the street! As no woman had ever successfully completed the challenge, her progress was widely reported in the newspapers and followed keenly by supporters and critics alike. Sometimes many thousands of people turned up at the course to cheer her on. For some reason she chose to dress like a man for the walk with the only indication of her sex being the large drooping straw hat she wore which was ornamented with a white feather and other girlie accessories.

Like all these events, it was heavily wagered upon. Huge bets were placed against her and there were no end of shady characters lining up to try and influence the result. Apart from the constant jeering in an effort to try and break her spirits, some of her more unscrupulous detractors also tried tripping her up, attacking her with chloroform, drugging her food and even throwing burning embers at her! Things got so bad that she had to ask a friend to walk in front of her with a loaded shotgun and undercover police officers were sometimes employed to mingle with the crowds to keep a watchful eye on her and find the ruffians responsible for the assaults. For the final two days of her walk, Emma packed a pistol herself and reportedly had to fire it 27 times to fend off over enthusiastic fans and potential attackers. It was rumoured at the time that Emma was the only person to bet on herself to finish the race in the time!

Despite all the obstacles, she still managed to complete the challenge. She crossed the line in front of a 25,000-strong crowd, a band struck up a little tune and one unlucky Ox was thrown on a fire and roasted in her honour. Her husband, who'd been a little embarrassed by his wife's manly endeavours had stayed out of the limelight until then, but after realising how much money she'd earned, suddenly appeared by her side to champion her achievements! During her walk Emma probably experienced less health problems than any of her supposedly fitter and much stronger male counterparts. Just a couple of swollen ankles, which quickly healed again once she'd stopped walking.

ALAN FERGUSON

the london garrotting panic

It was all a big fuss about nothing really.

It was meant to be a new type of crime and the streets of London in 1862 were meant to be full of criminal gangs attacking people and robbing them. Except, that wasn't really the case at all. There'd been a few isolated incidents but nothing on the scale being reported in the press. Reading the newspaper coverage of events, it was easy to think that gangs of ruffians were lurking around every corner waiting to pounce.

The Times reported garrotting as a thoroughly 'un-British crime' and the *Observer* described the garrotting gangs very unfavourably to the more gentlemanly highway robbers of the past. Clearly, if the Great British public had to be robbed then they'd prefer to be fleeced of their valuables by a dashing highwayman waving a pistol in their faces!

The few garrotting gangs that actually were roaming the streets usually worked in groups of three – a 'nasty man' (the garrotter), a 'front-stall' (the robber) and the 'back-stall' (the lookout). While the garrotter crept up behind the victim and held them in a choke hold with a belt or a scarf, the robber would quickly relieve them of all their cash and valuables.

The fear of being garrotted was so great that people started travelling in small groups or even hiring bodyguards to walk alongside them whenever they left the house. Some individuals armed themselves or wore strange, convoluted anti-garrotting contraptions like huge spiked collars, which were probably more of a danger to themselves than any garrotter! One of the more discreet devices was the Anti-Garrotter Belt Pistol which consisted of a little half-cocked pistol mounted onto a flat piece of metal which was then strapped into the small of the back and activated by pulling a cord fastened around the waist. If attacked, the wearer would simply give the cord a tug and shoot the garrotter in the balls!

On 17 July 1862, the MP Hugh Pilkington (1804-1890) was attacked and robbed in Pall Mall as he walked from the Houses of Parliament to his club. He turned out to be the most famous victim of the so-called garrotting gangs and the newspapers became even more hysterical in their coverage of the crime. Politicians and the police were seen as being completely ineffective in trying to stop the attacks. Even though there weren't actually that many attacks to stop! The politicians quickly rushed through The Garrotter's Act 1863, which restored flogging for criminals convicted of a violent robbery, and the police responded by redefining some minor felonies as garrotting crimes. There simply weren't enough of the real crimes for them to investigate, so some unlucky pickpockets and thieves were labelled garrotters and given a much harsher sentence, just so it looked like they were doing something to protect the public. In some cases, even innocent men were picked out as being potential 'nasty men' just because they were seen wearing a scarf!

Although the newspapers positively loved reporting on the garrotting gangs and their victims, there were plenty of other newsworthy crimes to report in Victorian London and eventually they tired of the story. Unsurprisingly, the public stopped panicking about being garrotted too, just as soon as reports of the non-existent crime wave faded from the front pages!

the man in the bottle hoax

In the first few weeks of January 1749 the following advertisement appeared in many of the London newspapers:

> *At the New Theatre in the Haymarket, on Monday next, the 16th instant, is to be seen a Person who performs the several most surprising things following, – viz., 1st. He takes a common walking Cane from any of the Spectators, and thereupon plays the music of every Instrument now in use, and likewise sings to surprising perfection. 2dly. He presents you with a common Wine Bottle, which any of the spectators may first examine; this Bottle is placed on a Table in the middle of the Stage, and he (without any equivocation) goes into it, in the sight of all the Spectators,*

and sings in it; during his stay in the bottle, any Person may handle it, and see plainly that it does not exceed a common Tavern Bottle. Those on the Stage, or in the Boxes, may come in masked habits (if agreeable to them); and the performer, if desired, will inform them who they are. Stage, 7s. 6d. Boxes, 5s. Pit, 3s. Gallery, 2s. Tickets to be had at the Theatre. To begin a half an hour after six o'clock. The performance continues about two hours and a half.

The advertisement generated an amazing public response and on the night of the performance, every seat in the theatre had been sold. But as the start time came and went the excitable crowd became rather less excitable and a lot more restless, stomping their feet and yelling for the show to commence. Eventually, a theatre employee appeared on stage, asking the audience to remain calm and assuring them that they would all have their money refunded if the performer failed to appear.

But then someone threw a lighted candle onto the stage and a few of the more vengeful members of the audience took this as their cue to start smashing up the theatre. Whilst many people ran out the doors, abandoning hats, wigs and cloaks in their haste to escape the violence, the rioters started tearing up seats, destroying scenery and demolishing the boxes. Someone stole the box-office takings and then the debris from the theatre was dragged outside into the street and burnt on a huge bonfire.

Suspicion immediately fell upon the theatre's manager, a notorious prankster called Samuel Foote (1720-1777) as having organised the event. But he denied all knowledge of it. The theatre's owner was then blamed for the fiasco but he too pleaded his innocence, claiming that a man unknown to him had made all the arrangements for renting the theatre.

The Man in the Bottle Hoax instantly became the target of newspapers and pamphlets which published satires about the conjurer's non-appearance. One newspaper explained that he'd been ready and willing to present his show but was asked by a gentleman beforehand for a private performance, and as he'd crawled inside, the gentleman 'corked up the bottle, whipped it in his pocket and made off.'

Other practical jokers jumped on the bandwagon; taking the piss out of all those people stupid enough to fall for such an obvious ruse and even proposing their own outlandish stage shows. One guy claimed that if an audience was willing to pull out their own eyeballs, he'd pop them back in their sockets again and somebody else promised to jump down their own throat if people would pay him lots of money to watch!

Meanwhile, the identity of the practical joker remained unknown. However, in his book *The Handy-book of Literary Curiosities* (1893), American William Shephard Walsh identified the perpetrator as William Bentinck, 2nd Duke of Portland (1709-1762). After discussing the gullibility of the man in the street with his chum, the Earl of Chesterfield, he'd been convinced that it was possible to find 'fools enough in London to fill a playhouse and pay handsomely for the privilege of being there' even if he advertised a show featuring an unknown performer staging some preposterous and totally impossible task.

Guess he was right.

the festival of art, amusements & entry-level anarchism

The dystopian theme park Dismaland which was organised and funded by the English street artist/social activist Banksy was located inside a derelict seaside lido in Western-super-Mare and proudly advertised itself as Britain's most disappointing visitor attraction! The pop-up art exhibition in the form of an apocalyptic theme park featured a vast collection of bizarre new works of art with distressing imagery and adult themes by 58 world-renowned artists and sculptors including Damien Hirst (1965-), the American Jeff Gillette, whose series of paintings is often cited as being the inspiration behind the event, and Banksy himself, who contributed 10 new pieces of art to the darkly humorous exhibition.

It was advertised as an 'alternative to the sugar-coated tedium of the average family day out.'

In addition to the dystopian artwork, there was also a shabby Disney-style castle, a mini golf course, a Ferris wheel, various traditional fairground attractions, a few musical shows, and some totally uninspiring games to keep everyone unamused. Particularly challenging was the Topple the Anvil game by the visual artist David Shrigley (1968-) where visitors had to try and knock over an anvil using just a handful of ping pong balls!

The park was staffed by surly and unhelpful people just to make sure everyone had a thoroughly miserable time!

Local residents had been told that a Hollywood film company was using the location to film a crime thriller called *Grey Fox* and needed to build a few sets. Likewise, the park's staff were originally recruited as extras for the film. Nobody was any the wiser until just a few days before the place was due to open on 21 August 2015.

Shortly after the website for Dismaland went live, it abruptly crashed, supposedly due to 'technical problems' because of the enormous demand for tickets. However, there has been much speculation since that those so-called technical problems were all just part of the visitor experience.

The exhibition proved incredibly popular with the great British public and visitors from all around the world. Many were prepared to queue for hours each day for the walk-in tickets and the chance to be completely underwhelmed. Over 150,000 people passed through the fake security gates at the entrance and then wandered around Dismaland looking confused and disappointed before exiting through the gift shop during the 36 days in which the 'bemusement park' was open.

the death of william shakespeare

Early in the morning of 8 December 2020, a 91 year-old inpatient at the University Hospital in Coventry called Margaret Keenan became the first person in the world to receive the Pfizer/BioNtech anti-Covid vaccine. It was the first of the 800,000 doses due to be administered in the coming weeks to the over-80s and the most vulnerable in Britain. The second person to receive the jab was an 81 year-old man by the name of William Shakespeare, who for understandable reasons was known to everyone as just Bill.

Then, on 20 May 2021, Bill sadly passed away after a stroke and the news was reported around the world.

In what can only be described as a comedy of errors, the newscaster Noelia Novillo on Argentina's Channel 26 evening news show reported that 'one of the most important writers in the English language had died' as old film footage of Bill receiving his Covid jab was played to the viewers. After the clip went viral, poor Noelia tried to explain away her gaffe by blaming it on poor punctuation! 'I actually knew what I was saying to people, just like I always do,' she boasted. 'I expressed myself badly. I missed out a full stop, a comma, [and] some brackets. I wanted to clear up something that was very unclear and of course people misinterpreted it.'

Yeah, right!

the holy maid of kent

In 1525, Elizabeth Barton (1506-1534) was working as a domestic servant for a local farmer when she suddenly started having visions!

As her revelations seemed to have some merit, her fame soon reached beyond her own parish with even the Archbishop of Canterbury William Warham (c.1450-1532) getting to hear about her. At first, he was a little concerned by the stories and appointed a commission to investigate that her prophecies weren't in any way detrimental to the king or contrary to the teachings of the Catholic Church. As it turned out, they were all seemingly in support of both and they all warned of heresy and condemned rebellion, so he invited her to enrol at the Benedictine convent of St Sepulchre Priory in Canterbury. She took up his offer and continued falling into trances and having visions. Not long afterwards, it appears that she also had the will and the way to work a few miracles and do a bit of public healing too! By now her fame had spread far and wide and many pilgrims were arriving at the convent to see the 'Holy Maid of Kent' for themselves and arrange private sittings with her.

All of a sudden, Elizabeth had become one of sixteenth-century England's biggest celebrities.

In 1528, she requested a meeting with the Lord High Chancellor of England and the so-called *alter rex* (other king) Cardinal Thomas Wolsey (1473-1530). He was a man of great religious influence, acting as a papal legate and enjoying precedence over all the other English clergy. He also had enormous secular power, having the ear of the king and being responsible for all matters of state. At the time, he was busy negotiating with Pope Clement VII for a divorce between Henry VIII (1491-1547) and Catherine of Aragon (1485-1536) but still found time in his busy schedule to meet with Elizabeth. She told him bluntly that such a move by the king to divorce his queen and banish her from court would be contrary to God's will and he'd be foolish to continue along this path. The Cardinal was impressed with the young nun and arranged for her to speak directly with Henry. Maybe if she could persuade him to change his mind, it might make his life a bit easier! Again, she spoke plainly and advised the king that an angel had told her of how he'd incur the wrath of God if he went ahead with his plans. But Henry just brushed off her warnings. He was desperate to start shagging Anne Boleyn (c.1501-1536) and not even the wrath of God could dissuade him!

But it seemed that Elizabeth was just as stubborn and strong-minded as Henry. She met with him again a year later and told him that his insatiable desires were a blatant disregard for God's laws and that if he divorced the queen and married that skank Anne Boleyn he'd die a shameful and miserable death within a month! Naturally, Henry was not amused and she was never invited to the palace again.

By 1530, Thomas Wolsey had fallen out of favour, having failed so spectacularly to convince the pope to grant Henry his much sought after divorce. Then, on 29 November 1530, whilst travelling from York back to London to stand trial for treason, he fell ill and died. Archbishop Warham went two years later and Elizabeth suddenly found herself without two of her greatest supporters.

However, Elizabeth seemed undeterred by her dwindling fan base. By now, she'd become obsessed with Henry's sex life and had even taken to stalking him! Later, in 1532, Henry and Anne had travelled to Canterbury and were enjoying a little stroll around a monastery garden when they were suddenly accosted by her. Dispensing with the usual formalities, she just blurted out that Henry would shortly die a horrible death and then burn in Hell if he didn't change his wicked ways!

Remarkably, Elizabeth went unpunished for her actions, with Henry seemingly content just to undermine her reputation by portraying her as the 'Mad Maid of Kent' after ordering his agents to spread false rumours of her insanity and her fondness for priests! Even her last high-profile follower, the statesman, author and anti-Protestant Reformation campaigner Thomas More (1478-1535) soon withdrew his support. But by 1533, Henry had lost patience with her altogether. Elizabeth was continuing to bad-mouth him and so he had her arrested on charges of heresy and treason. She was interrogated (and tortured) by Thomas Wolsey's successor Thomas Cromwell (c.1485-1540) and soon confessed that all her trances had been faked and all her prophecies were lies. She was viewed as a false prophet who'd continually made malicious and deceitful revelations in order to turn people against the monarchy and was condemned to death without trial.

On 20 April 1534, she was taken from her cell in the Tower of London and dragged behind a horse through the streets of London to the gallows at Tyburn where she was hung in front of a baying crowd. She was then decapitated and her head boiled in a cauldron before being taken to London Bridge and stuck on top of a long pole! The rest of her was buried at Greyfriars Monastery (1225-1538) in Newgate.

Elizabeth Barton remains the only woman ever to be dishonoured in death by having her head displayed on a pole on London Bridge.

Just how crazy was Elizabeth Barton? Taking on a tyrant like Henry VIII was surely the definition of madness!

the monkey hangers

Sometime during the Napoleonic Wars (1803-1815) a French warship was wrecked off the coast of Hartlepool during a storm. The only survivor appeared to be the ship's mascot; a monkey dressed in a miniature military-style uniform! It's doubtful if anyone in Hartlepool had ever seen a monkey or indeed a Frenchman, and since the satirical cartoons of the time often portrayed French soldiers as monkey-like creatures with claws and tails, the townsfolk probably thought they'd caught a real-life French spy!

At an impromptu trial, the monkey unsurprisingly refused to answer any questions and was sentenced to death, dragged through the streets and hanged.

However, there is an alternative and much more believable version of this story. It's entirely possible that the monkey was actually a small boy. At the time, children were employed on warships to prime the cannons with gunpowder and were known as 'powder monkeys'.

The first recorded mention of the hanging was in *The Monkey Song* (1855) written by the Victorian music hall entertainer Ned Corvan (c.1830-1865) and ever since then the good folk of Hartlepool have been nicknamed 'Monkey Hangers' after enthusiastically embracing the story involving the monkey ... and not the darker and much more sinister one involving the small child! They've even erected a couple of monkey statues around the town to celebrate this bizarre incident.

the celebrity who was a celebrity just for being a celebrity

The famous courtesan Catherine 'Kitty' Fisher (1741-1767) was a clever, witty and attractive young woman with an unrivalled capacity for self-publicity which soon attracted the attention of many well-to-do suitors. After charming her way into the fringes of English society, she soon attained celebrity status by collaborating with famous writers and artists who were seemingly queuing up to promote her image and publicise her life. Her appearance and fashion sense were widely reported and copied, and there were many kiss-and-tell magazine articles about her scandalous love life for the gossip-hungry public to enjoy.

Britain's first celebrities were usually prostitutes. They were the subject of poems and songs; scurrilous newspaper articles, and they even had racehorses named after them! Kitty was determined to be the most famous of them all by commissioning the celebrated artist Joshua Reynolds (1723-1792) to paint several portraits of her, including one where she famously posed as the Egyptian queen Cleopatra in 'Cleopatra Dissolving the Pearl' (1759). Prints were produced from the engravings, which were then sold in their thousands to her adoring fans, making Kitty one of the first pin-up girls! Some prints were so small as to fit inside a pocket watch or a snuff box allowing her many gentlemen admirers to catch a quick glimpse of her whenever they felt the need. It's always been assumed that Kitty was Joshua Reynolds's favoured model as he painted at least four different portraits of her between 1759 and 1766, prompting rumours that they were also lovers.

However, the most famous portrait of Kitty was painted by Nathaniel Hone (1718-1784) in 1765 at the height of her fame. The painting shows her posing with a kitten and is now on display at the National Portrait

Gallery in London.

On 12 March 1759, whilst riding through St James's Park (London), she fell off her horse and landed on the ground in such a way that her skirt billowed up, apparently exposing the fact that she wasn't wearing any knickers! This incident inspired a frenzy of songs, poems and drawings. One of the most famous drawings of the time, 'The Merry Accident' (1759) showed her lying sprawled on the ground and surrounded by a group of well-dressed gentlemen. It's uncertain whether her fall was just an unfortunate accident or a very skilfully staged publicity stunt, but whatever it was, it only served to increase her popularity further with the great British public.

Only the famous Italian lover Giacomo Casanova seems to have turned down the chance to get to know her better. In 1763, he was introduced to her on a visit to London and later wrote of their meeting: 'She was magnificently dressed, and it is no exaggeration to say that she had on diamonds worth 500,000 francs. [Pierre Ange] Goudar told me that if I liked I might have her then and there for 10 guineas. I did not care to do so, however, for, though charming, she could only speak English, and I liked to have all my senses, including that of hearing, gratified.' What a dick!

Her rapid rise through the echelons of London society earned her a marriage to the prominent politician John Norris (1740-1811) in 1766. She then moved to her new husband's family home in the village of Benenden where she devoted herself to local affairs and became well-liked by the villagers particularly for her generosity to the poor.

Sadly, she died only four months after her move to the country when she was only 25 years-old, possibly from consumption or smallpox. But Kitty was flamboyant right to the end, insisting that she was to be buried in her best ball gown!

the death of sweyn forkbeard

Sweyn Forkbeard (963-1014) was the first Viking king of England but he was also one of the lesser known English kings, possibly because he lived a long time ago and ruled for just five weeks before his death. Sweyn was a cruel and ruthless man; a fearless warlord who gained power after overthrowing the Saxon king Æthelred II (c.968-1016) and forcing him into exile. He was crowned King of England on 25 December 1013 and then died on 3 February 1014 after being killed by the ghost of Edmund the Martyr (c.841-869).

The monk/historian John of Worcester wrote about Sweyn's rather fanciful death in *Chronicon ex Chronicis* (1140). Apparently, he'd been bad-mouthing Edmund and then threatened to attack the town of Bury St Edmunds where 'the incorrupt body of the precious martyr Edmund lay' because the people there owed him money in unpaid taxes. Edmund had been reburied in the town in 902; thousands of pilgrims were flocking to his shrine every year to pay homage, and presumably his ghost was rather enjoying all the attention as England's favourite martyr, so the last thing he would have wanted was some jumped-up little Viking king destroying his shrine and putting an end to his celebrity status.

John of Worcester takes up the story …

'When the evening was approaching … he repeated the same threats, at a time when he was surrounded by Danish troops crowded together, he alone saw St Edmund, armed, coming towards him. When he had seen him, he was terrified and began to shout very noisily, saying "Help, fellow-warriors, help! St Edmund is coming to kill me!" And while he was saying this he was run through fiercely by the saint with a spear, and fell from the stallion on which he sat, and, tormented with great pain until twilight, he ended his life with a wretched death on 3 February.'

Of course, the Vikings claimed that he'd just fallen off his horse!

toshers

The journalist and social reformer Henry Mayhew (1812-1887) is best known for co-founding the satirical magazine *Punch* in 1841 and writing a series of newspaper articles detailing the trades, habits and daily life of the poor in London. These articles were later compiled and published in book form as the *London Labour and the London Poor* (1851), an extensive multi-volume encyclopaedia providing an overview of their everyday lives and vivid descriptions of the most bizarre and desperate jobs they were forced to undertake such as pure-finding, bone-grubbing, mud-raking and toshing.

Pure was a euphemism for dog shit and the pure-finders of the Victorian era were the poor bastards who made a living collecting it off the streets and then selling it to the local tanneries for use in curing leather. The bone-grubbers foraged in the bins and the back alleys of the city searching for discarded rags and bones and the mudlarks scavenged along the banks of the River Thames looking for coal, iron, copper, bones, coins, bits of canvas and anything else they could find that might be worth a few pennies to them.

However, according to Henry, the sewer hunters had the worst job …

These guys, who he called toshers, made their living by walking miles through the London sewers at low tide searching for bones, bits of metal, rope fragments, coins and other valuables that had been dropped in the street and then washed into the gutter and down the drains. Their work was dirty and very dangerous and they needed a detailed knowledge of the sewer network and its many hazards. They could quite easily be suffocated by poisonous gasses or become trapped under the crumbling brickwork; they might also wander too far into the endless maze of passages and get cut off by the rising tide or conversely, they could drown when the sluices were raised at low tide to release a wave of effluent-filled water. And, of course, they also had to avoid being bitten by the army of rats who inhabited the tunnels.

Most of the toshers worked in small gangs led by a veteran of the trade who knew all the best places to look. Their work was surprisingly lucrative and most earned a decent living from crawling around the 500 miles of tunnels under London's streets: 'Sometimes they dive their arm down to the elbow in the mud and filth and bring up shillings, sixpences, half-crowns and occasionally half-sovereigns and even sovereigns. They always find the coins standing edge uppermost between the bricks in the bottom, where the mortar has been worn away.'

They all seemed to be known to each other by a nickname, seemingly based on their physical appearance or whatever disability they might have, like the men Henry was told about – Lanky Bill, Long Tom, One-Eyed George and Short-Armed Jack.

Fair chance that Short-Armed Jack wasn't much use when it came to sticking his arms in the mud to search for coins!

Rather bizarrely, however, the toshers who did this dangerous and smelly work all seemed to be in good health. They were all strong and fit and Henry speculated that they were probably more likely to catch some horrible disease in the slums where they lived rather than down in the sewers where they worked!

There were many myths and legends associated with the tunnels like the wild hogs who lived in the sewers under Hampstead or the existence of a Queen Rat; an invisible, supernatural creature who followed the toshers around the tunnels as they worked. When she saw one of them she fancied, she'd turn herself into a sexy, scantily-clad woman and seduce him! If he was up to giving her a damn good seeing-to there and then, he'd be sure to have good luck in his work by finding plenty of money and other valuables. However, if he later blabbed to his mates about shagging the Queen Rat, his luck would change for the worse and most probably he'd meet with a nasty accident!

As if wading about knee-deep in human excrement and being hunted by killer pigs wasn't bad enough, they also had to contend with being stalked by a sex-mad, paranormal rat! It's no wonder Henry Mayhew thought they had the worst job of the lot.

the laughing lord

Simon Fraser, 11th Lord Lovat (c.1667-1747) was a keen supporter of Charles Edward Stuart (1720-1788) during the Jacobite Rising (1745). But whereas the 'Young Pretender' famously escaped over the sea to Skye and then to France after the failed rebellion, his Lordship wasn't quite so lucky. Despite being 80 years-old and crippled with gout and arthritis, he was ruthlessly hunted down across the Scottish Highlands by Prince William, Duke of Cumberland (1721-1765) and his Hanoverian army.

They eventually caught up with him at Loch Morar where he was found hiding in a hollowed out tree.

His Lordship was arrested and transported to London to stand trial for treason. There was never any doubt that he would be found guilty and on the final day of his trial he was sentenced to be beheaded. But in a way, he had the last laugh. Newspapers and pamphlets of the time reported that as he was being led out to the scaffolding at Tower Hill on 9 April 1747 a wooden stand that had been erected to seat the vast crowds collapsed, killing at least nine people and injuring many more. Their plight seemed to amuse his Lordship and he was still laughing about it when the axe fell!

His life ended there but the phrase 'laughing your head off' which is said to have originated from the occasion has lived on.

the playboy footballer

The Northern Irish footballer George Best (1946-2005) famously played for Manchester United between 1963 and 1974.

With his good looks and playboy lifestyle, George was the first media celebrity footballer; a sporting superstar who was as much a part of the Swinging Sixties scene as the pop stars and actors of the day. Commenting on his flamboyant and reckless lifestyle, he once famously remarked: 'I spent a lot of money on booze, birds and fast cars. The rest I just squandered.'

the great british tea robbery

The Scottish botanist Robert Fortune (1812-1880) was probably best known for introducing many new ornamental plants into the gardens of Britain from China and Japan. But he also pulled off the greatest theft of trade secrets ever known!

Back in the mid-nineteenth century, tea was grown in China ... and only in China. They zealously guarded the secrets of its cultivation, harvesting and production; they planted it, picked it, blended it, and then always kept the best of the crop for themselves. The tea they had left over was sold off to the rest of the world for a nice little profit with the shipments destined for Britain usually being bought and paid for by the East India Company (1600-1874) with large quantities of opium. Everyone was happy. We got to sip our tea and the Chinese got high! But then everything changed when the Chinese started growing their own opium. The Brits retaliated by trying to grow their own tea in the foothills of the Himalayas, an area of land in India that best resembled the tea-producing regions of China. However, their early attempts to beat the Chinese at their own game were far from successful. The tea leaves were bitter and not at all soft like the Chinese leaves and they didn't even smell like tea!

The East India Company needed to get their hands on the same seeds and plants as they used in China ... and they'd have to acquire the technology and the expertise to cultivate them too. To succeed in their task they decided to employ Robert Fortune. He was the curator of the Chelsea Physic Garden, he'd already worked in China and he'd spent his whole life studying plant biology.

He seemed like the perfect man for the job ...

Robert thought so too and it wasn't long before he'd set sail for China. He shaved his head, wore a false ponytail and dressed himself in a traditional costume to become, in his own words, 'a very fair Chinaman'. Calling himself Sing-Wa, he then travelled along the Yangtze River to the remote and mountainous Sung-Lo region of the country with a few local sherpas he'd paid to hump his bags around and keep their mouths shut! Not only was he risking the wrath of the Chinese authorities by travelling outside the designated areas for foreigners, he was also on a mission to steal the secrets of their most precious export!

Along his journey, he stopped off here and there to wander around the fields and villages and pick up a few plants. He was a very tall man, almost 1-foot (0.3m) taller than the average 'Chinaman', but this (and his slightly iffy Chinese appearance) were explained away easily enough. Amazingly, the peasants he encountered seemed to accept his explanation of being from a distant province 'beyond the Great Wall' and he was never rumbled.

After arriving at the first tea factory, his servant, a man called Wang, asked if they'd graciously consent to a visit from an honoured and wise man who'd travelled a great distance to see how their glorious tea was produced. The factory manager fell for his bullshit and welcomed Robert inside. It was here that he discovered how black tea and green tea were both produced from the same plant but then followed a very different fermentation process to create their unique and quite different tastes. Back in Britain everyone had always assumed the leaves came from two different plants. But more importantly, he also realised how the Chinese had been slowly poisoning the British tea-drinkers by adding an artificial colouring to the tea marked for export. They'd somehow got it into their heads that the Brits liked their green tea leaves to look a lot greener than they actually were and so they'd been busy adding a dye and a form of cyanide called Prussian Blue to make them look more attractive!

He visited many plantations and was usually allowed to wander around to collect soil samples, saplings and as many seeds as he could carry away with him. His precious booty was later packed into boxes and crates ready for the journey to India by steamer from Hong Kong. After arriving in Calcutta they were transported to Allahabad and then onwards towards their final destination in the foothills of the Himalayas.

In total, 13,000 saplings and 10,000 seeds were shipped off to India. However, the vast majority of them didn't survive the journey. One particularly overenthusiastic Indian government official couldn't resist breaking the seal on the Wardian cases to take a peek inside but in doing so he exposed all the plants to the air and destroyed most of the valuable crop! Only 1,000 plants survived and just 80 were healthy enough to take root. The seeds didn't fare much better. Every one of them was rotten because one of the scientists accompanying the cargo had decided to water them and store them in the shade. The exact opposite of what he should have done! The glass cases in which they were packed were self-sustaining and all they needed was a bit of sunlight.

The first attempt to rob the Chinese of their tea had turned out to be a bit of a disaster.

Luckily, Robert Fortune was having such a good time of it travelling around China disguised as Sing-Wa, he'd already headed off to the south of the country to continue his mission. It was an area controlled by warlords and blighted by peasant uprisings but he didn't seem at all deterred, filling up his sedan chairs with all the plants he could find growing in the fields. At a temple, he learnt more tea-making secrets from the orange-robed monks; he studied the ways of their planters, tasters and tea makers, and then walked away with a huge batch of their seeds and plants! This time, all the cargo made it back to India intact. The stolen harvest was successfully transplanted onto the Indian hillsides and soon began flowering and producing the finest teas in the world.

Robert Fortune also smuggled a few so-called tea experts out of China to help build the fledgling industry in India and within a generation or so, much to the relief of the East India Company, their tea was beating the Chinese stuff hands down for quality, flavour and price.

Back in Britain tea suddenly became very affordable and it was now completely poison free too!

TRIAL BY COMBAT

The *Wager of Battle* was introduced into common law in England after the Norman Conquest in 1066 and remained in use until the late- Middle Ages. It was a method of settling disputes between two people in the absence of witnesses or a confession and involved them just fighting it out until a winner was declared. The winner was automatically considered to be in the right as it was believed God would always grant victory to the innocent party.

The main flaw with this system of justice was that some people were just better fighters than others, and the rich folk of the day would often employ some other poor sap to do their fighting for them!

TRIAL BY ORDEAL

When fire or water determined a person's guilt.

A *Trial by Ordeal* was an ancient judicial practice by which the accused was subjected to a painful and potentially fatal punishment in order to determine their guilt or innocence. This type of sentence was considered a 'judgement of God' and it was assumed that if the person was innocent of the crime, a miracle would occur and they would survive their injuries. The most common forms of torture always seemed to involve fire or water …

An *Ordeal by Fire* involved the accused holding a red-hot burning object for a determined length of time or walking barefoot over heated plowshares or hot coals. Innocence was established by the extent of the wounds to their hands or feet. In the rare instances when there were no apparent signs of injury then the accused was immediately acquitted of the crime, but usually the wounds were bandaged and re-examined by a priest after a few days, who would then determine if God had intervened to heal them. If not, then the accused would be deemed guilty of the crime and immediately exiled or put to death.

Most famously, Emma of Normandy (c.984-1052), the mother of the last King of Wessex Edward the Confessor (c.1003-1066), had been accused of adultery with the clergyman Ælfwine of Winchester (fl.1032-1047) but proved her innocence by walking over nine burning plowshares without sustaining any injuries.

An *Ordeal by Water* was the oldest form of judgement and involved either hot or cold water.

The cold water punishment was the easiest and simplest to administer with the accused being tied and bound and just thrown into a river. If they sank, they were deemed to be innocent (after being accepted by the water) but if they floated, they were thought to be guilty (after being rejected by the water) and then presumably subjected to some other hideous form of medieval punishment to actually kill them off. Hopefully the innocent people were rescued before they drowned otherwise it was a bit of a flawed system!

The hot water punishment usually involved the accused having to retrieve a stone from the bottom of a pot of boiling water. The depth of the water depended on the severity of the crime. The ordeal would usually take place in a church, with those in attendance to watch the trial, praying to God to reveal the truth. Afterwards, the accused's hand would be bandaged and re-examined after three days to judge the extent of their injuries. If God had not healed the wounds, the suspect was assumed to be guilty of the crime.

In 1215, Pope Innocent III banned their clergymen from participating in any *Trials by Ordeal* and by 1219, Henry III (1207-1272) finally recognised the need to abolish these barbaric practices. Without the legitimacy of the Catholic Church, the system collapsed with juries of 'twelve good men and true' being asked to decide a person's guilt instead.

the celestial bed

The Scottish showman and self-styled doctor James Graham (1745-1794) was also a pioneering sex therapist and one of the first people to practice a form of 'electric medicine' to cure the idle rich of their ills.

In 1780, he opened the Temple of Health clinic in Aldwych, London where his privileged patients could wander around the ornately furnished rooms, breathe perfumed air, listen to soothing music or just gawp at the scantily-clad young ladies he employed to pose amongst the marble statues. They could also indulge in a little electric shock treatment, listen to various medical lectures and buy all the lotions and potions they could possibly need to cure any impotency problems or just improve their sex lives. It has been rumoured that Emma, Lady Hamilton (1765-1815), who later become the mistress of Horatio Nelson (1758-1805), was once employed as one of those aforementioned scantily-clad young ladies moping about amongst the statues.

The Temple of Health was a great success. It was raking in the money and James Graham soon became the talk of the town, hobnobbing with the rich and famous of London society, and featuring in satirical plays, poems and newspaper articles.

In June 1781, he opened a second health centre, the Temple of Hymen at Schomberg House, Pall Mall in London featuring his newly built celestial bed as its main attraction. Aristocratic couples were asked to part with £50 a night for the chance of trying to make babies on it! The large fertility-inducing 12 foot (3.6m) x 9 foot (2.7m) bed was surrounded by magnetic fields, mirrors, erotic paintings and perfumes to get them in the mood. The bed's tilting inner frame placed the woman in the best possible position to conceive with the couple's movements setting off music from organ pipes pumping out celestial sounds, which increased in intensity as their exertions in bed became more and more intense. The mattress was filled with 'sweet new wheat or oat straw, mingled with balm, rose leaves, and lavender flowers' and the headboard was inscribed with the inspiring words 'Be fruitful. Multiply and Replenish the Earth.'

His famous lecture *On the Generation Increase and Improvement of the Human Species* (1783) promoted sex as patriotic and procreation as a duty. One of his tips involved the man regularly washing his genitals with cold water. He described how this daily ritual would 'lock the cock and secure all for the next rencontre.' It would also considerably improve the general state of the testicles, as he explained: 'Certain parts which next morning after a laborious night would be relaxed, lank, and pendulous, like the two eyes of a dead sheep dangling in a wet empty calf's bladder, by the frequent and judicious use of the icy cold water, would be like a couple of steel balls, of a pound apiece, enclosed in a firm purse of uncut Manchester velvet.'

He certainly had a way with words!

However, despite all that early success, by 1784, James Graham was knee deep in debt and forced to sell most of his possessions and close his temples. By this time, he had attracted a few critics and people were generally a little more sceptical of his practices. Presumably it was also pretty obvious by then that his fancy celestial bed just didn't work! But no worries, he had another idea up his sleeve. He gave up trying to cure the rich and stupid of their impotency problems and started to tackle the slightly trickier issue of immortality instead by promoting his 'earth bathing' treatment which involved immersing people neck-deep in a big bath full of smelly mud and claiming that it was the secret of everlasting life!

the lord of the rings

There's nothing more expressive than a roundabout: it's English in its good manners, with people giving way to each other, whereas a set of traffic lights is fascist in its demands that you stop and go only when it allows you to – Kevin Beresford (1953-)

Roundabout Spotting was popularised by Kevin Beresford with his *Round-A-Bouts of Redditch 2003* calendar showcasing twelve of the Worcestershire town's most attractive roundabouts. Kev followed this up with the spectacularly dull book *Roundabouts of Great Britain* (2004) featuring over eighty of his favourite roundabouts! He continued producing other similar-themed calendars each year but eventually there just weren't enough new roundabouts left in Redditch to feature in any more calendars, so in 2006, he went national with the *Best of British Roundabouts* (2006) and then international ten years later with *Roundabouts of the World* (2016).

In 2003, he formed the Roundabout Appreciation Society for other dreary, like-minded people who get a thrill out of this particular type of road traffic management system. Apparently, they meet up twice a month in a Redditch pub and just sit around looking at photos of roundabouts and discussing their design and safety features over a few pints. They also organise days out to visit a few must-see roundabouts around the country, but most importantly, once a year they decide the winner of their annual *Roundabout of the Year Award* with the nominee roundabouts being judged on their appearance, quirkiness or historical significance.

Although Kev has since been involved in many projects celebrating other very boring subjects such as car parks, telephone boxes, park benches, rubbish dumps, post boxes and even village hall notice boards and mobility scooters (specifically the *Mobility Scooter Riders of Benidorm 2025* calendar), roundabouts remain his first love and he has since adopted the nickname of *Lord of the Rings.*

Only in Britain!

the great balloon riot

Ballooning was very popular in the mid-nineteenth-century. Probably because aeroplanes hadn't been invented yet!

One of Britain's greatest balloonists was Henry Tracey Coxwell (1819-1900). His most notable achievement occurred on 5 September 1862 when he and the meteorologist/astronomer James Glaisher (1809-1903) set a new world altitude record. They'd been tasked by the British Science Association to investigate the conditions in the upper atmosphere by going as high in the sky as they dared just to see what happened. But what happened was both men barely escaping with their lives! James went blind and lost consciousness and Henry, who could no longer feel his gloveless hands, was forced into pulling the balloon's valve-cord with his teeth in order to begin their descent, just a few seconds before he too would have passed out. It was later estimated that they'd reached a maximum altitude of 35,000-37,000 feet (10,700-11,300m).

Henry was lauded as a hero after his daring flight to the heavens and back, so when he agreed to appear at a fair organised by the Foresters Friendly Society at Victoria Park in Leicester two years later on 11 July 1864 to show off his new, larger and much fancier balloon *Britannia,* a crowd of around 50,000 people flocked to see him.

Thirteen lucky tickets holders had paid handsomely for the chance to accompany Henry on a flight around the park at 5.30pm.

Early in the afternoon, he was still completing all his pre-flight checks when some dickhead in the crowd started a rumour that Henry's balloon wasn't new, large or fancy at all. According to him, Henry was trying to fob them off with a really naff, small and very old one! The excitable good-natured crowd suddenly turned nasty and at 2.00pm they broke into the balloon's enclosure. The ticket holders clambered into the basket and demanded to take off immediately but Henry explained to them that he hadn't yet finished his checks and such reckless behaviour would only delay their departure time further.

Henry's appeals for calm fell on deaf ears. The crowd started pushing and shoving their way closer and closer to the balloon, throwing bottles at Henry and scuffling with the few police officers on duty that afternoon. In an attempt to diffuse the escalating tension, Henry then announced that he'd let all the air out of the balloon if they didn't calm down and move away. But the crowd continued shouting abuse and throwing bottles at him, so he followed through with his threat and started deflating the balloon.

And that's when things really kicked off ...

As the balloon collapsed, the crowd ripped the fabric and set fire to the basket; Henry's car was set alight, and Henry himself was then attacked. The rioters were baying for his blood and yelled 'finish him' and 'knock him on the head' as they started throwing punches and tearing at his clothes. A bleeding Henry eventually made his escape, finding sanctuary inside a nearby pub. Which is always a good place to seek sanctuary! The crowd then rampaged through the streets of the town triumphantly waving around pieces of the torn balloon with a few of the more entrepreneurially-minded hooligans trying to sell them to passers-by as souvenirs of the riot.

The *London Review of Politics, Society, Literature, Art and Science* described the crowd as 'a horde of savages as fierce and untamed as South Sea Islanders.' And a letter-writer to the *Leicester Chronicle* complained: 'I never witnessed such barbarous ignorance, baseness and injustice in my life. I feared Mr Coxwell would be killed. I was knocked down thrice myself simply for endeavouring to defend him.'

But the good folks of Leicester refused to accept the blame for the rioting. Instead, they accused the out-of-towners for all the trouble. Especially the ones from Nottingham!

THE MILE HIGH CLUB

The earliest reference to having sex in the sky appeared in the famous betting book held at Brooks's (London), one of the world's oldest and most exclusive gentlemen's clubs. The club's main attraction was their gambling rooms where members could sit and play cards or bet on other games of chance. Some of the more unusual and eccentric bets between members, however, were usually written in the club's betting book and it was one of these entries from 1785 recording a wager between George Cholmondeley, 1st Marquess of Cholmondeley (1749-1827) and Edward Smith-Stanley, 12th Earl of Derby (1752-1834) that first referenced what would later become known as the Mile High Club: 'Ld. Cholmondeley has given two guineas to Ld. Derby, to receive 500 Gs whenever his lordship fucks a woman in a balloon one thousand yards [900m] from the Earth.'

Unfortunately, there's no further indication of how the bet was to be verified.

Or even if it was ever paid.

the life and times of charles peace

Charles Peace (1832-1879) was a pickpocket, burglar, stalker and murderer!

At 14 years-old, he was crippled in an accident at a steel-rolling mill after a piece of red-hot metal got stuck in his leg just below the knee and left him with a permanent limp. Perhaps because of this disability he was unable to find work and decided to make ends meet by embarking on a life of crime. He started off small with a bit of pickpocketing here and there but soon worked his way up to burglary, recording his first conviction in 1851 for which he served six months in prison.

Immediately after his release, he took up his old thieving ways again and was later jailed for four years in 1854, six years in 1859 and then eight years in 1866. It was during this last stretch behind bars at Wakefield Prison that he attempted a daring prison break. After somehow gaining the trust of his guards, he was allowed to do some repair work around the cells. He managed to get hold of a ladder, make a hole in the ceiling in his own cell using a handmade tin saw and then clamber outside onto the roof. He scrambled along the rooftop and onto the prison wall but was then forced to take refuge inside the Governor's house after losing his footing on some loose bricks, and falling back inside the prison yard! He'd been spotted by the guards and decided to lie low in the Governor's house and wait it out for another opportunity to escape. But things didn't work out quite the way he'd planned because he was recaptured shortly afterwards.

After being released from prison in 1875, he returned to his long suffering family in Sheffield. He tried to go straight after taking up picture-framing as a trade; his wife Hannah adopted the role of the dutiful little housewife, and the kids were enrolled in Sunday School. For a while, they seemed like a perfectly normal family.

That same year, they moved from the city centre of Sheffield to the suburb of Darnall where Charlie met Mr and Mrs Dyson and became good friends with them … particularly Mrs Dyson! The two of them went out to the pubs and music halls together and he began putting it about that she was his mistress. The poor woman was mortified when she found out, claiming they were just friends, and anything more repulsed her! It seems that she may have rejected his clumsy sexual advances and this had made Charlie mad because he then spent the rest of his life orchestrating a campaign of harassment and intimidation against her …

He insulted her, shouted obscenities at her, made threats against her, stalked her and tripped her up in the street.

In June 1876, Mr Dyson delivered a little card to Charlie stating: 'Charles Peace is requested not to interfere with my family' but unsurprisingly he just ignored it. A few very polite words on a nice bit of stationery wasn't really going to hold much sway over a man like Charlie. If anything, it had the opposite effect because he then stepped up his hate campaign against Mrs Dyson by threatening to shoot her! This latest incident forced Mr Dyson to take out a court injunction against him, which seemed to have the desired effect because shortly afterwards he and his family moved to Hull. Hannah began managing an eating-house and Charlie resumed his career as a burglar …

On the night of 1 August 1876, he was confronted by two policemen after they'd spotted him entering the grounds of a house in Whalley Range, Manchester. Charlie tried to make his escape but he was chased by PC Nicholas Cock, so he pulled out his revolver and fired a warning shot at the young constable. But police officers must have been a lot stupider or a lot braver back then because PC Cock continued giving chase armed only with his truncheon! So, Charlie shot him for real this time! Fortunately for him, two brothers living nearby, John and William Habron were later arrested for the PC's murder. John was acquitted for a lack of evidence but William got life imprisonment. Charlie even attended their trial just to make sure that he wasn't in any way implicated in the murder!

Charlie then switched his attention back to bullying the Dysons again ...

Clearly the court injunction was no longer having the desired effect, so Mr and Mrs Dyson tried to outsmart him by moving house. On 29 November 1876, they upped sticks into their new home in the Sheffield suburb of Banner Cross, safe in the knowledge that they'd finally escaped their tormentor. But who should turn up on their doorstep the very next day? That's right, it was Charlie! He confronted them and boasted: 'You see. I am here to annoy you and I'll annoy you wherever you go!'

Things came to a head later that evening. True to his word, Charlie had spent the day hanging around outside their house and making a nuisance of himself. Then, at around 8.00pm, he spotted Mrs Dyson coming out of the back door on her way to the outhouse. When she was making her way back to the house again a little later, he challenged her, pointed his revolver at her head and yelled: 'Speak or I'll fire!' He presumably meant to say something like 'Scream and I'll shoot!' but he completely muffed his lines! Mrs Dyson must have been equally as confused because she screamed her pretty little head off and fled in terror back inside the outhouse. Alerted by his wife's screams, Mr Dyson arrived in the backyard and after spotting Charlie running away, he foolishly gave chase. Without a second thought, Charlie just shot him in the head. And as Mrs Dyson ran to his aid crying 'Murder! Murder! You have shot my husband!' Charlie made his escape back to Hull.

Mrs Dyson identified her husband's killer and the police began a manhunt. But when they arrived at the Hull eating-house, Charlie's incredibly understanding wife and their stupidly loyal customers covered for him, giving him time to escape onto the roof and hide behind a chimney. For the next three weeks, the police kept turning up at his door and Charlie kept avoiding them by heading to the rooftop!

The police offered a £100 reward for information leading to Charlie's capture and issued a description of him so the public knew who to look out for: 'He is thin and slightly built, from fifty-five to sixty years of age. Five feet four inches or five feet high; grey (nearly white) hair, beard and whiskers. He lacks use of three fingers of left hand, walks with his legs rather wide apart, speaks somewhat peculiarly as though his tongue were too large for his mouth, and is a great boaster.' No wonder Mrs Dyson wasn't all that excited about jumping into bed with him!

Charlie always seemed to be one step ahead of the police. He shaved off his beard, dyed his hair, donned a pair of specs and even kitted himself out with a fake arm so he appeared to have all his fingers. He also moved around the country to avoid detection. It was whilst he was staying in Nottingham that he met Susan Thompson, and soon after, he declared his undying love for her in his own inimitable way by threatening to shoot the poor woman if she didn't become his mistress! His unique courting style seemed to work because it wasn't long before they'd shacked up together. One night the police raided their house when they were lying in bed together but Charlie gave them a false name and refused to get up until he had a little privacy to dress himself. Obligingly, the police then waited downstairs for him as Charlie made his way across the rooftops again!

As his house was now being watched by the police, Charlie headed south to London and settled in Peckham. He'd always been a keen music lover and set himself up as a dealer in musical instruments. Although he was now a respectable businessman, he couldn't resist the urge to dabble in a little bit of housebreaking now and again. Just to keep his hand in. On some occasions he even carried his burglary tools around with him in a violin case when he went out on a job! He lived in style and had enough money to keep two houses, so he sent for his mistress Susan Thompson and then for his wife and kids. Unbelievably, both women agreed to join him in London and live in his two houses. Life was good for Charlie for a couple of years until his luck finally ran out on the night of 10 October 1878 when he was caught red-handed by PC Robinson as he was robbing a house in the affluent London suburb of Blackheath. Charlie obviously did his best to avoid capture, firing off five shots at the chasing policeman and hitting him in the arm, but he was eventually overpowered and wrestled to the ground. The gun was taken off him and Charlie was marched away to the nearest police station.

Meanwhile, the women in his life packed their things and moved back up north. When the police later raided Susan Thompson's house and discovered some stolen goods, she struck a deal with them and spilled the beans on poor Charlie. But then she had the audacity to try and claim the £100 reward money too! Charlie was subsequently charged with burglary and the attempted murder of PC Robinson before standing trial at the Old Bailey. It was a fairly open and shut case and he was sentenced to life imprisonment.

Charlie also had to appear in court in Sheffield to stand trial for the murder of Mr Dyson. On the journey from London, he managed to escape his captors by jumping from the train … but was then found lying unconscious by the trackside a little while later during a police search. Apparently, it was a lot easier to escape across rooftops than it was from moving trains! The Sheffield trial was postponed for eight days whilst he recovered from his injuries and didn't begin until the morning of 4 February 1879. Mrs Dyson gave her evidence and by the afternoon, the jury had convicted him of murder, taking just ten minutes to reach their verdict.

As an act of atonement, Charlie finally admitted to the murder of PC Cock, exonerating William Habron, who later walked out of prison with £800 compensation in his back pocket after serving three years in prison.

On the day before his execution, Charlie seemed in good spirits and was visited for the last time by his family. Out of deference for their feelings, he didn't ask to see Susan Thompson, although it was reported that he very much wanted to say goodbye to her too. On the day of his execution, 25 February 1879, he enjoyed a hearty breakfast of bacon and eggs and was then escorted to the gallows. Charlie was defiant to the end, sure of his place in Heaven, and seemingly totally unrepentant for any of his crimes. At 8.00am, the public executioner, William Marwood (1818-1883), pulled the lever and one of Victorian Britain's nastiest villains fell to his death.

the moving staircase

The Moving Staircase was the original name for Britain's first escalator and it was a pretty big deal when it opened for business in the fancy, high-end department store of Harrods in London on 16 November 1898. Hopping on and off the 40 ft (12.2m) long mechanical conveyor belt was meant to be an exciting experience but the shop owners were smart enough to realise that it might be a frightening one too, and so any traumatised customers were offered smelling salts and a shot of brandy at the top of the escalator just in case they needed a little pick-me up after their ordeal.

Note: Britain's first modern-style electric escalators (with moving stairs) were installed at Earls Court Underground Station in London. Two different escalators linking the Piccadilly line platforms with a subway leading to the Circle & District lines were opened on 4 October 1911 with a one-legged man called William 'Bumper' Harris employed to ride up and down on them as a way of demonstrating to any apprehensive passengers how safe and secure they were to use.

If some poor soul with just one leg wasn't afraid of them, then nobody else should be either!

the rules of cricket

The origins of the game of cricket can be traced back to Tudor times in the early sixteenth century.

Originally it was played by children but by the early-seventeenth century it had become very popular with adults too. The first recorded mention of 'creckett' was in a 1597 court document making reference to the sport being played in Guildford sometime around 1550. The case involved a dispute over the ownership of a small piece of land with the court hearing from a gentleman working as a coroner for the county of Surrey, who had been a scholar at the Free School of Guildford [Royal Grammar School] fifty years earlier, that 'hee and diverse of his fellows did runne and play at creckett and other plaies' on that piece of land.

The first parish teams were established in the mid-seventeenth century. Mitcham Cricket Club was formed in 1685 and is the earliest known cricket club whilst Sussex CCC, which was formed in 1839, is the oldest county club and also the oldest professional sporting club anywhere in the world.

The original *Laws of the Game of Cricket* (1744) were compiled at the Star and Garter pub in Pall Mall by players from various local cricket clubs and many of these rules have remained unchanged and are still used in the modern game. From 1788 these laws have been maintained and updated by the Marylebone Cricket Club in London.

Below is a simplified and easy to understand summary of the rules for anyone not acquainted with the game:

You have two sides, one out in the field and one in.
Each man that's in the side that's in, goes out, and when he's out, he comes in and the next man goes in until he's out.
When they are all out, the side that's out comes in and the side that's been in goes out and tries to get those coming in, out. Sometimes you get men still in and not out.
When a man goes out to go in, the men who are out try to get him out, and when he is out he goes in and the next man in goes out and goes in.
There are two men called umpires who stay out all the time, and they decide when the men who are in are out.
Depending on the weather or the light, the umpires can also send everybody in, no matter whether they're in or out.
When both sides have been in and all the men are out, and both sides have been out twice after all the men have been in (including those who are not out), that's the end of the game!

the first cycle lane

The 2½ mile (4km), 8-feet (2.5m) wide concrete pathway running along both sides of the A40 Western Avenue in west London between Ealing and Greenford became Britain's first purpose-built cycle lane when it was opened by the Minister of Transport Leslie Hore-Belisha (1893-1957) on 7 June 1934. But not everyone was happy about it. The fiercest critics of the new scheme were actually the cycling groups of the day who claimed that the pathway was just another blatant attempt by car drivers to push everyone else off the roads!

There's just no pleasing some people!

john the painter

JAMES AITKEN, alias JOHN the PAINTER.

After leaving school, James Aitken (1752-1777) trained to become a house painter but soon discovered that it didn't pay very much and there weren't actually that many people around who wanted their houses painted! To supplement his income, he turned to a life of crime as a highwayman, burglar, shoplifter and thief. Fearful that anytime soon he might be arrested for his crimes, he fled England and travelled to America where he drifted around for a while and became exposed to revolutionary rhetoric and anti-British propaganda.

After his return to England in 1775, he got it into his head to become an arsonist. He was convinced that the Royal Navy dockyards were particularly susceptible to attack and quickly cobbled together a plan to destroy them, believing that he'd be handsomely rewarded for his actions by the Americans. Despite being a wanted man, he was able to travel freely around the country selecting his targets and assessing their vulnerability. He even travelled to Paris where he'd arranged to meet with the American diplomat Silas Deane in an effort to convince him to back his wild scheme. The American apparently listened with interest but it's doubtful if he ever believed he could pull it off. Although he probably offered him a few words of encouragement and gave him a big hearty slap on the back as he left his office, he didn't offer any financial aid. Nonetheless, James came away convinced that he had the full support of their government and set about his task with relish …

Back in London he then made contact with the American spy, the eminent physician/chemist Edward Bancroft (1745-1821) who again offered him his best wishes but nothing more. Presumably he too believed that James was just some kind of nutter seeking a bit of attention and doubted that he would ever go through with his wild plan.

Using his training as a painter, James started mixing together various cocktails of chemicals and solvents to make crude incendiary devices and then set about destroying all of England's dockyards …

On 5 December 1776, he sneaked into a storehouse at the Portsmouth dockyard and soaked a bale of hemp with turpentine and gunpowder. But then he changed his mind about setting it alight. Instead, he looked around for something much bigger and better to burn down. Satisfied that a fire in the huge, 1,000 feet (304m) long rope house would do the trick, he meticulously built a little tinder pile and again added turpentine and gunpowder. But when he attempted to ignite it the tinder proved to be too damp! However, he didn't give up and kept trying to set it ablaze. In fact, he spent so long trying to set the damn thing alight that he ended up being locked inside the building for the night and was forced to bang on the door, hoping that someone would hear his cries for help and let him out! Eventually someone did come along and open the door for him. They even believed his cock-and-bull story about just being a curious bystander who'd lost his way before escorting him to the main gate and waving him on his way! The wannabee anarchist was determined to burn something to the ground that night, so he attempted to set his boarding house alight instead. But he failed at that too!

James returned to the dockyard the following night, retraced his steps and successfully set the whole place alight. Then he ran from the scene of the crime out into the countryside from where he just sat and watched the flames lighting up the night sky.

Feeling rather pleased with himself he immediately rode off to London to inform his co-conspirator Edward Bancroft. But Edward was horrified by his tales of treachery and threatened to inform the authorities. You see ... Edward was a double agent!

Fearing for his safety, James fled London and moved to Plymouth. There was a nice big dockyard there to burn down but the security was too tight, so he moved on to Bristol. They weren't quite so security conscious there, so he was able to light a few more fires and destroy a few more warehouses.

Although his one-man arson campaign did a lot of damage, his ability to cause panic amongst the public was far greater and much more dangerous. A few copycat fire starters, whose destructive work had been incorrectly attributed to James, helped give the impression that a gang of highly-organised foreign saboteurs were roaming the country with impunity. People were convinced that they were under attack from a foreign power, instead of just one slightly deranged Brit ... who wasn't all that good at what he did anyway! At the height of the crisis, a reward was offered for the capture of James Aitken aka 'John the Painter' and even George III (1738-1820) received frequent updates about the arson attacks.

Eventually James's luck ran out. But rather disappointingly, he wasn't caught red-handed with a smouldering match in his hand. Instead, he was apprehended in Odiham, Hampshire, by a local constable after a botched robbery! For whatever reason, he suspected the thief of also being the notorious arsonist everyone was looking for and when told to turn out his pockets, his suspicions were confirmed. James pulled out a primed and fully-loaded pistol, a pistol tinderbox, powder, matches, a bottle of turpentine and a snuffbox of tinder. So even when the silly arse wasn't setting fires, he was still running around the countryside with all his fire starting paraphernalia!

He was transported to London to face trial. At first, he proved to be uncooperative during questioning, even refusing to give his name, but they had ways of making you talk back then, and sooner rather than later, he confessed to being James Aitken the fugitive firestarter.

His trial began and ended on 6 March 1777. The result was never in any doubt and he was sentenced to death by hanging. On 10 March 1777, a 64-foot (19.5cm) mast from the frigate HMS *Arethusa* was taken from the ship and positioned at the entrance to the Portsmouth dockyard. It was the highest gallows ever erected for an execution in England. After being placed in a cart and paraded around in front of the large crowd who'd gathered to watch the show, he was ran up the mast like a flag and left to hang there for an hour as a gruesome warning to any other potential saboteurs and traitors out there.

rock, paper, scissors

When the Japanese electronics company Maspro Denkoh Corporation decided to sell off some of their fabulous art collection, which included works by Paul Cézanne, Pablo Picasso and Vincent van Gogh worth around $20 million, they couldn't decide which of the two world famous British auction houses of Sotheby's and Christie's to trust with the sale, so they left it up to them to decide by arranging a high-stakes game of Rock, Paper, Scissors between representatives of the two companies at their Tokyo HQ.

The winner would earn the right to hold the auction.

The rival auction houses approached the game quite differently. Christie's took the challenge very seriously with their chosen player, Kanae Ishibashi studying the psychology of the game, consulting colleagues and their kids (who she believed would have more of an insight) and praying for guidance. On the night before the bizarre contest, her husband even appeared to her in a dream advising her of what choice to make and on the day itself she carried a lucky charm and even sprinkled salt everywhere for good luck!

Sotheby's, on the other hand, just viewed it all as a silly little game of chance and didn't give it a moment's thought.

On game day itself everyone assembled at the Tokyo offices of the Maspro Denkoh Corporation as arranged. But instead of playing the game in the traditional way by waving their arms in the air, the players were asked to write their chosen object on a piece of paper. Kanae Ishibashi dutifully wrote down 'scissors' as all the evidence had suggested that was the dominant strategy ... and it was also her husband's choice too. The Sotheby's player foolishly chose 'paper' and lost the contract on the very first go!

the fight that changed boxing forever

The world's first world championship boxing match took place in a field somewhere near Farnborough in Hampshire between the Englishman Tom Sayers (1826-1865) and the American John C Heenan on the morning of 27 April 1860. The much publicised bareknuckle fight had captured the public's imagination on both sides of the Atlantic and vast crowds arrived on special trains from London to watch the two men slug it out.

The contest began at around 7.30am with the American fighter commenting beforehand: 'We have a fine morning for our business. If a man can't fight and win on such a crisp morning, then he can't fight at all.'

It was a fairly uneven contest with the British champ conceding 4lbs (18kg) in weight, 5 inches (12cm) in height and 8 years in age. The American also won the coin toss and placed himself at an advantage in the corner with his back to the sun. He then dominated the opening rounds, knocking down his opponent on many occasions. In the sixth round, Tom injured his right arm blocking a shot and was forced to fight one-handed for the rest of the contest. *The Times* later reported that he'd continued with a broken arm! In the seventh round, Tom seemed to stage a bit of a comeback, reigning down several punishing blows onto John's right eye which swelled up and remained closed for the remainder of the fight.

So now it was a one-armed boxer against a one-eyed one …

In the thirty-seventh round, the ring ropes snapped and the fight descended into chaos after the crowd invaded the boxing arena. Each man was bloodied and bruised but neither showed any sign of throwing in the towel. The referee tried to bring the contest to an end but the ring was soon reformed and the two fighters continued for another five rounds, although neither man was boxing proficiently at this stage. The match was eventually declared a draw but only because the police had raided the field …

The fighters and most of the estimated crowd of around 12,000 people managed to escape with many crossing a nearby river into Surrey where they knew they couldn't be pursued by the local Hampshire constabulary. A report in the sports newspaper *Bells' Life* described the scene: 'The final round was merely a wild scramble, both men ordered to desist from fighting. The Blues being now in force, there was, of course, no chance of the men continuing, and adjournment was necessary. Heenan had rushed away from the ring, and ran some distance with the activity of a deer, and although he was fit as ever, he was obviously totally blind. Sayers, although tired, was also strong on his pins and could have fought some time longer, although by then the authorities were up in arms in all directions, so it would be a mere waste of time to go elsewhere.'

The two men shared the purse of £400. They also became good friends and later toured the country together staging exhibition fights.

The boxing match had been the most talked about sporting event of the year. Just like modern-day fights, the ringside seats were full of celebrities, politicians, sportsmen and other VIPs enjoying the show. But they too were forced to scatter when the police arrived. Seen fleeing the scene that day were a young Prince of Wales (Edward VII) (1841-1910), the novelists

William Makepeace Thackeray (1811-1863) and Charles Dickens (1812-1870), and rather worryingly ... the Prime Minister, Henry John Temple, 3rd Viscount Palmerston (1784-1865), who was later forced to answer some very awkward questions in Parliament about his presence at the event.

Note: The brutality of the fight forced politicians to seek out a new code of conduct for the sport and by 1865 the Dozen Rules drawn up by the Amateur Athletic Club had been adopted. These twelve rules later became the basis for which all modern boxing matches would be governed and were more commonly known as The Queensberry Rules after receiving a public endorsement from John Douglas, 9th Marquess of Queensberry (1844-1900). They were the first set of rules to mention gloves, the ten-second count and three-minute rounds. Even today, in popular culture, the term 'Queensberry Rules' is still used to refer to a sense of sportsmanship and fair play.

the way we were

A WELCOME PRESENT FOR FRIENDS AT THE FRONT

Up until the early-twentieth century it was possible to buy cocaine and heroin over the counter at some of Britain's department stores!

In 1916, Harrods in London even began selling gift packs marketed as *A Welcome Present for Friends at the Front* containing cocaine, morphine, needles and syringes which people could send to the British soldiers fighting on the frontline in World War I (1914-1918).

WHEN BUYING A BOOK WAS NEVER SO HARD

Foyles was once the world's largest bookstore. The famous shop in London's Charing Cross Road was founded in 1903 by William Foyle (1885-1963) and Gilbert Foyle (1886-1971) and at one time operated the most eccentric and archaic business practices ever devised by a retailer. It was almost as if they didn't want you to buy a book!

Customers were required to queue up three times - once to collect an invoice for the book, once to pay the invoice and then for a third time to actually collect the damn book! Equally mystifying was their shelving arrangement, categorising the books by the name of the publisher rather than by topic or the author's name like any normal bookshop!

Unfortunately, this quirky little way of doing things was abandoned in the late-1990s after an extensive re-modernisation program.

Shame.

THE TODDLERS' TRUCE

The Toddlers' Truce was the colloquial name given to the government policy requiring a daily early-evening break in transmissions on the BBC TV service. The policy was in place from 1946 until 1957 and required the BBC to interrupt broadcasts for an hour each weekday evening between 6.00pm and 7.00pm (marking a division between the end of kids TV and the start of the evening schedule for adults) so that young children could be put to bed.

The rules were even more draconian on a Sunday because no children's programmes were allowed at all in the early afternoon in case it stopped the kids from studying their bibles!

The BBC had always been rather keen on the hour's break. As they were funded by the licence fee, the fewer hours they had to broadcast the cheaper it was for them. However, that wasn't the case for ITV when they started broadcasting in 1955. They immediately petitioned the government to abolish the Toddlers' Truce because they were losing valuable advertising revenue during the transmission downtime. The new Postmaster General, Charles Hill (1904-1989), who took over the job that same year agreed with the ITV proposal claiming: 'It was the responsibility of the parents, not the state, to put their children to bed at the right time' and took steps to abolish the rule.

The Toddlers' Truce finally came to an end on Saturday, 16 February 1957.

The BBC created two new programmes for the vacant time slot: the pop music show *Six-Five Special* (1957-1958) and the news and current affairs show *Tonight* (1957-1965). The first was shown on a Saturday night and the second from Mondays to Fridays. It's probably fair to assume that parents still didn't have much of a problem dragging their kids away from the TV on a weekday night. Faced with the prospect of watching stuffy old men in suits banging on about politics and current affairs for a whole hour probably sent them up the stairs to Bedfordshire even quicker than before!

On Sundays, transmissions continued to stop between 6.15pm and 7.25pm for another year or so to allow viewers to attend church!

the duke takes his revenge

The soldier/statesman Arthur Wellesley, 1st Duke of Wellington (1769-1852), was appointed as Britain's ambassador to France in August 1814. Napoleon Bonaparte was in exile on Elba after his defeat in the War of the Sixth Coalition (1813-1814) and the Bourbon king Louis XVIII was back on the throne of France.

However, the duke's tenure as ambassador was brief, after leaving the post six months later in February 1815 to represent Britain at the Congress of Vienna (1814-1815), an international conference of European states chaired by the Austrian Empire's Foreign Minister Klemens von Metternich in Vienna to agree a long-term peace plan for Europe after the Napoleonic Wars (1803-1815).

It's been said that at one particular reception (either in Paris in 1814 or Vienna in 1815) the duke was confronted by a group of rather rude and embittered French officers who turned their backs on him as he'd entered the room. A lady standing nearby apologised to him for their bad manners but he cut her short and waved off her excuses, before nonchalantly replying: 'I have seen their backs before, Madam.'

the fat bastard pie-eating goalkeeper

William 'Fatty' Foulke (1874-1916) was the first celebrity footballer.

He is remembered primarily for his long and distinguished career at Sheffield United [1894-1905] although he also played a few seasons for Chelsea [1905-1906] and Bradford City [1906-1908] too.

Willie was reportedly 6ft 3in (1.90m) tall and weighed about 26 stone (165kg) at the height of his 14 year career! He was a temperamental man known for his gamesmanship: he was hugely popular with the fans, and for many years he was also the best goalkeeper in the country. He might have had difficulty in reaching the low shots but there was never any chance of him being barged over the goal line!

Willie was the subject of much derision and name calling from the opposition fans due to his enormous bulk and sometimes from his own fans too. It has even been suggested that the chant *Who Ate All the Pies?* was originally aimed at him by the Sheffield United supporters. But it was all water off a duck's back for Willie: 'I don't mind what they call me as long as they don't call me late for lunch!'

During his time at Sheffield United he won a league championship medal in 1898 and two FA Cup winner medals in 1899 and 1902.

As well as being a big man, he also had a big personality. Opposing players who incurred his wrath were often unceremoniously picked up and dumped into his goalmouth; he'd walk off the pitch if he thought his own players weren't trying hard enough; he liked to swing from the crossbar during matches and on one occasion actually pulled down the goal, and was known to turn up early for pre-match lunches so he could scoff all the food meant for his team-mates.

Most famously, in the 1902 FA Cup Final against Southampton, he fiercely contested the equalising 88th minute goal scored by Harry

Wood (1868-1951), playing for Southampton, and after the game he ran naked from the Sheffield United dressing room to confront the referee, chasing him into a broom cupboard, where he'd taken refuge in fear of his life. As the poor chap begged for mercy from behind the locked door that Willie was trying to rip off its hinges, a group of equally as scared Football Association officials approached the big man and eventually persuaded him to return to the dressing room ... and put some bloody clothes on!

Although he was a big hit with the fans, the stuffy old codgers at the FA didn't take kindly to his antics which might explain why the Selection Committee only picked him once to play for England in a game against Wales in 1897.

In 1905, he was transferred to Chelsea for a fee of £50; he was made captain, and helped the newly formed club to finish the 1905-1906 season in third place. Nobody had ever thought of employing kids around the ground to retrieve the ball when it went out of play until they signed Willie. To draw even more attention to their larger-than-life goalkeeper, Chelsea employed two little boys to stand behind his goal in every home game to make him look even bigger and more fearsome than he actually was and to distract the opposition strikers as they charged towards him. Because Willie wasn't the most agile player in the later stages of his career, the boys were also used to retrieve the ball whenever it went out of play so he didn't have to. In effect they were the first ever ball boys.

After playing only thirty-five games for Chelsea he then moved to Bradford City where he finished his career.

Willie made the headlines again in an FA Cup-Second Round match against Accrington Stanley on 2 February 1907. Apparently, he turned up wearing the same red jersey as the Accrington players. The referee postponed the kick-off and asked everyone to look around for an alternative shirt for him. But finding a different coloured shirt that would fit a man of his size proved impossible and he was forced to play the game wrapped in a white bedsheet tied like a Roman toga which had been acquired from a nearby house. Willie kept a clean sheet that day with Bradford winning 1-0 and also kept his sheet clean too as he was never called upon to make a save in the whole game. It has sometimes been suggested that the phrase 'clean sheet' may have originated from Willie's performance that day.

Willie retired from first-class football at the end of the 1907-1908 season and bought himself a pub. He also made a few guest appearances in beat-the-goalie competitions at the amusement arcades along the Blackpool seafront. And when he wasn't pulling pints or making an arse of himself at the seaside, he was to be seen just walking around the streets of Sheffield wearing his cup final medals!

William 'Fatty' Foulke remains in the record books as the heaviest ever first-class footballer to play anywhere in the world.

the jakarta incident

British Airways flight 009 was a scheduled flight from London Heathrow to Auckland in New Zealand. On 24 June 1982, the Boeing 747-200 flew into a cloud of volcanic ash being thrown up by Mount Galunggung, about 110 miles (180km) south-east of Jakarta, resulting in the failure of all four engines on the aircraft.

Engine number 4 had surged and then flamed out. As the flight crew began their emergency shutdown drill, cutting off the fuel supply to the stricken engine, the other three engines suddenly flamed out too, leaving the plane completely without power!

The cabin quickly filled with an acrid sulphuric smoke, oxygen masks dropped down from the ceiling and the frightened passengers began writing notes to their families in the belief that the plane was about to crash. Despite this overwhelming sense of fear and the urgent need to try and re-start the stricken engines, Captain Eric Moody took a few moments to make an announcement to the 248 passengers, which has since been described as the perfect example of British understatement: 'Ladies and Gentlemen, this is your captain speaking. We have a small problem. All four engines have stopped. We are doing our damnedest to get them going again. I trust you are not in too much distress.'

The flight crew did get them going again, one at a time and were able to land the plane safely at Jakarta airport.

the wise men of gotham

Sometime in the early thirteenth century, King John (1166-1216) suddenly felt the need to build a new hunting lodge somewhere near the village of Gotham in Nottinghamshire. But the villagers weren't awfully keen on the idea. It would somehow cost them a lot of money and a fair chunk of their land too no doubt. They knew perfectly well that any appeals to make him change his mind would fall on deaf ears, so they decided to adopt a far more radical plan to try and dissuade him ...

When an advance party of royal officials arrived in Gotham to survey the area and make arrangements for the king's future visit, the villagers all feigned imbecility! Everywhere the officials travelled, they came across them acting strangely or engaged in some bizarre and pointless task; trying to drown eels that had apparently eaten all the fish in a river, dragging carts of wood into a barn to protect them from the sun, and most famously, trying to trap a cuckoo by building a fence around the bush in which the bird had built its nest! One official even witnessed a daft old man kill his horse after it had swallowed the Moon! The poor animal just happened to be drinking from the village pond when the Moon's reflection in the water disappeared, so he'd picked up his sword and chopped the horse in two to release it from its belly. Just then a cloud which had been obscuring the Moon drifted away and the man seemed content that he had released it back into the sky.

The officials were convinced that they'd stumbled across a village inhabited entirely by fools and quickly advised the king to stay well away and build his hunting lodge somewhere else!

bad medieval animals

Although animal trials were more popular in Europe, quite a few of them took place in England too.

From as early as the thirteenth century, all kinds of animals could be charged with a crime, assigned a lawyer and sent for trial in either a secular or ecclesiastic court. The biggest villains were the domesticated animals such as pigs, cows, bulls, horses, donkeys and mules which were usually charged with criminal damage, murder or even bestiality! But occasionally a colony of rats and even insects like locusts were carried into court to answer for their crimes. Wild animals such as wolves and bears were never prosecuted. They seemed to be above the law. Probably because they were bit harder to catch!

A trial normally followed the same formal criminal proceedings as those for humans. Both sides put their case, witnesses were called and then a clergyman or a lay judge delivered their verdict.

It seems that pigs found themselves in the dock more often than any other animal. Their most common crime appears to be homicide. Occasionally they were let off lightly and just exiled from the village if found guilty but more often than not they were executed. Sometimes they were tortured beforehand and even dressed up in human clothes before being burnt, hanged or made into sausages!

In 1379 a gang of pigs stood trial for infanticide after rampaging through the village of Saint-Marcel-le-Jeussey in France and in 1492 a piglet was hung for murder in the French town of Abbeville. It's doubtful that juvenile animal courts existed so it was presumably tried as an adult.

One of the most famous cases involving a murderous pig occurred in Rouen, again in France, in 1386 when a sow was found guilty of killing and eating a small child; she confessed through an interpreter (some kind of medieval Dr Dolittle-type character who could evidently talk to the animals!) and was then hanged in the local marketplace still wearing her court attire of jacket and trousers.

Another famous case, this time involving a rooster in Basel, Switzerland, in 1474, was described by the Swiss theologian Johann Georg Gross in *Kurtze Baßler Chronik* (1624). The confused bird was apparently accused of the 'heinous and unnatural crime of laying an egg.' The townsfolk feared that the egg had been spawned by Satan and likely to contain a cockatrice (a malevolent winged reptile) so he was tried and convicted of colluding with the Devil and summarily executed. He probably ended up on someone's dinner plate after that!

In 1750, in France, a man and his donkey were charged with bestiality. Witnesses testified to the good character of the donkey and the animal was ultimately acquitted. The man wasn't quite so lucky though.

beside the seaside, beside the sea

Natural spring water was discovered running down the cliffs at

Scarborough in North Yorkshire in the late-seventeenth century. The water tasted slightly bitter because it contained a high level of *magnesium sulphate* but was found to cure many minor ailments and so it soon became a widely accepted medicine for the townsfolk. A treatise by the eminent physician Robert Wittie (c.1613-1684) published in 1660 further extolled the healing qualities of the water and also promoted the health benefits of bathing in the sea. The resulting publicity encouraged many visitors to the town and by the early-eighteenth century, it had become a fashionable seaside resort with activities such as boating and horseback riding taking place along the beach.

In 1750, Benjamin Beale (1703-1775) invented the bathing machine, a little wooden hut on wheels which could be rolled out across the sand into the sea enabling bathers to retain their modesty whilst taking a dip and these were first used in Scarborough.

The first package holiday was arranged by the businessman Thomas Cook (1808-1892) but was nothing more than just a day trip by rail for a group of around 500 temperance campaigners from Leicester attending a meeting in Loughborough on 5 July 1841. The rail ticket and some food for the journey was included in the price of the excursion. During the next three summers further trips were arranged between Leicester, Nottingham, Derby and Birmingham for other local temperance societies and Sunday schools. The first overseas trip organised by Thomas took place in the summer of 1855 when he accompanied a group of British tourists on a grand tour of northern Europe through Belgium, Germany and France, ending with a visit to the *Exposition Universelle* in Paris.

The Victorians continued the craze for seaside holidays throughout the nineteenth century. After the rapid expansion of the rail network and the Bank Holidays Act 1871 which established certain days of the year as official holidays, day trippers and the working class families from the factory towns flocked to the ever-expanding coastal resorts of Blackpool, Scarborough, Llandudno and others to enjoy the sunshine and fresh air.

The first modern overseas package holiday was organised by Vladimir Raitz (1922-2000) (Horizon Travel) with the inaugural group of tourists flying out of London-Gatwick on 20 May 1950. For the price of £32.10s they had a return flight to the sun-soaked Mediterranean island of Corsica, tented accommodation at *Club Franco-Britannique*, the chance to sample the local wines and twice-a-day meals that were guaranteed to contain meat! This was especially attractive due to the rationing and austerity measures still present in post-war Blighty. From those first tentative overseas steps back in 1950 to what it's like today ...

Sitting down to dinner in a fancy restaurant in one of the most exotic locations in the world with the choice of the most exotic dishes to choose from and then overhearing the Brit at the next table saying: 'Can I have chips with that?'

the bradford sweets poisoning

The adulteration of food during the nineteenth century with cheaper, more available substances was common practice and unscrupulous sweet manufacturers would often use a sugar substitute because the real thing was too expensive. Typically, they used a mixture of substances such as powdered limestone and gypsum plaster known colloquially as 'daff'. Not particularly tasty but perfectly safe.

William Hardaker, known to his customers as 'Humbug Billy' sold sweets from a market stall in Bradford and always purchased his stock from Joseph Neal, who used daff supplied by a local pharmacist called Charles Hodgson.

On one particular occasion in 1858, however, there was a bit of a mix up at the pharmacist when Joseph was mistakenly given 12 pounds (5.4kg) of arsenic trioxide, an odourless and tasteless white crystalline powder that closely resembled daff. He was none the wiser even when he began manufacturing his peppermint humbugs, although he did notice that the finished sweets looked a little different from usual. 40lbs (18kg) of these sweets were then sold to Humbug Billy, who also noticed how different they appeared and was able to negotiate a discount on the price. He was also the first to pop one in his mouth and fell ill immediately. But he didn't connect the dots and began selling the contaminated sweets from his market stall …

Within a few days, twenty people had died and a further 200 people had fallen seriously ill with arsenic poisoning.

It was later proved that each contaminated sweet contained enough arsenic to kill two people, so the poor buggers that just fell ill after sucking on the humbugs got off lightly!

The growing number of casualties led the authorities to William Hardaker's stall and from there to Joseph Neal and Charles Hodgson. All three men were arrested and sent for trial. Apparently, Joseph had sent a lodger James Archer to collect the daff from the pharmacy. When he arrived, he was served by the shop assistant, William Goddard, who was told by his boss that the daff was stored in a cask in the attic. Unfortunately, the arsenic trioxide was also stored in a cask right next to the daff and the assistant picked up the wrong cask. An easy mistake to make. And the jury thought so too because everyone was acquitted.

However, the question remains: how stupid do you have to be to keep two identical looking powders right next to each other in the same type of unlabelled containers when one of those powders could kill you?

a time of war, destruction and death

The Dark Ages (500-1000) began after the fall of the Western Roman Empire in the late-fifth century. It was a time of political upheaval, plagues, violent conflict, religious persecution and a lack of any cultural achievement or scientific advancement, where everyone was either a fire-and-brimstone preacher, a swashbuckling knight or some wretched peasant who was poor, miserable or oppressed (usually all three) with a life expectancy in their late-twenties!

Definitely not the greatest time to be alive.

THE LEGEND OF URSULA AND THE ELEVEN THOUSAND VIRGINS

Ursula was a Romano-British princess and the daughter of King Dionotus of Dumnonia, now Devon and Cornwall. Sometime in the late-fourth century, she set sail for Europe accompanied by boatloads of virginal maidens to meet up with her future husband Conan Meriadoc of Armorica (a region in France between the Seine and the Loire), the legendary leader of Brittany. The king had apparently received a request from the young nobleman asking him to send over some wives for his followers who'd recently settled in Armorica, so he'd dutifully despatched his daughter for him and another 11,000 virgins for all the other guys. Unfortunately, the women never made it to their destination …

After landing in Gaul, Ursula suddenly felt the need to go on a pilgrimage before her wedding day. So everyone trooped south-east towards Rome for a meeting with the pope.

Sometime later, after heading north again towards Germany, they were attacked by the Huns, a nomadic race of people from Central Asia who spent most of the fourth century raping, pillaging and killing their way around Europe. The Huns were busy besieging Cologne in Germany at the time but took time off from their bloody rampaging to welcome the virgins … in their own inimitable way. However, Ursula and her young ladies refused their clumsy advances, the Huns inevitably took offence and then killed the lot of them!

Or so the story goes …

There must have been an Ursula because the Basilica Church of St Ursula in Cologne was built in her memory by the Roman Senator Clematius in around 400 BE on the very site where the bodies are thought to be buried. However, it's highly likely that the number of virgins might have been exaggerated a bit. It's doubtful that there were even 11,000 people in the whole of Cornwall at that time, never mind 11,000 young maidens so eager and willing to play the v-card. There might have only been eleven of them but through time the abbreviation 'M' used in transcripts of the event has been incorrectly interpreted as meaning the Roman numeral M (thousand) instead of M for martyr. Or there might have been just one of them … someone called Undecimilla, whose name is pronounced and spelt very similarly to *undecim milia* in Latin, or *undicimila* in Italian, and which means 11,000.

Perhaps it wasn't such an exciting story after all.

THE WIHTWARA MASSACRE

The Wihtwara were a Jutish people who'd migrated to the Isle of Wight (then called Wihtland) during the settlement of Britain by the Germanic people from northern Europe; a confederacy of seven tribes, living in peace, working the land and praying to their Pagan gods.

The island had already been invaded once, in 661, by the first Christian King of Mercia, Wulfhere (c.640-675) during his campaign to conquer the neighbouring Saxon kingdom of Wessex. He'd installed his godson Æthelwealh of Sussex (fl.660-685) as Wihtland's overlord with the remit to convert the inhabitants to Christianity and this he did with some degree of success.

But after a while the Wihtwara just went back to being Pagans again …

Twenty-five years later, in 686, it was the turn of the Wessex king, Cædwalla (c.659-689) to try his luck at bringing a bit of Christianity to Wihtland. He was more of a man of his time and adopted a slightly more practical approach than his Mercian predecessor. Instead of going to all that time and effort in trying to persuade them to change their ways, he just killed the lot of them and moved his own Christian followers from Wessex onto the island!

Job done.

A PESTILENCE RAGING FAR AND WIDE

The plague of 664 was the first recorded pandemic in British history.

It caused widespread death, social upheaval and a loss of religious faith, and was described by the English monk/historian Bede (c.672-735) as a 'pestilence raging far and wide' that 'destroyed a great multitude of men.'

According to the Irish clergyman Adamnán of Iona (c.624-704) the plague was present everywhere except in the very north of the island (Scotland). He firmly believed that it was a divine punishment with the Picts and the Irish being spared God's wrath because St Columba (521-597) had founded many monasteries in their lands and had therefore warranted protection. Just to prove his point, he and his followers then travelled south to England and spent a lot of time walking amongst the plague victims but never became sick themselves.

The urge to say 'I told you so' must have been unbearable!

the eighth power

The Welsh mathematician/physician, Robert Recorde has been credited with inventing the equals sign (=) and introducing the plus sign (+) to England in 1557.

In *The Whetstone of Witte* (1557) he also suggested using the mathematical notation, 'zenzizenzizenzic' to represent the eighth power of a number. At the time there was no easy way of denoting the powers of numbers and they were always written out in words, so Robert just chose the word 'zenzic' (the German spelling of the medieval Italian word *censo* meaning 'squared') and then kept adding to it until he'd invented something that 'doeth represent the square of squares squaredly.' The word is now obsolete and is only mentioned in the *Oxford English Dictionary* as a curiosity and linguistic oddity having contained more Zs than any other English word!

the wrong diagnosis

The famous Victorian surgeon Joseph Bell (1837-1911) is believed to be the inspiration for the character of Sherlock Holmes. Apparently, he had the uncanny knack of identifying a patient's illness just by looking at them! He was well-known for his extraordinary observational skills and could often deduce the occupation and the recent activities of a patient as a means of forming a more accurate diagnosis.

But he didn't always get it right ...

After gathering a group of his students around a patient's bed, he proceeded to question him: 'Aren't you a bandsman?' The patient nodded his agreement and Joseph turned back to his students: 'You see, gentlemen. I am right!' he boasted, 'It is quite elementary. This man has a paralysis of the cheek muscles, the result of too much blowing into wind instruments. We need only inquire to confirm. What instrument do you play, my man?'

'The big drum, doctor,' replied the patient.

the brown lady of raynham hall

According to legend, the ghost of the English aristocrat Dorothy Walpole (1686-1726) haunts Raynham Hall, Fakenham, in Norfolk. She was the sister of Robert Walpole (1676-1745), the *de facto* first Prime Minister of Great Britain and the wife of her childhood sweetheart Charles Townshend, 2nd Viscount Townshend (1674-1738).

Charles was a politician and an important man in his brother-in-law's government, serving off-and-on for ten years as the Secretary of State for the Northern Department. He was also a man renowned for his fiery temper. There is a common belief that when he discovered that Dorothy was having a fling with the politician Thomas Wharton, 1st Marquess of Wharton (1648-1715), he imprisoned her in the top floor rooms of Raynham

Hall where she purportedly remained for the rest of her life! Although the official cause of her death was listed as smallpox, it's been said that she was either starved to death or pushed down the house's grand staircase.

Years after her death, there were many unsettling reports of her ghost haunting the house. One of the first sightings involved the Prince Regent (George IV) (1762-1830) when he stayed there overnight. He'd been awoken by the presence of 'a little lady all dressed in brown with dishevelled hair and a face of shy paleness' standing by his bedside and had apparently fled the scene yelling: 'I will not pass another hour in this accursed house, for I have seen that what I hope to God I may never see again!'

Another famous sighting occurred in 1835. Two guests had stayed up late to play chess after a party at the house. As they'd finally made their way up the staircase to bed, their attention was drawn to a lady in a brown dress standing on the landing. They didn't recognise her as one of the other guests and when they went to talk to her she just disappeared. The following night, one of these men reported seeing her again but to his horror, he noticed that she had luminous skin and empty eye-sockets which appeared 'dark in the glowing face'.

A year later, the writer Frederick Marryat (1792-1848) visited Raynham Hall on a hunting trip. He'd previously dismissed all those ghostly stories as poppycock and had insisted on sleeping in the most haunted room of the house, the one containing a portrait of Dorothy Walpole, in order to disprove them. As he was getting ready for bed on the third night of his stay, two other guests arrived at his room to ask his advice about a gun they wanted to use on the shooting party the following day. He went with them to see it but took his revolver with him, joking that it was just in case he met the Brown Lady! On his way back to his room, he spotted a ghostly figure floating towards him along the hallway. He quickly hid in a vacant room and watched her through a chink in the door getting closer and closer until he could distinguish the colours and style of her costume. The ghost stopped outside the room and he could clearly see that it resembled the portrait of Dorothy Walpole hanging in his room. After later claiming that she then smiled at him in 'a malicious and diabolical manner', he flung open the door, drew his revolver and fired off a shot. The bullet passed straight through her and the door of the bedroom opposite and lodged in the wall. And then the Brown Lady just disappeared. Afterwards, the brave Frederick wasn't quite so brave and slept with the revolver under his pillow for the remainder of his stay!

In 1926, Gwladys, Marchioness Townshend (1884-1959) reported how her son and his friend, as young boys, had met a lady on the staircase when they'd been playing. They were more puzzled than scared because they could see right through her!

Then, on 19 September 1936, the most famous sighting of the Brown Lady was recorded, resulting in one of the most celebrated ghostly images ever captured on film …

The photographer Hubert Provand and his assistant Indre Shira had arrived at Raynham Hall to take shots of the house for use in a future article for *Country Life* magazine. Having taken one photograph of the Hall's main staircase, they were busy setting up a second shot when Dorothy suddenly appeared. Hubert had his head under the camera's focusing cloth but Indre was standing beside him holding the flashlight pistol when he suddenly spotted 'a vapoury form gradually assuming the appearance of a woman' gliding down the stairs towards them. Realising that he was witnessing something quite extraordinary, he yelled at Hubert to remove the lens cap and take the shot. Luckily, Hubert didn't ask any questions and did as he was told. Later, when the negative was developed, the famous image of a translucent, ethereal female figure in a flowing brown dress thought to be the ghost of Dorothy Walpole was revealed.

The Brown Lady photo was first published in *Country Life* magazine on 26 December 1936 and later in the American magazine *Life* on 4 January 1937.

the cruel and unhappy marriage of effie gray

John Ruskin (1819-1900) was a leading art critic, draughtsman, watercolourist, author, philosopher, social thinker and philanthropist. He was also a bit of a weirdo too! Today, he's more famous for falling in love with Effie Gray (1828-1897), marrying her and then doing everything in his power to make her life a misery, than any of the writings or paintings he ever produced.

He was 22 years-old and she was only 12 when he first started having feelings for the young Effie. To demonstrate his love, he wrote his only work of fiction for her, a fairytale called *The King of the Golden River* (1841). Effie's family knew Johnny Boy's father, John James Ruskin (1785-1864) and actively encouraged a match between the two of them despite the rather inappropriate age difference.

They eventually married seven years later on 10 April 1848 when he was 31 and she was 19 years-old.

It's been said that Johnny Boy had never seen a naked woman before his wedding night except in paintings or sculptures, where their naked forms rarely included pubic hair. On their wedding night, when Effie undressed in front of him, he was so horrified by her enormous bush, he assumed that she was in some way deformed, and ran out of the bedroom! Sexual relations were then postponed indefinitely until the marriage collapsed in 1854. In a letter to her father, Effie wrote about his reluctance to consummate the marriage: 'He alleged various reasons, hatred to children, religious motives, a desire to preserve my beauty, and, finally this last year he told me his true reason ... that he had imagined women were quite different to what he saw I was, and that the reason he did not make me his Wife was because he was disgusted with my person the first evening.' Johnny Boy seemed to confirm this in a statement to his lawyers during the court proceeding to annul the marriage: 'It may be thought strange that I could abstain from a woman who to most people was so attractive. But though her face was beautiful, her person was not formed to excite passion. On the contrary, there were certain circumstances in her person which completely checked it.' His obvious disgust with certain 'circumstances in her person' remains unknown but it's always been assumed that he was referring to her pubic hair or possibly menstrual blood.

A year after their marriage, in the winter of 1849, the unhappy couple travelled to Venice where he locked himself away to write his three-volume treatise on Venetian art and architecture *The Stories of Venice* (1851-1853) and she went out partying and had a bit of a fling with some passing Austrian soldier. Many people later claimed that Johnny Boy had deliberately encouraged their friendship in an attempt to compromise her and end the marriage.

When Effie met the painter/illustrator John Everett Millais (1829-1896) four years later she was still a virgin. He'd been hired by her husband to paint his portrait and the three of them had travelled to Scotland together. During their time spent at Brig o' Turk in Stirlingshire, she fell in love with John and he made many drawings and sketches of her. She even posed for his painting *The Order of Release, 1746* (1853) in which she was depicted as the loyal wife of a Jacobite soldier. On their return to London, Effie left Johnny Boy to go and stay with her family, sent her wedding ring back and announced that she'd be filing for an annulment due to his cruel and distrustful behaviour towards her. With the support of some influential friends, she pursued her case through the courts and the marriage was finally annulled on the grounds of 'incurable impotency' in 1854.

In 1855, Effie married John and finally had her first shag! They had eight children together and as far as anyone knows they lived happily ever after. Johnny Boy, on the other hand, never remarried. Who the hell would have him?

the fake princess

On the evening of 3 April 1817, a young woman was found wandering around the village of Almondsbury in Gloucestershire dressed in exotic clothing and speaking gibberish. She was given some bread and milk by a kindly cobbler before being placed in the care of a local magistrate, Samuel Worrall and his American-born wife Elizabeth.

To cut a long story short, she then spent time in and out of hospital and various care homes before being handed back to the Worralls. A few days after her return, she was introduced to a Portuguese sailor called Manuel Eynesso who claimed to speak her language. He told the Worralls that her name was Princess Caraboo and that she'd lived on the Indian Ocean island of Javasu before being captured by pirates and brought to England. Apparently, she'd jumped ship somewhere in the Bristol Channel, swam ashore and had been wandering around the country dazed and confused ever since.

The young woman had some very peculiar habits. She liked to swim naked in lakes, she slept on the floor, she often climbed onto the roof to pray to a God called 'Allah-Talla' and she continued talking in her own mysterious language that nobody else could understand. She also and had some very odd looking scars on the back of her head, which a local know-it-all physician, known only as Dr Wilkinson, had described as being the handiwork of inexperienced oriental surgeons. He also claimed to have identified her language using a book on writing systems and typography called *Pantographia* (1799) by Edmund Fry (1754-1835).

Within a very short time Princess Caraboo had become something of a local celebrity. Her portrait was painted and reproduced in local newspapers and she even attended a grand ball held in her honour in Bath. Everyone was fascinated by her exotic background and her very peculiar habits, and she soon became the most talked about person in English high society. By all accounts, she was having a grand old time of it, hobnobbing with the posh folks and enjoying all the attention they afforded her.

But then it all turned to shit ...

A boarding-house keeper from Bristol recognised her from an illustration in the *Bristol Journal* and informed the Worralls of her true identity. The mysterious princess was in fact just plain old Mary Willcocks (c.1792-1864), a cobbler's daughter from Witheridge in Devon. She was a servant girl who'd been working around England but had found no permanent place to stay. She'd dressed extravagantly and invented her own language from gypsy words and made-up phrases to create a more glitzy and believable backstory for her character, and the odd marks on the back of her head were just scars from a botched cupping operation carried out in a London poorhouse hospital.

No mention has ever been made of just how stupid Dr Wilkinson must have felt after these revelations!

Mary was ridiculed in the press but Elizabeth Worrall took pity on the girl and shipped her off to America, out of harm's way, where she continued to play the part of the exotic princess by touring the country and appearing in various stage shows. In 1824, she returned to England and began exhibiting herself as Princess Caraboo again ... but by this time nobody really cared anymore!

the thames tunnel

The Thames Tunnel was the world's first underwater tunnel built under a navigable river when it opened on 25 March 1843.

The 1,300 feet (396m) long tunnel between Rotherhithe and Wapping was constructed by Marc Isambard Brunel (1769-1849) and his son Isambard Kingdom Brunel (1806-1859) over an eighteen-year period between 1825 and 1843 to provide carriage drivers in that part of the city with an alternative and much quicker route across the River Thames.

Progress was slow with only 10-12 feet (3-3.6m) of ground being cleared each week and the project went so far over-budget that the company management were forced to open the tunnel to fee-paying visitors, charging them a shilling a time to wander around and gawp at the building work! Surprisingly, they attracted hundreds of people a day but the extra money still wasn't enough to prevent the site from temporarily shutting down in 1828. It took another six years before the necessary finances were in place to start again. Conditions inside the tunnel were dire; the water leaking through the roof contained sewage which produced methane gas and made the workers ill, and the tunnel was prone to flooding with at least six men losing their lives during construction.

Then, after all that, when it was finally finished, the company bosses realised there wasn't enough money left over to build the access ramps needed to allow horse-drawn carriages to enter and exit the tunnel. Which was the whole point of the damn thing in the first place!

So it was just used as a pedestrian walkway.

For the cost of a penny, people were allowed to stroll around inside the tunnel under the River Thames and browse amongst the many market stalls selling goods and souvenirs or refreshments that had opened up. However, it wasn't quite as idyllic as it all sounds. Thieves would often wait in the darker passages and rob passers-by and prostitutes did a roaring trade in the even darker passages!

It wasn't until 1869 when the tunnel was finally used for something like its intended purpose when the East London Railway Company (1865-1925) began operating a train service through the tunnel.

Today it forms part of the infrastructure for the Windrush Line (London Overground).

the first marathon race

Marathon races had been held at the Olympic Games since the very first meeting in 1896 but the course distance was never standardised until the Games of the IV Olympiad held in London in 1908.

The official distance for a marathon race was set at 26 miles, 385 yards (42km, 195m) by the British Olympic Association for no other reason than it was convenient for the Royal Family. The course distance was originally 25-miles (40.2km) but it was lengthened by them to 26 miles (41.8km) because the race was due to start at Windsor Castle in Berkshire and end underneath the royal box at the White City Stadium, Shepherd's Bush in London. It was then lengthened again by just another 385 yards (352m) to its present distance of 26 miles, 385 yards (42km, 195m) after the Queen Consort Alexandra of Denmark (1844-1925) asked for the starting point to be moved to the East Lawn of Windsor Castle so the royal children could watch proceedings from the window of their nursery.

The International Association of Athletics Federation later adopted this distance for all official races from 1921.

Previous Olympic marathon races had been plagued with drama, intrigue and controversy. In Athens in 1896, the Greek runner Spyridon Belokas finished in third place but was later disqualified after completing part of the course riding in a carriage! In Paris in 1900, the course markings were so bad that many athletes got confused and ran off in the wrong direction and in St Louis in 1904, Frederick Lorz romped home a full sixteen minutes ahead of his nearest rival but without ever crossing the halfway line! He'd retired from the race with exhaustion after only 9 miles (14.5km) but his manager had then given him a lift in his car, driving the next 11 miles (17.7km) and dropping him off near the stadium, so he could complete the race!

The London Olympic Games marathon was held on the final day of the athletics tournament on 24 July 1908 with 55 competitors from sixteen nations setting off along the course at precisely 2.33pm. Every five minutes, after each mile or so of the race, a broadcast was made to the 100,000-strong crowd gathered inside the White City Stadium announcing the current race leader ...

Two Englishmen, Thomas Jack (1881-1961) and then Jack Price (1884-1965) led during the early part of the race but the South African Charles Hefferon became the race leader for most of the latter part. He only lost the lead 1½ miles (2.4km) from the stadium because he stopped to drink Champagne and accept the congratulations of all the spectators lining the streets! He was overtaken by the Italian runner Dorando Pietri who later staggered into White City in first place and was welcomed by the cheering crowd ...

'As I entered the stadium the pain in my legs and in my lungs became impossible to bear,' he later told the Italian magazine *Sport Illustrato.* 'It felt like a giant hand was gripping my throat, tighter and tighter. Willpower was irrelevant now. If it hadn't been so bad I would not have fallen the first time. I got up automatically and launched myself a few more paces forwards ... They tell me that I fell another five or six times and that I looked like a man suffering from paralysis stumbling with tiny steps towards his wheelchair. I don't remember anything else. My memory stops at the final fall.'

The second-placed runner the American Johnny Hayes then entered the stadium and began catching the diminutive Italian, who was still staggering around but was now being aided by the clerk of the course and the chief medical officer Michael Bulger (1867-1938). They were massaging his legs, helping him to his feet and willing him on every time he faltered. On one occasion, he was so disorientated after getting to his feet that he stumbled off backwards around the track and had to be re-directed and pointed in the right direction by the officials! The writer Arthur Conan Doyle (1859-1930), who was reporting on the race for the *Daily Mail* noted: 'He has gone to the extreme of human endurance ... It is horrible, and yet fascinating, this struggle between a set purpose and an utterly exhausted frame.'

Eventually Dorando toppled through the tape to win the race in a time of 2 hours, 54 minutes and 46.4 seconds. It had taken him ten minutes just to complete the final lap of the track!

Johnny Hayes finished in second place in 2 hours, 55 minutes and 18.4 seconds and immediately lodged a protest with the race officials. His opponent had been helped around the track and that was surely against the rules. However, the Press Association claimed that he too had received some assistance when he'd entered the stadium and so the third-placed athlete Charles Hefferon, emboldened by all that Champagne no doubt, quickly seized the opportunity to claim a gold medal by lodging a complaint of his own against both the Italian and the American. Dorando Pietri was later disqualified with Johnny Hayes being declared the winner much to the dismay of the stadium crowd who'd been supporting the little Italian runner. Meanwhile, Charles Hefferon just had to be content with second place because nobody had taken a blind bit of notice of his appeal.

It could be argued that the two race officials who'd assisted Dorando around the track had cost him the gold medal. But it's doubtful if he would have even finished the race without their help. The final result was (1) Johnny Hayes [USA] - 2:55:18.4 OR, (2) Charles Hefferon [RSA] - 2:56:06.0, (3) Joseph Forshaw [USA] - 2:57:10.4. The highest placed British runner was William Clarke (1882-1960) in twelfth place with a time of 3:16:08.6. Of the original 55 runners only 27 of them completed the race, with another 27 being classified as DNF and of course, the unfortunate Dorando Pietri being listed as DSQ.

Dorando later blamed his failure to complete the race unaided on eating too much steak for breakfast!

The New York Times reported: 'It would be no exaggeration to say that the finish of the marathon at the 1908 Olympics in London was the most thrilling athletic event that has occurred since that marathon race in ancient Greece, where the victor fell at the goal and, with a wave of triumph, died.'

Despite Johnny Hayes winning the world's first 26 miles, 385 yards (42km, 195m) marathon race, it was Dorando who proved to be the more popular athlete and went on to enjoy worldwide fame, especially after he seemed to gain royal support. Queen Alexandra, who'd watched the race from the stadium's royal box and had enthusiastically cheered him on, had insisted that he should receive some kind of reward for his heroic efforts, and so during the closing ceremony, she presented him with a small specially-made silver cup. 'When I was called to see Her Majesty, I was trembling all over,' recounted Dorando. 'I felt as if I should fall as I did in the race. Then she spoke to me very kindly. "Bravo" was the only word I could understand, but I knew she meant it by her smile. This cup is balm to my soul. I shall treasure it to the end of my life.'

All of the Olympic officials at the 1908 London Games had been British but the marathon race incident and all the whinging from the American team prompted the International Olympic Committee to start appointing judges and referees from neutral countries for future Olympic Games.

Note: Two months after that race, Dorando accepted a challenge to race against Johnny Hayes again. He travelled to New York for an indoor, 262-lap race around Madison Square Garden. Despite a huge home crowd of 20,000 spectators cheering on Johnny, the tobacco smoke-filled air and a lack of any real training, Dorando won the race easy enough by half a lap! *The New York Times* later described it as 'the most spectacular foot race that New York has ever witnessed.'

THE OLYMPIC WALKOVER

The first and only Olympic Games 'walkover' occurred on 25 July 1908 in a re-run of the 400m final.

Two days earlier, the American runner John Carpenter had been accused by a race official of obstructing the British guy Wyndham Halswelle (1882-1915). The race was ordered to be re-run but this time without the American. Although the blocking manoeuvre he'd used was perfectly legal under American rules, the Games of the IV Olympiad were being held in accordance with British rules, and so John Carpenter was promptly disqualified and barred from competing in the re-run. As two out of the three remaining athletes were also American, and they refused to take part in the re-run as a protest against the ruling handed down to their teammate, Wyndham was left to jog around the track on his own and pick up the gold medal.

puffing devil

Puffing Devil was the name of the world's first full-size, steam-powered road locomotive and passenger vehicle.

Unlike the earlier steam engines of James Watt (1736-1819), the design pioneered by the inventor/engineer Richard Trevithick (1771-1833) used high-pressure 'strong steam' allowing him to develop smaller, more powerful and very versatile engines which could easily be used in the mines and factories or built into ships and locomotives.

The *Puffing Devil* engine weighed more than 1½ tonnes and was built with four wheels on a square frame chassis with a small passenger platform at the rear. It was successfully trialled by Richard and another engineer Andrew Vivian (1759-1842) when they took it for a spin around the streets of Camborne in Cornwall on 24 December 1801. The townsfolk had never seen anything quite like it; a huge metal monster that chugged through their streets belching out great clouds of steam, and rather predictably for that time, they gave the vehicle its demonic nickname. Their little jaunt around town is widely accepted as being the world's first public demonstration of any steam-powered passenger vehicle and the first time that people in Britain had travelled under mechanical power. It was also the inspiration for the popular Cornish folk song 'Camborne Hill' (1801).

The lads went for another joyride on Christmas Day and then again on 28 December 1801.

It was this third outing which also proved to be the vehicle's last. Richard Trevithick was tending the engine and Andrew Vivian was steering when they hit a gully in the road and the machine toppled over. They managed to heave it upright again with a little help from some passers-by and then went to drown their sorrows in the local pub.

Unfortunately, the fire was left burning, the water boiled away causing the engine to overheat and the locomotive blew up!

the deadly experiment

The English scientist Francis Bacon, 1st Viscount St Alban (1561-1626), is often referred to as the 'father of modern science' after being the first person to outline a process of designing and implementing carefully planned experiments as a basis for all scientific research which later became known as the Scientific Method.

He was also one of the few scientists to die as a result of one of his own experiments!

Francis was travelling by coach to Highgate in London through a blizzard when he suddenly had the idea that snow could be used to preserve meat. He ordered the coach to stop and barged into a nearby house, buying a chicken from the householder and asking her to gut it for him. After standing around in the cold and stuffing the bird full of snow, he soon realised that his experiment had failed. The chicken didn't look in the least bit frozen and he'd caught pneumonia.

Three days later he was dead!

design failure

The logo chosen for the Games of the XXX Olympiad in London held in

2012 was possibly the worst of all time!

Four garish fuchsia coloured jagged shapes that looked like broken bits of a jigsaw puzzle clumsily arranged to spell out the numbers 2-0-1-2. It was supposed to be an edgy, youthful and unforgettable logo reflecting the energy of the world's greatest sporting event but it was mocked by the public as being just plain ugly.

Then somebody noticed that it looked exactly like Lisa Simpson from the cartoon series *The Simpsons* giving someone a blowie!

skewered in the arse

Edward II (1284-1327) was a weak, effeminate and rather unpopular and ineffectual king and his reign was marked by much internal strife, baronial wars and lots of military failures, most notably the humiliating defeat against the Scots at the Battle of Bannockburn (1314) during the First War of Scottish Independence (1296-1328).

Even his wife, Isabella of France (1295-1358) didn't like him very much! By 1325, their marriage was on the rocks and she'd pissed off back to her homeland to start screwing around with the nobleman Roger Mortimer, 1st Earl of March (1287-1330). She then returned to England a year later with a small army of mercenaries to depose him. Edward's forces quickly deserted him and by 1327 Isabella had gained power, imprisoned her husband in Berkeley Castle (Gloucestershire) and had their young son Edward of Windsor (Edward III) (1312-1377) crowned as England's new king.

Edward II was never seen again after that. How he died has never really been determined but there are plenty of theories and conflicting stories surrounding his demise. Some medieval historians wrote that he'd died of natural causes; others were convinced that he'd died from an illness, strangulation, suffocation or even sorrow, whilst the chronicler Thomas Grey rather unhelpfully noted that he'd died 'by what manner was not known but God knows it.'

However, the most horrific and often quoted cause of his death involved a red hot poker ...

On 21 September 1327, the king was lying in bed when a group of unknown men suddenly burst into his bedchamber. They grabbed hold of him, held him down under the mattress and then one of them shoved a red-hot poker up his arse! Some believe that Isabella had arranged the murder and so she may well have decided how he should die too! The king was known to have had a few homosexual affairs in his time and perhaps Isabella thought he might appreciate the irony of her methods!

the worst kept secret

The 37-floor, 627 feet (191m) tall Post Office Tower (now known as the BT Tower) became Britain's tallest building when it was officially opened on 19 May 1966. Britain's first revolving restaurant, The Top of the Tower was opened on the 34th floor and offered diners a 360° panoramic view of London as it completed a full rotation every 23 minutes.

But despite this futuristic-shaped building being an unmissable addition to the London skyline which attracted the social elite to its fancy restaurant, its existence was actually considered an official secret for many years due to its importance to the national communications network. It wasn't until February 1993, when its location was finally revealed to the public! The Labour MP Kate Hoey (1946-) used the BT Tower as an example of trivial information being kept a secret when debating a Bill in the Houses of Parliament:'... An example that has not been mentioned, but which is so trivial that it is worth mentioning, is the absence of the British Telecom tower from Ordnance Survey maps. I hope that I am covered by parliamentary privilege when I reveal that the British Telecom tower does exist and that its address is 60 Cleveland Street, London ...'

the battle of lake nyasa

The first naval action of World War I (1914-1918) took place in the tranquil waters of Lake Nyasa (also known as Lake Malawi) in Tanzania rather than the more obvious and less tranquil waters of the North Sea.

The British Empire territory of British East Africa [Malawi] was guarded by one steamship, the SS *Gwendolen*, captained by Edmund Rhoades and on the other side of the lake in German East Africa [Tanzania], the SS *Hermann von Wissmann* captained by a man known only as Berndt guarded the German territory. The two captains were drinking buddies. Having been posted to the middle of Africa where not a lot happened from one day to the next, they'd spent most of their time hanging out together and knocking back the beers!

But then war broke out. The British captain obviously heard the news first because he immediately set course across the lake, opened fire on the German ship and put a shell through its hull. The German captain had just assumed his pal was drunk and rowed out to the SS *Gwendolen* to confront him. Once it was explained to him that their two countries were now at war and that he would have his ship's gun confiscated, he seemed to accept his lot and duly surrendered.

Then the two captains just carried on as before, seeing out the rest of the war getting pissed together!

ALAN FERGUSON

the english dandy

George 'Beau' Brummell (1778-1840) was born into a wealthy, middle-class family and educated at Eton College where he became friendly with the Prince of Wales (George IV) (1762-1830). After attending only one term at Oriel College (University of Oxford), he returned to London in 1794 to take up a commission in the Prince's own regiment, the 10th Royal Hussars. Throughout his military career, he used his friendship with the prince to great effect; shirking his duties and generally doing whatever the hell he liked, but then in 1797, when the regiment was about to be posted to Manchester, he immediately resigned, citing the city's poor reputation, undistinguished ambience and its lack of culture and civility as his reasons!

Beau was one of those rich playboy-types with too much money and too much time on his hands! He continued to exploit his friendship with the Prince of Wales and soon became an iconic figure of Regency England; an arbiter of men's fashion, must-have party guest, celebrity man-about-town and one of the most famous and influential men of early nineteenth-century London.

He was the originator of dandyism, a more subdued and much less eccentric alternative to the foppish culture of the day. The fops were the effeminate rich folks influenced by the Italian and French fashion of wearing powdered wigs, make-up, perfume, elaborate fabrics and silk stockings, whereas Beau championed bespoke tailoring and sombre fabrics; a look based on dark coats, full-length trousers (rather than knee breeches and stockings), immaculate white shirts and elaborately knotted cravats. As such, he is often credited with popularising the modern men's suit and necktie. Many people began copying his style and it wasn't long before London was full of both dandies and fops with a sort of early-nineteenth century Mods vs Rockers-style rivalry emerging between the two groups.

If he was around today, Beau would be one of those celebrity influencers with millions of followers!

He bathed, shaved and brushed his teeth regularly (which was a bit of a novelty for the time) and replaced all those ridiculous hair powders and perfumes with a simple daily soak in the tub. His obsession with immersing himself in hot water every day was nothing short of revolutionary! He once claimed that it sometimes took him five hours a day to dress and recommended that boots must always be cleaned with Champagne! However, it should be noted that the Napoleonic Wars (1803-1815) were raging at the time and cleaning boots with France's finest export might have just been a personal act of patriotism on his part.

Beau was a member of various London clubs; he had a string of lady friends, and his impeccable style, manners and grace made him one of London's most eligible bachelors and the most talked about celebrity of the time. He was famous for his wit but just as infamous for his rudeness and it was this rudeness which eventually led to a falling-out between him and the Prince of Wales, when Beau called him a big fatty at a party in 1813. This loss of royal favour would have been a disaster for anyone else but Beau's lofty societal position was completely unaffected and he continued to maintain his old friendships.

The beginning of the end only came three years later when he was finding it more and more difficult to maintain his exuberant lifestyle and pay off his mounting debts. He wasn't an aristocrat with seemingly limitless funds and he'd been gambling away his father's fortune, partying and generally living the highlife for many years, so eventually he just ran out of money. He fled to Calais in France to escape his creditors and then moved to the nearby town of Caen. He spent his final days in a state of depression and self-delusion, dressing up and hosting parties for non-existent guests before being admitted to the town's sanatorium where he died penniless and insane.

dolly the sheep

Dolly (1996-2003) became the world's most famous sheep when she was born on 5 July 1996.

Dolly was the first mammal ever cloned from an adult somatic cell using the process of nuclear transfer. The procedure was undertaken at the Roslin Institute at the University of Edinburgh by the biologists Keith Campbell (1954-2012) and Ian Wilmut (1944-2023). She was named after the well endowed country singer Dolly Parton. On being asked about their choice of name for the sheep, Ian Wilmut commented: 'Dolly is derived from a mammary gland cell and we couldn't think of a more impressive pair of glands than Dolly Parton's!'

the angels of mons

Britain declared war on Germany on 4 August 1914 and deployed a British Expeditionary Force of about 80,000 to 130,000 soldiers to the continent. Their first major engagement of the Great War was the Battle of Mons (1914) with the fighting beginning on the morning of 23 August 1914. Although the British Forces were heavily outnumbered, they still succeeded in inflicting heavy casualties on the enemy before being forced to retreat.

The Welsh author Arthur Machen (1863-1947) had been inspired by the accounts he'd read of the fighting at Mons and wrote *The Bowmen* (1914) which was first published in the *London News* on 29 September 1914. The newspaper story described an unnamed British soldier cowering in the trenches and recalling a picture of Saint George and the motto *Adsit Anglis Sanctus Georgius* (May St George be a present help to the English) he'd seen in a London restaurant before the war. After reciting a prayer, he suddenly experienced an electric shock and heard a voice calling the men to arms. 'Array! Array! Array!' He turned around and saw a long line of phantom bowmen from the Battle of Agincourt (1415) suddenly appear in the sky above and behind the British lines and then fire their arrows ceaselessly into the German trenches. Both sides appeared bewildered as the German soldiers dropped to the ground, one after the other, with only the story's main character, the unnamed British soldier, knowing the truth that God and St George had answered his prayers and intervened to save the lives of the British troops.

The story wasn't labelled as fiction and was written in the first person, inadvertently leading the reader to believe that it was actually a true account of events. Despite many declarations to the contrary from Arthur, nobody wanted to believe that he'd just made the whole thing up! Much to his amazement there were many witnesses who then came forward to confirm that things had really happened just the way he'd said they happened in the story. *The Bowmen* was later republished in many parish magazines, seemingly as proof that God was on the side of the British Empire. Soon afterwards, similar spooky tales of angelic intervention on the battlefield featuring medieval archers, cavalrymen, St George or just strange luminous clouds, which all claimed to be based on true-life experiences, started appearing in the newspapers.

Arthur republished his original story in book form in 1915 and again attempted to quell the hysteria by including a long preface stating that everything he'd written was the result of his very fertile imagination. Nevertheless, the book was still a bestseller and resulted in a series of copycat publications recounting stories of angels and their presence on the World War I battlefields. A few critics may have tried to dismiss these celestial apparitions as some form of collective hallucination but they were deemed unpatriotic and any attempt to lessen the impact of the inspiring and morale-boosting stories was viewed by many as an act of treason.

One of Arthur's fiercest critics was the journalist and author Harold Begbie (1871-1929) who accused him of sacrilege: 'Mr Machen in his quieter and less popular moments will feel a very sincere regret and perhaps sharp contrition for his attempts to deprive good people of their hope.' He'd just published his own book, *On the Side of the Angels* (1915) which recounted testimony from soldiers who he believed had witnessed the angels helping the retreating British troops at Mons, so beginning a war of words with Arthur was probably just a clever ploy on his part to increase sales of his own book.

Another prominent believer in the existence of the angels was Phyllis Campbell, a British Red Cross volunteer in France, whose essay *The Angelic Leaders* (1915) first appeared in the illustrated monthly magazine *The Occult Review*. She'd first heard about the incident at Mons when an injured British soldier had asked her for a picture of Saint George because he'd just seen him in person on the battlefield!

By 1916, music, art and films had all been produced promoting the Angels of Mons story. Angels then started appearing on postcards and drawings, and inevitably the British government began producing propaganda based on the story, featuring angels on recruitment posters and advertisements encouraging the public to buy war bonds.

the groom of the stool

According to *A Collection of Ordinances and Regulations for the Government of the Royal Household* (1790), the first guy appointed to the role of 'Yoman of the Stoole' (Groom of the King's Stool) was the politician/courtier William Grimsby (1420-1482) during the reign of Henry VI (1421-1471). However, it wasn't until Henry VII (1457-1509) was sitting on the throne that it became an official role within the royal household.

The job holder, unofficially known as the King's Most Intimate Servant, was expected to assist the king in his bedchamber, help him with dressing and undressing, undertake a variety of administrative tasks within the private rooms, monitor the king's diet and record his bowel movements, and liaise with the royal physician whenever there was cause to do so. It's unclear whether he was also expected to wipe the king's arse. There's still some debate amongst historians as to whether this duty was part of the job description or not.

The job was usually awarded to the sons of noblemen and rather surprisingly it was a highly prized position within the palace.

It was only abolished when Edward VII (1841-1910) acceded to the throne in 1901.

Presumably he preferred to wipe his own arse!

the perilous life of alice de lacy

The medieval noblewoman Alice de Lacy, 4th Countess of Lincoln (1281-1348) had a long and eventful life.

Married three times. Widowed three times. Abducted and imprisoned twice.

Edward I (1239-1307) arranged for her betrothal 'in her ninth year' to his nephew Thomas, 2nd Earl of Lancaster (c.1278-1322). They were married on 28 October 1294 when Alice was 13 years-old and Thomas was 16 years-old. But it was a loveless and childless marriage. She lived alone in a remote castle somewhere and he spent all his time drinking, whoring and pissing about in Europe.

Alice was first abducted from her manor at Canford in Dorset in the spring of 1317 by some knights loyal to John de Warenne, 7th Earl of Surrey (1286-1347), a long time enemy of her husband. Unsurprisingly, Thomas didn't bother to come to her rescue. There's no record that he even asked for her back, never mind fighting for her! He obviously felt that she was a damsel in distress not worth saving. However, he did go to war with John de Warenne but only because the two men couldn't wait to start scrapping with each other and his wife's abduction seemed like a good enough reason as any.

As was so often the case in the Middle Ages, it was only a matter of time before one of them was executed for treason. In this case, it was Thomas. His luck run out at the Battle of Boroughbridge (1322), a little known battle during an even lesser known war, the Despenser War (1321-1322), in which he'd led an army of rebellious barons against the Royalist forces of Edward II (1284-1327). At his trial, he wasn't allowed to speak in his own defence, nor was he allowed to have anyone speak for him, so obviously he was found guilty. Although to be fair, in this particular case, the evidence against him did look pretty overwhelming! The king must have been in a compassionate mood because he had his sentence commuted to a beheading, as opposed to the usual hanging, drawing and quartering which was so popular for such a crime. On 22 March 1322, he lost his head in front of a jeering crowd in front of Pontefract Castle in West Yorkshire.

Meanwhile, Alice had escaped her captor ... or maybe he'd just got bored with her and let her go after her husband's death. The history books are a little vague about what happened. But poor Alice didn't remain a free woman for very long. The king had her imprisoned in York Castle and threatened to have her executed unless she agreed to pay him a huge ransom and sign over the majority of her husband's estates. Ironically, many of these lands were then handed over to her kidnapper John de Warenne in recognition of his loyalty to the crown.

In 1324, Alice married Eubulus le Strange, 1st Baron Strange (c.1286-1335). By all accounts their marriage was a happy one with Eubulus describing her as a 'dear and loving companion.' But this was medieval England and so no one was allowed to stay happy for very long. Twelve years later, Eubulus was killed during the Second War of Scottish Independence (1332-1357).

Around about the same time, Alice announced she'd taken a vow of celibacy.

Since Eubulus had been involved in the 1330 plot organised by Edward III (1312-1377) to bring down the *de facto* rulers of England, Isabella of France (1295-1358) and Roger Mortimer, 1st Earl of March (1287-1330), Alice had been rewarded for her husband's loyalty to the crown with the return of some of her old estates. By 1335, Alice was 54 years-old and probably hoped to live out the rest of her life just pottering around the garden at her castle in Old Bolingbroke in Lincolnshire but the nobleman Hugh de Freyne, Baron Freyne (c.1251-c.1337), had other ideas. In early 1336, he abducted her, dragged her back to his castle and raped her! To add insult to injury, she was later rebuked by Pope Benedict XII for breaking her vow of celibacy!

As so often happened in medieval rape cases, the rapist then married his victim. By now, Alice was getting on a bit, so it's highly likely that Hugh had been more attracted by her vast wealth than her beauty. But he never really had much time to enjoy his new found fortune. The marriage had taken place without a licence granted by the king, so all her land, property and wealth were seized again ... and then he went and died a year later! Alice had her land returned to her on the death of her husband but only after she'd paid a hefty fine and then agreed to resume her vow of celibacy.

On 4 May 1337, she was imprisoned again. This time it was her own family that held her captive! Her second husband's nephew Roger le Strange (c.1326-1382) and her illegitimate half-brother John de Lacy stormed into her castle, stole a few horses, assaulted the staff and made off with her and as much of her stuff as they could carry away with them. Nobody tried to rape her and nobody wanted to marry her anymore but they still kept her prisoner for a month until she'd agreed to give away some of her land to Roger.

For around ten years she was finally allowed to live in peace.

She was 66 years-old when she died which wasn't too bad considering the time and the place. Alice was buried alongside Eubulus le Strange, the only man she ever loved, in the grounds of Barlings Abbey in Lincolnshire.

the south sea bubble

The South Sea Company (1711-1853) was an international trading company created to manage Britain's national debt in exchange for the monopoly on trade with Spain's colonies in South America and the West Indies. There weren't actually that many trading opportunities to be had with these countries but this little inconvenient truth didn't seem to stop them from making extravagant claims about their ever-expanding activities in the region prompting many politicians, clergymen, bankers and other wealthy types to buy shares in the company.

The South Sea Company's share price increased from about £100 at the beginning of 1720 to almost £1,000 in August of that year.

Having seen the rich get richer, the less well-off investors then sank all their money into the stock market which led to a nationwide share buying frenzy ...

Share prices in other companies rose sharply, some by as much as ten times their original value; speculation ran wild and all sorts of dubious and fraudulent joint-stock companies were quickly set up to take advantage of the sudden demand for speculative investments. Many of these new companies made rather outrageous or fraudulent claims about their business activities for the purpose of raising capital and boosting their share price. One company advertised its ambition to improve the art of making soap and another had plans to manufacture a cannon that could fire square-shaped balls ... or cubes! But the most outlandish and deceitful company of them all has to be the one that advertised itself as 'carrying-on an undertaking of great advantage but no-one to know what it is' which unbelievably still attracted investments totalling around £2,000.

The public couldn't wait to part with their hard-earned cash because everyone was making a shitload of money out of buying shares in these companies.

But then the bubble burst ...

Everyone starting selling ... and the share prices started tumbling, resulting in a catastrophic loss of money across the whole country. Almost overnight, investors were ruined, businesses went bankrupt, company directors were arrested, corrupt politicians were jeered and attacked, there was a marked increase in suicides and there were riots in the street.

Even the famous scientist Isaac Newton (1642-1727) had been duped into parting with his money. It's been said that he invested heavily in the stock market but bought low and sold high, managing to cash in when the prices were at their peak. But then the silly arse went and invested all of his money again and ended up losing around £20,000 causing him to remark that '[he could] calculate the motions of the heavenly bodies, but not the madness of people.' He might have seemed quite calm about it all at the time but he refused to discuss the affair for the rest of his life.

Investor outrage led to Parliament conducting an inquiry into the matter in December 1720.

All the South Sea Company directors were eventually arrested and their estates seized. The Chancellor of the Exchequer John Aislabie (1670-1742) was found to have accepted £20,000 of South Sea Company stock in exchange for promoting the company. He was expelled from Parliament and forced to resign from the Privy Council after being found guilty of the 'most notorious, dangerous and infamous corruption' before being imprisoned in the Tower of London. Although many other prominent politicians were named and shamed in the parliamentary report, two of them managed to escape conviction for fraud and corruption. The Postmaster General James Craggs the Elder (1657-1721) opted to kill himself to avoid the fallout, and his son, the Secretary of State for the Southern Department, James Craggs the Younger (1686-1721) also avoided being caught up in any scandal by fortuitously contracting smallpox ... falling ill ... and dying off too.

Just to make sure something like this could never happen again, the government passed the Bubble Act 1720 which prohibited the formation of any joint-stock companies unless approved by a royal charter.

the pluckiest of all the plucky brits

The XV Olympic Winter Games in Calgary are remembered more for the heroic failure of the plasterer turned British ski jumper Michael 'Eddie the Eagle' Edwards (1963-) than for any of the medal winners or their achievements.

Having failed as a downhill skier, Eddie had turned his attention to ski jumping mainly because Britain didn't have a ski jumping team so there was no one to compete against him for a place in the Olympic team.

He was a working class lad who'd only been jumping for two years when he rolled up in Calgary, whilst his fellow competitors from Austria, Switzerland and all those other counties with a long tradition of winter sports were all posh and privileged, and had been poncing about on the ski slopes since before they could walk! He had no funding, he used borrowed skis, his helmet was tied in place with string and he wore nerdy supersized specs which would mist up at altitude! The other ski jumpers ridiculed him and the British Olympic Committee thought he was an embarrassment to the team. But against all the odds, Eddie won them over and achieved worldwide fame. But not because he proved them all wrong. There was no fairytale ending to his struggle against the odds; he didn't win a gold medal and he didn't set any world records. In fact, he did the complete opposite, finishing last in both of his events! Eddie had done what British sportsmen do best at a Winter Olympic Games: putting in a plucky performance but getting nowhere near the podium! Nevertheless, he was so enthusiastic and happy-go-lucky about the whole thing that it was impossible not to admire his commitment and showmanship.

On 14 February 1988, in the 'Normal Hill Individual' event, he finished in 58th place with a grand total of only 69.2 points (against a gold medal winning points total of 229.1) and on 23 February 1988, in the 'Large Hill

Individual' event he managed to secure 55th place with 57.5 points (against a gold medal winning points total of 224.0). In both events he had less than half the points of his nearest rivals in 57th and 54th place!

Eddie was so hopelessly bad at ski jumping that the International Olympic Committee changed the qualifying criteria for future competitions to ensure nobody quite as bad as him could compete at the highest level ever again. Needless to say Eddie then failed to qualify for the next three Olympic Games in 1992, 1996 and 2000.

putting two feet on the top of mount everest

The 1953 British Mount Everest Expedition was the ninth British attempt to reach the summit of Mount Everest. And it was ninth time lucky! The expedition was led by the mountaineer/explorer John Hunt (1910-1998) but it was New Zealander Edmond Hilary and Nepalese sherpa Tenzing Norgay who became the first men to set foot on the summit of the world's highest mountain at 11.30am (local time) on 29 May 1953. They stayed there just long enough to admire the view and take a few snapshots. After returning from the summit, Edmond Hilary's first words to a fellow member of the team, George Lowe were: 'Well George, we knocked the bastard off!'

However, there was another man who managed to put two feet on the top of Mount Everest before them …

He was the British army officer Andrew Scott Waugh (1810-1878). In 1852, he was working as the Surveyor General of India when a Bengali mathematician Radhanath Sikdar who was part of the team surveying the Himalayan region, advised him that the mountain known as Peak XV (aka Mount Everest) had been measured and was the highest in the area and therefore probably the highest in the world. The two men checked their calculations again and again before Andrew finally informed the Royal Geographical Society of their findings. The height of Peak XV was originally calculated at exactly 29,000 feet (8,839.2m) but was initially publicised as being 29,002 feet (8,839.8m) high by Andrew to avoid the impression that the exact height was nothing more than just a guess. As a result, he is often credited as being the first person to put two feet on the top of Mount Everest!

Note: In 1856, Andrew Scott Waugh proposed that Peak XV should be named after his predecessor in the job, the esteemed surveyor and geographer George Everett (1790-1866). Although George objected to his name being used for the mountain because it couldn't be written in Hindi and was totally unpronounceable for the Indians, the proposal was eventually accepted by the Royal Geographical Society after a decade of debate with Peak XV finally being officially renamed Mount Everest in 1865.

the hollinwell incident

On 13 July 1980, about 500 children from eleven different marching bands were preparing to take part in a contest at the annual Hollinwell Show being held near Kirkby-in-Ashfield in Nottinghamshire when they suddenly began fainting. At around 10.30am, one or two of the kids collapsed and then they started dropping like flies! In total, around 300 adults and children were affected by this bizarre fainting epidemic with many complaining of headaches, sore throats, dizziness and nausea before falling unconscious. Over 200 casualties were ferried by ambulance to four different local hospitals for treatment. Although most of the victims made a fairly quick recovery, nine of the kids were kept in overnight.

The exact cause of the illness is still disputed. Initial investigations ruled out food poisoning, radio waves, contaminated water supplies and the effects of breathing in pesticides used to spray crops in a nearby field. Many of the young musicians had travelled a long way to the showground, they were tired, it was a hot day and they were probably over-excited and very nervous about performing, so the official inquiry concluded that mass hysteria was most likely the cause. But that doesn't explain why some of the less vulnerable adults and a few babies lying in their prams (who were far too young to be influenced by what was happening around them) also fainted that day too!

The strange events at the Hollinwell Show have continued to baffle the local community. Many have accepted the mass hysteria theory whilst others have continued to argue that their sickness was very real and the reason behind it was something a lot more sinister.

the invasion of sark

In August 1990, the unemployed French nuclear physicist André Gardes attempted to invade the little island of Sark in the Channel Islands. Believing that he was the rightful ruler of its 600-odd inhabitants, he decided to forcefully take control of the island and set himself up as the *Seigneur* or Lord of the Manor. It was probably the stupidest invasion in history!

Unable to convince anyone of his claim to sovereignty, he then launched a one-man invasion of the island. He arrived the night before his planned attack and posted notices all over Sark, advising the residents that he would seize control from noon the following day! Most people thought it was all just a silly joke, but André was deadly serious …

The local constable decided to investigate the threat. On the morning of the invasion, he went looking for the eccentric Frenchman and found him sitting on a park bench dressed in army fatigues and loading his gun! The constable complimented him on his choice of weapon and eventually convinced him to remove the clip and let him examine it further. As soon as he handed it over, the constable punched him on the nose and wrestled him to the ground. He was then taken into custody and eventually kicked off the island.

The invasion was over before it had even begun.

Undeterred, André Gardes then attempted another coup the following year but was intercepted in Guernsey and sent back to France again. His gun is now a permanent exhibit in the island's tiny museum.

indecent exposure

Winston Churchill (1874-1965) is widely regarded as being amongst the most influential people in British history and possibly the greatest Briton of all time. As well as being a politician and statesman, he was also a prolific writer and an accomplished artist, winning the Nobel Prize for Literature in 1953 and producing over 500 works of art. He also enjoyed a spot of bricklaying too. In his spare time he liked nothing better than to build a few brick walls in his back garden!

Winston was the first person to be presented with the Honorary American Citizen award on 9 April 1963 in a ceremony presided over by the US President John F Kennedy. The prize is granted to non-US citizens deemed to be people of exceptional merit warranting honorary citizenship of the USA and to date, only eight people have received the honour.

He was also one of the finest orators of the twentieth century and the undisputed master of the eloquent insult. One of his most famous remarks was aimed at the MP Nancy Astor (1879-1964) when she'd commented, 'If you were my husband, I'd poison your tea' to which he very nonchalantly replied 'Madam, if you were my wife, I'd drink it.' He also had a few less than complimentary remarks to make about his political opponents too, describing Clement Attlee (1883-1967) as 'a modest little man with much to be modest about' and famously claiming that Stafford Cripps (1889-1952) had 'all of the virtues I dislike and none of the vices I admire.' Of Ramsay MacDonald (1866-1937) he once remarked: 'We know that he has, more than any other man, the gift of compressing the largest amount of words into the smallest amount of thought.'

It wasn't just other politicians he quarrelled with, he also seemed to have a long running feud with George Bernard Shaw (1856-1950) too. The Irish playwright had apparently sent him a letter: 'I am enclosing two tickets to the first night of my new play; bring a friend … if you have one' to which Winston had replied: 'Cannot possibly attend first night, will attend second … if there is one.'

Regrettably, his best jibe is most likely apocryphal. Winston had been napping on a train when a woman entered his carriage and noticed that his flies were undone. A little taken aback, she shook him awake and said 'Mr Churchill, your penis is sticking out!' to which he replied, 'Madam, don't flatter yourself. It is merely hanging out.'

black monday

The Hundred Years' War (1337-1453) was a series of intermittent wars between the Kingdoms of England and France during the late-Middle Ages which actually lasted 116 years! It was a war started by England and lost by England, and a war that famously included Henry V (1386-1422) leading his troops to victory at the Battle of Agincourt (1415) and Joan of Arc being burnt at the stake after the Siege of Orléans (1428-1429). It was also a war that featured Edward of Woodstock (1330-1376) (better known as Edward, the Black Prince) in a starring role as England's most successful and chivalrous commander, most notably after his win at the Battle of Poitiers (1356) which earned him his reputation as one of the greatest knights of the age.

The Black Death (1346-1353) also played a big part in the war. The catastrophic global epidemic struck Europe in the mid-fourteenth century … right in the middle of all the fighting! Things got so bad that the war had to be put on hold for a few years because both sides didn't have enough men to be killed on the battlefield as they were all being killed by the plague!

Possibly the strangest event of the Hundred Years' War occurred on Easter Monday, 13 April 1360 when a freak hailstorm resulted in more English casualties than any previous battle! The English army, commanded by Edward III (1312-1377) was camped out in a field outside Chartres in France laying siege to the town. As night fell, a sudden drop in temperature was followed by a lightning storm, freezing rain, high winds and hailstones. One-by-one the soldiers were struck down as they had nowhere to hide or take shelter; the horses scattered across the field in panic, and the tents and baggage trains were torn apart and ended up strewn across the open plains. In just half-an-hour, the hailstones and the intense cold had killed over 1,000 English soldiers and 6,000 horses! It's been said that during the storm, the king had fallen to his knees reciting a vow of peace and pleading with God for mercy.

Edward III was convinced that the storm was a sign from God to make peace with France and so he quickly rushed through the Treaty of Brétigny on 8 May 1360, in which he renounced any claim to the throne of France (in return for sovereignty over Aquitaine and Calais) and agreed to release the French king Jean II who was being held captive in England. This treaty marked the end of the war's first phase, usually referred to as the Edwardian War (1337-1360).

However peace was fairly short-lived with war breaking out again just nine years later with the start of the Caroline War (1369-1389).

the calendar girls

The Rylstone & District Women's Institute started the craze of stripping off and posing nude for a charity calendar.

Their calendar featured twelve sepia-tinted photographs of naked old women engaged in typical Women's Institute activities such as baking, knitting and sewing with their modesty concealed by a few well-placed kitchen utensils, teapots and houseplants! All the women were from the quaint little village of Cracoe in North Yorkshire and the project was originally intended as a light-hearted way of raising funds for the Leukaemia Research Fund. The calendar was conceived by Tricia Stewart, an active member of the Women's Institute who featured as Miss October, and dedicated to John Baker, who died of leukaemia in 1998, and whose wife Angela also featured in the calendar as Miss February. John had enjoyed growing sunflowers and each month's photograph also featured one or two of the flowers with their intense yellow colouring acting as a stark contrast against the bleached, sepia coloured images.

People seemed to want a calendar full of naked old ladies adorning their walls. It was a huge success after selling 88,000 copies in Britain when it was first launched in 1999. Then, in May 2000, a nineteen-month version of the calendar was released which sold over 200,000 copies worldwide! The ensuing public attention brought with it a series of radio and TV interviews, bookstore signings, a US publicity tour and even a movie deal.

the ealdorman of mercia

The Ealdorman of Mercia Eadric Streona (c.990-1017) was one of medieval England's greatest villains!

He was appointed as the Ealdorman in 1007 and then married Edith, the daughter of Æthelred II (Æthelred the Unready) (c.968-1016) in 1009. Acting as the king's chief adviser, he had his finger in every pie and played an important role in the affairs of the kingdom, enforcing the king's will, quashing any rebellious noblemen, and advising on policy matters such as the payment of *Danegeld* to the Vikings. As a perk of the job, he helped himself to church land, appropriated their funds and generally acted the part of the tyrant.

He was also the go-between and the king's chief negotiator with the Danes but spectacularly failed to win the release of the Archbishop of Canterbury Ælfheah (c.953-1012) after he was kidnapped and held to ransom during the Siege of Canterbury (1011). Not only did they collect the payoff, they held onto him for months afterwards and then just killed him anyway! But knowing Eadric's reputation as a ruthless, cold-hearted bastard, he probably didn't give two shits anyway!

Only Æthelred seemed to have any faith in him and only Æthelred seemed to like him. The medieval chronicler, John of Worcester described him in *Chronicon ex Chronicis* (c.1130) as '… a man [who] surpassed all his contemporaries in malice and perfidy, as well as in pride and cruelty' and that other great English historian William of Malmesbury (c.1095-1143) said of him: 'This fellow was the refuse of mankind, the reproach of the English; an abandoned glutton, a cunning miscreant; who had become opulent, not by nobility [but] by specious language and impudence.'

Eadric was most famous for his traitorous actions during the Danish conquest of England in 1016 …

The Danish prince Cnut (994-1035) arrived with an army of 10,000 men in 200 longships and had set out to conquer England once and for all. Æthelred was completely unprepared. He'd been unable to deal with the Viking threat in the past and it didn't look like he was going to have much luck this time either. His court was deeply divided with Eadric wanting to negotiate with the invaders and his hothead son Edmund Ironside (c.990-1016) champing at the bit to kick their arses all the way back to Denmark!

What happened next was fairly predictable …

Eadric defected to the Vikings and Edmund tried unsuccessfully to halt the invading army's advance through Wessex and Mercia.

Then the Saxons caught a break. Æthelred died and Edmund became king. He turned out to be the inspirational leader the Saxons needed and it wasn't long before their armies were having a bit of success on the battlefield. They were only small victories which hardly altered the course of the war, but at least they seemed to halt the enemy's advance. By now, Edmund was being hailed as the new Alfred the Great (c.849-899) prompting the slippery, cowardly and opportunistic Eadric to change sides again and fight alongside the Saxons. But Edmund really needed to inflict one big defeat on Cnut and his army if he wanted to win this thing once and for all and drive the Vikings out of England …

The Battle of Assandun (1016) definitely took place in Essex but nobody is quite sure exactly where, although Ashdon in the north or Ashingdon in the south of the county seem like the two most probable locations. There was no *Bayeux Tapestry* or any other pretty little paintings of this battle, so nobody really knows how it unfolded, although most contemporary accounts of the battle agreed that the Vikings won, the Saxons suffered heavy casualties, Edmund ran away to Wales and … yep, you've guessed it … Eadric Streona changed sides again!

The pro-Viking account of events in *Encomium Emmae Reginae* (c.1041), which was written in honour of Cnut's future queen Emma of Normandy (c.984-1052), claimed that 'all the best of the English nation' fell in battle that day, and the pro-Saxon account of things in the *Anglo-Saxon Chronicle* noted Eadric's betrayal, even suggesting that the beginning of the end for the Saxons came when he and his men deserted the battlefield: 'Then Eadric the Ealdorman did as had so often done before, and first began the flight with the Maisevethians, and so betrayed his king and lord and all the

English nation. There Cnut had the victory, though all England fought against him.'

Cnut had followed Edmund westwards and caught up with him somewhere in the Forest of Dean. There may have been one further battle after which the two kings decided to negotiate a peace. It was agreed that Edmund could keep Wessex but Cnut could rule over the rest of England, and when one of them died, the other would become king of the whole country.

Just over a month later on 30 November 1016, Edmund died and Cnut became the new undisputed king of all England. He may have died from wounds sustained in battle, he may have been poisoned or, as the medieval scholar and historian Henry of Huntingdon (c.1088-1157) claimed in *Historia Anglorum* (c.1154), he may have been impaled from below with a spike when sitting on the toilet! According to him, Edmund was stabbed twice with a sharp dagger by someone hiding in the cesspit below him, who then made their escape leaving 'the weapon fixed in his bowls.'

Although Cnut was never directly implicated in Edmund's death, speculation was rife that he'd given the order to have him killed.

Meanwhile, Eadric had sworn allegiance to the new Viking king and was promising to serve him just as he'd served the Saxon kings before him. But Cnut knew perfectly well that he wasn't to be trusted because he hadn't fought faithfully for anyone during the war. Cnut had respected Edmund Ironside for his leadership and courage, even laying a wreath at his tomb, so he wasn't all that impressed watching Eadric, a man whose character traits were the complete opposite of those he admired in a man like Edmund, still living the good life and going about his business without a care in the world. Eadric's promise to serve him as he'd served Æthelred and Edmund certainly wouldn't have persuaded him to change his opinion of him!

According to *Encomium Emmae Reginae,* Eadric was invited to the Tower of London on Christmas Day in 1017. Then, during the festivities Cnut quite unexpectedly gave the order to have Eadric killed after accusing him of being 'deceitful, and to have hesitated between the two sides with fraudulent tergiversation.' His head was hacked off and his body was just dumped over the palace walls and left unburied. The severed head was then 'placed upon a pole on the highest battlement of the Tower of London' for all to see.

standard time

It wasn't until 2 August 1880 when all the clocks in Britain showed the same time!

In the early-nineteenth century most people still relied on the position of the Sun in the sky to tell the time. This was called Local Mean Time (LMT) and varied across the country from east to west, meaning that some towns and cities had different times to others. Just because it was midday in London, it didn't necessarily mean that it was midday everywhere else! In fact, LMT in Plymouth was about 16½ minutes behind LMT in London!

These local time differences were of little importance to most people as travel and communication were so slow. Journey times by coach between the larger towns and cities could take many hours or even days, so nobody really cared if they arrived a few minutes sooner or a few minutes later than when they were supposed to. People overcame the time differences by adjusting their pocket watches accordingly but as most people didn't have a pocket watch to adjust it was even less of a problem than you might think!

But then someone invented the railways and these local time differences suddenly became a bit inconvenient. It soon became apparent that even tiny discrepancies in the time could cause confusion, disruption and even accidents.

A nationwide time was first introduced by the Great Western Railway (GWR) (1833-1948) in 1840 and quickly became known as 'Railway Time'. Train timetables and station clocks across the GWR network were all brought into line with Greenwich Mean Time (GMT) or 'London Time' as it was more commonly known. This was the first recorded occasion when different local times were synchronised and a single standard time applied across the whole country. Now, if it was midday in London, it was also midday in other places along the GWR network like Bristol and Bath.

Other railway companies soon followed the GWR's lead and adopted GMT ... but other railway companies did not. On those lines where they continued using local times, trains travelling east to west still appeared to be travelling slower than when they were travelling in the opposite direction! These time differences caused scheduling problems with travellers often missing their connections and forcing some companies to install public clocks in their stations with two minute hands! One set to local time and the other set to GMT.

With the growth of the railway network and its importance to the economic prosperity and the social life of the nation, Railway Time soon extended far beyond the railways and by 1855 it was estimated that 98 percent of the public clocks in Great Britain and Ireland had been set to display GMT. However, it wasn't until the Statutes (Definition of Time) Act 1880 became law that all clocks in the British Isles were obliged to display the same standard time, putting an end to time travel in Britain forever!

the ancient scorton silver arrow

The Ancient Scorton Silver Arrow Tournament is the world's longest established non-equine sporting event. The competition is named after the village of Scorton in North Yorkshire where the competition involving England's finest archers first took place on 14 May 1673.

Targets are placed at a distance of 100 yards (91m) from the archer and the winner or 'Captain of the Arrow' is the first gentleman to hit the target's centre black spot which, even to this day, is still set 'at about the height of a Frenchman's heart'. It's unclear if French soldiers in the seventeenth century were any shorter or taller than their English counterparts but it was probably the case that a gentleman's aim would have been improved if he was seduced into thinking that the target was a Frenchman! The tournament winner is then expected to organise the following year's event, assisted in his task by the 'Lieutenant of the Arrow' or the first competitor to have hit the target's red band.

The Ancient Scorton Silver Arrow Tournament is one of the few sporting fixtures where the competitors are trusted to mark their own scorecards. Only gentlemen may enter the competition, so there's no need for any independent checks because gentlemen don't cheat. Right? That may well be the case but it's still a little suspicious that the first recorded winner just happened to be the same guy who donated the prized silver arrow trophy, a gentleman archer from Eryholme in North Yorkshire called Henry Calverley (1641-1684).

spaghetti trees

'Spaghetti Trees' was the name for a three-minute spoof report broadcast on April Fools' Day in 1957 as part of the BBC's flagship current affairs show *Panorama* which purportedly showed women in Switzerland harvesting strands of spaghetti from trees and laying them out in the sun to dry. It was narrated by Richard Dimbleby (1913-1965), an authoritative and well-respected journalist usually associated with more serious and much weightier projects. He began his commentary by informing the viewers how the end of March was a particularly worrying time for Europe's spaghetti farmers as a severe frost could impair the flavour of the pasta and drive down prices but ended his report on a more upbeat note with the news that the recent mild winter and the virtual disappearance of a pasta eating parasite called the Spaghetti Weevil had led to a good harvest that year. The report seemed credible due to the involvement of such a distinguished journalist and because pasta was relatively unknown in Britain at that time. Very few people seemed to know that it didn't grow on trees because after the show had aired, the BBC were inundated with calls from people asking where they could buy a spaghetti tree!

This April Fools' Day joke is thought to be the first of its kind to be televised and has been called 'the biggest hoax that any reputable news establishment ever pulled' by CNN.

WASHING THE LIONS

On 2 April 1698, the *Dawks's News-Letter* reported: 'Yesterday being the first of April, several persons were sent to the Tower Ditch to see the Lions washed.' This was the earliest recorded reference to the oldest known and longest running April Fools' Day joke. It seems that the unsuspecting victims had been invited to attend something called the 'Annual Ceremony of the Washing of the Lions' at the Royal Menagerie in the Tower of London. Although there were lions kept in the Tower back then as part of the monarch's private collection of exotic animals, there certainly wasn't any ceremony to watch them getting a bath in the castle's moat!

The joke was such a success that it was repeated again in 1848, 1856 and 1861.

The English author Gustave Louis Maurice Strauss (c.1807-1887) related his part in organising the 1848 prank in his autobiography *Reminiscences of an Old Bohemian* (1882): '[We] had a great number of order-cards printed, admitting "bearer and friends" to the White Tower, on the 1st day of April, to witness ... the famous grand annual ceremony.' There was pandemonium when hundreds of people turned up only to realise they'd been tricked: 'In the midst of the turmoil someone spotted me to whom I had given an order of admission, and he would have set the whole mob upon me. Knowing of old that discretion is, as a rule, the better part of valour ... I had to skedaddle, and keep dark for a time, until the affair had blown over a little.'

a damn good thrashing

The first round Scottish FA Cup tie between Arbroath FC and Bon Accord FC played at Gayfield Park, Arbroath on 12 September 1885 ended in a 36-0 win for the home team and the biggest margin of victory ever recorded in any professional football match.

Arbroath were already 15-0 up against Bon Accord FC by half-time and then scored another 21 goals in the second half. It's been claimed that their goalkeeper Jim Milne (1855-1919) didn't actually touch the ball in the entire game and spent most of his time sheltering from the rain under an umbrella lent to him by a spectator! The *Scottish Athletic Journal* later reported: 'The leather was landed between the posts forty-one times, but five of the times were disallowed. Here and there, enthusiasts would be seen with scoring sheet and pencil in hand, taking note of the goals as one would score runs at a cricket match.'

There were no goal nets back then and many people thought the scoreline could have been even higher if they hadn't wasted so much time retrieving the ball after every goal. The Arbroath striker Jocky Petrie (1867-1932) scored 13 goals and unsurprisingly still holds the British record for the most goals scored by one player in any senior football game.

Note: Coincidentally, on the same day, Dundee Harp FC were involved in an equally bizarre one-sided SFA Cup game after beating local rivals Aberdeen Rovers FC 35-0. The referee had actually recorded a score of 37-0 but this was disputed by the Dundee Harp club secretary after the game when he claimed that his side had only scored 35 goals. Presumably, he thought he was being awfully sporting about the whole thing, but as it turned out, he should have just kept his big mouth shut because his goody-two-shoes attitude cost his team a place in the record books! The referee acknowledged that it had been very difficult for him to keep an accurate score with such a deluge of goals and quickly accepted the lower 35-0 scoreline before wiring the result to the Scottish Football Association's HQ in Glasgow.

the ride to york

John Nevison (1639-1684) was a gentleman highwayman. He was tall, charming and a bit of a dandy; always very polite, rarely violent and only robbed from the rich.

He's most famous for an epic horse ride across England in 1676 which has often been erroneously attributed to another highwayman, Dick Turpin (1705-1739). One summer's day, early in the morning, he robbed a traveller at Gad's Hill in Kent. Realising that he'd been recognised, he immediately set off on his horse to ride all the way to York. He rode through Chelmsford, Cambridge and Huntingdon and then along the Great North Road, stopping only to rest his horse for short periods. After arriving in York at the end of his 200-mile (322km) dash, he stabled his exhausted horse and found himself lodgings for the night. After a quick wash and change of clothes, he then walked into the town centre where he'd been told the Lord Mayor was playing a game of bowls. He then made a point of striking up a conversation with him and at around 8.00pm he even placed a bet on the match. He was very loud and boisterous, leaving no one in any doubt of his presence at the bowling green.

John was later arrested for the robbery in Kent but after the Lord Mayor of York provided him with an alibi, all charges against him were dropped as the authorities mistakenly believed it was impossible for anyone to ride from Kent to York in one day. He'd got away with it but then started blabbing about his little adventure to anyone who'd listen. Charles II (1630-1685) got to hear about it and summoned John to the palace. On asking him how he'd managed to accomplish such a journey on one horse in less than a day, John replied that he'd ridden so ferociously that even the Devil himself 'Old Nick' couldn't have caught him. The king was so impressed by the audacious rogue standing before him that he nicknamed him 'Swift Nick' and upheld his pardon!

John Nevison was arrested and imprisoned several times during his long and undistinguished career as a highwayman but he always managed to escape his captors. In 1674, he broke out of Wakefield Prison; in 1676, he reportedly jumped from a prison ship, and in 1684, he famously escaped from prison in Leicester after an accomplice masquerading as a doctor pronounced him dead from the plague. Nobody would have wanted to go near his body to double-check the diagnosis for fear of being infected themselves, so his body was packed into a coffin and carried out of the prison as quickly as possible. Needless to say, he soon took up his thieving ways again, and many people were convinced they'd been robbed by a ghost! However, his luck finally ran out when he was apprehended on 6 March 1684 at the Magpie Inn in Sandal near Wakefield after being betrayed by the landlady.

His execution was never in any doubt and he was hanged on 4 May 1684.

the man who stole the crown jewels

The Irish trickster and self-styled colonel, Thomas Blood (1618-1680), spent most of his early life in England. He fought on the side of the Royalists when the English Civil War (1642-1651) began, but when it became clear he was fighting for the losing side, he switched his allegiance to the Parliamentarians. After the war, he was made a Justice of the Peace and gifted a big chunk of land in Ireland as a reward for his services, but after the Restoration (1660) he was identified as a Cromwellian supporter and that land was then confiscated under the Poor Relief Act 1662. Thomas then fled back to the old country and hatched a plan with a few other likeminded anti-British rebels to storm

Dublin Castle, overpower the government and kidnap the Lord Lieutenant of Ireland James Butler, 1st Duke of Ormond (1610-1688). But their dastardly plan was discovered and Thomas made his escape to the Netherlands. He didn't return to England again until 1670 when he set himself up as a physician called Dr Thomas Alyliffe in Romford, Essex, despite having no medical training whatsoever!

After another unsuccessful attempt to kidnap the poor old Duke of Ormand, Thomas then turned his attention to a new get-rich-quick scheme. The theft of the Crown Jewels ...

He disguised himself as a clergyman and visited the Tower of London along with an accomplice who played the part of his wife, where he met Talbot Edwards, the 75 year-old ex-soldier and Keeper of the Jewels, who lived with his family in an apartment above the basement room where the Crown Jewels were stored. Over time, Thomas and his wife met frequently with the Edwards family and they became good friends. Talbot was delighted when Thomas then proposed a meeting between his wealthy (but non-existent) nephew and his new friend's pretty daughter ...

On 9 May 1671, Thomas arrived at the Tower with his so-called nephew (who was actually his son) and two other men. Whilst the nephew and the daughter were supposedly getting to know each other better, Thomas expressed a wish to see the Crown Jewels. Of course, Talbot was only too happy to oblige and led the three men downstairs but after unlocking the door, Thomas threw a cloak over his head, struck him with a mallet to subdue him and then stabbed him with his sword to subdue him even further. And then he just helped himself to the precious royal regalia. The crown was flattened with the mallet and shoved into a bag; he stuffed the orb down his breeches, and then tried to saw the sceptre in half because it was too long to fit in his bag! At which point, Talbot suddenly regained consciousness and started yelling 'Murder! Treason! The Crown is stolen!' The sceptre was abandoned and Thomas and his accomplices tried to make their escape. But they didn't get very far as they were arrested by the wardens attempting to leave the Tower.

In custody, Thomas refused to answer any questions, telling his captors that he'd answer only to the king. He knew that Charles II (1630-1685) had a reputation for liking rogues and scoundrels, and reckoned that he could use his Irish charm to escape punishment. He wasn't wrong either! The king was amused by his audacity after he'd claimed that the Crown Jewels were only worth around £6,000 instead of the £100,000 they were valued at. Not only did the king spare him his life, he also awarded him another huge chunk of land in Ireland! So much for crime not paying!

Thomas soon became a familiar figure around London and a frequent visitor at court. Meanwhile, Talbot Edwards, having recovered from his injuries, was also rewarded by the king and then continued his work at the Tower of London, regaling visitors with stories about the attempted theft and his part in foiling it.

the welsh not

The Welsh Not was a piece of wood or lead often inscribed with the letters 'WN' which was hung around the neck of the first schoolkid heard speaking Welsh at the start of the day. It was then passed along to the next kid who spoke Welsh, and so on and so on until whoever was in possession of it at hometime got a damn good thrashing from their teacher! Although the Welsh Not was thought to have been used in Welsh schools as early as the eighteenth century, incidents of its use increased considerably in the decade after the British government appeared to endorse the findings outlined in the *Reports of the Commissioners of Enquiry into the State of Education in Wales* (1847).

The parliamentary report was published in three large, blue-coloured books and outlined the findings of a government inquiry into Welsh schools and the general standard of education in the country. The report ('Blue Books') concluded that the schools were inadequate and the Welsh people were generally ignorant, lazy and immoral because they had the audacity to speak Welsh! 'The Welsh language is a vast drawback to Wales, and a manifold barrier to the moral progress and commercial prosperity of the people. It is not easy to over-estimate its evil effects … It disserves the people from intercourse which would greatly advance their civilisation, and bars the access of improving knowledge to their minds. As a proof of this, there is no Welsh literature worthy of the name.'

Blimey!

the time travellers party

Stephen Hawking (1942-2018) was a leading theoretical physicist/cosmologist and the greatest scientist of his generation, best known to the public for his bestselling book *A Brief History of Time* (1988) in which he tackled everything from the origins of the universe to the possibility of time travel and the mystery of black holes.

On 28 June 2009, he famously held a party at the Gonville & Caius College (University of Cambridge) for time travellers!

He decorated a room with balloons and laid on some Champagne and a few nibbles … and then waited patiently for his guests to arrive …

The invitations read, *You are cordially invited to a reception for Time Travellers* and included the date, time and even the coordinates for the event. But they weren't actually sent out until the following day so only someone from the future would be able to attend. Stephen waited in the room for a couple of hours but unfortunately nobody turned up and he was forced to admit that time travel wasn't possible.

But maybe travelling back in time creates a parallel timeline that has no impact on the original, the invitations were all lost or destroyed, or, for whatever reason, the time travellers decided not to attend?

Of course, it's also entirely possible that someone might still turn up …

the shipwrecked football team

Raith Rovers FC finished the 1922-1923 season in third place behind Celtic and Rangers in Scottish Division One. It was their highest ever finish and as a reward the club splashed the cash for a post-season tour of the Canary Islands.

Thirteen players, five club officials and the team manager James Logan (1885-1961) boarded the steamer *Highland Loch* at Tilbury in Essex. The service was operated by the Nelson Line Steam Navigation Company (1880-1932) and ran between London and Buenos Aires with the players due to disembark at Vigo in Spain where they would watch a bullfight and stay overnight whilst the ship was replenished, before continuing their journey to Las Palmas in the Canary Islands.

The voyage was literally plain sailing until the *Highland Loch* rounded Cape Finisterre into the Bay of Biscay on 1 July 1923 …

The ship had sailed headlong into a violent storm and the wind, rain and high waves sent it crashing onto rocks. It was early on a Sunday morning and many of the passengers were still in their PJs when they were ordered to grab their lifejackets and abandon ship. The players demonstrated remarkable composure and bravery and helped ensure the strict maritime tradition of 'women and children first' was adhered to before abandoning ship themselves. In fact, they were amongst the last passengers to leave the *Highland Loch.*

Spanish fishermen helped in the rescue and towed the lifeboats into various ports along the coast.

A few of the players were separated from the rest of their team and ended up in a tiny village after five hours at sea where nobody spoke a word of English and nobody could offer them any help, so they had to set off again in a motorboat to reach the port of Vilagarcia de Arousa further along the coast where the rest of the team had gone ashore.

After contacting the Nelson Line agent, the players were told to take a train to Vigo where they would be met by the company's representative who would arrange alternative transport for them. Amazingly, the first ship they saw sitting in the harbour when they arrived was the bloody *Highland Loch*. The ship had been badly damaged but the crew had somehow managed to refloat it and reach the harbour. So, abandoning ship and embarking on a long hazardous lifeboat journey and then ending up disorientated and starving hungry in the middle of nowhere in a foreign land had all been a gigantic waste of time. They could have just as easily stayed onboard!

The passengers were eventually ferried out to the ship by motor launch and allowed to go aboard to retrieve their belongings with the players managing to rescue most of their luggage and the chests containing their football kits.

The following day everyone boarded the steamer *Darrow* which took them on the rest of their journey to Las Palmas. According to the Rovers player Tom Jennings (1902-1973) their party was invited to dine at the captain's table as a reward for their bravery during the evacuation of the *Highland Loch*.

A few days later than expected, they finally made it to their destination. Their traumatic experience at sea didn't seem to affect the players too much as they went on to win all of their matches.

To this day, Raith Rovers FC remains the only football team ever to be shipwrecked!

mr winstanley's lighthouse

The first Eddystone lighthouse, known as *Winstanley's Tower* was constructed on a small rock in the open sea near Plymouth in 1698 by the English engineer and showman Henry Winstanley (1644-1703), who was more famous at the time for his Winstanley's Water-works aquatic and pyrotechnics show which was one of London's most popular attractions.

Construction on the wooden, 120-foot (36.5-metre) tall octagonal tower began on 14 July 1696 and took two years to complete. Due to the treacherous seas, work was only possible during the summer months, with the materials and workmen being ferried out to the site from Plymouth on a boat every day. For the first few months, it wasn't even possible to leave all the construction materials overnight on the rock because they'd be washed away! As Britain was at war with France at the time, the government positioned a warship near the rocks on the days when construction was taking place, such was the importance of the Henry's lighthouse. One day in June 1697, however, the British warship didn't turn up but a French one did and Henry was whisked away to France against his will. But when the French king Louis XIV heard of Henry's abduction, he immediately ordered his release after recognising the importance of the lighthouse, claiming that 'France was at war with England, not with humanity.'

The first candles were lit by Henry on 14 November 1698 … but then the weather turned nasty and he was stuck on the rock for another five weeks. He almost starved to death before finally being rescued!

Henry undertook some much-needed improvements to his tower in the summer of 1699; bolstering the foundation, raising its height, and even enhancing its look by adding some fancy ornamental features. It looked more like a fairground helter-skelter now than a lighthouse! From an architectural perspective, it looked very elegant but from an engineering point of view, the seamen of Devon never really believed that it would last very long. However, Henry dismissed their concerns claiming that he was 'so very well assured of the strength of his building' and hoped to be inside it when 'the greatest storm that ever blew under the face of the heavens' hit the rock so 'he might see what effect it would have upon the structure.'

It wasn't long before he got his wish …

From 26 November until 29 November 1703, high winds and heavy rain caused extensive damage and prolonged flooding across central and southern England; windmills were destroyed; chimney stacks were blown down; 4,000 oak trees in the New Forest were lost, and at sea, hundreds of ships were blown off course or wrecked with the loss of many thousands of lives. It has been estimated that between 8,000 and 15,000 people were killed. The Royal Navy alone lost thirteen ships and upwards of 1,500 men drowned. The Great Storm of 1703 was unprecedented in its ferocity and duration; the Church of England declared that it was God's vengeance for the sins of the nation and it subsequently remained a topic of moralising in sermons well into the next century. As an act of atonement, the government later declared 19 January 1704 as a day of fasting, saying that it 'loudly calls for the deepest and most solemn humiliation of our people.' The novelist Daniel Defoe (1660-1731) described the storm as 'the Greatest, the Longest in Duration, the widest in Extent, of all the Tempests and Storms that History give any Account of since the Beginning of Time' and firmly believed it was a divine punishment for the country's poor performance against the Catholic armies in the War of the Spanish Succession (1701-1714). He compiled a collection of around sixty first-hand accounts of the storm after placing adverts in the newspapers, asking people to send him their recollections of the terrible event. It was an innovative method of collating reliable information and opinion, occurring long before first-hand reports from the public became commonplace and for this reason *The Storm* (1703) is often referred to as the first substantial work of journalism.

Just before the storm hit, Henry had arrived at the lighthouse to carry out a few repairs and had then found himself stranded on the Eddystone Rock as the fierce winds raged around him. Exactly as he'd wished for. Unfortunately for him, however, it turned out to be his dying wish! On the last night of high winds on 27 November 1703, Henry, five workmen, and the lighthouse keeper and his family along with the lighthouse itself were all blown away … never to be seen again!

the field of the cloth of gold

The biggest pissing contest in history!

On 7 June 1520, two young kings, Henry VIII of England (1491-1547) and Francis I of France began a momentous eighteen-day summit full of pomp and ceremony in a specially landscaped valley near the town of Balinghem in France in an effort to strengthen the friendly and peaceful relations between the two countries following the signing of the Treaty of London (1518). The lavish event was the brainchild of the Lord Chancellor Cardinal Thomas Wolsey (1473-1530) and was designed to be a grand festival of entertainment, religious ceremony, feasting and sport.

It also turned out to be the perfect opportunity for each king to try and outdo the other by dominating proceedings with crass displays of extravagance and wealth. They both set up huge camps to house the royal courts and organised lavish banquets, music shows, games, archery displays, wrestling matches and jousting contests. The meeting was so named because of the many tents and pavilions which were made from a cloth of gold (an expensive fabric woven with silk and gold thread). The clothing worn by the estimated 10,000 guests was equally as opulent, made from delicate materials and decorated with gold and exquisite jewels.

The most lavish facilities were obviously reserved for the two kings. Henry had an army of 6,000 workers build him his own temporary palace covering an area of 12,000 sq yards (10,000 m^2) made from timber and covered with a canvas painted to resemble real stone. The palace was constructed in four blocks with huge stained glass windows and a central courtyard. It was decorated with the most sumptuous fashions and furnished with a profusion of gold ornaments, carvings and paintings. There were even two ornate fountains at the entrance which flowed with wine!

Henry also brought with him two royal monkeys to entertain his guests which were a present from the ruler of the Ottoman Empire, Sultan Selim I. They were a big hit with his opposite number with Thomas Wolsey recounting: 'The French king was overcome with much curiosity, playing with those little knaves that did all they could to steal and pester his advisers, yet he willed them to be present at ever banquet.'

When the kings competed in the tournaments themselves, their advisers were astute enough to have them competing on the same side. No point in going to all that time and expense of arranging such a festival, if the two protagonists were then going to declare war on each other because one of them lost a jousting match! Having said that, the boisterousness of the occasion did prompt a pissed-up Henry to challenge Francis to a wrestling match. 'Brother, let us wrestle!' he announced with great bravado. They grappled only briefly before Francis overthrew Henry with a fancy, rapidly executed hip throw known as the *Tour de Bretayne*. According to the Irish novelist/literary critic Francis Hackett (1883-1962) in his book *Henry the Eighth* (1929), the English king was said to be 'purple with rage' when stumbling to his feet again after having been so easily beaten. He was a man who was so confident of his masculinity, his strength and dexterity, and to be humiliated in front of everyone must have left him feeling like a bit of a dick.

The summit had been a great success. Following a religious service presided over by Thomas Wolsey the festivities came to an end on 24 June 1520, presents were exchanged and after a final banquet, the two kings departed as the best of friends.

Then, less than two years later, the two countries and the same two kings were at war!

Henry had joined forces with Charles V (who seemed to be the Billy Big Bollocks of most of Europe at that time, holding the titles of Emperor, Archduke, King and Lord in the Holy Roman Empire, Austria, Spain and the Netherlands) against Francis in the Italian War (1521-1526). Maybe, Henry had never really gotten over that wrestling match?

very british people

THE BUNGEE JUMPER

David Kirke (1945-2023) was a member of the Oxford University's Dangerous Sports Club and made the world's first recognised bungee jump from the Clifton Suspension Bridge (Bristol) on 1 April 1979 wearing a top hat and tails, and clutching a bottle of Champagne! He later commented: 'We hadn't tested it, or anything like that. We were called the Dangerous Sports Club, and testing it first wouldn't have been particularly dangerous!'

THE WORLD'S MOST ENTHUSIASTIC AUTOGRAPH HUNTER

Tommy Scullion (1924-1996) collected over 40,000 autographs of popes, dictators, murderers, royalty, politicians, artists, Nobel Prize winners and the usual assortment of movie stars, singers, sporting superstars and celebrities, which he kept in various old shoe boxes at his home in the village of Broughshane in Co. Antrim. Some of the more famous and infamous people who offered up their autographs were Pablo Picasso, Robert Kennedy, Martin Luther King, Pope John Paul II, Charles Manson, Grace Kelly and the 'Napalm Girl' Phan Thi Kim Phuc.

He started collecting autographs after leaving school when he was only 15 years-old. He wrote about twenty-five letters a week to the famous people of the day, scouring newspapers and magazines for their names, and then firing off a request for an autograph. He only made a half-hearted attempt to catalogue them but whilst his filing system might have left a lot to be desired, his enthusiasm for the task in hand never faltered. For example, not content with getting the autograph of the ex-sportsman O J Simpson during his murder trial in 1995, he also collected autographs from all the lawyers on the defence and prosecution teams too!

When he passed away in 1996, he left a will bequeathing his collection to the village museum. Which was all very well and good but it left his family with a bit of a dilemma because the village didn't have a museum!

THE MOLE MAN OF HACKNEY

William Lyttle (1931-2010) lived in a four-storey, twenty-room Victorian mansion at 121 Mortimer Road, Hackney in London. Sometime in the early-1960s he started digging holes under his house and over a period of four decades he succeeded in excavating a network of tunnels and caverns that extended up to 65 feet (20m) in all directions. Although the neighbours had frequently complained to the local council about the noise, they didn't act until 2006 when a double-decker bus fell into a sink hole that had opened up outside his house.

The council ordered William to stop his illegal digging and then obtained a court order to evict him whilst their engineers moved in to assess the damage.

The tunnels had to be filled in with cement to prevent his house and all the other houses in the street from collapsing. As well as being a committed tunneller, it seems that William was also a committed hoarder because the council first had to remove around 40 tons of excavated gravel, household refuse and other assorted junk (including four cars, a boat, old TV sets, refrigerators and bathtubs) from his back yard before the cement trucks could move in.

When asked by journalists why he'd done what he'd done, William explained that his 'home improvements' had all started when he'd dug himself a wine cellar. And then he'd just kept on digging because he'd always fancied a big basement!

William was put-up in a hotel for a couple of years before being moved into another council-owned flat. As a precautionary measure his new home was in a tower block … on the top floor!

the source of the nile

Much like finding the illusive North West Passage, Victorian explorers were equally as obsessed with finding the source of Africa's longest river, the River Nile. There were many famous names who tried their luck but it was the British Indian Army officer John Hanning Speke (1827-1864) who finally discovered the source on 30 July 1858.

In 1856, he set off for East Africa with fellow explorer Richard Burton (1821-1890) in an expedition financed by the Royal Geographical Society initially with the aim of exploring the Great Lakes but with the hope of finding the source of the River Nile too.

Their journey began in Zanzibar in June 1857 and after an arduous 600-mile (965 km) trek inland, with both men succumbing to various nasty diseases along the way, they finally reached the settlement of Kazeh in Tanzania. By then, Richard was gravely ill and John was rapidly going blind! Nevertheless, the two men struggled on, even deeper into the interior of Africa, and arrived in the town of Ujiji becoming the first Europeans to reach Lake Tanganyika. Although John couldn't actually see very much of it because of his failing eyesight!

The lake was vast, over 400 miles (644 km) long from north to south, nevertheless they decided to explore as much of it as they could. But first they had to get hold of a bigger boat. There were only small canoes available to them and they were no bloody use to anyone. John opted to make the short 30-mile (48 km) hop across to the western side of the lake where the Arabs had settled, hoping to buy a larger boat from them whilst Richard remained at the base camp. By now, he was too sick to go anywhere! However, halfway across the lake, John was marooned on an island for a short time and whilst there a beetle crawled into his ear. After foolishly trying to remove it with a knife, he became temporarily deaf. Now the poor bugger was half blind and half deaf too! As if things couldn't get any worse, when he finally reached the lake's western side, the Arabs refused to sell him any of their boats.

As a consequence, the two men were prevented from exploring the lake any further and were forced to start making their way back to Kazeh. They'd been told of a second Great Lake lying to the north-east of the town and John wanted to try and explore that one instead. Richard was too sick to continue and so he went off on the 47-day, 452-mile (727 km) round trip without him. On 30 July 1858, he finally got his reward, sighting Lake Victoria and becoming the first European to map the area and discover the source of the River Nile.

The two men were never pals. John was more of a leader and Richard more of an explorer. They never really got on that well and their relationship deteriorated even further once it became clear that John might have found the source of the River Nile without Richard. After returning to Zanzibar, they travelled by ship to Aden and then John continued on to England alone, as Richard was still struggling with his health. He arrived back in Blighty on 8 May 1859 and immediately started blabbing about their discovery, even though Richard later claimed that they'd agreed to make any announcement together. At which point, Richard got his revenge by announcing that there wasn't any definitive proof that Lake Victoria was the source of the Nile and that it was more likely to be Lake Tanganyika. The bad feeling between the two men was fuelled even further by their respective circle of friends and various rival newspapers squabbling about who was right and who was wrong.

John was then chosen by the Royal Geographical Society to lead a second expedition to Africa to gain the actual proof of where the River Nile began.

He departed for Africa again on 27 April 1860, this time with the explorer James Augustus Grant (1827-1892). However, the expedition was constantly delayed and they didn't actually reach Lake Victoria until 28 July 1862. There was an atmosphere of distrust towards any foreigners in Africa at that time due to the many Arab slave traders operating in the region and the expedition was constantly having to bribe local tribes and negotiate a passage through their territories. They travelled north around the western side of the lake until they discovered the River Nile and a waterfall which John later named Ripon Falls after the Royal Geographical Society president George Robinson, 1st Marquess of Ripon (1827-1909). By January of the following year, the two men had begun mapping the river northwards but were unable to follow it for their whole journey to Gondokoro in Southern Sudan because of travel restrictions, angry slave traders, local wars and the difficulty of the terrain. They then continued to Khartoum and John sent a telegram to the Royal Geographical Society in London stating: 'The Nile is settled.'

But not according to Richard Burton. He argued that John hadn't followed the river for its entirety and so he couldn't be absolutely sure of his findings. He was relentless in his criticism and a very good public speaker, so he was easily able to convince others that he was the person they should believe. A debate was arranged between the two men for 16 September 1864 but John managed to shoot himself in the neck the day before and then died from his injuries! It was a simple hunting accident although many at the time suspected suicide. Never one to miss an opportunity to slag off his old sparring partner, even when he was dead, Richard was vocal in spreading the suicide rumour, claiming that John had feared their debate!

It was down to the explorer Henry Morton Stanley (1841-1904) to finally settle the dispute. A few years later, he took a boat trip along the Lake Victoria shoreline and discovered that the River Nile did indeed flow from Lake Victoria via the Ripon Falls and from there northwards to Gondokoro proving John Hanning Speake's theory to be correct and Richard Burton's alternative Lake Tanganyika theory to be total bollocks!

the cottingley fairies

Elsie Wright (1901-1988) (16) and Frances Griffiths (1907-1986) (9) were young cousins and would often play together beside a stream at the bottom of the garden at Elsie's house in the village of Cottingley near Bradford.

On one particular occasion in the summer of 1917, Elsie returned home soaking wet. After her mother demanded to know why she looked so bedraggled, Elsie claimed that she'd fallen in the stream when they'd been playing with fairies! Her mother didn't believe a word of it of course, so the girls headed off back to the stream to take a photograph of the fairies to prove that Elsie had been telling the truth.

Elsie's father was a keen amateur photographer and had set up his own darkroom in the house. The picture he developed showed Francis with several dancing fairy figures in the foreground and would later be called *Alice and the Fairies* (photo #1). Two months later, the girls took another photo. This time it was Elsie who was photographed sitting on a lawn next to a gnome in *Iris and the Gnome* (photo #2). Elsie's father dismissed the photos as a silly practical joke but her mother thought they were authentic and showed them to members of the Bradford Theosophical Society. A prominent member of the society, Edward Gardner realised the potential significance of these photographs to their movement and was intrigued enough to send the prints and the original glass plates to a photography expert called Harold Snelling for examination. He concluded that the two photographs were entirely genuine with no trace of any studio work involving card or paper models.

The novelist Arthur Conan Doyle (1859-1930), who was also a prominent spiritualist, came to hear about the photos and obtained the family's permission to include them in an article he was writing about fairies for *Strand Magazine*. With such an eminent writer advocating the existence of fairies and seemingly being able to prove it with photographs, it wasn't long before the great British public believed that fairies were living at the bottom of Elsie's garden too. By now the girls were only known as Iris (Elsie) and Alice (Frances) to protect their anonymity due to all the publicity the photographs were receiving.

Another three photos were taken in the summer of 1920: *Alice and the Leaping Fairy* (photo #3); *Fairy Offering Flowers to Iris* (photo #4); and *Fairies and their Sun-Bath* (photo #5).

Despite various interviews given by the women in the Sixties and Seventies hinting at the possibility of the photos being fakes, it wasn't until 1983 in an article for the magazine *The Unexplained* when they finally admitted it. They both maintained that they'd seen fairies but the photos were just a silly prank. Elsie had copied the pictures of some dancing girls from a book and drawn wings on them, then she'd cut out the cardboard figures and used hatpins to support them so they stood upright. However, the women disagreed about the fifth and final photograph *Fairies and their Sun-Bath* (1920). Elsie claimed that it was a fake just like all the others but Francis insisted that it was genuine: 'It was a wet Saturday afternoon and we were just mooching about with our cameras and Elsie had nothing prepared. I saw these fairies building up in the grasses and just aimed the camera and took a photograph.'

that famous stiff-upper-lip moment

Keeping a stiff-upper-lip has been described as remaining resolute and calm in the face of adversity, self-restraint in expressing emotion and interpreting any moment of crisis as just 'a bit of a pickle.' It has always been considered a particularly British trait, possibly because we're so good at it.

A typical example of a British stiff-upper-lip moment occurred on 29 July 1588 when the Spanish Armada was sighted off the coast of Cornwall. The fleet of around 130 ships (including 28 purpose-built warships) carrying 8,000 sailors and 18,000 soldiers had set sail from Lisbon across the English Channel with the purpose of invading England, overthrowing Elizabeth I (1533-1603) and restoring Catholicism to the country. According to legend, the famous explorer/privateer and the Vice Admiral of the English fleet, Francis Drake (c.1540-1596) was busy playing a game of bowls in Plymouth (Devon) when news of the invasion threat reached him. He was then said to have remarked: 'We have time enough to finish the game and beat the Spaniards too.' Which is exactly what happened. He calmly finished his game of bowls and then proceeded to blow the Spanish fleet out of the water!

But perhaps the most famous stiff-upper-lip moment involved poor old Henry Paget, 1st Marquess of Anglesey (Earl of Uxbridge) (1768-1854). He was injured after cannon fire hit him in the right leg during a cavalry charge at the Battle of Waterloo on 18 June 1815. He was standing near to Arthur Wellesley, 1st Duke of Wellington (1769-1852) at the time and was reported to have quipped: 'By God, Sir. I've lost my leg!' on realising the seriousness of his injuries. The duke, whose lip seemed equally as stiff at the time, apparently replied quite coldly: 'By God, Sir. So you have!' The unfortunate Earl of Uxbridge was then whisked away from the battlefield to a nearby house for medical treatment. His leg needed to be amputated above the knee and the operation was quickly performed without anaesthetic. According to his aide-de-camp Thomas Wildman (1787-1859) he just smiled and remarked: 'I have had a pretty long run. I have been a beau these forty-seven years and it would not be fair to cut the young men out any longer.'

Henry Paget later had an artificial limb fitted and continued with his highly successful military career.

Note: His severed limb then went on to enjoy an equally successful life of its own as a macabre tourist attraction in the village of Waterloo in Belgium. Mr Paris, the owner of the house where the amputation had taken place, had granted permission for the leg to be buried in his back garden with a little tombstone bearing a long, rambling inscription detailing the Earl's heroism marking the spot: 'Here lies the leg of the illustrious and valiant Earl Uxbridge, Lieutenant-General of His Britannic Majesty, Commander in Chief of the English, Belgian and Dutch cavalry, wounded on the 18 June 1815 at the memorable Battle of Waterloo, who, by his heroism, assisted in the triumph of the cause of mankind, gloriously decided by the resounding victory of the said day.'

The tourists were shown the blood splattered chair in which the Earl of Uxbridge had sat for the amputation and then led out into the back garden to visit the spot where the severed limb was buried. It was a nice little earner for Mr Paris and his family. But in 1878 all that changed when the Earl's son visited the house and was horrified to discover that the bones had been dug up and put on display! He demanded their immediate return but the Paris family refused his request and a minor diplomatic incident developed between Britain and Belgium which was only resolved after the Belgian Minister of Justice intervened and ordered the Paris family to rebury the bones.

They might have disappeared from public view but the bones were never reburied. In 1934, after the last Mr Paris had died, his widow found them hidden in his study. She was so appalled at the thought of another scandal that she incinerated them there and then in her furnace.

standing for the chorus

Messiah (1741) is a three-part, English language oratorio composed by George Frideric Handel (1685-1759).

The London premiere was held at the Covent Garden Theatre (Royal Opera House) in London on 23 March 1743 in the presence of George II (1683-1760). Legend has it that during the oratorio's majestical choral piece 'Hallelujah'. the king suddenly stood up, and since it was protocol to stand whenever the monarch did, and remain on your feet until they sat down again, everyone else in the audience got to their feet too!

There has since been much speculation as to why the king had suddenly stood up but ever since that day the audiences for a performance of *Messiah* have continued the tradition by standing during the 'Hallelujah' chorus. He was either enthralled by the beauty of the music and couldn't contain his enthusiasm or he was just a bit of an old fidget and felt the need to stretch his legs a bit.

the first dictionary

A Table Alphabeticall (1604) was the very first English language monolingual dictionary and was compiled by the clergyman Robert Cawdrey (c.1538-fl.1604) 'for the benefit and helpe of Ladies, Gentlewomen, or other unskillful persons.' At a time when many new words were entering the English language due to the fast-moving advancements in the sciences, medicine and the arts, Robert was apparently concerned that many people (particularly women it would seem) were becoming a little confused. And he might have had a point ... William Shakespeare (1564-1616) was busy scribbling his wonderful plays at this time and he alone has been credited with introducing almost 3,000 new words into the English language!

He was also alarmed by the 'far journied gentlemen' who'd 'pouder their talke with over-sea language.' He reckoned they were picking up far too many foreign words and phrases on their travels around the world causing them to 'forget altogether their mother's language, so that if some of their mothers were alive, they were not able to tell or understand what they say.'

Subsequently, Robert set about compiling his dictionary so all the dim people may 'better understand many hard English words' which they were likely to hear in their everyday lives in the hope that it would popularise knowledge and improve their reading and writing skills. But the end result was just a little on the disappointing side. His expected *magnum opus* was actually only 120 pages long and listed just 2,543 words so it probably wasn't much use to anyone! He didn't even bother listing any words beginning with the letters J, K, U, W, X and Y. Although there was a very brief definition for each word, more often than not, this was just a one-word explanation.

In effect the dictionary was little more than a long list of synonyms. Swallowing it wouldn't have improved anyone's vocabulary!

At that time, even the most literate readers wouldn't have been that skilled at handling a book with an alphabetical listing and so Robert was careful to explain how to navigate around his book in the preface: 'Nowe if the word, which thou art desirous to finde, begin with (a) then looke in the beginning of this Table, but if with (v) looke towards the end.'

Thanks, Robert!

the great storm

The meteorologist and BBC TV weatherman Michael Fish (1944-) gained notoriety on 15 October 1987 with a career-defining gaffe made during a daytime bulletin: 'Earlier on today, apparently, a woman rang the BBC and said she'd heard there was a hurricane on the way ... well, if you're watching, don't worry, there isn't.'

That evening, the worst storm for three centuries hit the south-east of England!

The Great Storm of 1987 was the most destructive weather front to hit Britain since The Great Storm of 1703 causing extensive damage over much of London and southern England. Buildings were ripped apart by gusts of winds raging at over 100mph (160km/h); fallen trees blocked roads and railway lines; cars were crushed; numerous small boats were wrecked or blown out to sea; scaffolding and billboards collapsed, and electricity lines were brought down leaving several hundred thousand homes without power. Schools were closed, all forms of public transport were cancelled and eighteen people lost their lives!

The damage caused by the storm was estimated to be around £2 billion.

Good one, Michael!

the legend of sawney bean

A macabre Scottish folktale about Britain's most gruesome and infamous killer!

Alexander 'Sawney' Bean married a woman called Agnes Douglas and they set up home together in a coastal cave at Bennane Head near Ballantrae in Ayrshire where they murdered and cannibalised up to 1,000 people to feed their insatiable desire for human flesh!

Sawney had originally supported himself and his new bride by carrying out a few robberies. It was easy enough to ambush travellers along the local roads as they were narrow and isolated, and people were still stupid enough to travel along them after dark! Then he had the idea of murdering his victims so they couldn't identify him ... then he had the idea of butchering the bodies and eating them to avoid the need for grocery shopping! The bodies were dragged back to the cave where they were dismembered and cooked by Mrs Bean; the leftovers were pickled in large barrels, and all the bones were scattered around the countryside and along the beaches as a way of fooling the local people into thinking that wild animals were responsible.

As well as being a thief, a killer and a cannibal, Sawney Bean was a lover too! The happy couple had fourteen kids together and then the kids had another 32 kids of their own! But because nobody ever dated outside of the family, they just had all their babies amongst themselves!

The fact that so many people had disappeared around the nearby villages of Girvan and Ballantrae hadn't gone unnoticed by the people who hadn't yet gone missing. The local authorities must have been keeping the longest list of missing persons ever produced! But the Bean family were very secretive and very clever, staying put in the cave during the day and only hunting for food at night. The villagers searched for the missing people but nobody ever thought to search the cave at Bennane Head with its miles of passageways and tunnels so the killings continued. The Bean menfolk would go out hunting and the womenfolk would do all the cooking ... and the pickling!

Then one fateful night, the menfolk ambushed a man and his wife as they were returning home from a fair. The wife was easily pulled from her horse, stripped and quickly disembowelled but the husband managed to hold off his attackers long enough to attract the attention of a large group of other fair-goers who were travelling home along the same road. Realising that they were outnumbered the Bean menfolk retreated back to their cave.

A local magistrate was informed of the incident and he informed the king …

James VI of Scotland (1566-1625) promptly arrived in Ayrshire with a small army of men and cadaver dogs, and together with a few enthusiastic local volunteers, began one of the biggest manhunts Scotland has ever seen. When the dogs picked up the scent of decaying human flesh near the cave entrance, the hunting party entered the labyrinth of tunnels to conduct a search. The Bean family were found sitting around a large cooking pot; human limbs were hanging from hooks on the walls like hams in an Italian deli and in other areas of the cave there were barrels full of body parts and piles of clothes, stolen jewellery and discarded bones! After a brief scuffle, all 46 Bean family members were taken into custody and marched off to Edinburgh to stand trial.

Except they never had a trial. Their crimes were considered so heinous that the notion of wasting time and money on a court case was quickly abandoned and the entire family were just sentenced to death. The menfolk had their genitalia cut off and thrown into the fires, their hands and feet were severed and then they were just left to bleed out. After being made to watch them die, the women and children were then burnt alive at the stake.

the first anti-smoking campaign

Tobacco had been smoked by Spanish and Portuguese sailors for many years and it's highly likely that their British counterparts may have copied the habit of smoking a pipe long before the English adventurer Walter Raleigh (c.1554-1618) returned home from the New World in 1586 with a few pouches of his precious 'brown gold'. The use of tobacco in some parts of Europe was already widespread at this time with the noted Spanish physician Nicolás Monardes [ESP] writing: 'To seek to tell the virtues and greatness of this holy herb, the ailments which can be cured by it, and have been, the evils from which it has saved thousands would be to go on to infinity … this precious herb is so general a human need not only for the sick but for the healthy.' He recommended sucking on a pipe for toothache, worms, halitosis, lockjaw and even as a cure for cancer!

Nevertheless, Sir Walter has always been thought of as the man who popularised the practice of smoking tobacco in England. He was the most prominent and celebrated smoker in the land and introduced the habit at court. It's been said that he was even able to tempt his beloved queen, Elizabeth I (1533-1603) into taking a few puffs on his pipe and once she'd been seen doing it, everyone wanted to do it.

However, not everyone was aware of his celebrity status as England's greatest smoker. There's that famous story of Sir Walter having a bucket of water thrown over him by a confused servant who was unaware of his master's new habit and thought he was on fire after seeing him engulfed in a cloud of thick smoke!

By the early seventeenth century it seemed like everybody in the land was now smoking tobacco but the new guy on the throne, James I (1566-1625) wasn't one of them. He detested the habit and, as was so often his way, he quickly put his thoughts down on paper by scribbling a pamphlet on the subject. In *A Counterblaste to Tobacco* (1604) he wrote about the evils of tobacco and expressed his distaste for the new fad of smoking by describing it as 'a custome lothsome to the eye, hatefull to the Nose, harmefull to the braine [and] dangerous to the Lungs.' He even complained about passive smoking and claimed that the use of tobacco was sinful. It was probably the world's first anti-smoking campaign! Just to ram home his point, he then banned the growing of tobacco in Britain and increased the duty on tobacco being imported from the New World by a whopping 4,000 percent.

But nobody really took much notice of what he had to say. Everybody just kept happily puffing away on their pipes. Smoking became more and more popular because people were convinced that it was beneficial to their health! During the spread of the Great Plague in 1665, tobacco smoke was widely advocated as a defence against the bad air and at the posh boys school of Eton College, pipe smoking was even made compulsory for the pupils! It wasn't until the English Restoration (1660) when the popularity of pipe smoking began to wane a little. But that was only because everyone had found a new way of enjoying tobacco. Now they were stuffing it up their noses instead.

female hysteria

The disease of 'female hysteria' was a catch-all diagnosis for women showing symptoms of faintness, shortness of breath, anxiety, insomnia, irritability, sexual desire, lack of sexual desire, loss of appetite, fluid retention, nervousness or even just the need to make trouble for others!

The signs of this so-called complaint were so wide ranging that almost any woman could be diagnosed with it. In fact, the physician Thomas Sydenham (1624-1689) claimed that it accounted for a sixth of all human disorders after becoming the second-most commonly diagnosed complaint in seventeenth-century England.

Basically, any medical condition that couldn't be easily identified was assumed to be female hysteria!

The first person to describe this strange medical phenomenon was the Greek physician Hippocrates in around 500 BCE. The Athenian philosopher Plato believed that the womb was an animal that goes 'wandering in every direction through the body, closes up the passages of the breath, and, by obstructing respiration, drives them [women] to extremity, causing all varieties of disease.' A few hundred years later, the Roman physician Galen wrote that hysteria was caused by sexual deprivation and prescribed a good roll in the hay for married women and pelvic massages for unmarried women, widows and women devoted to the church.

The English surgeon Nathaniel Highmore (1613-1685) was one of the first physicians to publicly acknowledge that a pelvic massage could end with a hysterical paroxysm (orgasm) but noted that it was no easy task to achieve, likening it to 'that game of boys in which they try to rub their stomachs with one hand and pat their heads with the other.'

By the nineteenth century, manual sexual relief was being mentioned in medical journals as an effective way of curing the hysteria and doctors found themselves treating it with increasing regularity. It was quite common for a woman to visit the family GP and have him manually stimulate her genitalia to the point of orgasm. She would happily pay him his fee and leave the surgery with a big smile on her face, safe in the knowledge that she'd been cured of hysteria ... at least, until she began suffering from the symptoms again and it was time to book another appointment!

However, the treatment wasn't always quite so fulfilling or straightforward. In some of the more extreme cases, the woman may have been committed to an insane asylum or dragged away by the men in white coats for a hysterectomy!

Note: The first portable electro-mechanical vibrator was patented by Joseph Mortimer Granville (1833-1900) in 1882. Whilst he disapproved of using it to treat female hysteria, his fellow doctors couldn't wait to try it out on their patients. Treating hysterical women was a very labour-intensive and time-consuming task and the new machines could achieve hysterical paroxysm in a matter of minutes rather than hours.

the theft of the duke of wellington

During the Peninsular War (1808-1814), a victorious Arthur Wellesley, 1st Duke of Wellington (1769-1852) arrived in Madrid in August 1812 after winning the Battle of Salamanca (1812). In between undertaking all his usual military duties, he found time to have his portrait painted by the Spanish artist Francisco Goya. That painting later came into the possession of Francis D'Arcy Osborne, 7th Duke of Leeds (1798-1859) and it remained in the family until 1961 when it was put up for sale at auction by his distant cousin John Osborne, 11th Duke of Leeds (1901-1963).

After being bought for £140,000 by the American art collector Charles Bierer Wrightsman it seemed that *Portrait of the Duke of Wellington* (1812-1814) was about to leave the country forever. There was a public outcry and so the American graciously agreed to sell the painting back to the British government for the same price as he'd paid for it. The money was eventually put up by the British government and The Wolfson Foundation with the painting going on display at the National Gallery (London) on 2 August 1961.

Then, just nineteen days later it was stolen from under the noses of the museum staff ...

No intruders were spotted, there were no signs of a break-in, no damage had been done, no other paintings were missing and no tools or equipment had been left behind at the scene.

This was the first theft ever recorded at the National Gallery and the museum's director Philip Hendy (1900-1980) immediately tended his resignation. A reward of £5,000 was offered for the painting's safe return but in the meantime, a review was launched into security measures at all of Britain's museums and galleries and a police investigation launched to track down the thief. The newspapers reported that even Interpol were involved in the manhunt as the authorities had assumed a professional art thief or some sophisticated international cat burglar had been responsible. A bit like Cary Grant (1904-1986) in *To Catch a Thief* (1955) or David Niven (1910-1983) in *The Pink Panther* (1963).

But they couldn't have been more wrong ...

The thief was actually a retired bus driver from Newcastle called Kempton Bunton (1904-1976), so called because his father once had a big win on the horses at Kempton Park racecourse! He'd stolen the painting because he was pissed off with the British government partially funding the acquisition of the painting at a time when he and so many other OAPs were struggling to pay for a TV licence out of their meagre pensions. According to his own account, he'd learnt from chatting to the guards that the museum's elaborate system of alarms and infrared sensors is deactivated in the early mornings to allow the cleaning staff to go about their duties more freely. So, at around 5.50am on 21 August 1961, Kempton sneaked around the back of the gallery building, propped a ladder up against the wall, loosened a window in a first-floor toilet and sneaked inside. He then made his way to the room where the painting was hanging, lifted it off the wall, exited the building through the same toilet window ... and just calmly walked away.

Over the next couple of years, a few letters arrived at various news agencies promising the painting's safe return in exchange for a charitable donation of £140,000 to assist poorer people in paying for their TV licences and an amnesty for the thief. But no ransom was ever paid, the police investigation continued and the painting remained missing for another four years. However, the public's interest in the crime never really diminished in all that time and the theft was even referenced in the *Dr No* (1962) movie. In one particular scene James Bond spots the painting propped up on an easel in Dr No's secret hideaway and remarks: 'Ah, so there it is.'

During all this time the *Daily Mirror* had continued with its campaign for the painting's safe return and was finally rewarded for it's efforts in June 1965 when a letter arrived at it's Fleet Street offices detailing the painting's exact whereabouts. The rolled-up and frameless painting was eventually found in the left-luggage office at Birmingham New Street station.

Six weeks later on 19 July 1965 Kempton Bunton handed himself into police.

At first, the police were a little reluctant to accept that the 61 year-old, 17-stone (110kg) pensioner standing before them was the international man of mystery they'd been chasing for all this time. It was difficult for them to believe that such a gangly-looking and heavily-built old man could have scaled the museum's outer wall, squeezed himself through a first-floor window and then gone wandering around the National Gallery without being detected. However, Kempton told the police that he'd opened the window on a previous visit, he'd found a discarded ladder to use on a nearby building site, and he already knew that the guards would most likely be off duty at the time he was there. His story, however fanciful it seemed, was supported by forensic evidence found at the scene and the confirmation by a handwriting expert that he'd most likely been the author of all those letters. Kempton also told the police that he'd only confessed to the theft because he was fearful that after one too many pints in the pub one evening, he may let something slip and was anxious that the £5,000 reward money wasn't collected by one of his drinking buddies!

Kempton was prosecuted for theft, making demands with menaces and causing a public nuisance. But luckily, he'd had the good sense to retain the top criminal barrister Jeremy Hutchinson (1915-2017) who cleverly argued that his client couldn't be prosecuted for theft because he'd never intended to permanently deprive the owner of the painting. He was always going to return it and had only intended to draw attention to the fact that the government's £140,000 could have been better spent helping OAPs who couldn't afford to pay for a TV licence rather than spaffing it away on some old painting! The jury acquitted him of all the charges, except for the theft of the picture frame valued at £100 which had never been recovered. The judge, who was clearly irked by their unexpected verdict, then sentenced Kempton to three months in prison.

To make sure nobody else could get away with such an obvious theft and still be acquitted for the crime, the government quickly passed the Theft Act 1968 to close the loophole in the law.

Then came the twist in the tale …

A few years later, it was discovered that Kempton wasn't the thief after all. Neither was Dr No. It was Kempton's son John Bunton.

After Kempton had left prison, it was reported that John had sent out letters to various newspapers and other media outlets touting the true story behind the heist including the film rights with the tantalising message that even his father's 'defence advisors knew as little about the truth as you do.' It's unclear if any of them bothered to contact him but certainly his story never made it to the big screen!

In 1969, it was reported that a man from Leeds had apparently confessed to stealing the painting and then in 2012 (after the release of files held at The National Archives) it was discovered that the mysterious man from Leeds was none other than John Bunton. He'd told police that it had all been a spur of the moment thing; he saw the ladder, he saw the open window and saw the opportunity to draw attention to his father's campaign and at the same time earn some extra money for his cash-strapped family by demanding a ransom for the painting's safe return. He'd then given the painting to his father for safe keeping. Kempton had started writing all those letters in the hope they'd put John in a better light should he be arrested and then insisted on taking the blame for the crime himself. The authorities had decided against prosecuting him because there was no real evidence, only his word for it, and it was simpler just to brush the matter under the carpet. If they had another trial, they'd have to call Kempton back to the stand and the feeling was they'd already afforded him enough publicity for his silly campaign. The British legal establishment were determined to avoid any further embarrassment.

The police always had their doubts about Kempton squeezing through that first-floor toilet window and it seems they were proved right in the end.

the london beer flood

The most bizarre and tragic industrial accident in the history of London!

At around 5.00pm on 17 October 1814 disaster struck at the Meux & Company brewery located at the corner of Great Russell Street and Tottenham Court Road (at the present day site of the Dominion Theatre) in London when one of the iron rings fixed around a huge 22-foot (6.7m) tall fermentation tank holding the equivalent of 3,500 barrels of beer snapped. An hour or so later, the tank burst open releasing a powerful tsunami of beer which blasted open several more vats and smashed into the back wall of the brewery. The wall collapsed under the force resulting in around 320,000 gallons (or 2.5 million pints) of beer being released into the surrounding streets.

Three brewery workers were rescued from the flood and another was pulled alive from the rubble.

The 15-foot (4.6m) high wave of beer and debris flooded the basements of some neighbouring houses, including one where a wake was being held, resulting in five of the mourners being killed. Eleanor Cooper, a 14-year-old barmaid at the nearby pub The Tavistock Arms was killed after being buried under a collapsed wall while washing pots in the pub's yard. In another instance the *Scots Magazine* described a mother and daughter being 'washed out of a window' with the daughter 'swept away by the current … and dashed to pieces.'

In total there were eight fatalities from the flood.

The *London Morning Post* described the events as being quite horrific: 'The surrounding scene of desolation presents a most awful and terrific appearance, equal to that which fire or earthquake may be supposed to occasion.'

However, it wasn't all bad news. The streets of one of London's poorest areas had suddenly been flooded with what seemed like a near-limitless supply of free beer and the vast majority of people who lived in the area (and hadn't been drowned or crushed to death) suddenly found themselves wading about knee-deep in the stuff. These lucky people collected it up in pots and pans to take home or just scooped it up there and then in their hands and got drunk. Literally enjoying a piss up in (what remained of) a brewery! This led to reports of a ninth victim dying a few days later from alcohol poisoning!

Watchmen at the brewery later charged people to view the remains of the destroyed beer vats and relatives of the dead charged people to gawp at their bodies in the hope that the money raised would be enough to cover the funeral costs. At one particular house, this macabre show resulted in the floor collapsing under the weight of all the visitors, plunging everyone into a beer-flooded cellar.

A coroner's inquest was held on 19 October 1814 with the jurors listening to witness testimony as they were shown the scene and the dead bodies. The inquiry later concluded that the beer flood had been an act of God and that the deaths had occurred 'casually, accidentally and by misfortune' meaning the brewery didn't have to pay out any compensation.

the bang on the head

John Lambie (1941-2018) was the no-nonsense, cigar-chomping and slightly eccentric manager of Partick Thistle FC on four different occasions between 1988 and 2005. During one particular match his star striker, Colin McGlashan (1964-) was involved in a clash of heads with an opponent and led off the pitch for treatment. On being told by his assistant Gerry Collins (1955-) that the player was concussed and didn't know who he was, he replied: 'Great. Tell him he's Pelé and get him back on!'

Pelé, of course, was the legendary Brazilian footballer widely regarded as one of the greatest players of all time after winning three FIFA World Cups in 1958, 1962 and 1970.

the prophetess of devon

Joanna Southcott (1750-1814) lived a quiet and fairly uneventful life as a domestic servant in Exeter until one day in 1792 when she suddenly started having visions and hearing heavenly voices. Convinced that she now possessed supernatural powers, she collated all of her premonitions in a book *The Strange Effects of Faith with Remarkable Prophecies* (1792).

She was then lured to London by the followers of Richard Brothers (1757-1824). He was another religious nut who'd had visions but he'd just been carted off to an asylum and so presumably his followers were looking around for another prophet to follow. Joanna convinced them that she was the real deal and they started following her instead; she then published more of her prophetic writings, and founded the Southcottian Movement which soon attracted around 20,000 members.

In 1814, when she was 64 years-old and still an unmarried virgin, she shocked everyone by announcing her pregnancy! Pretty amazing stuff considering her age and her virginity but it became even more amazing when she claimed to be pregnant with the Second Messiah! Despite her rapid weight gain and her ever-expanding belly, nobody really believed her. The public ridiculed her and she was subjected to some rather savage criticism in the press.

Unsurprisingly, the due date of 19 October 1814 came and went with no sign of the new Messiah. Luckily, Joanna knew what the problem was. She'd omitted to provide the baby with a father and so she quickly married some poor sap called John Smith, an elderly friend and a devoted Southcottian Movement member who'd selflessly agreed to be Joseph to her Mary.

But even a shotgun wedding still couldn't coax the little Messiah to show his face.

Then, on 27 December 1814, Joanna Southcott died. Her followers were convinced that she was just in a trance and there was still a possibility that the new Messiah might appear, so her body lay undisturbed for four days whilst they all crossed their fingers and sat around waiting for a miracle. They only agreed to her burial after the corpse began to decay and the stench became unbearable. But firstly, the body was taken away for a post-mortem. There was absolutely no trace of a pregnancy but one of the attending doctors did describe her abdomen as 'the largest I ever saw, being nearly four times the usual size and appeared [to be] one lump of fat.' So she wasn't the next Virgin Mary after all, just a big old fatty! Who'd have thought it?

The Southcottian Movement didn't end with the old bird's death. At the time of her demise there were around 100,000 members and they continued her good work, babbling on about whatever it was they believed in and conning people out of their money.

But Joanna couldn't stop giving … even when she was dead …

She'd left the world with what would become known as *Joanna*

Southcott's Box, a small wooden container stuffed full of her prophecies that was only to be opened in the presence of all twenty-four Church of England bishops at a time of national crisis. Attempts were made to persuade the churchmen to open it during the Crimean War (1853-1856) and again during World War I (1914-1918) but to no avail. In 1927, the psychic researcher Harry Price (1881-1948) claimed to have got hold of the box and opened it, revealing its contents as just a bunch of meaningless papers and a few knick-knacks. However, one of the more prominent Southcottian Movement groups, the Panacea Society, which was formed in 1919, claimed that Harry's box was a fake because they had the real one in their possession and it was stored in a secret location.

In 2012, the Panacea Society was dissolved after the death of its last surviving member Ruth Klein (1932-2012) but the box is supposedly still locked away somewhere in a safe place!

the cowardly spaniard

Thomas Cochrane, 10th Earl of Dundonald (1775-1860) was a gallant, swashbuckling Royal Navy officer. His heroic exploits on the high seas during the Coalition Wars (1792-1815) were so well known to Britain's enemies that he was nicknamed *Le Loup des Mers* (The Sea Wolf) by none other than the diminutive French dictator himself, Napoleon Bonaparte.

On 6 May 1801, during the War of the Second Coalition (1798-1802) he famously attacked and captured the 32-gun Spanish frigate *El Gamo* with a crew of 319 men, whilst captaining the old 14-gun sloop-of-war HMS *Speedy* with a crew of just 54 men.

The *Speedy* drew alongside the *El Gamo* so it couldn't fire its guns into the British ship's hull and every time the Spanish tried to board it, the *Speedy* would pull away and fire on the boarding party. Sometime during the fighting, the Spanish captain was killed and replaced by his incompetent second-in-command ... who promptly surrendered!

After realising that he'd capitulated to an enemy they'd outnumbered by six-to-one, the cheeky Spaniard then demanded a letter from Thomas describing how bravely he'd fought during the battle, which he could then show to his bosses back in Madrid. Thomas was only too happy to oblige and wrote a very nice letter stating that the Spaniard had conducted himself like a true Spaniard!

To his amusement, Thomas later discovered that the Spanish officer had interpreted his remark as a compliment and had actually used his letter to try and gain a promotion!

the amazing lady nithsdale

The Scottish nobleman William Maxwell, 5th Earl of Nithsdale (1676-1744) fought with a Jacobite army commanded by Thomas Forster (1683-1738) at the Battle of Preston (1715) but was captured and taken to London to face charges of treason. He was found guilty at his trial and sentenced to death on 9 February 1716.

Winifred Maxwell, Countess of Nithsdale (c.1680-1749) was advised of her husband's fate at their family home in Terregles in Scotland on 8 December 1715 and then bravely decided to set off on horseback with her faithful servant Cecilia Evans for the very long and arduous 400-mile (644km) journey to London to try and free him from prison.

William didn't seem at all optimistic about her chances of setting him free but she was already concocting a plan to do just that …

Plan A was to visit the king and ask for clemency. Unfortunately, when she was finally able to arrange an audience with George I (1660-1727) he refused to read her petition or listen to her appeals for mercy. It has been said that when she knelt before him and took hold of his coat in a desperate last attempt to gain a pardon for her husband, the king walked away and dragged her halfway across the room before he could break free of her.

Plan B was a lot riskier but there was no Plan C, so it had to work …

On 22 February 1716, two days before the execution date, she visited William in prison to explain that Plan A had failed and she was now going ahead with Plan B.

The following night she returned again along with Celia and two other women she'd become acquainted with at her lodgings known only as Mrs Morgan and Mrs Mills. Lady Nithsdale and Celia entered the cell whilst the two women waited in another part of the Tower and took it in turns to make their entrance. First up was Mrs Morgan. She was wearing an extra petticoat and a cloak, which she quickly removed after entering the cell. She wished everyone good luck and then made her leave. Then it was the turn of Mrs Mills to enter the cell. She appeared tearful and was holding a handkerchief to her face as she passed the guards and went inside. She quickly took off her clothes and put on the petticoat and cloak left behind by Mrs Morgan and then walked out of the cell, with her head held high looking like a different woman!

Finally, William dressed himself in the clothes left behind by Mrs Mills and dabbed a bit of make-up on his face to cover his beard. As he left the cell arm-in-arm with his wife and Celia, he appeared agitated and began sobbing into a hanky which he held to his face, just as the real Mrs Mills had done on her way in, hoping that the warders would assume it was the same hysterical woman making her exit. The guards were their usual half-pissed selves, and with the poor light and all the comings-and-goings, they weren't sure who was who anymore ... and probably didn't care much either.

Lady Nithsdale then returned to the cell, shut the door and pretended to talk to her husband as if he was still there by impersonating his gruff voice. She then waited just enough time for her husband and co-conspirators to leave the Tower before appearing to promise him that she would return later that same evening, leaving the cell again and shutting the door behind her. She then advised the guards that her husband didn't want to be disturbed any further because he was saying his prayers.

After a few days in hiding, William was smuggled out of the country to France. Despite being suspected of aiding her husband's escape from prison, Lady Nithsdale made the perilous journey back to Scotland to collect their daughters and some family papers before escaping across the English Channel to join her husband.

The family ultimately settled in Rome where they all lived happily ever after.

sin-eaters

A grieving family would employ the services of a Sin-Eater to rid the dearly departed of their sins as a way of ensuring their souls safely ascended to Heaven. The practice was prevalent in North Wales and in the villages along the England-Wales border from the seventeenth to the nineteenth centuries.

A piece of bread or pastry was placed on the dead body and the Sin-Eater would consume it, literally eating the sins of the deceased. The family believed that the bread soaked up the sins and once it had been eaten by someone else, all those sins were somehow magically passed onto that other person. The bread would normally be washed down with a few tankards of ale before the Sin-Eater read out a little prepared prayer: 'I give easement and rest now to thee, dear man. Come not down the lanes or in our meadows. And for thy peace, I pawn my own soul. Amen.'

The village Sin-Eaters were normally just the local drunkards or beggars who only accepted the role for a small payment and the offer of free food and drink. Nevertheless, the villagers were usually frightened of them. They feared anyone who was willing to absorb the sins of others as their own and often thought of them as heretics, blasphemers and devil worshipers. They also believed that these men became more and more evil after every ceremony they performed and nobody would look them in the eye, even for just a few seconds, as it was considered bad luck!

chasing ghosts

Ghostwatch (BBC) was a TV show hosted by Michael Parkinson (1935-2023) and the husband-and-wife team of Mike Smith (1955-2014) and Sarah Greene (1958-) to investigate the alleged poltergeist activity detected at a house on a council estate in Northolt, London, on the night of Halloween in 1992. Despite having been recorded many weeks in advance, the show was presented as live TV complete with a studio audience, outside broadcasts and interviews with people on the street. Michael Parkinson even urged viewers to phone in with their own ghost stories on 081 811 8181 which was the usual BBC phone-in number used on all their other live shows at the time such as *Crimewatch* and *Going Live*. Michael Parkinson was a trusted and respected broadcaster and his involvement in the show was designed to deceive viewers into thinking it was a serious investigation into the paranormal instead of the scripted (by Stephen Volk), mockumentary-style drama that it really was.

The reporters at the so-called 'most haunted house in Britain' where Pamela Early and her two daughters lived, were there to investigate the existence of a malevolent ghost nicknamed Pipes, the spirit of a psychologically disturbed man called Raymond Tunstall, who molested and abused children before committing suicide. Sarah Greene followed the ghostly activity around the house and the tension mounted as the family were subjected to increasingly more terrifying paranormal experiences, culminating with the spirit of the dead man apparently entering the children.

At the end of the 90-minute show, Sarah Greene had been dragged away by Pipes screaming her little head off, police and paramedics had rescued the family from the house and the audience had abandoned the BBC TV studio, leaving only Michael Parkinson wandering around the set looking dazed and confused and seemingly exhibiting the first signs of being possessed!

It all sounds a bit daft now but at the time it all felt so real.

The BBC received around thirty thousand complaints after the programme was aired.

the coughing major

On 20 November 2000, after answering the fifteenth and final question on *Who Wants to Be a Millionaire?* (ITV), the former garden designer Judith Keppel (1942-) became the first contestant to win a jackpot prize of £1,000,000 on a British TV gameshow. She knew her stuff and went home with a big, fat cheque after knowing: Which King was married to Eleanor of Aquitaine?

It was Henry II (1133-1189) by the way.

Someone who definitely didn't know their stuff was the former British Army officer Major Charles Ingram (1963-). Less than a year after Judith's historic win, he tried to claim the jackpot prize unfairly by attempting one of the most extraordinary acts of deception ever witnessed on British TV.

He wasn't exactly looking like much of a winner at the end of filming on the first day, after stumbling his way to the £4,000 mark and using two of his three lifelines, with the show's production team doubting he'd progress much further when filming resumed the following day. But they didn't know about the cunning little plan he'd hatched to win the jackpot prize ...

He continued answering questions in a seemingly erratic manner, often flipping between one answer and another, settling on one and then opting for an entirely different answer, in some cases without any explanation or any obvious knowledge of the subject. But he always got them right and continued triumphantly all the way to the final £1,000,000 question.

However, as it turned out, he'd had a bit of help from his wife Diana and their mutual friend and co-conspirator Tecwen Whittock who were sitting in the audience. Every time the Major had been asked a question, he pretended to contemplate each of the four possible answers and then listen out for a little cough from the audience after reading out the correct one. At which point, he would proceed to offer it as his final answer. After correctly answering the fifteenth question - A number one followed by one hundred zeros is known by what name? - the show's host Chris Tarrant (1946-) handed him a cheque for £1,000,000.

It's called a googol by the way.

At the time, nobody had guessed what was happening but by the time he'd left the set, the show's production team were already beginning to have doubts that he'd won fairly and suspended the pay-out until after they'd completed an investigation. After reviewing the tapes, the matter was handed over to the police who later charged the Major and his two collaborators with procuring the execution of a valuable security by deception.

Everyone pleaded not guilty to the charges and a four-week trial at Southwark Court (London) followed ...

A video recording of the amplified coughing was played for the jury and various witnesses were called, most significantly, another contestant called Larry Whitehurst who testified that he too had detected a pattern of coughing and was entirely convinced that this had helped the defendant. It was also alleged by the prosecution that Tecwen Whittock used a total of nineteen strategically placed coughs to help him. But good old Tecwen claimed that he'd always suffered from a persistent cough because of hay fever and a dust allergy. According to him, it was pure coincidence that his coughing fits just happened to coincide with the correct answers being called out! However, it was noticeable that his cough seemed to miraculously disappear when he immediately followed the Major as the next contestant on the show! The Major testified that he neither 'listened for, encouraged, nor noticed any coughing' but nobody seemed to believe him and on 7 April 2003 he and his two collaborators were convicted of fraud.

The Ingrams had been heard arguing in the TV studio's Green Room shortly after filming. It has since been speculated that the Major was supposed to get a question wrong, possibly around the £64,000 half-way mark. Bowing out then would have made their deceitful little plan a lot less obvious. If only he'd exercised a little self-restraint, they might have got away with it.

the calculus conspiracy

The two eminent scientists,Englishman Isaac Newton (1642-1727) and German Gottfried Wilhelm Leibniz, both claimed the glory for inventing calculus and then spent the rest of their lives trying to discredit each other's claims.

The German was first to publish his work in his *Nova Methodus pro Maximis et Minimis* (1684) but it was well known that Isaac had begun his research several years earlier and his conclusions may have influenced Gottfried. The initial claims and accusations were primarily made by the students and supporters of the two scientists but both men soon became personally involved in the controversy, each accusing the other of plagiarism. Then, in 1711, the Royal Society issued a report proclaiming that Isaac was the true inventor and labelling the German scientist's findings as fraudulent.

It was just a pity that the author of this report was later revealed to be none other than Isaac Newton himself! It wasn't until the two men were dead and buried that they were both credited with inventing calculus independently. However, it was only the German who came up with the name *Calculus* for the new science. Isaac wanted to call it 'the science of fluents and fluxions' which was never going to catch on!

THE MOST IMPORTANT WORK IN THE HISTORY OF SCIENCE

After eighteen months of scribbling, Isaac Newton finally produced the first draft of *Philosophiæ Naturalis Principia Mathematica* (1687), the most important and critically acclaimed work in the history of science! The book contained all his theories from the previous twenty years including the Laws of Motion and the Law of Universal Gravitation for which he has become most famous.

His devotion to his work during the time he was researching and writing the *Principia* was recounted later by his secretary and copyist of the period Humphrey Newton (no relation). Apparently, he was so absorbed in his studies that he would sometimes forget to eat and sleep or to change his clothes. When walking around the garden at his family's home of Woolsthorpe Manor near Grantham in Lincolnshire he would sometimes run back to his study with some thoughts or new ideas and wouldn't even sit down first before putting quill to paper! No doubt it happened exactly like that when that apple fell on his head.

The three volumes of *Principia* were eventually presented to the Royal Society for publication and the society's president Samuel Pepys (1633-1703) gave the green light on 30 June 1686 ... but then promptly changed his mind again after realising that they'd already spent all of their budget funding the spectacularly unsuccessful *De Historia Piscium* (Of the History of Fish) (1686) by the ornithologist and ichthyologist Francis Willughby (1635-1672). This book had proved to be a much costlier venture than anyone had ever imagined mainly due to its lavish illustrations and the fact that nobody was actually interested in reading a book about fish! It was a complete flop and dear old Samuel was reluctant to spend even more of what little money they had left in their coffers. Especially on a book about mathematics!

Isaac was a very private and cautious person when it came to publicising his work. It had been one of his great friends, the astronomer Edmond Halley (1656-1742), who'd originally encouraged him to present *Principia* to the Royal Society, so when they declined to publish, Isaac would have probably just forgotten about the book if it hadn't been for his friend's continued involvement in the project. The so-called most important and critically acclaimed work in the history of science would never have seen the light of day if it hadn't been for Edmond deciding to pick up the tab himself.

Principia was finally published on 5 July 1687 thanks entirely to Edmond's generosity.

He was working as a clerk for the Royal Society at the time and they couldn't even afford to pay him his annual £50 salary, so they offered to pay his salary arrears in leftover copies of *De Historia Piscium,* forcing him to fund the printing costs of *Principia* from his own savings! Poor old Edmond had risked his career and reputation to get *Principia* published and all because of some crap book about fish that nobody has ever heard of since!

But at least it was worth it in the end.

In 1747, the French mathematician/astronomer Alexis Clairaut stated: 'The famous book [*Principia*] ... marked the epoch of a great revolution in physics. The method followed by its illustrious author Sir Newton ... spread the light of mathematics on a science which up to then had remained in the darkness of conjectures and hypotheses.'

the old price riots

On 20 September 1808, the original Covent Garden Theatre (aka the Royal Opera House) was burnt to the ground. With little or no means to fight the flames, the historic old building was completely gutted in only three hours. At the time, it was one of only two theatres in London licensed to stage full-length, spoken plays with all the other non-licensed theatres having to make do with putting on song and dance acts or acrobatic performances. If they did want to hire actors for a theatrical production, they were only allowed to mime the words!

The insurance money didn't cover the reconstruction costs but after a successful public fundraising campaign, building the new theatre designed by the famed architect Robert Smirke (1780-1867) began on 2 January 1809 when the future George IV (1762-1830) laid the first stone. The need for a new theatre was already an urgent matter with all the toffs in a hurry to get it built but on 24 February 1809, it became even more urgent when London's only other licensed theatre, the Theatre Royal in Drury Lane also went up in flames!

The new Covent Garden Theatre finally opened for business on 18 September 1809.

It was a much posher affair than its predecessor. The third tier of seating, which had previously been available to the general public, had been converted into large boxes for wealthy patrons to rent out at a cost of around £300 a year. These boxes could be curtained off so the rich folk might invite prostitutes and actresses (often the same thing back then) for a little bit of hanky-panky during the interval! To offset the building costs and pay for all these fancy new boxes, the theatre's manager John Philip Kemble (1757-1823) raised the ticket prices. Only the prices for the gallery seats with the restricted views remained unchanged but nobody wanted to sit in those seats because they could only see the legs of the performers and nothing else!

The plebs who normally occupied the cheap seats began protesting against the price hikes as soon as the curtain came up on the opening night's performance of *Macbeth* (1606). Things got so bad that John Philip Kemble had to send for the Bow Street Runners after the protesters refused to leave the theatre at the end of the show. But they just seemed to make things worse. The peaceful protests soon turned into violent protests and the crowds didn't disperse until around 2.00am.

The protesters were back the following night and every night after that, disrupting the plays, unfurling huge banners, yelling abuse and demanding a return to the old ticket prices. They sneaked in drums, bells and rattles to make as much noise as possible, drowning out the actors on stage and making it impossible for the toffs in the posh seats to enjoy the show. Sometimes they started dancing in the aisles, stomping on the wooden benches and screaming for a return to the old prices.

The protests continued each night with John Philip Kemble forced to address the angry crowd on 23 September 1809. He tried to placate them by explaining that a committee of gentlemen would be convened to examine his decision to increase the prices and then determine if it was justified or not. Until such a time as they returned their verdict, the theatre would remain closed. But since this committee consisted almost entirely of the theatre's shareholders, it wasn't particularly surprising that the hike in prices was deemed as being perfectly reasonable when the honourable gentlemen eventually returned their verdict.

After the theatre was re-opened, the protests resumed …

Newspapers were now regularly reporting on the nightly chaos inside the Covent Garden Theatre. People across the country quickly took sides, with the protesters and their supporters now calling themselves the OPs and their opponents who sided with the theatre's management calling themselves the NPs. Meanwhile, the protests had become more and more elaborate. The OPs dressed up in outlandish costumes, farm animals were sneaked inside the theatre, flocks of pigeons were released, mock fights were staged and on one occasion a coffin and a banner announcing 'Here lies the body of the new price' were paraded through the auditorium in an attempt to distract the audience from what was happening on the stage. When the OPs weren't protesting in the theatre, they were gathering outside John Philip Kemble's home chanting 'Original Prices!' and singing crude songs about him.

At this point, John hired some thugs led by the famous ex-boxer Daniel Mendoza (1764-1836) to try and keep order inside the theatre. But when they tried to evict the OPs, fights broke out and caused even more commotion than before. Daniel Mendoza had been one of the most popular and respected fighters of his time but his perceived support for the NPs lost him most of his fans as he was seen to be fighting on the side of the rich folks against the poor.

After almost three months of unrest and with no end to the protests in sight, John Philip Kemble finally gave in to the demands of the OPs. On 15 December 1809, he issued a public apology to the crowd gathered outside the theatre and promised to restore the old ticket prices. He also agreed not to press charges against all the OPs who'd been arrested during the protests.

And just like that, the protests stopped and everything went back to normal.

the honourable member for shrewsbury

As a young boy, the eccentric upper-class twat, John Mad Jack' Mytton (1796-1834) was expelled from two of England's fanciest schools but somehow managed to gain entry into Trinity College (University of Cambridge). He soon abandoned his education and, after inheriting his father's wealth, he then abandoned his highly unremarkable military career to take on the altogether more enjoyable role of squire at the family's country house at Halston Hall in Shropshire.

He often hunted naked, fed steak and Champagne to his dogs, allowed his favourite horse to roam about inside the house and tormented his few friends with practical jokes. It's been said that 'Mad Jack' spent his whole life drinking, gambling and trying to injure himself! He positively loved being involved in accidents, often driving his gig along narrow country lanes like a man possessed, deliberately steering it towards ditches, rabbit holes and potholes just to see if he'd have a crash! On one occasion, he purposely raced his horse and gig towards a tollgate, to see if the horse would jump over the gate. It didn't and he crashed into it. On another occasion he was driving his gig in his usual reckless manner with a terrified companion by his side who'd foolishly admitted that he'd never been involved in a road accident before. 'What a damn slow fellow you must have been all your life!' exclaimed 'Mad Jack' before driving off at high speed up a sloping bank, overturning the gig and tipping them both out onto the road.

In 1819, he stood for parliament as a Tory MP in Shrewsbury and secured his victory by offering bribes of £10 to anyone promising to vote for him, spending a total of around £10,000. He then attended his first session of Parliament but walked out after just half-an-hour because he was bored … and never went back!

Needless to say his over indulgent lifestyle soon took its toll on his health and his finances.

He died when he was only 38 years-old in a debtors' prison in Southwark with one contemporary account describing him as a 'round-shouldered, tottering, old-young man bloated by drink, worn out by too much foolishness, too much wretchedness and too much brandy.'

ALAN FERGUSON

the rebecca riots

The first of the many individual acts of parliament establishing Turnpike Trusts to collect road tolls was passed in 1707. In theory the tolls were meant to be collected by the local authorities and used for repairing and maintaining specified parts of an existing road, but in reality, many of the trusts were operated by fat-cat businessmen whose only interest in the scheme was doing as little repair work as possible whilst raking in as much money as possible. Very little of the revenue they collected was actually used for its intended purpose.

The Rebecca Riots were a series of violent protests by the peasant folk of rural Wales between 1839 and 1843 against the collection of these tolls. The local farmers and agricultural workers were angered by the high fees they were being forced to pay when transporting their crops and livestock along the roads to market and organised themselves into little gangs to smash up the tollgates. These gangs became known as Rebecca's Daughters. It's believed they took their name from a passage in the Bible (Genesis 24:60): 'And they blessed Rebekah and said unto her, thou art our sister, be thou the mother of thousands of millions, and let thy speed possess the gate of those which hate them.' Men would dress up as women, blacken their faces and attack the tollgates at night. One man would be dressed as an old crone called Rebecca and the others as her daughters. Arriving at the tollgate, they would then act out a little play!

Rebecca – What is this my children? There is something in my way. I cannot go on …

Daughters – What is it, Mother Rebecca? Nothing should stand in your way.

Rebecca – I do not know my children. I am old and cannot see well.

Daughters – Shall we come and move it out of your way, Mother Rebecca?

Rebecca – Wait! It feels like a big gate put across the road to stop your old mother.

Daughters – We will break it down, mother. Nothing stands in your way.

Rebecca – Perhaps it will open … Oh my dear children, it is locked and bolted. What can be done?

Daughters – It must be taken down, mother. You and your children must be able to pass.

Rebecca – Off with it then, my children.

At which point everyone would then smash up the tollgate!

However, it has to be assumed that the guys working the nightshift at the tollgate would have cottoned on to this little pantomime fairly quickly and after the first couple of attacks, Rebecca and her daughters probably just turned up and swung their axes and sledgehammers around without all the theatrical shenanigans beforehand!

the world's funniest joke

The British Science Association conducted a survey to find the world's funniest joke. It was one of the largest and most unusual scientific experiments ever undertaken. A special website called *LaughLab* was set up which encouraged people from different countries, cultures and demographics to post a joke and then rate a random selection of five other jokes already posted. Over the course of a year the website received 40,000 jokes and 1,500,000 ratings. The funniest joke was submitted by someone called Gurpal Gosall from Manchester and announced on 3 October 2002.

Two hunters are out in the woods when one of them collapses. He doesn't seem to be breathing and his eyes are glazed. The other guy whips out his phone and dials 999. 'My friend is dead! What can I do?' he gasps. The operator says, 'Calm down. I can help. First, let's make sure he's dead.' There is a moment of silence and then a gunshot! Back on the phone, the guy says, 'OK, now what?'

the trial of nicholas throckmorton

The English diplomat/politician Nicholas Throckmorton (c.1515-1571) had been indicted for treason for his alleged involvement in the uprising led by the politician Thomas Wyatt (1521-1554) against the forthcoming marriage of Mary I (1516-1558) to the future Spanish king Philip II. He was accused of being 'a principal, deviser, procurer and contriver' of the rebellion and was brought to trial at the Guildhall in London on 17 April 1554.

The trial was just a formality. Every VIP in Tudor England seemed to be accused of treason or heresy at some point or another in their lives, so this trial shouldn't have been any different from all the others. It was clearly just a case of being seen to go through the motions, hanging the bastard and then moving on to the next guy.

Nicholas Throckmorton wasn't allowed council and defended himself. Something he apparently did with bravura, wit and elegance, running rings around the prosecution with his masterful arguments and knowledge of the law. Eventually, the twelve good men of the jury were asked to consider their verdict ...

When they returned to court and were seated, they confirmed that a verdict had been reached and a foreman appointed to speak on their behalf. The court clerk then asked the jury foreman: 'How say you? Is Master Throckmorton ... guilty of the treasons whereof he hath been indicated and arraigned in manner and form, yea or no?' Rather surprisingly he replied 'No.' After all the other members of the jury confirmed the not guilty verdict, the judge angrily interjected: 'Remember yourselves better ... Have you considered substantially the whole evidence ... as it was declared and recited?' Then, he added rather ominously: 'The matter doth touch the queen's highness, and yourselves also, take good heed what you do.' But the foreman, who was either a very principled man or a very stupid one, assured the judge and everyone else in the packed courtroom that the jury stood by their decision.

Nicholas Throckmorton then demanded to be acquitted as the judge pondered how to resolve the matter. Eventually, he agreed that the verdict should be respected and acquitted him of committing the crimes he'd been charged with. However, he then turned to the jailer and said: 'Take him with you again, for there are other matters to charge him with.' So Nicholas was marched back to the Tower of London until such a time as the authorities could think of something else to accuse him of. He remained a guest in the Tower until 1557 when he somehow contrived to win a pardon from the very queen he'd been plotting against! Then, after Elizabeth I (1533-1603) acceded to the throne in 1558, he managed to wheedle his way back into favour at court and was eventually appointed as England's ambassador to France.

But what of the twelve men of the jury? Well, the judge had ordered them to be imprisoned too! Just for returning a verdict he didn't agree with. They didn't come to trial until 26 October 1554 when they appeared before the Star Chamber, the tyrannical high court of Privy Councillors who sat in the Palace of Westminster, who ordered their houses to be sealed and payment of a huge fine, due within an impossibly short time period of just a few weeks. So, presumably they all ended up destitute and living on the streets!

The oppressive punishment handed down to this particular mutinous jury served as a timely reminder to anyone else thinking about going rogue when summoned to do their duty! They weren't expected to think for themselves. Just follow the judge's direction and return the verdict he wanted.

the death train

London's population had more than doubled from 1,000,000 people in 1801 to around 2,500,000 by 1851. This posed a problem for the authorities because nobody was quite sure what to do with all these extra people when they died. All the churchyards were full and cremation wasn't really a thing yet. Between 1846 and 1849, the situation was made even worse by a devastating cholera epidemic which swept through the city, resulting in the early deaths of an extra 14,000 Londoners.

Parliament then passed the Burials Act 1852 which made it illegal for any new burials to take place in the built-up areas of London and encouraged private companies to establish new cemeteries in the city's leafy suburbs, far from the overcrowded and over-buried parts of central London.

The grandly named London Necropolis and National Mausoleum Company (LNC) was formed to develop a new cemetery at Brookwood in Surrey with the aim of becoming the go-to place for Londoners to bury their loved ones. But their new cemetery was located around 25 miles (40km) from London and the horse-drawn hearses would take an eternity to reach it. To overcome the problems of transporting the coffins and the accompanying mourners all the way out to Surrey, the company proposed using the newly built London & South Western railway.

However, this ingenious plan was not welcomed by everyone. The owners of the railway weren't all that thrilled about having their trains stuffed full of dead people and the church objected that the noise and speed of the railways was incompatible with the solemnity of a burial service. One of the most vocal opponents of the scheme was Charles Blomfield, Bishop of London (1786-1857) who argued that the families of people from different social classes shouldn't be expected to share the same 40-minute train journey to the cemetery. It was quite intolerable that the upper-classes should have to mingle with the lower classes at such an emotional time!

The LNC announced they would use separate, unscheduled trains leaving from a newly built terminus next to Waterloo Bridge Station and each train would have first, second and third class carriages to ensure that the posh people never had to mix with the peasants! However, there was nothing they could do about the noise and speed of the trains, so they just ignored that little detail.

In June 1854, the LNC started construction of their new station. It was completed a few months later and the company began operations on 13 November 1854. The mortuaries were located on the ground floor; the company's offices and the second and third class passenger waiting rooms on the first floor, and the first class waiting room and the platforms were located on the second floor, with steam-powered lifts being used to move the coffins between floors. The coffins were loaded into the carriages and the doors labelled with the family name, ensuring that each of the funeral parties travelled with the right one! First and second class mourners were boarded first and only when they were seated comfortably were the third class lot allowed out of the station and on to the train.

One train departed from Waterloo Bridge Station late in the morning every day. After arriving at Brookwood Cemetery, it first pulled into the South Station (for Anglican burials) and then into the North Station (for any other type of burial). The mourners would attend the burial service and then a wake at one of the cemetery's two stations before jumping back on the train back to London in the late afternoon.

By 1856, over 2,000 people a year were being laid to rest in Brookwood Cemetery with the vast majority of them making their final journey courtesy of the Necropolis Railway. The company originally used established High Street undertakers to arrange the funerals but soon started offering to do the whole thing themselves at a discounted price. Burying people in bulk might not have been particularly cheerful but it was certainly cheap, allowing them to pass along these savings to their customers.

By the end of the nineteenth century, business was booming but by the beginning of the twentieth century it was starting to tail off a bit. The invention of the motor car and the increased competition from new municipal cemeteries operated by the various London councils inevitably led to a downturn in the need for the LNC's unique services. By the 1930s, the number of trains leaving London for Brookwood Cemetery had been reduced to just one or two a week.

Then, on the night of 16/17 April 1941, a Luftwaffe bombing raid on central London destroyed the company's Waterloo station and all their rolling stock, and on 11 May 1941, the station was officially declared closed forever.

For 87 years, this bizarre train service had run an almost daily service from London to Surrey, transporting dead bodies on a 40-minute journey to Brookwood Cemetery. In total, 203,041 people were buried there during this time.

the devil's footprints

After a heavy overnight snowfall, the people of South Devon woke up on the morning of 9 February 1855 to find a trail of hoof-like tracks outside in the snow. The cloven hoof prints reportedly continued in a straight line for 40 to 100 miles (64-160km) seemingly going through high walls and haystacks, across gardens, through locked gates, and inexplicably up drainpipes and even across snow covered rooftops! They were between 8-16 inches (20-40cm) apart, 4 inches (10cm) long and 3 inches (7cm) across and were reported in about thirty different locations across the county. They appeared to have been left by a hoofed beast but walking upright like a human!

The Exeter & Plymouth Gazette published a letter from one of their readers describing in great detail the unusual event and commented: 'Everyone is wondering, but no one is able to explain the mystery; the poor are full of superstition, and consider it little short of a visit from old Satan or some of his imps.'

Many people did indeed believe they'd been visited by the Devil during the night, as no bird or beast could have possibly made such tracks in such a straight line for such a distance. The footprints had almost completely cleared the snow, giving the impression that they'd been branded into the ground, making it easy to imagine that the Devil's red hot hooves had made the marks as he'd stalked their towns and villages looking for sinners. As many of the tracks seemingly led directly to people's front doors, they were even afraid to leave their houses afterwards, fearful of being dragged away by Old Nick.

the dreadnought hoax

One of the most celebrated hoaxes in British military history!

Famous at the time and still well known today, due largely to the participation of a young Virginia Woolf (1882-1941) and the renowned prankster Horace De Vere Cole (1881-1936). The hoax was orchestrated by six members of the Bloomsbury Group, a loose London-based collective of young artist, writers and intellectuals, who lived, worked and studied together in Bloomsbury and were united by an abiding belief in the importance of the arts.

The 'Dreadnought Six' as they became known were able to gain access to the pride of the British naval fleet ...

HMS *Dreadnought* was the first of the 'dreadnought' class of battleships which entered service with the Royal Navy in 1906. It was faster, stronger, better equipped and more heavily armed than any other warship afloat and became a symbol of the British Empire's strength and dominance at sea. It also became a much loved cultural icon through songs and advertising. Oxo famously used the punchline 'Drink OXO and dread nought' to sell their stock cubes!

One of the pranksters sent a telegram to the Commander-in-Chief of the Home Fleet supposedly signed by someone called 'Harding' of the Foreign Office advising: 'Prince Makalen of Abbysinia [sic] and suite arrive 4:20 today, Weymouth. He wishes to see *Dreadnought*. Kindly arrange meet them on arrival.'

On 7 February 1910, they all travelled by train from London to Weymouth in Dorset. Four of them had darkened their faces with stage makeup and donned false beards, turbans and exotic costumes to disguise themselves as members of the Abyssinian royal family while the other two had just put on their best suits and were pretending to be the accompanying Foreign Office officials. They were welcomed aboard the ship with an honour guard. Presumably, nobody could find an Abyssinian flag for the occasion, because the Royal Navy flew the one from Zanzibar instead ... and played the Zanzibar national anthem too! The fake VIPs were then given a 40-minute guided tour of the ship. They appeared to talk in their native tongue (which was actually just a mixture of Latin, Greek and a few words of Swahili) and exclaimed 'Bunga! Bunga!' every now and again, which was interpreted as a way of them showing their appreciation. Although they enjoyed their tour, they refused any refreshments because they were worried that their beards might fall off. At one point, it began to rain and the FO chaps only just got their African visitors undercover in time. A few moments longer outside and their face makeup would have started to run.

The Royal Navy were horrified to learn of the hoax and the newspapers delighted in their embarrassment. The Admiralty wanted to bring formal charges against the pranksters but soon dropped the idea, fearing that a court case might attract even more unwanted publicity. Instead they just ordered the ship to sea until all the fuss had died down.

the world champions from county durham

Before the first official FIFA World Cup in 1930, the English businessman Thomas Lipton (1848-1931) invited the best club teams from Italy, Germany, Switzerland and England to compete for the Sir Thomas Lipton Trophy, an inter-club competition to be held in Turin in

Italy. The first three countries duly complied with his request and sent their strongest teams but the old farts at the Football Association refused to have anything to do with his little competition and declined his request to take part. Not wishing to see England excluded, however, Sir Thomas then asked West Auckland FC, an amateur side from County Durham playing in the Northern League, to represent their country.

Why they should have got the invite, nobody really knows!

The part-time players of West Auckland were mostly coalminers and struggled to raise the funds for their journey to Italy with many of them forced to pawn their own possessions to find the money. Most of them had never been out of County Durham before, let alone the country, so the journey itself was already a fairly daunting experience for them. They crossed the English Channel and then took a train through France to Turin, where they were greeted by the tournament organisers as Woolwich Arsenal FC. They'd been expecting a big club to arrive from England and had been told that WAFC were on their way, so when the players eventually turned up, it was just assumed they'd be from the more famous north London club. Nobody had been expecting a bunch of part-time Geordie miners! The tournament organisers were disappointed but still had to let them play. What kind of a football competition would it be without a representative from the country that invented the sport?

The lads met their opponents and then they watched a few of their training sessions but they came away feeling pretty downbeat about their chances as all the other teams seemed more prepared, more skilful and much fitter than them.

But all that nervousness and self-doubt soon disappeared when they started playing football ...

On 11 April 1909, they met their first opponents Sportfreunde Stuttgart from Germany and secured a fairly comfortable 2-0 victory. They'd started slowly but grew in confidence after scoring an early goal in the 10th minute. Their second goal came two minutes before the final whistle when their goalkeeper James Dickenson converted a spot-kick to secure the team's place in the final.

The final was played the very next day on 12 April 1909 against the Swiss champions and the tournament favourites FC Winterthur who had just beaten Torino XI from Italy in the other semi-final. It was expected to be a pretty easy game for them but things didn't work out that way because the lads from County Durham beat them 2-0 too.

Tiny West Auckland FC were suddenly the first and the most unlikeliest champions of the world!

Note: As the cup holders, West Auckland were invited back to Italy two years later in 1911 to defend their title. They beat Switzerland's FC Red Star 2-0 and then met the Italian giants Juventus in the final on 17 April 1911. But this time they didn't win 2-0. This time they won 6-1 and were awarded the trophy outright. It's difficult to believe that a bunch of poorly equipped and under-funded coalminers had just beaten the mighty Juventus team to become champions of the world for the second time!

Note: The team didn't hold onto the Sir Thomas Lipton Trophy for very long though. The club had serious financial problems after all their gadding about in Europe and they were forced to pawn the trophy to pay off a £40 debt to the landlady of a local pub. The trophy remained in her possession for almost fifty years until the club were able to buy it back from her for £100 in 1960. Then in 1994, the trophy was stolen. Despite an extensive police investigation and the club offering a substantial reward for its safe return, it has never been recovered.

little kinsey

The first national survey into the sexual behaviour of both men and women ever undertaken in Britain was dubbed Little Kinsey after the American Kinsey Report, a similar survey into the secret sex lives of American men undertaken in 1948. A cross-section of just over 2,000 people were asked their opinions on sex education, divorce, birth control, prostitution and their personal sexual habits. The findings showed the remarkable truths behind the prim and proper façade of post-war Britain and were considered so scandalous that the social research group who undertook the survey never published their results! One-in-five men said they'd had a homosexual experience, one-in-four men admitted to having sex with a prostitute, and one-in-five women claimed to have had an extra-marital affair!

However, the Little Kinsey results were still a lot less promiscuous than the American survey results, which seemed to confirm the popular establishment opinion at the time that oversexed GIs stationed in Britain during World War II (1939-1945) had been responsible for the decline in British morals.

The survey results only came to light when they became the subject of a BBC documentary film in 2005.

mother prodgers

Caroline Prodgers (1829-1890) was famous for her seemingly endless hate campaign against London cab drivers.

She first went to court in 1871 to divorce her Austrian husband Giovanni Battista Giacometti, and appeared to enjoy the experience so much that she couldn't wait to get back there again!

For some inexplicable reason she then vented her anger against the London cab drivers to get her day in court.

She would memorise their tariff and then stop a driver, even if she hadn't arrived at her destination, just before they were entitled to charge her for the full fare. If they failed to stop immediately or attempted to overcharge her, she'd threaten to take them to court. In her nineteen year reign of terror against the drivers, she took 50 of them to court … and won most of the cases. It wasn't long before even the magistrates were sick of seeing her standing before them in their courtroom, with one particularly confused judge commenting that it would be much cheaper and convenient for her to buy a horse and carriage rather than having to pay the court costs of all her frivolous lawsuits. Her notoriety soon spread throughout London's cab ranks. If one cabbie spotted her approaching, he'd shout a warning to the others: 'Mother Prodgers! Mother Prodgers' and they'd all scatter.

Caroline Prodgers was featured in cartoons and poems in satirical magazines and it's rumoured that she was such a despised figure that cabbies even burnt effigies of her on Bonfire Night.

The comedian, actor and music hall entertainer Herbert Campbell (1844-1904) penned this little verse about her:

All great men have their statues and its but their due,
But I wonder why the ladies don't have them too;
If they did, to the Academy I'd like to send,
A bust of Mrs Prodgers the Cabman's friend.
Of all the strong-minded females she's the worst I ever saw,
Oh, wouldn't she be lovely as a mother-in-law?
At the corner of every cab-rank her flag should be unfurled,
As a horrible example to this wicked world.

the invasion of iceland

Possibly the easiest military invasion of all time!

Iceland was of strategic value to both the Allies and the Axis powers during World War II (1939-1945) but after failing to persuade their government to join the Allied war effort, the British didn't take no for an answer and invaded on the morning of 10 May 1940. Over 700 Royal Marines commanded by Robert Sturges (1891-1970) disembarked at Reykjavik and quickly disabled communication networks, secured strategic locations and arrested any German citizens they stumbled across. After requisitioning local transport, the troops then moved quickly to secure other possible landing areas on the island susceptible to a German counter attack.

The whole thing lasted a few short hours and without a shot being fired!

The Icelandic government protested and claimed that their neutrality had been violated and its independence threatened; they demanded compensation and made a point of letting the whole world know that Iceland was on the side of nobody in the war. But their complaints were ignored and more British troops arrived followed by the first contingent of 2,500 Canadian Army troops on 16 June 1940.

Even the Americans sent troops to occupy the island and they hadn't even entered the war yet!

finding a wife

Finding a wife in the old days sometimes meant placing an ad in the local newspaper and hoping for the best!

Lonely Hearts columns or Matrimonial Advertisements, as they were more commonly known, have been a regular feature in British newspapers for over 300 years, and were incredibly popular with the public back in the days before you could just swipe right and hope for the best.

Originally the advertisements were only placed by young gentlemen seeking a wife.

The earliest known example was placed by a man who rather curiously described himself as being 'about 30 years-old' in the popular magazine *Collection for the Improvement of Husbandry and Trade* on 9 July 1695. He went on to explain that he had 'a very good estate' and that he was seeking 'some good young gentlewoman that has a fortune of £3,000 of thereabouts.'

Examples from the eighteen-century were either very romantic or very business-like but always very specific. In 1750, one lonely man placed an ad in *The Daily Advertiser* for a wife with 'good teeth, soft lips [and] sweet breath ... neat in her person, her bosom full, plump, firm and white; a good understanding, without being a wit, but cheerful and lively in conversation, polite and delicate of speech.'

Note: The first ad placed by a woman was in 1727 by a young lass called Helen Morrison who professed her desire to meet a gentleman in the *Manchester Weekly Journal*. Unfortunately for her, the only gentleman she actually met was the mayor of the town who promptly had her committed to a mental hospital for four weeks!

It wasn't until the late nineteenth century when it became more acceptable for women to place ads for a husband and this change in social attitudes came in quite handy for anyone brave enough to be homosexual back then. They published their ads using female names with codewords to protect themselves and get around the law. Nobody who wasn't that way inclined was none the wiser and the gay folk of the day could meet up safely and securely without being dragged off to jail.

selling a wife

In eighteenth and nineteenth century England, married couples who'd fallen out of love faced a real dilemma. It was impossible to get a divorce and an annulment was far too expensive, so most married couples just carried on living together unhappily ever after ... unless the husband could find another man willing to buy his wife off him! Although the practice was actually illegal, the authorities usually turned a blind eye and during the golden age of wife selling (1780-1850) some 300 sales were recorded.

In most instances the sale was announced in advance, usually through an advertisement in the local paper. The wife was usually led to the local marketplace by a rope tied around her neck or arm and made to stand on an auction block; a crowd would gather, and the husband would start taking bids. Once the deal was struck, everyone would gather in the nearest pub to celebrate with a few pints. In fact, quite often the price would also include a pre-agreed quantity of beers and spirits! Sometimes, she was even sold to an existing lover after a fee had been agreed between the two men beforehand.

In the vast majority of cases the wife was just as happy as the husband to go along with the auction.

The first recorded wife sold at auction was a young lady called Mary Whitehouse. Her husband Samuel sold her to a Thomas Griffith at a Birmingham market for one guinea sometime in 1733. As part of the deal the buyer was to accept the woman 'with all her faults'.

the shakespeare hoax

In December 1794, a young lad called William Henry Ireland (1775-1835) told his father Samuel Ireland (1744-1800) about a cache of old documents in a friend's possession which were purportedly written by William Shakespeare (1564-1616).

Samuel was a successful publisher and a keen collector of anything old, curious or valuable. He was also a big fan of England's greatest playwright and had been collecting Shakespearean memorabilia for many years. Although, in truth, there wasn't actually a lot of it around to collect. Nobody had ever uncovered any original manuscripts, documents or correspondence written by the Bard, so imagine his delight at suddenly being presented with such an historic find by his son.

He was overjoyed when he saw the various documents and papers which included letters and poems scribbled in faded ink on yellowed paper to his future wife Anne Hathaway (1556-1623), a statement of his Protestant faith, a letter from Queen Elizabeth I (1533-1603), old books with his handwritten notes in the margins, a few pages of *Hamlet* (1609) and an original full manuscript for *King Lear* (1606).

But none of them were real. William had forged the lot as part of a desperate plan to win a little affection and respect from his cold and judgemental father.

In February 1795, many literary scholars, antiquarians and dignitaries including the Poet Laureate Henry James Pye (1744-1813), the playwright and theatrical impresario Richard Brinsley Sheridan (1751-1816) and the famous diarist James Boswell, 9th Laird of Auchinleck (1740-1795), were invited into the family home to inspect the historic find. It seems that all the so-called experts of the day were easily fooled because they all complimented Samuel on his discovery and later publicly declared their belief that it was all authentic. It's been said that James Boswell studied them for a long time in-between sips of hot brandy and water. Finally, he set the documents on a table, got down on his knees and kissed the top pages, exclaiming 'I shall now die contented.' Which is exactly what he did three months later!

But not everyone was quite as excited about the discovery as Samuel and his new friends ...

One visitor noted that a letter supposedly written by the statesman Robert Dudley, 1st Earl of Leicester (1532-1588), had been dated in 1590, two years after his death! Two leading academics, Richard Porson (1759-1808) and Joseph Ritson (1752-1803) then correctly recognised the documents as being phoney, with the latter commenting that they were 'a parcel of forgeries, studiously and ably calculated to deceive the public.' Suspicion was further aroused as Samuel hadn't invited the two greatest Shakespearean scholars of the day, Edmond Malone (1741-1812) and George Steevens (1736-1800) to examine the documents. He'd invited everyone else, so why not them?

To counter the cynics, however, a core group of fans including James Boswell then issued a *Certificate of Belief* stating that they 'entertained no doubt whatsoever as to the validity of the Shakespearian production.'

Meanwhile, Samuel enthusiastically continued promoting his son's discoveries and many more people turned up at his house to view them. He even brought out a little book about it all, a lavishly illustrated and expensively produced set of facsimiles and transcriptions of his precious documents called *Miscellaneous Papers and Legal Instruments under the Hand and Seal of William Shakespeare* (1795).

Then, in March 1795, William presented his father with the promised manuscript for a previously unknown play called *Vortigern and Rowena* which was also part of his friend's seemingly inexhaustible supply of Shakespearean memorabilia. Previously he'd just copied the original printed texts for the *Hamlet* and *King Lear* manuscripts onto the flyleaves he'd torn from antique books, omitting a few lines and adding a few passages of his own every now and again, but now he'd become much bolder, writing an entirely new play himself and passing it off as one of the Bard's long-lost masterpieces.

The rights to stage the play were sold to Richard Brinsley Sheridan (1751-1816). He was the owner of London's Theatre Royal, Drury Lane and had just spent a small fortune on having the place renovated, so he was badly in need of a hit to offset all the building costs. Knowing full well that staging the first new Shakespeare production in almost 200 years would fill his 3,500-seat theatre night after night, he jumped at the chance to stage the play despite finding it a little simplistic and unpoetic. He wasn't totally convinced that it was the work of the Bard but hey ... what the hell, it looked old enough, an extra 'e' had been added to the end of enough words to make it seem Elizabethan in origin and all the other stuff had been authenticated by greater minds than his, so he handed over £300 for the rights and lined up the esteemed actors John Philip Kemble (1757-1823) and Sarah Siddons (1755-1831) in the lead roles.

Vortigern and Rowena opened to a full house on 2 April 1796. The first two of the five acts went well with little of the customary heckling from the audience. They even applauded a few of the speeches. But in the third act, a bit player overplayed his lines for comic effect, and in the fifth act, John Philip Kemble, who'd also been a little sceptical about the play's authenticity and had previously suggested that it would be more appropriate if it opened on April Fools' Day, began repeating the line 'and when this solemn mockery is o'er' in a ghoulish and drawn-out voice, which provoked several minutes of laughter and whistling from the audience. When the final curtain came down, the audience cheered and booed in equal numbers. Many believed they'd just witnessed a lost Shakespearean play being performed whilst others believed they'd sat through a pile of old dross that clearly wasn't the work of England's greatest playwright. The audience was clearly split between believers and non-believers and the animosity between the two groups resulted in a bit of fisticuffs in the orchestra pit afterwards!

Newspaper reviews were fairly damning. The critics had clearly taken their cue from Edmond Malone who'd recently added his voice to the growing list of sceptics by publishing a 424-page exposé of the documents and manuscripts, describing them as a 'clumsy and daring fraud' riddled with errors and contradictions.

The debate over Samuel Ireland's papers and the authenticity of the play persisted for many months afterwards. By now, William was beginning to feel a bit stressed-out by it all, and eventually he confessed to the fraud. His father refused to believe that his simple-minded son had planned something quite so elaborate and continued disbelieving it right up until his death four years later.

Despite William's public admittance of guilt, some people were unwilling to accept that an 18 year-old kid could have misled so many distinguished people and they began to suspect Samuel of being the real mastermind behind the fraud. Naively, William had expected to be praised for his ingenuity and brilliance but instead he was either denied the recognition or harshly criticised for the deception. Something he just dismissed as a way of his critics coping with the embarrassment of being so easily fooled.

William never expressed any real regret, in fact he was rather proud of everything he'd done and later wrote *The Confessions of William Henry Ireland* (1805) in which he described in great detail how he perpetrated the fraud. This book helped him win publication for some of his own original novels and poetry, but ultimately any real success eluded him and he will only be remembered for committing one of the most audacious literary hoaxes in history.

lost trophies

Compared to some of England's other big football clubs like Arsenal, Liverpool and Manchester United, Aston Villa haven't won that many trophies. Probably just as well because they're not very good at looking after them. Not only did they manage to lose the FA Cup in 1895 they also lost the European Cup for a few hours in 1982 too ...

THE FA CUP

Aston Villa won the FA Cup after beating West Bromwich Albion 1-0 on 20 April 1895 at Crystal Palace Park in London. At that time, the FA Cup competition was still English football's greatest prize and the Football Association (FA) generously allowed the winning team to keep the trophy for a year until the winners of the following season's final took possession.

William Shillcock was a shoemaker and sportswear retailer who'd supplied the winning Villa team with their boots. He was also a lifelong fan, so when he'd asked for their permission to display the FA Cup in the window of his Birmingham shop, the club readily agreed to his request. The trophy attracted huge crowds and no doubt resulted in a lot of extra business for William too.

After locking up his shop at around 9.15pm on the evening of 11 September 1895, he returned the following morning at 8.00am only to discover that he'd been burgled overnight. Although the till had been emptied, the two safes and many other valuables remained untouched. It was only when he checked the window display that he discovered the true reason for the break-in.

To his horror the FA Cup had been stolen!

William informed the police and distributed handbills around the city offering a £10 reward for the trophy's safe return. However, it was ultimately Aston Villa who were responsible for the cup's safety and they were ordered by the FA to pay for a replacement. The police never solved the crime, the FA Cup was never recovered and a replica trophy had to be used until 1911.

Fast forward 63 years ...

In an exclusive interview with the *Sunday Pictorial* published on 23 February 1958 under the headline I STOLE THE FA CUP, an 80 year-old, career-criminal called Harry Burge claimed to have stolen the trophy with two of his mates. According to Harry, they'd broken into the shop, snatched the cup and then calmly walked back to his house a few streets away to melt it down and make fake half-crown coins. Ironically, most of these coins were then spent on booze in a city centre pub owned by the Villa striker Dennis Hodgetts (1863-1945) and frequented by many of his team-mates. In the newspaper article, Harry speculated that the players would have almost certainly handled the dud coins not knowing that they were actually holding a bit of the melted down FA Cup in their hands!

THE EUROPEAN CUP

Villa had beaten Germany's Bayern Munich 1-0 in the final of the UEFA European Cup in Rotterdam on 26 May 1982 and twenty-four hours later they'd somehow managed to lose the trophy in a Birmingham pub!

Two of the Villa players Colin Gibson (1960-) and Gordon Cowans (1958-) had taken the giant silver cup into the Fox Inn near Tamworth in Staffordshire, which was a popular pub with the Villa players at the time, so the fans could see it, touch it and have their photos taken with it. The players downed a few pints and sometime later got involved in a game of darts, taking their eyes off European football's most treasured prize long enough for it to be stolen! Nobody had the slightest idea what had happened to it, least of all the two red-faced players, and eventually the police were informed of the theft.

It wasn't until 3.00am the following morning when there was a break in the case …

A hundred miles away, a man had walked into a Sheffield city-centre police station, identified himself as Mr Sykes and then informed the officer on duty at the front desk that he had the European Cup stashed in the boot of his car. He'd then gone outside again and returned a few minutes later with the cup, still with the claret and blue ribbons attached. He'd admitted taking it from the pub but had then had a change of heart and was now returning it and handing himself in.

The South Yorkshire cops informed their colleagues in the West Midlands force, who then informed the players and the pub staff still anxiously pacing around the Fox Inn. The cup was eventually returned, Aston Villa were saved the cost and embarrassment of having to pay for another one and the mysterious Mr Sykes was apparently released without charge.

It was later revealed that Mr Sykes was actually a 28 year-old Fox Inn regular called Adrian Reed, who'd swiped the cup and taken it home to show his flatmates. They eventually persuaded him to hand it in to the police, and then for some strange reason, he'd decided to drive all the way to Sheffield and return it to a police station there.

Note: The South Yorkshire police officers on duty at the Sheffield police station that night acted no differently from anyone else who might have suddenly found themselves in possession of the European Cup. They wanted their photograph taken with it but in 1982, mobile phones hadn't yet been invented, so they had to call in their Scenes of Crime Officer who was the only person they knew with easy access to a camera!

the convict police force

A fleet of 11 ships captained by Arthur Phillip (1738-1814) sailed from Portsmouth to Australia on 13 May 1787 with over 1,400 sailors, marines, convicts, government officials and free settlers. On 26 January 1788, the Union Jack was raised at what is now Sydney Cove, Port Jackson, NSW where Britain established the first permanent European settlement on the continent.

A year later, the best-behaved convicts were chosen to serve as members of Australia's first police force!

Although the marines had originally assumed responsibility for law enforcement, there just weren't enough of them to do it effectively. At the time, Australia had many more convicts than free settlers, so Arthur had no choice but to enlist the help of the most trusting and best-behaved thieves and petty criminals to patrol the streets after dark, in order to protect the law-abiding folks from the nastier and more violent thieves and petty criminals!

a reindeer called pollyanna

HMS *Trident* was a British submarine assigned to patrol the waters of the North Sea during the early days of World War II (1939-1945).

In August of 1941 it stopped off at the Russian naval base at Polyarny in Russia for repairs and in the spirit of Anglo-Soviet cooperation, the ship's captain Geoffrey Sladen and his officers were invited to dine with their Soviet counterparts. As a way of showing his country's appreciation for Britain's help in fighting the Nazis, the Soviets presented Geoffrey with a little gift at the end of their meal, and not wishing to appear rude, he gratefully accepted it ... albeit through gritted teeth.

During the dinner he'd foolishly mentioned how his wife had been struggling to push the pram through the snow back home in England and now all of a sudden he was the proud owner of a bloody great reindeer!

The reindeer was named Pollyanna after the name of the Russian naval base. The next day, she was lowered into HMS *Trident* via the torpedo tubes, the British said *dasvidaniya* and then sailed away to patrol the Norwegian fjords again.

Pollyanna soon got used to the sights and sounds of life at sea and was free to wander around the submarine at will. She quickly adopted the captain's cabin as her rest area and lay under his bunk for most of the day, although when the submarine was resurfacing she would often stand under the hatch and breathe in the fresh air.

Pollyanna dined on moss donated by the Soviets and buckets of leftovers, jam and condensed milk donated by the submarine's crew.

When HMS *Trident* finally returned to her home port at Blyth, after six weeks at sea, Pollyanna was too fat to fit inside the torpedo tubes again. All that lying around and gorging on scraps had taken its toll and she had to be winched out of the hatch. Pollyanna never got the chance to pull any prams through the snow because as soon as her hooves hit dry land, she was whisked off to her new home at the Regent's Park Zoo in London.

piltdown man

The greatest scientific hoax of the twentieth century!

The amateur archaeologist Charles Dawson (1864-1916) claimed to have found some bone fragments in a gravel pit in Piltdown, East Sussex. He contacted his old friend Arthur Smith Woodward (1864-1944), who just happened to be the curator of the geology department at the National History Museum in London and together they excavated the gravel pit looking for more bones between June and September 1912. After uncovering further human skull fragments, some teeth, half of a lower jaw bone, and a few primitive stone tools buried in the pit's spoil heaps, they presented their findings to the prestigious Geological Society of London at a meeting on 18 December 1912.

The two men hypothesised that the remains belonged to a previously unknown early human from around 500,000 years ago and it was given the Latin name of *Eoanthropus Dawsoni*. Arthur had reconstructed Piltdown Man's skull (containing characteristics that were both human and apelike) which led them to believe that they'd now found the missing evolutionary link between the two species!

Whilst some fellow anthropologists such as Grafton Elliot Smith (1871-1937) sided with Charles and Arthur, others such as Pierre-Marcellin Boule and Franz Weidenreich argued that the Piltdown Man discovery was just a scam and nothing more than a modern human skull and a monkey's jaw bone.

However, for the most part, the scientific community accepted their findings in good faith as a new species of human - the illusive so-called missing link which marked the point at which humans and apes began their separate evolutionary development, especially as their reconstructed skull with an ape-like jaw seemed to support the erroneous theory of the time that human evolution began with the brain.

In 1915, more bits of more bones were unearthed by Charles at a second site around 2 miles (3.2km) away from the original excavation. The three skull fragments labelled 'Piltdown II' were then made public by Arthur after his colleague's death in 1916 and were viewed as conclusive proof of the original discovery's authenticity.

Then in 1953, the whole thing was exposed as just a very elaborate scientific hoax …

The anthropologists Kenneth Oakley (1911-1981) and Joseph Weiner (1915-1982) and the human anatomist Wilfred Le Gros Clark (1895-1971) ran a new advanced fluorine absorption test which demonstrated that the fossils were in fact a composite of three very different species. The skull was human, the jaw was from an orangutan and the teeth once belonged to a chimpanzee, and all of them were more likely to be around 500 years old instead of 500,000! They also discovered that all the Piltdown finds had been artificially stained with an iron solution and chromic acid to match the colour of the local gravel and the scratches on the teeth revealed that they'd been filed down to make them look more human.

The identity of the Piltdown hoaxer still remains unknown but there have been many names in the frame over the years including the celebrated pranksters Horace de Vere Cole (1881-1936) and Arthur Conan Doyle (1859-1930). However, the prime suspect has always been Charles Dawson himself. There's evidence that he may have perpetrated other archaeological hoaxes in the past; his publications were often plagiarised or demonstrated naïve research, and his antiquarian collection contained many fake specimens including the teeth of a reptile/mammal hybrid *Plagiaulax Dawsoni* which he'd claimed to have discovered in 1891 and whose teeth had also been filed down in the same way as the teeth of Piltdown Man.

It was almost as if the Piltdown Man hoax had been the culmination of his life's work!

the royal institution hack

Most people think that hacking is a modern phenomenon but the world's first known public hack took place way back in 1903 …

On 4 June 1903, the physicist John Ambrose Fleming (1849-1945) was preparing to deliver a lecture at the Royal Institution (London) featuring a demonstration of a new wireless communication system pioneered by the Anglo-Italian engineer Guglielmo Marconi (1874-1937) which could transmit secure Morse code messages over long distances.

Guglielmo was extremely proud of his invention and had previously boasted in the London newspaper, *St James Gazette*: 'I can tune my instruments so that no other that is not similarly tuned can tap my messages.'

He was over 300 miles (482km) away at a clifftop radio station in Poldhu, Cornwall, and was getting ready to send a signal back to the audience in London but before the show could start, the apparatus used to receive the transmission began tapping out a rather unexpected (and unauthorised) message which was then projected onto a screen at the front of the lecture hall. At first, it tapped out the word 'Rats!' over and over again but then a little poem: 'There was a young fellow of Italy, who diddled the public quite prettily …[etc etc]' followed by a few more insulting rhymes!

It was obvious that somebody had hacked into the fancy new system to prove that anyone could eavesdrop on private messages and it wasn't quite as wonderful as Guglielmo had claimed.

The disruptive signals stopped just before Guglielmo's message was due to arrive from Cornwall but the damage had been done. If some anonymous trickster could hack into the apparatus whilst its inventor was busy showcasing it to the public then anyone could do it at any time and no message was ever going to be that safe or secure.

John Ambrose Fleming was furious at the intrusion and the embarrassment it had caused his friend. He fired off a letter to *The Times* describing the hack as 'scientific hooliganism' and demanded the public's help in identifying the saboteur. But his appeal proved unnecessary as the man responsible couldn't wait to blab about his mischief-making …

Four days later, *The Times* published a letter from the magician and music hall entertainer Nevil Maskelyne (1863-1924) in which he gleefully admitted to the hack, claiming that he'd acted in the public good, justifying his actions as the only way of exposing the security issues involved with the new-fangled technology. But what he'd failed to mention was that he'd been paid to do so by the Eastern Telegraph Co Ltd. They'd hired him to make trouble for Guglielmo because they'd just invested heavily in the use of undersea cables and stood to lose a great deal of money if everyone suddenly switched to using wireless communication.

the d-day crosswords

The Normandy Landings on 6 June 1944 by US, British and Canadian forces was the largest seaborne invasion in history.

In the months leading up to D-Day, the solutions 'Gold' and 'Sword' (which were the codenames allocated to the beaches where British forces would land) and 'Juno' (the codename for the Canadian beach) had appeared in *Daily Telegraph* crossword puzzles. The first two words were obviously in common usage and had appeared in the puzzles before so the incident was treated as just a rather unfortunate coincidence by the boys at MI5.

Then, on 2 May 1944, 'One of the US' appeared as the clue for 17-down. The answer was 'Utah' (codename for one of the US beaches). Slowly but surely it seemed like all of the Allied codenames for the Normandy beaches were being disclosed! The fifth and final beach of 'Omaha' (the other US beach) then appeared as the answer to the clue 'Red Indian on the Missouri' for 3-down on 22 May 1944.

By now, the boys at MI5 were beginning to get a bit suspicious ...

In the crossword of 27 May 1944, the clue for 11 across read 'bigwig' The answer was 'overlord', as in Operation Overlord, the codename for the whole D-Day operation! Then on 30 May 1944, 'Mulberry' appeared as the answer for another 11-across clue: 'The bush is the centre of nursery revolutions.' But Mulberry was also the name for the temporary portable harbours developed by Britain to facilitate the rapid offloading of cargo onto the beaches during the landings. Finally, on 1 June 1944, the clue: 'Britannia and he hold to the same thing' appeared at 15-down. The answer was 'Neptune' as in Operation Neptune, the British mission name for the initial seaborne landings of Operation Overlord.

Clearly there was a spy at the *Daily Telegraph* ...

Suspicion immediately fell on the crossword compiler Leonard Dawe (1889-1963).

He was the headteacher of a posh London all-boys grammar school which had been re-located to Effingham, Surrey, after the outbreak of World War II (1939-1945). He was also a keen crossword enthusiast and had been compiling the cryptic puzzles published in the *Daily Telegraph* since 1925. The boys from MI5 turned up at the school and hauled him away. They ransacked his home and his office, and then subjected him to days of intense interrogation. But they couldn't break him. They'd demanded to know why he'd hidden those words in his crosswords but he'd continued to deny any knowledge of their significance.

No one would ever have imagined that the puzzle pages of such a well-respected British newspaper could have been used by fifth columnists and subversives but that's exactly what might have happened. The schoolboys were just as shocked. There'd been a Nazi spy in their midst and it had been their loveable, mild-mannered headmaster Mr Dawe!

After keeping him in custody until after D-Day, MI5 were eventually forced to release him and accept that it had all been an unfortunate coincidence. Leonard Dawe was allowed to return to his school ... and allowed to continue compiling crosswords for the *Daily Telegraph.*

Surely, the greatest coincidence ever known in the whole of history!

Until one day in 1984 when it suddenly wasn't …

After the *Daily Telegraph* ran an article celebrating forty years since the great D-Day Crossword Puzzle Mystery, an old student of the school called Ronald French got in touch to explain what had really happened. Mr Dawe was apparently in the habit of inviting sixth-formers into his study to suggest words that he could use as answers in his crossword puzzles with the boys competing amongst themselves to see who could come up with the most unusual and imaginative words. Only later would Mr Dawe then devise the clues to match the answers he'd been given. The teenage boys were obviously obsessed with the war and they'd previously suggested solutions like 'warden', 'aircraft' and other well-used, war-themed words of the time. The school was also right next to a US army base and the boys would often hang out with the soldiers. They'd struck up a close friendship with some of the men and would often just sit around and chat and eat chocolate with them, so it was inevitable that they'd pick up some of their vocabulary and overhear some loose talk. Ronald claimed that everyone knew about the invasion plan and the soldiers frequently talked about Operation Overlord and the Omaha and Utah beaches.

It was only afterwards, when Leonard Dawe had asked him how he and his friends had thought of the words, that he'd admitted to overhearing his army buddies at the camp using them and had then written them down in his notebook. Mr Dawe went apeshit when he was told! He accused Ronald of jeopardising national security, ordered him to burn his notebooks and made him swear on the bible never to talk about the incident again! Poor little Ronald was mortified to learn how he may have unwittingly endangered the war effort.

skeletons in the cupboard

This little story concerning a practical joke played by the famous English writer Arthur Conan Doyle (1859-1930) appeared in the weekly magazine *Tit-Bits* published on 18 September 1897:

> 'This story has been attributed to Mr Conan Doyle: A friend of his had often been told that there is a skeleton in the cupboard of every household, no matter how respectable that household may be; and he determined to put this opinion to a practical test. Selecting for the subject of his experiment a venerable Archdeacon of the Church, against whom the most censorious critic had never breathed a word, he went to the nearest post-office, and dispatched a telegram to the revered gentleman: "All is discovered! Fly at once!" The Archdeacon disappeared, and has never been heard of since!'

san serriffe

The islands of San Serriffe were featured in a special seven-page travel supplement published in *The Guardian* on 1 April 1977. It was one of the most elaborate newspaper April Fools' Day jokes ever conceived and has been credited with fuelling the British media's obsession for these jokes in subsequent years.

The obscure archipelago with its two main islands of Caissa Superiore (Upper Caisse) and Caissa Inferiore (Lower Caisse) was shaped like a semi-colon and was supposed to be located in the Indian Ocean, somewhere north-east of the Seychelles. The supplement provided an elaborate description of the islands as a tourist destination celebrating ten years of independence and very cleverly featured a load of themed advertisements from major companies who were in on the joke to make the articles seem all the more realistic.

Kodak sponsored a photography competition, with the best snaps forming part of a future *The Legendary Beauty of San Serriffe* exhibition; Texaco organised a competition to win a vacation with the Formula One racing driver James Hunt (1947-1993) at one of San Serriffe's Cocobanana Beach resorts, and Guinness placed an ad detailing how the San Serriffe version of their famous beverage was a little different from the one on sale in the rest of the world:

> *How San Serriffe turned Guinness upside down: It was after the freak barley crop of '56 that the local inhabitants of San Serriffe first began to notice a change in their beer. The taste was the same. It still poured slowly and evenly. But the white head turned out black and the strong dark body was white. Experts put it down to the novice farm helpers who spent their holiday in San Serriffe that year. Knowing little about crops, they sowed the barley seeds upside down.*

The Guardian itself invented a fake ad for the position of 'Reader in Lunar Spectroscopy' at the University of San Serriffe, with the successful applicant being expected to spend their time extracting energy from moonbeams. Rather surprisingly, they were inundated with applications!

There were many in-depth articles about the island's history, geography, culture and economy including: *Three Point Key to Prosperity* describing how the island's economy was reliant on tourism, oil and the phosphate industry; *The Leader's Rise to Power* reporting on the bloodless 1971 coup which saw the island's president-for-life General Maria-Jesu Pica come to power; *Spiking the Cultural Roots* focusing on the cultural heritage of the indigenous San Serriffe people, their relationship with the European immigrants, and the annual *Festival of the Well Made Play* when the islanders stage the complete works of the prolific but fairly mediocre and largely unknown playwright William Douglas Home (1912-1992); and *Transposed by the Tides* detailing the island's unique geological characteristics, particularly it's coastal erosion problem. Due to the sand and silt disappearing from the west coasts and mysteriously reappearing on the east coasts, the islands were gradually moving through the Indian Ocean at a rate of 0.86 miles (1,400m) each year. It had been estimated that they would eventually collide with Sri Lanka in 2011 and to slow down the erosion and hopefully avoid a collision, boats were continually ferrying all that sand and silt from one coast to the other!

Everything connected with the story was named after printing and typesetting terms such as the capital city of Bodoni (a typeface), the president's name, Pica (a typographic unit of measurement) and the indigenous islanders who were known as Flongs (a mould for making type). The public weren't familiar with the industry's professional terms and at the time they didn't know one typeface from another.

The majority of people were completely fooled by the fake travel supplement. Only a few smart-arse readers spotted the joke and many of them wanted to be part of it. *The Guardian* received hundreds of letters supposedly describing memorable holidays in San Serriffe and one particular letter purportedly from the San Serriffe Liberation Front slagging off the newspaper for their pro-government stance!

wooden warfare

The Nazis liked nothing better than constructing phoney airfields. They were made almost entirely of wood and included aircraft, hangers, oil tanks, gun emplacements, the odd truck or two and anything else that might be found at an airfield, all meticulously crafted to look like the real thing from the air. They were meant to trick the Allies into thinking that they had more resources at their disposal than was actually the case and fool them into mounting worthless raids and wasting their precious bombs and ammunition.

A well-repeated wartime story, which may or may not be true, is the one about the fake airfield built in occupied Holland. The Nazis had taken so long to build the bloody thing that the Allies had lots of time to observe its construction. They knew exactly what was going on, and so when the day finally arrived when it was supposed to be open for business, a lone RAF plane crossed the English Channel, came in low, circled the airfield and dropped a large *wooden* bomb!

the war of jenkins' ear

When Britain and Spain went to war just because one man had his ear cut off by another man!

The Royal Navy ship HMS *Rebecca* was returning home after a voyage to the West Indies when it was stopped off the coast of Florida on 9 April 1731 and boarded by the crew of the Spanish coastguard sloop *La Isabela.* After being accused of smuggling, the *Rebecca's* captain Robert Jenkins was tied to a mast and had his left ear sliced off by his cutlass-wielding Spanish counterpart, Juan de León Fandiño.

Seven years later, in the spring of 1738, Robert recounted the incident before a special committee of MPs at the House of Commons and dramatically produced his severed ear which he'd kept pickled in a jar for all that time!

The British public were outraged and Parliament later voted for the king to seek redress from Spain. The Spanish couldn't be allowed to go around cutting the ears off Englishmen whenever they felt like it and should be made to pay for their barbaric actions! By the summer of 1739, however, all diplomatic efforts to win any form of recompense from the Spanish government had been exhausted and so George II (1683-1760) directed the Royal Navy to initiate maritime reprisals against their ships.

A formal declaration of war was made on 23 October 1739.

Then, after nine years of war and the loss of over 400 Royal Navy ships with around 20,000 British personnel (declared dead, wounded, MIA or captured) and any territorial changes deemed *status quo ante bellum,* both governments decided to call it quits!

The conflict was only named The War of Jenkins' Ear by the Scottish historian Thomas Carlyle (1795-1881) when he published *History of Friedrich II of Prussia* (1858), possibly as a way of telling it apart from all the other Anglo-Spanish wars of that period.

the man who destroyed everything in the name of art

Having compiled an exhaustive inventory of his 7,227 possessions, the performance artist Michael Landy (1963-) then decided to destroy them all as a protest against today's consumerist society in an exhibition he called *Break Down* (2001). Everything was placed into yellow trays and sent around a large figure-of-eight conveyor belt in a two-week public exhibition held at the old C&A store at 499 Oxford Street in London. During the course of the show, workmen would systematically remove each item and then destroy it. Everything from clothes, old love letters, photographs, furniture, artwork and household items to his beloved Saab 900 was stripped, shredded, crushed or smashed to pieces before being sent off to a landfill site somewhere.

And when it was all over, the artist was literally left with just the clothes on his back!

The exhibition attracted 45,000 visitors, many of whom were just confused shoppers looking for a bargain. According to the artist, a couple of little old ladies even turned up trying to return some clothes they'd bought in C&A's closing down sale!

MORE ARTY-FARTY NONSENSE

My Bed (1998) was a piece of confessional artwork by the controversial English artist Tracey Emin (1964-); a dirty, unmade double bed in which she'd spent several days of her life drinking, smoking, sleeping and shagging at a time when she was suffering from depression brought on by a relationship breakup. The bedsheets were ruffled and stained and the floor around the bed was littered with empty bottles, condoms, dirty underwear with menstrual blood stains and many everyday objects such as her pair of slippers.

My Bed generated considerable media attention. It was shortlisted for the Turner Prize in 1999 and then displayed at the Tate Gallery (London) where pretentious twats could pontificate over it and dismayed normal people could shake their heads at it and wonder how the fuck something so ridiculous could possibly be considered a piece of art.

Then, in 2014, someone was daft enough to pay £2.5 million for it at auction!

a game of skill

In the early twentieth century it was illegal to play any games of chance in a pub. Card games, darts, pool and probably even dominoes were all banned. One night in 1908, the police turned up at the Adelphi Inn in Leeds only to find some of the patrons blatantly flouting the law by playing a game of darts. The landlord, James Garside, was promptly arrested and charged with contravening the licencing laws.

When the case came to court, the defendant argued that darts was a game of skill and not a game of chance and asked one of his regular patrons and one of the best darts players in Leeds, William Anakin to prove the point. A dartboard was mounted onto the courtroom wall, Willie stepped up to the makeshift oche and threw three single-twenties. The defence lawyer then challenged the judge to do the same as a way of demonstrating that an untutored player couldn't match the same level of skill and precision. The judge declined but ordered one of the court clerks to throw the darts instead. As expected, the clerk's darts landed nowhere near the target. Then Willie started showing off a bit by throwing three double-twenties! At which point, the judge asked him to do it again. So he did. He probably could have continued throwing double-twenties all day if that's what the judge had wanted.

But the judge had seen enough. He banged his gavel and yelled 'Case dismissed!'

Darts was now officially a game of skill.

the frost airship

It's generally accepted that Americans Wilbur Wright and Orville Wright were the first to fly a powered, heavier-than-air aircraft on 17 December 1903. But it might be the case that a humble Welsh carpenter, who nobody's ever heard of, beat them to it seven years earlier!

On 25 October 1894, William 'Bill' Frost (1848-1935) filed a patent for 'a flying machine' and then spent the next couple of years building it at his home in Saundersfoot in Pembrokeshire. The Frost Airship Glider was a 30-foot (9.1m) long vertical take-off and landing cross between a glider and an airship made of bamboo, canvas and wire and propelled by two reversible fans kept aloft by gas-filled tanks.

According to the patent description: 'When sufficient height is gained, wings are spread and tilted by means of a lever, causing the machine to float onward and downward. When low enough, the lever is reversed causing it to rise upward and onward. When required to stop it the wings are tilted so as to hold against the wind or air and lowered by the reversible fans. The steering is done by a helm fitted to front of machine.'

On 24 September 1896, he took to the Pembrokeshire skies to try out his invention. Unfortunately, the event was not recorded except in the memories of the local people who witnessed the flight. It has been claimed that he flew in his glider for around 500 yards (457m) before the undercarriage got caught in a tree and the plane crashed into a field. If this is true, then he'd stayed airborne for a considerably longer distance than the 40 yards/120 feet (36.6m) that Wilbur and Orville managed in 1903.

Although he was able to repair his machine, there would be no second flight. That night, it was destroyed in a violent storm and the pieces were scattered far and wide. He then applied to the government for funding to continue his research and development but received a rather brusque reply from the Under-Secretary of State at the War Office William St John Brodrick, 1st Earl of Midleton (1856-1942), denying his request as the British government had no intention of using aircraft either for navigation or for warfare!

Bill Frost had neither the money nor the time to continue with his project and then he allowed the patent to lapse when it was due for renewal four years later in 1898. He died in 1935 without wealth or recognition for his achievement.

THE FIRST AVIATOR

The engineer/inventor George Cayley (1773-1857) was a pioneer of aeronautical engineering and the first person to really understand the principles of flight. He has been credited with identifying the four forces of flight (weight, lift, drag and thrust) and inventing the concept of modern aeroplanes being fixed-wing flying machines with separate systems for lift and propulsion.

His design for a glider called The Governable Parachute was first described in an article written for *Mechanics' Magazine* on 25 September 1852 and finally tested a year later at Brompton Dale near Scarborough. Workmen hauled the glider down the hill's steep slope with ropes until it lifted into the air. Apparently it flew for about 500 feet (153m) before crash landing in a nearby field. By then, the 'father of aviation' was 79 years-old, so he'd let one of his employees have the honour of being Britain's first aviator in a heavier-than-air machine. Most probably it had been his butler/groom/coachman John Appleby (c.1833-1901), who, according to many reports, didn't appreciate the experience and resigned immediately after his feet touched the ground again!

THE FLYING PIG

J T C Moore-Brabazon (1884-1964) was a prominent member of the Aero Club of Great Britain and the proud owner of the first British pilot's licence, who took to the skies above the Isle of Sheppey on 2 May 1909 in his biplane *Bird of Passage* to complete the first recognised heavier-than-air flight in England. The pioneering aviator then went on to disprove the myth that pigs can't fly. After placing a bemused piglet in a wicker basket and strapping it to his plane's wing strut, he went for another little jaunt on 4 November 1909 solely with the intention of proving that the little porkers definitely could fly! A handwritten sign was attached to the basket proudly proclaiming 'I am the first pig to fly'. Unfortunately, there's no record of the brave little piggy's name. But it's probably fair to assume that he was called Percy or Porky or some other name beginning with a P.

the train that brought down a plane

Possibly the most unlikely kill in the history of aerial warfare!

On 27 November 1942, a Southern Railways train was tootling along the Lydd & New Romney Branch Line in Kent at a sedate 25mph (40km/h) when it was suddenly attacked by a low-flying German fighter plane. Gunfire from the plane hit the locomotive's boiler, the boiler exploded and a powerful jet of steam shot into the air hitting the plane as it passed overhead.

The plane was downed and the Luftwaffe pilot Heinz Bierwirth killed instantly. But the train driver survived and the locomotive was back in service a few months later!

the dogger bank incident

The time when Britain almost went to war with Russia!

In 1904, the Russo-Japanese War (1904-1905) was in full swing with Russia and Japan fighting each other over their rival imperial ambitions in Korea and Manchuria. Following a number of humiliating defeats, Russia decided to bolster its naval presence in the Sea of Japan by re-routing a large number of its Baltic Fleet ships under the command of Admiral Zinovy Petrovich Rozhestvensky to the Far East warzone.

It was a long journey with the planned route taking the ships through the North Sea, the English Channel, the Mediterranean Sea, the Suez Canal and the Red Sea, and then onwards through the Indian Ocean towards Japan. Right from the off the sailors were nervous about the voyage. They'd heard rumours that areas of their route had been mined and Imperial Japanese Navy ships were lurking along the Danish coast or hiding in the Norwegian fjords just waiting to attack them.

On the night of 21/22 October 1904, a fleet of British trawlers were fishing in the Dogger Bank – an area of the North Sea approximately 60 miles (96.5km) from their home port of Hull. Through the thick fog, they suddenly spotted the Russian ships steaming towards them and used lights and sent up flares to identify themselves as civilian fishing vessels. But the Russian ships interpreted their signals incorrectly, assumed they were Japanese torpedo boats and opened fire! It obviously never occurred to them how unlikely it would be for Japanese boats to stray some 20,000 miles (30,000km) from their own waters!

Using powerful searchlights to light up their targets, the Russians pounded the defenceless fishing boats with gunfire and shells. Tragically, the British boats all had their nets down and couldn't escape the unprovoked attack. The trawler *Crane* was sunk, killing two of its crew, and at least four other boats including the *Mino, Moulmein* and *Snipe,* were all shelled and badly damaged injuring the fishermen aboard.

As if mistaking British trawlers for Japanese torpedo boats wasn't bad enough, the Russians then opened fire on themselves! Some ships had been spotted arriving from the east and the warships then turned their fire on them. Except the new arrivals were the stragglers in their own Baltic Fleet convoy. For a short time the two groups of Russian ships exchanged friendly fire. Two of the stragglers, the cruisers *Aurora* and *Dmitrii Donskoi* were bombarded by the first group of battleships and were severely damaged, killing two sailors and wounding many others. Some Russian vessels reported seeing torpedoes in the water and at one stage during the pandemonium, the sailors aboard the battleship *Borodino* seemed convinced they were about to be boarded and readied themselves for hand-to-hand combat. More serious losses on both sides were only avoided because the Russian gunners were such lousy shots! The battleship *Oryol* reportedly fired more than 500 shells and never hit a damn thing!

The bombardment of the British trawlers lasted for around twenty minutes. Eventually, Admiral Rozhestvensky must have realised that they weren't shooting back and gave the order to cease firing. You might have expected them to help the fisherman once they'd realised their mistake but instead they hightailed it out of there as fast they could go!

The Dogger Bank Incident led to a serious strain in diplomatic relations between Britain and Russia. Some British newspapers described the Russians as 'pirates' with *The Times* commenting: 'It is almost inconceivable that any men calling themselves seamen, however frightened they might be, could spend twenty minutes bombarding a fleet of fishing boats without discovering the nature of their target.' The Royal Navy diverted its cruiser squadrons to shadow the Russian fleet making its way through the Bay of Biscay and ordered the battleships of the Home

Fleet to raise steam and prepare for war!

For a short while it looked like a conflict between the two countries was inevitable …

But then the Russian government suddenly adopted a policy of appeasement. They quickly issued an apology and agreed to cooperate with an independent commission of inquiry into the incident to be held in Paris.

Meanwhile the Russian fleet had continued on their journey and by now they'd reached Tangiers. Yet again, they'd managed to lose a ship along the way. This time it was the frigate *Kamchatka* which had suffered engine damage and had been limping along behind. After eventually re-joining the fleet, the crew of the frigate claimed to have fired over 300 shells at attacking Japanese warships, forcing them to retreat. In reality, they'd fired on a Swedish merchant ship, a German trawler and a French schooner! But because the Russians were such crap shots, no loss of life was ever reported in these incidents! When the Russian fleet eventually left Tangiers, one of the ships accidentally severed an underwater telegraph cable, preventing communication between Europe and the North African city for four days! Not only couldn't they shoot straight, they could steer straight either!

When they finally reached the Sea of Japan, unsurprisingly they were soundly beaten by the Japanese at the Battle of Tsushima (1905). Two-thirds of their fleet were sunk with the loss of many thousands of lives whilst the remaining Russian ships surrendered. The Imperial Japanese Navy, who could obviously shoot a lot better than their opponents, lost only three torpedo boats in the whole battle!

The international commission met in Paris from 9 January to 25 February 1905 to discuss the Dogger Bank Incident.

Rather predictably, the Russians claimed they'd been justified in their actions that night. They'd received credible reports of Japanese ships operating in the area, they hadn't recognised the lights and flares used by the British trawlers to identify themselves as civilian fishing boats because that type of signalling wasn't used in Russia, they were still worried about being attacked, and they'd only abandoned the trawlers because there were plenty of other ships in the vicinity who could have come to their aid.

Britain rejected all their arguments … and so did the international commission who ordered them to pay £66,000 in compensation.

swimming the channel

The craze for swimming the English Channel began with someone called J B Johnson on 23 August 1872. He was a professional swimmer based in Leeds who came to prominence in 1871 after winning a race across the Brent Reservoir in Hendon.

He'd already attracted some media attention a few days earlier when he'd jumped off London Bridge to rescue a drowning man who'd fallen from a passing steamship into the River Thames. Although it wasn't quite as heroic as it seemed since the drowning man of the story was actually his brother who was also an accomplished swimmer and the whole thing had just been a cleverly staged publicity stunt.

In August 1872, he plastered posters around Dover announcing that the 'hero of London Bridge and champion swimmer of the world' would swim across the English Channel from England to France. He was none of those things of course but nobody seemed to mind. Such a feat was generally deemed impossible and so a large crowd gathered at the town's Admiralty Pier to see him off on 22 August 1872. A brass band struck up a tune ... and then everyone went home again! For whatever reason, J B had decided to postpone his swim until the following day ...

The same brass band led J B Johnson from his hotel, through the town and onto the pier. Cheered on by another large crowd (or possibly the same one from the day before), he jumped into the water at 10.40am. His heroic long distance swim was now underway. But after about an hour it was already clear to everyone on the steamship that was accompanying him on his epic journey that he was struggling a bit. And by 11.45am he was out of the water altogether and standing on the deck of the ship. According to *The Times,* he'd been suffering from hypothermia and was in such a bad way that he couldn't even drink the beef tea offered to him when he was rescued. The steamship continued towards Calais where yet another large crowd was waiting to see him swim ashore. J B was a showman and he was determined not to disappoint his fans. Seemingly fully recovered from his hypothermia, he jumped back into the sea again as the steamship approached the French port and triumphantly swam ashore!

The first person to actually complete a swim of the English Channel was the seaman Matthew Webb (1848-1883).

He'd read about J B Johnson's exploits and it had inspired him to try his luck. He quit his job and began a rigorous training schedule. He first built up his stamina with regular visits to Lambeth Baths and then began practising for the long-distance swim in the cold waters of the River Thames. Finally, on 12 August 1875, he took the plunge and waded into the English Channel. But seven hours into the swim he was forced to abandon his record breaking attempt because of strong winds and the poor sea conditions.

Undeterred, he tried again 12 days later …

On the morning of 24 August 1875 he enjoyed a big plate full of bacon and eggs washed down with some claret and then made his way to Admiralty Pier in Dover. At exactly 12.56pm, he dived into the water and set off on his 22 mile (35km) swim towards France accompanied by a couple of boats full of family and friends, supporters and newspaper reporters. Occasionally he'd stop and tread water to take on some nourishment: cod liver oil, beef tea, coffee, brandy or some ale, or wave to cheering passengers on passing ships. Eight hours after the start he was stung by a jellyfish but after a quick brandy to calm his nerves, he was soon on his way again. After spotting land he then had to swim back and forth along the French coast for another five hours as the strong currents were preventing him from reaching the shore! It wasn't until 10.40am the following morning, after 21 hours and 45 minutes of swimming the equivalent of 39 miles (63km), when he finally crawled ashore at Calais totally exhausted. He'd done it but he'd done it the hard way!

Matthew Webb never returned to his old job. Instead, he made a good living as a professional swimmer. He wrote a book *The Art of Swimming* (1875), licensed his name for merchandising purposes and performed in many shows and exhibitions. He was having a great time of it. Then in 1883, he announced his attention to swim through the Niagara Whirlpool in the Niagara River. Everyone thought he was mad. It was suicidal to attempt such a dangerous swim. And they were right …

At 4.25pm on 24 July 1883, he jumped from a small boat into the river and died ten minutes later!

eyes on the road

The Cat's Eye retroreflective road stud was invented by the businessman Percy Shaw (1890-1976) in 1934. Nobody is quite sure how he got the idea, as there are a number of different stories doing the rounds, but the most famous of these involves him driving down a steep road in Halifax and seeing a cat sitting on a fence by the roadside. The cat's eyes were reflected back in the headlights of his car, allowing him to take corrective action and remain on the road.

This explanation of events seems to have been confirmed by the comedian Ken Dodd (1927-2018): 'The man who invented Cat's Eyes got the idea when he saw the eyes of a cat in his headlights. If the cat had been going the other way, he would have invented the pencil sharpener!'

the fantasist assassin

Marcus Sarjeant (1964-) fired six shots at Queen Elizabeth II (1926-2022) as she rode along The Mall on horseback during the Trooping the Colour ceremony in 1981. He later claimed that he'd been inspired to kill her after reading about the assassinations of John Lennon (1940-1980) and John F Kennedy and the assassination attempts on Ronald Reagan and Pope John Paul II. He was particularly obsessed with the notoriety afforded to Mark David Chapman after he'd shot John Lennon and was determined to emulate that assassination with one equally as shocking of his own.

But unfortunately for him he couldn't get hold of a proper gun!

He tried and failed to buy ammunition for his father's old service revolver and then joined a local shooting club because he thought it would help him obtain a gun licence and ultimately a gun. But Britain's strict gun laws meant he had to settle for buying a blank-firing handgun from a mail order company! Despite the overwhelming handicap of not actually having a working firearm, he didn't seem at all put off and charged ahead with his plan regardless. He sent letters and photos of himself posing with his gun to magazines and even sent a note to Buckingham Palace in which he warned the queen not to attend the Trooping the Colour ceremony because he'd be there to shoot her! Which was nice of him. He didn't have to give her the heads-up.

On 13 June 1981, he joined the crowds along The Mall. When the queen rode past him, he raised his arm … pointed his toy gun … and fired off all six shots. He was immediately apprehended by a soldier, pulled over the crowd control barriers and wrestled to the ground as he yelled: 'I wanted to be famous. I wanted to be somebody!' The queen was completely unfazed by the incident, calming her horse and riding onwards towards Horse Guards Parade as if nothing had happened.

At his trial he was found guilty under Section 2 of the Treason Act 1842 in that he 'wilfully discharged at or near Her Majesty the Queen a gun with the intent to alarm or distress Her Majesty' and got five years in jail for his actions.

On his release from prison in October 1984, Marcus very wisely chose to change his name and start a new life somewhere else.

THE WORLD'S SECOND WORST ASSASSIN

Somebody else tried to kill Queen Elizabeth II in 1981. It really wasn't her year! This guy had a real gun and real ammunition but luckily he was such a crap shot that nobody was really quite sure if an assassination attempt had taken place or not! The queen was on a tour of New Zealand and on 14 October 1981 she visited the city of Dunedin. As her motorcade came to a halt and she stepped out of the car, self-styled terrorist Christopher

Lewis, who was hiding in a building across the street, fired his rifle through an open window at Her Majesty standing five storeys below him. The bullet landed nowhere near her or anyone else in the royal party ... or anyone else in the crowd! Everyone heard a loud crack but nobody had any idea that it was a gunshot. The local police initially tried to cover up the story by telling British journalists that it was just a sign falling over and then later claimed it was a firecracker being let off.

The world's second worst assassin was arrested eight days later. Despite admitting to the shooting and declaring that a mysterious Englishman known only as 'The Snowman' had instructed him to kill the queen, the police continued keeping the assassination attempt under wraps. He was only charged with possessing a firearm because the authorities were concerned that the incident would show New Zealand in a bad light and possibly endanger future royal visits.

Two years later, in 1983, when Charles, Prince of Wales (1948-) and Diana, Princess of Wales (1961-1997) toured the country, he unsuccessfully attempted to escape from prison to assassinate them too! He really didn't like the Royal Family.

In 1995, the queen returned to New Zealand, but this time the police weren't taking any chances. They apprehended Christopher and sent him on an all-expenses ten-day trip to the idyllic Great Barrier Island in the north of the country out of sight and out of mind.

Christopher Lewis killed himself in prison two years later whilst awaiting trial for murder.

the hangman and the execution of mary ann cotton

Mary Ann Cotton (1832-1873) looked like a sweet old lady but she was actually Britain's first recorded serial killer! She is thought to have murdered as many as twenty-one people between 1860 and 1872 - three husbands, eight of her children, seven stepchildren, her mother, a lover and a friend before being arrested, tried and hanged. No doubt she would have carried on killing if she hadn't been caught.

Her hangman was William Calcraft (1800-1879), one of Victorian Britain's most prolific executioners, estimated to have carried out some 450 hangings in his 45-year career. Although his services were always in demand up and down the country, many considered him to be incompetent, whilst others believed him to be a cruel and sadistic showman! He insisted on using the short-drop hanging method which meant the condemned prisoners slowly being strangled to death (instead of having their necks broken instantly) and sometimes taking several minutes to die. To expedite death, William would often jump on their shoulders or pull on their legs in an effort to snap their necks. But it has often been speculated that he only did so to entertain the large crowds who'd turned up to watch him perform!

In the early morning of 24 March 1873 Mary Ann Cotton was hanged at Durham County Gaol.

She was only dropped about 2 feet (0.6m) and ended up kicking her legs and swinging her arms about in a desperate attempt to wriggle free from her restraints. The sadistic (or bungling) executioner then lent down and pushed down on her shoulders in an effort to stifle her last attempts at life. As he felt her rearing up and down, he pushed down even harder but she continued writhing around and endured a slow and agonising throttling for almost three minutes!

By law, she was then left to hang there for another hour as the police dispersed the crowd. Meanwhile, William and the other dignitaries withdrew to the Governor's office for a slap-up breakfast!

the overbury murder scandal

Frances Howard (1590-1632) was married to Robert Devereux, 3rd Earl of Essex (1591-1646), in 1604. She was only 14 years-old and he was only 13. The marriage was primarily a political union between their two powerful families but because the happy couple were so young it was thought prudent to keep them apart for a while, so young Robert was sent away on a Grand Tour, a little jaunt around Europe which young, upper-class men took when they came of age to acquaint themselves with the music, art and culture of the continent.

Unfortunately for Robert, when he was travelling around Europe, Frances fell head-over-heels in love with another man and another Robert, Robert Carr, 1st Earl of Somerset (c.1587-1645), a young Scottish nobleman who'd quickly established himself as one of the king's favourite courtiers since moving south of the border.

By the time her husband returned from his European adventure, Frances wanted nothing more to do with him and in 1613, she sought to annul the marriage through the courts for non-consummation due to his impotence, claiming that she'd made every attempt to be sexually compliant, but through no fault of her own, she was still a virgin. To prove her case, she agreed to a medical examination. According to the English statesman/philosopher, Francis Bacon, 1st Viscount St Alban (1561-1626), who followed the court proceedings, the matrons and midwives who undertook the examination later reported that 'the Lady of

Essex is a woman apt to have copulation, to bring forth children and that the said Lady is a Virgin and uncorrupted.' However, for the sake of her modesty, Frances had insisted on wearing a veil throughout the medical examination and there was much speculation at the time that a body double had been used! The subterfuge seemed so obvious to many people that the exam results were greeted with derision and someone even made up a little rhyme about it all:

The Dame was inspected, but fraud interjected
A Maid of greater perfection
Whom the midwives did handle whilst the knight held the candle
O there was a clear inspection

The court case quickly attracted a lot of unwanted public attention and Robert Devereux was mocked for his inability to satisfy Frances, even though he strongly denied her accusations of impotence. According to him, he was perfectly capable of performing with other women and it was only with Frances that he seemed to have a problem because 'she reviled him, and miscalled him, terming him a cow, and coward, and beast.' It was claimed by one of his friends, that he once stood up in front of a group of male companions, removed his nightshirt and whipped out his dick ... which was anything but limp, proving that he was more than capable of arousal.

Meanwhile, the other Robert, Robert Carr, had been promoted to serve on the Privy Council and had taken up his new position as the Groom of the Bedchamber. He'd also found himself a new best friend in the poet/essayist Thomas Overbury (1581-1613). They made a good team. Thomas was a wise and influential man and Robert had the king's ear. Poor Robert was more famous for his good looks than his brains and often allowed Thomas to organise his affairs and help him with his government work. The only thing that could have threatened their successful double act was Robert's infatuation with Frances. Thomas had been against their liaison right from the start and had tried to warn him that she was 'noted for her injury and immodesty' but when Robert had ignored his warnings, he did what any concerned friend would do ... he wrote a poem! In his little ditty *A Wife* (1613) he described all the qualities of a virtuous woman and seemed to imply that Frances lacked all of them!

Robert Carr's role as the favourite courtier wasn't going to last forever. Things were already starting to look a bit shaky for him after the arrival at court of George Villiers, 1st Duke of Buckingham (1592-1628), and so he thought it prudent to marry Frances as soon as possible to secure himself a valuable position inside the all-powerful Howard family. Again, Thomas tried to dissuade him from tying the knot, implying that he knew secrets about Frances and her liaisons at court, which he was willing to make public if he decided to go ahead with the wedding. Either he fancied Robert himself or he was like that friend from *Love Actually* who was secretly in love with Keira Knightley.

Obviously, Frances was not happy with Thomas continually meddling in their lives and slagging her off. She was a bit of devious cow, so she persuaded her family to convince the king, James I (1566-1625), to offer Thomas the post of ambassador to the court of Michael I of Russia, knowing full well that he'd refuse the job in order to stay in England to be by Robert's side and therefore displease the king. Sure enough, he turned it down and the king had him locked away in the Tower of London. Thomas was an egotistical and arrogant man so nobody batted an eyelid when he was incarcerated. Similarly, when he died on 14 September 1613, nobody appeared that concerned and just assumed it was the poor prison diet, the harsh conditions or any one of the popular diseases of that time that had killed him off. More people died in prison than were ever released, so the authorities weren't too concerned when another dead body was added to the pile.

Ten days after his death, the marriage of Frances and Robert Devereux was finally annulled and she and Robert Carr were married on 26 December 1613. It was the society event of the season and was even celebrated in verse by the great Jacobean poet John Donne (1572-1631). Everyone had to write a bloody poem about everything in those days!

Eighteen months passed and all was well with the happy couple ...

By September 1615, however, there were some unsettling rumours about the death of Thomas doing the rounds. The Secretary of State, Ralph Winwood (c.1563-1617) brought the matter to the king's attention but at first he didn't seem all that interested, dismissing the rumours as mere tittle-tattle. It was only when they persisted and his involvement in a murderous plot was beginning to be implied that he urged the Privy Council led by the Lord Chief Justice Edward Coke (1552-1634) to investigate further.

The inquiry quickly established that Thomas had been poisoned and unmasked Frances as his killer ...

Apparently, her great uncle, Henry Howard, 1st Earl of Northampton (1540-1614), had arranged for the Lord Lieutenant of the Tower William Wade (1546-1623) to be relieved of his duties and replaced with one of his lackeys Gervase Helwys (1561-1615) in the hope that he might be able to persuade Thomas to retract his opposition to the marriage of Frances and Robert, but when that didn't work, Frances had decided that a more drastic and permanent solution to the problem of Thomas Overbury was needed and started working on a plan of her own ...

Her lady-in-waiting and companion Anne Turner was ordered to procure poisons from an apothecary, later named as James Franklin. Frances then had some pies, tarts and jellies laced with white arsenic smuggled into the jail and delivered to Thomas in his cell. Prison meals were so bad that when his gaoler Richard Weston arrived with the extra food, Thomas never thought to query why somebody was being so kind to him and just gobbled it all up! The slow-working poison soon made Thomas ill and the king became so alarmed by his worsening condition that he authorised medical help for him. To sort out his digestive problems, which weren't particularly uncommon amongst prisoners at that time, he was prescribed an enema. Unfortunately for Thomas, that had also been poisoned. All those toxic substances squirted up his arse and into his gut killed him instantly and any secrets he may or may not have known about Frances and her sexual conquests at court were lost forever.

Frances Howard admitted to her part in the murder but her husband did not, despite the king being fearful that he could be implicated in the scandal if the case ever went to court and pleading with him to admit his culpability in return for a pardon and a shitload of money. However, Robert was adamant that he had done nothing wrong and promptly rejected the king's offer by replying: 'Life and Fortune are not worth the acceptance, when honour is gone' before defiantly announcing his intention to prove his innocence at trial.

Robert and Frances were eventually found guilty and condemned to death. Believe it or not, one of the Privy Council's distinguished gentlemen deciding their fate was none other than Robert Devereux who couldn't wait to find Frances guilty and see her hanging from the gallows, however, the king seemed to take pity on them and their death sentences were later commuted by royal decree to a prison term.

The trial also concluded that the prison governor Gervase Helwys had known about Thomas being poisoned but had made no attempt to discover who had done the poisoning. The gaoler Richard Weston, after having admitted to delivering the poisoned food, claimed that he was just following orders, although he was a little vague as to whose orders he was actually following. Both men were found guilty of being accomplices to murder, as were the lady-in-waiting Anne Turner and the apothecary James Franklin, but as none of these co-conspirators were rich and famous like Frances and Robert, they were actually hanged for their crimes!

Six years later, Frances and Robert were released from prison, given a state pension and a big house in Oxfordshire and allowed to live out the rest of their lives in relative obscurity.

Love had triumphed in the end!

the shredded painting

The classic painting known as *Girl with Balloon* (2006) created using spray paint on canvas by the anonymous British street artist Banksy was sold at Sotheby's Auction House (London) on 5 October 2018 for £1,042,000. But as soon as the auctioneer banged his gavel to confirm the sale, something rather unexpected happened …

An alarm sounded and the painting started rolling downwards and out of its frame. As it passed through the bottom part of the casing, a built-in shredder began tearing it into strips and partly destroying the painting before the mechanism could be stopped. It was probably the first instance ever seen of a self-destructing painting!

In a video posted afterwards on the artist's Instagram page, he demonstrated how the custom made shredding device was positioned into the large gilt frame just in case the painting was ever sold. In a separate post he quoted Pablo Picasso: 'The urge to destroy is also a creative urge.'

The staff of Sotheby's denied any prior knowledge of the stunt. But conspiracy theorists have since pointed out that the painting and the frame must have seemed much heavier than expected (which appears to have been ignored during the routine pre-auction inspection) and most importantly, the painting was conveniently the last item in the sale (therefore avoiding any disruption to the proceedings) and hung on the wall instead of being placed on a podium like all the other paintings offered for sale that day (so increasing the dramatic effect of the destructive process).

The buyer later commented: 'When the hammer came down … and the work was shredded, I was at first shocked, but gradually I began to realise that I would end up with my own piece of art history.'

Both Banksy and Sotheby's have since confirmed that the partly shredded painting is now considered to be a new original piece of artwork entitled *Love Is in the Bin* (2018).

the theft of the jules rimet trophy

The Victory trophy was the original prize awarded to the winners of the FIFA World Cup and was renamed the Jules Rimet Trophy in 1946 after the third FIFA president Jules Rimet of France who established the competition back in 1930.

In January 1966, the Football Association (FA) took possession of the trophy in preparation for the FIFA World Cup finals tournament due to be held in England later that year. It was usually kept at their HQ in London but occasionally the trophy was loaned out to the organisers of various events. One such event was the Stampex Exhibition held at the Westminster Central Hall beginning on 19 March 1966 where the stamp dealer Stanley Gibbons Ltd had arranged for it to be displayed on their stall.

There were tight security measures in place with two uniformed police officers guarding the trophy around the clock, backed up during the day by two plainclothes detectives. However, on Sunday 20 March 1966, when the exhibition was closed to the public and the building was being used for Methodist Church services, it soon became apparent that the tight security measures weren't quite as tight as the organisers had hoped. Thieves had forced open the rear doors of the building, calmly removed the padlock from the display case and swiped the trophy. And none of the guards had seen or heard a damn thing!

A short time later, the chairman of the FA, Joe Mears (1905-1966), received a ransom note demanding £15,000 for the trophy's safe return and then an undercover police officer codenamed 'McPhee' arranged to meet a man called 'Jackson' in Battersea Park for the pay-off. The fake notes were handed over and Jackson then agreed to get into McPhee's car and lead him to the trophy. At some point during their journey, however, Jackson spotted the police vans following them and jumped out of the car. He made a run for it, McPhee gave chase and eventually caught up with him, at which point he revealed himself to be a police officer and made an arrest. Jackson turned out to be Edward Betchley, a used car salesman and petty thief from South London. He denied stealing the trophy and claimed that someone he knew only as 'The Pole' had offered him £500 to act as a middleman. He was later convicted of demanding money with menace and sentenced to two years inside. The man known only as 'The Pole' was never identified and nobody else was ever convicted of the theft.

With just a few months before the start of the tournament, the police were no nearer to catching the thieves. And it didn't look like they were going to catch them any time soon either, so the FA started drawing up plans to have a duplicate trophy made. At least the teams would have something to play for when the tournament kicked off on 11 July 1966.

But nobody could have imagined what happened next ...

Step forward a black-and-white Collie called Pickles. On his evening walk in Upper Norwood, he spotted something lying under a hedge, wrapped in newspaper and bound with string. His owner, David Corbett, opened the mysterious package and realised immediately that it was the missing Jules Rimet Trophy. Although he took it to the nearest police station and collected the £5,000 reward, it was Pickles who received all the credit and adulation from the public. He became a national hero overnight, he was voted 'Dog of the Year' and appeared on the children's TV show *Blue Peter* (BBC) before starring in his own big-screen comedy *The Spy with a Cold Nose* (1966).

Sadly, his fame and fortune didn't last very long. A year later he was strangled to death by his own choke chain after it got snared on a tree branch while he was chasing a cat near his new home in Surrey.

A plaque was unveiled at the very spot in Upper Norwood where Pickles found the trophy in 2018.

Note: Brazil won the FIFA World Cup for the third time in 1970 allowing them to permanently keep the Jules Rimet Trophy. It was subsequently placed inside a bulletproof glass cabinet and displayed at the Confederação Brasileira de Futebol offices in Rio de Janeiro. On 19 December 1983, thieves broke into the building, forced open the case with a crowbar and made off with the trophy. Although four men were later tried and convicted in absentia for the crime, the trophy has never been seen again!

the great fire

The Great Fire of London started in Thomas Farriner's bakery in Pudding Lane just before midnight on Sunday, 2 September 1666 and spread rapidly westwards across the city.

Fires in the city were quite common and were usually extinguished fairly quickly. So when the Pudding Lane bakery went up in flames, nobody really took much notice of it at first. It was only when things started to get a bit out of hand that the Lord Mayor Thomas Bloodworth (1620-1682) was summoned to the scene. The most effective firefighting technique of the time was to pull down buildings adjacent to the burning ones to stop the fire from spreading, but the Lord Mayor was reluctant to give such an order. According to the noted diarist Samuel Pepys (1633-1703) he apparently expressed a lack of concern about the fire spreading, commenting that 'a woman might piss it out' before returning home and going back to bed! It was actually the king, Charles II (1630-1685) who eventually gave the order to start tearing down buildings. Then he rolled up his royal sleeves and joined the line passing buckets of water to the firefighters!

But the fire spread through the city quicker than the buildings could be demolished. So then they started using gunpowder to blow them up. But then the sound of the explosions convinced everyone that the French were invading and caused even more panic! England was busy fighting the Second Anglo-Dutch War (1665-1667) at the time and anyone looking a bit French (or Dutch) was set upon, accused of setting fires and lynched in the street!

People fled into the River Thames or took refuge in the fields on the outskirts of the city. The fire could be seen from 30 miles (48km) away. Eventually it was brought under control and by 6 September 1666 it had been extinguished altogether. But only one fifth of London was left standing! The fire famously destroyed St Paul's Cathedral, around 13,000 houses, 87 parish churches and virtually all of the public buildings, jails, markets, halls and landmarks, and left 70,000 of the city's 80,000 inhabitants homeless.

In the immediate aftermath of the fire, a demented French watchmaker named Robert Hubert who claimed to be a French spy and an agent of the pope confessed to starting the fire. According to one contemporary account of his trial, he was 'only accused upon his own confession; yet neither the judges nor any present at the trial did believe him guilty, but that he was a poor distracted wretch, weary of his life, and chose to part with it in this way.' Nevertheless, someone had to be the scapegoat and a doolally Frenchman was as good a person as any. Justice was swift and poor Robert was hanged at Tyburn on 27 October 1666. It only came to light after his death that he wasn't even in the country when the fire started!

In 1667, the fire was officially attributed to 'the hand of God, a great wind and a very dry season.'

It wasn't until 320 years later, in 1986, when the Worshipful Company of Bakers finally admitted that Thomas Farriner had started the fire and apologised on his behalf for setting London ablaze!

very underwhelming first times

THE FIRST PHONE BOOK

The first British telephone directory was published on 15 January 1880 by The Telephone Company (Bells Patent) Ltd and contained the 248 names and addresses of various individuals and businesses in London. But not their phone numbers!

All calls needed to be routed via an exchange with the subscribers then asked for by name.

THE FIRST ARMOURED VEHICLE

The Motor Scout was the world's first petrol-powered armoured vehicle and was designed and built in 1898 by the nineteenth-century's most famous petrolhead F R Simms (1863-1944) for supporting infantry or cavalry charges ... but only if they were charging along smooth, well paved roads! Because the Motor Scout was actually just a bicycle; a single-seat quadricycle with a standard Maxim machine gun fitted into an iron shield placed above the front wheels, and a 1½ hp motor and petrol tank mounted on the rear with the driver expected to just crouch behind that iron shield and fire the gun as he peddled into battle!

THE FIRST HOLE IN THE WALL WITH MONEY INSIDE

The world's first ATM was installed outside the Enfield branch of Barclays Bank PLC and the first person to withdrawal any money from the new *Barclaycash* branded machine was the TV sitcom actor Reg Varney (1916-2008) during the unveiling ceremony on 29 June 1967. Was he really the best they could get?

The inventor, John Shepherd-Barron (1925-2010), stated that he'd been inspired by a vending machine dispensing chocolate bars and then set about devising a similar machine which could distribute cash. However, early ATMs were only designed to receive hole-punched vouchers to the value of £10.00 which the customer had to queue up for and purchase beforehand. Not the least bit convenient for anyone!

spending a penny

The Great Exhibition of the Works of Industry of All Nations ran from 1 May to 15 October 1851. It was the world's first international exhibition of culture, industry and manufactured products. The fair boasted 14,000 exhibitors from all over Britain and its colonies and dependencies as well as many European and American states, and was intended as a celebration of modern industrial technology and design. Around 6 million people (equivalent to one third of Britain's population at the time) visited the Crystal Palace, the fancy newly constructed exhibition centre designed by Joseph Paxton (1803-1865) in Hyde Park where the fair was staged with an average daily attendance of nearly 43,000 people.

The world's first public flushing toilets known as Monkey Closets were installed at the exhibition site. They were devised by the sanitary engineer/plumber George Jennings (1810-1882) who specialised in designing toilets that were 'as perfect a sanitary closet as can be made.' The fancy new toilets caused a great deal of excitement - possibly more excitement than any of the exhibits! They were the first public toilets that some people had ever seen and they couldn't wait to have a dump and watch it all being flushed away! In total, 827,280 visitors paid one penny to use the Monkey Closets and for their money they were guaranteed a clean seat, a free shoe shine and use of a towel and a comb too. It was the door lock mechanism invented by John Nevil Maskelyne (1839-1917) which required the insertion of a one penny coin which led to the phrase 'spending a penny' becoming a national euphemism for going to the toilet.

the most boring day in history

On 18 April 1930, the BBC Radio newscaster presenting the 8.45pm bulletin announced: 'Good evening. Today is Good Friday. There is no news.' Light piano music then played for the remainder of the fifteen-minute bulletin before the normal schedule was resumed.

Could this be the most boring and insignificant day in history? Apparently not. Despite the worrying lack of any news to report on that day, it's not considered the most uneventful. According to research undertaken in 2010 by the Cambridge-based technology firm, Evi (formerly True Knowledge), that honour goes to Sunday, 11 April 1954 when there were no key news events, and no births or deaths of any famous people recorded!

the tennis match that would never end

The longest match in the history of the sport occurred at the 2010 Wimbledon Championships.

The record breaking first round Men's Singles match between John Isner of America and Nicolas Mahut of France lasted 11 hours and 5 minutes and consisted of 183 games played over three days! It was finally won by the American – 6-4, 3-6, 6-7 (7-9), 7-6 (7-3), 70-68.

The match began on 22 June 2010 at 6.13pm on Court 18 but was suspended at 9.07pm just before the start of the fifth set due to bad light. After play resumed the following day at 2.05pm fading light yet again forced the game to be suspended, this time at 9.09pm with the final set tied at 59-59. Play then resumed on the third day at 3.40pm with John Isner finally claiming victory at 4.47pm.

On the second day of play, the IBM scoreboard crashed as it had only been programmed to record a maximum score of 47-47 and the Swedish umpire Mohammed Lahyani was forced to provide a running commentary on the match to the crowd. The IBM tech guys had then worked through the night and the scoreboard was functioning perfectly again for the third day of play. Luckily, the umpire remembered to add on twelve more games to each player's score when the match resumed.

The first four sets had passed without any significant incidents. John won the first set 6-4 and Nicolas took the second set 6-3. Both the third and fourth sets were decided by tiebreaks; Nicolas winning the third set (9-7) and John the fourth set (7-3) leaving the score tied at two sets each. John Isner then failed to convert four match points in the fifth set, the first when the score was 9-10, the second and third at 32-33 and the fourth in the dramatic last game of Day Two when the score stood at 58-59. It was his fourteenth break point of the match and his fifth match point, a down-the-line backhand passing shot which finally proved to be the winner after 67 minutes of play on Day Three. The 138-game fifth set lasted 8 hours and 11 minutes, which on its own would have beaten the previous record for the longest match, a 7 hour and 2 minute Davis Cup game between the Czech Republic and Switzerland in 2013.

This match also set the record for the most games played (183), the most points scored (980) and the highest number of aces by any one player (113).

Immediately after the match, the players and the umpire had their photos taken in front of the Court 18 scoreboard and were presented with a crystal bowl as a memento of the historic occasion by the All England Lawn Tennis and Croquet Club. This match is likely to remain the longest ever played during a Wimbledon Championships. In 2018, the club changed their rules to introduce a final set tie-break game to avoid any more matches like this one. It might have made history and delighted the fans but it played havoc with their scheduling.

the holy maid of leominster

The faithful flocked to the Priory of Leominster in Herefordshire to see the girl known only as Elizabeth who'd been sent by God. She lived in the priory's loft and had no need to descend from there as she could survive solely on 'angel food' (communion bread). During Mass the congregation were astonished to see the wafer bread miraculously rise from the priest's plate, up into the loft and into her mouth. According to the social philosopher/statesman Thomas More (1478-1535) it wasn't long before thousands of people were arriving from all over the country seeking cures and blessings from this 'strange wenche'.

Then Margaret Beaufort (c.1441-1509), the mother of Henry VII (1457-1509), got to hear about the newly-christened 'Holy Maid of Leominster' and convened a council to investigate the cult surrounding her. And it didn't take them long to figure out that it was all a scam. On visiting her living quarters in the loft they discovered a well-used chamber pot that had 'no saintly savour', meat bones hidden under her bed, and most damning of all, a thin wire extending down from the loft to the altar used to convey her angel food through the air.

When questioned, Elizabeth confessed to the deceit. As always, it was all to do with sex and money. She was shagging the priest and he'd planned the whole thing, convincing her that they could make their fortune from false miracles!

the three-hundred-and-thirty-five year war

The longest war in British history lasted 335 years after Holland declared war on the Isles of Scilly in 1651.

The conflict began during the English Civil War (1642-1651) when Holland offered their support to the Parliamentarians. The Royalists felt betrayed and set about raiding Dutch ships in the English Channel from their base in the Isles of Scilly. The Dutch then sent a fleet of twelve warships to the islands to demand reparations but after receiving no satisfactory reply, Admiral Maarten Tromp declared war on the Isles of Scilly on 30 March 1651.

Not a lot happened after that and then three months later, the Royalist forces on the Scillies surrendered and the Parliamentary forces occupied the islands. Immediately afterwards, the Dutch fleet sailed back home but in their haste to leave the war zone, nobody thought about declaring peace.

A local historian uncovered the story in 1985 and wrote to the Dutch Embassy in London asking them to confirm if a state of war still existed between Holland and the Isles of Scilly. The embassy staff found some documents somewhere which seemed to suggest that was still the case and then accepted an invitation for their ambassador to attend a peace treaty signing ceremony on the islands. After 335 years and 18 days of 'hostilities' resulting in no casualties and no loss of life, the Dutch ambassador Rein Huydecoper finally signed the treaty on 17 April 1986 and joked: 'It must have been awful to know we could have attacked at any moment!'

the leinster gardens illusion

The world's first underground passenger railway service was operated by the Metropolitan Railway (1863-1933) and opened between Farringdon and Paddington in London on 10 January 1863. .

Although the locomotives were fitted with condensers to reduce the smoke and steam in the tunnels, there was still a need for a place above ground to vent-off the engines. Rather bizarrely, the railway company chose to do this right in the middle of a long, upmarket terraced street called Leinster Gardens in Bayswater by demolishing the houses at number 23 and 24. However, to hide the tracks and the belching fumes, two false house façades were erected which exactly matched the houses on either side to create the illusion of a continuous frontage along the street. Even today behind the painted-on windows and the doors without post boxes there is nothing but a birds-eye view of the Circle Line trains passing by!

ALAN FERGUSON

the dancing clown

A tale from Elizabethan England that doesn't involve acts of treason, war, religious persecution and gruesome executions.

So that's something to celebrate!

William Kempe (c.1560-c.1603) was an eccentric and flamboyant actor and dancer specialising in comic roles, best known for being a member of the famous acting troupe The Lord Chamberlain's Men along with William Shakespeare (1564-1616) and the esteemed actor Richard Burbage (1567-1619). He was highly revered by his peers, much loved by the public and widely acclaimed by critics as a worthy successor to the greatest of all the Elizabethan clowns Richard Tarlton (1530-1588). He would have played the parts of Lancelot Gobbo in *The Merchant of Venice* (c.1596) and Bottom in *A Midsummer Night's Dream* (c.1596) and it's believed that William Shakespeare created the characters of Dogberry in *Much Ado About Nothing* (1598) and Peter in *Romeo and Juliet* (c.1595) especially for him.

However, sometime during 1598 he fell out of favour with England's greatest playwright after claiming that his plays just weren't funny enough anymore! He also started going off-script, stealing scenes and improvising his own dialogue, prompting the Bard to write these lines in *Hamlet* (1599) which were almost certainly aimed at him: 'And let those that play your clowns speak no more than is set down for them.' By the end of that year there were no further records of him ever playing the fool for The Lord Chamberlain's Men ever again. It's uncertain whether he was fired or just left the acting troupe of his own accord.

Whatever the reason, he was then free to perform one of the cleverest but daftest acts of self-promotion ever attempted …

He'd dance his way along the 125-mile (201km) route from London to Norwich.

Even though he'd set himself the target of completing the dance within nine days, he was also allowed to rest up for any number of days in-between … which probably explains why his little stunt actually took him almost a month to complete.

It all began early in the morning of 10 February 1600 when he turned up outside the Lord Mayor of London's house in Whitechapel dressed in an elaborate clown's costume and accompanied by a servant, a musician and a referee. As he set off towards Mile End he was cheered and waved off by a great crowd offering him 'bowed sixpences and groats and hearty prayers.'

He danced his way through Stratford and Ilford and then along the roads of Essex, Suffolk and Norfolk, stopping off along the way many times to rest up or for something to eat and drink. Bad weather, difficult terrain and exhaustion sometimes hampered his progress and after stumbling over a pothole near Braintree he strained his hip resulting in 'exceeding paine' and had to lie low for a couple of days. However, he was enjoying all the attention and his spirits seemed buoyed by the huge crowds who regularly turned out along the roads to cheer him on or offer him refreshments or a place to stay for the night. Although, on one occasion, his host in Rockland left him a little bemused by his rather odd words of welcome as he was ushered into his house: 'Thou art even as welcome as the Queen's best greyhound.'

Many of his more enthusiastic fans wanted to dance alongside him. However, they weren't always that adept at matching the great man's style and elegance. A butcher, who despite being described as a 'lusty tall fellow' collapsed with exhaustion after only half-a-mile (0.8km) and two overly-excited youths misjudged a puddle in their excitement and fell into a muddy pothole! William was more impressed with the young country girls, whose company he appears to have appreciated the most! He seemed particularly infatuated by one 'comely lass' who'd witnessed the butcher's piss poor attempt at keeping pace with him and had decided to dance alongside him herself for the next mile or two. William was so appreciative of her efforts that he bought her a few pints of ale at the next tavern and even penned a little poem for her:

A Country Lasse browne as a berry,
Blith of blee in heart as merry,

Cheekes well fed and sides well larded,
Every bone with fat flesh guarded,
Meeting merry Kemp by chaunce,
Was Marrian in his Morrice daunce.

After a delay of three days, so the good folk of Norwich could organise a welcoming committee for him, William finally entered the city on 8 March 1600 and was greeted by musicians, more cheering crowds and a man called Thomas Gilbert who read out a little poem in his honour. William then continued dancing through the marketplace towards the mayor's house but his progress was slow due to the sheer number of well-wishers who'd turned out to greet him, and at one point he accidentally stepped on a girl's petticoat, ripping it and causing it to fall down, leaving her red-faced with embarrassment. Eventually he reached the mayor's house, took off his dancing shoes and donated them to the city. It's unclear if the city actually wanted his shoes but he left them there nonetheless!

For some time afterwards, William was the most talked about man in England. He cashed in on his fame and fortune by publishing the pamphlet *Nine Daies Wonder* (1600) recounting his time on the road dancing his way to Norwich before joining a touring company called The Earl of Worcester's Men for a short period in 1601.

And then he died in poverty and obscurity possibly during an outbreak of the plague a couple of years later.

good king richard

Richard I (aka Richard the Lionheart) (1157-1199) is remembered as being a chivalrous king and remains one of the few monarchs recognised by a flattering epithet rather than a regnal number. Although he was born and raised in England, he lived most of his adult life in the Duchy of Aquitaine in France and following his accession to the English throne in 1189, he chose to pass most of his time raising hell around Europe and the Holy Land rather than attend to his affairs at home. It's rumoured that he only spent about six months of his reign in England and it's doubtful that he even spoke a word of English! He once remarked that he would have sold the whole country if he could have found a buyer! Despite his obvious distain for England, he was still loved to bits by his people and hailed as a great military leader.

But he wasn't a great military leader. Not really. He might have led the Third Crusade (1189-1192) but he failed to regain control of Jerusalem and then, on his way home again, he managed to get himself kidnapped by the King of Germany Henry VI. The ransom was 150,000 marks (100,000 pounds of silver) which was two or three times the annual income of the English crown, so Richard's mum Eleanor of Aquitaine (1122-1204) raised the money by confiscating the church's gold and introducing new taxes for noblemen and landowners. Everyone was expected to find a few pennies to help raise the money needed to free her son. Richard has always been portrayed as a benevolent monarch and a paragon of Christian virtues but this was entirely due to the remarkable PR campaign waged by his mum to help raise the ransom money. Richard eventually returned to England where he was re-crowned king at Winchester on 17 April 1194 to divert attention away from the shame of the kidnap ordeal and reassert his authority as king after his younger brother John (1166-1216) had plotted against him to seize the throne. (Whilst his mum had been doing everything possible to free Richard from his kidnappers, John had been doing everything possible to keep him locked up! He'd been enjoying himself too much as 'interim king' and together with King Philip of France they'd offered King Henry 80,000 marks to keep him imprisoned for another few more years!)

It's also highly unlikely that Richard was best mates with the legendary outlaw Robin Hood. He might have visited Sherwood Forest but there's no historical evidence to suggest that the two men ever met. Probably because Robin Hood never actually existed!

Richard had an obligation to provide England with an heir to the throne, But he didn't do that either. He never really had much interest in women and wasn't in any hurry to get married despite the long line of eligible princesses queueing up to become Mrs Lionheart. There was no queen at his coronation with his mum standing by his side instead. The only woman to whom he really showed any consideration.

He didn't even die a glorious, heroic death befitting a medieval knight …

In March 1199, he was busy suppressing a revolt by King Philip's ally Viscount Aimar V of Limoges in southwest-central France. According to the medieval chronicler Ralph of Coggeshall he 'devastated the Viscount's land with fire and sword' and then lay siege to a fairly insignificant little fortress called Château de Châlus-Chabrol near Châlus. For three days Richard ordered the castle walls to be attacked and it was during this time that a French bowman, Pierre Basile spotted him wandering around outside the castle's perimeter not wearing his chain mail, so he fired off an arrow which hit him in the left shoulder. His wound was dressed with herbs and plasters but his condition worsened over the next few days and he died of septicaemia on 6 April 1199.

(Before his death, when the castle had fallen, Richard had asked to see the bowman. Pierre expected to be executed there and then but as a final act of mercy, Richard forgave him and ordered that he be set free with a 100 shilling reward. But Pierre's good fortune didn't last for very long. As soon as Richard had taken his last breath, the notorious Occitan mercenary Mercadier who was in Richard's service, had Pierre flayed alive and then hanged! Doubtless he kept the 100 shillings for himself too.)

As was the custom at the time, Richard's body was chopped up and buried in different parts of his kingdom. His heart was buried in Rouen, his entrails in Châlus and the rest of him alongside his father Henry II (1133-1189) at Fontevraud Abbey near Chinon. England didn't get any part of him with Richard seemingly just as absent in death as he was in life!

So, Richard the Lionheart didn't like England, he probably couldn't speak English and spent almost all of his reign outside of England; his crusade was a failure, he got himself kidnapped (and bankrupted England in the process), he was a bit of a mummy's boy and his brother thought he was a big wuss; he wasn't a friend of Robin Hood, his death was hugely embarrassing and he wasn't even buried in England.

Perhaps he wasn't quite as great as we all thought.

the long arm of the law

The ormer is a shellfish and is considered a delicacy in the Channel Islands. However, a decline in their numbers in recent years has led to a strictly controlled harvesting season and anyone caught illegally gathering them can expect a big fine or even a prison sentence.

On 31 December 1968, a passer-by spotted a diver off the coast of Castle Cornet in Guernsey about 40 feet (12m) under the water apparently collecting ormers out of season and dutifully informed the authorities. PC David Archer was then sent to the scene and dived into the water. He immediately spotted the culprit, tapped him on the shoulder and made the world's first underwater arrest!

operation mincemeat

Operation Mincemeat was coordinated by two British Intelligence officers Ewen Montagu (1901-1985) and Charles Cholmondeley (1917-1982) to fool the Germans into thinking that the Allied invasion of Europe during World War II (1939-1945) would begin with an attack on Greece and Sardinia.

They obtained the dead body of a homeless man, Glyndwr Michael (1909-1943), dressed him up as a Royal Marines officer, stuffed his uniform full of pocket litter, chained a briefcase full of fake secret documents to his wrist and then had him dumped in the sea off the coast of Huelva in Spain. The pocket litter included personal photographs, love letters from an invented fiancée called Pam, scraps of paper, a book of stamps, cigarettes, keys, an old ticket stub from a London theatre and a naval ID card identifying him as the fictitious Major William Martins. The briefcase he was carrying contained documents which appeared to detail a planned Allied invasion of southern Europe through Greece and Sardinia.

The body had been transported to the Spanish coastline on the submarine HMS *Seraph* and lowered into the sea. Early in the morning of 30 April 1943, it was discovered by local fishermen and the British Vice-Consul Francis Haselden was notified. He reported back to the Admiralty in London that the body had been found, knowing full well that his encrypted message would be intercepted by the Germans. In a series of planned and pre-scripted diplomatic cables, the Vice-Consul was then informed that the briefcase contained highly sensitive and secretive documents and had to be recovered at all costs.

Meanwhile, the local Spanish pathologists were cajoled by the Vice-Consul into giving the body of Major William Martins just a quick once over. As a consequence, they failed to spot that it was actually a three-month old corpse lying on their examination table and declared the cause of death as asphyxiation through immersion in the sea.

Karl-Erich Kühlenthal, one of the senior German military intelligence officers operating in Spain, got to hear about the dead marine and his briefcase full of top secret documents and persuaded his boss Wilhelm Canaris to contact the Spanish authorities and ask them to take a quick look inside the briefcase before handing it back to the British.

Despite a British request for the briefcase to be returned immediately, they knew perfectly well the Spanish would ignore them, examine the documents and report their findings to the German military. The Spanish didn't let them down. They removed the still-damp documents from the wax-sealed envelopes by tightly winding them around a cylindrical shaped probe and pulling them out through the envelope flaps. The documents were dried, photographed and soaked in salt water again before being carefully inserted back into the envelopes and placed in the briefcase. The photographs were then passed to the Germans and the briefcase returned to the British Vice-Consul, who forwarded it to London in a diplomatic bag.

Back in Britain, the documents were forensically examined. Fibres in the paper had been damaged but more importantly, a single eyelash which had deliberately been placed in one of the envelopes was missing! To complete the hoax, another encrypted cable which the British authorities knew would be intercepted and decoded by the Germans was sent from London to the Vice-Consul stating that the envelopes HAD NOT been tampered with and all was well. The Vice-Consul then leaked this information to German sympathisers in Spain just to make sure that everyone believed that the British had been duped into thinking their invasion plans hadn't yet been discovered.

On 14 May 1943, a German communication was decrypted by the good folks at the Government Code & Cypher School, Bletchley Park warning about a possible Allied invasion in the Balkans. A message was sent by the secretary of the Chiefs of Staff Committee Leslie Hollis (1897-1963) to Winston Churchill (1874-1965) who was visiting the USA at the time: 'Mincemeat swallowed rod, line and sinker by the right people and from the best information they look like acting on it.' The deception was further reinforced when a list of recent British casualties was published in *The Times* on 4 June 1943 and included amongst the names was Major William Martins of the Royal Marines.

Throughout June 1943, the German military began moving troops, U-boats, tanks and aircraft around Europe in preparation for Allied attacks in Greece and Sardinia. Then on 9 July 1943, 400,000 British and American troops invaded Sicily. The expected ninety-day *Operation Husky* lasted only 38 days with the island falling to the Allies on 17 August 1943.

the theory of space flight

More than three hundred years before the Soviet Union launched the first Sputnik satellite (1957) and the Americans put a man on the Moon (1969), the eminent English scientist and theologian John Wilkins (1614-1672) wrote the first serious description of space travel.

He was inspired by the great explorers of the time such as Francis Drake (c.1540-1596) and Walter Raleigh (c.1554-1618) who had embarked on epic voyages of discovery to unknown lands. In his book *The Discovery of a World in the Moone* (1638) he explained why he believed the Moon to be inhabited and outlined his design for a flying chariot (with flapping wings coated in feathers and powered by clockwork, springs and gunpowder boosters) which would be capable of reaching the Moon's surface. He also included a few handy tips for communicating with alien beings and even a process for setting up trade agreements with them!

John was a polymath and a founder of the Royal Society (1660) so presumably people just believed everything he wrote.

the last laugh

The Anglo-Irish comedian/writer, Spike Milligan (1918-2002) died on 27 February 2002. He was probably most famous for being the co-creator, writer and cast member of the BBC radio programme *The Goon Show* (1951-1960) and for writing seven autobiographical novels beginning with *Adolf Hitler: My Part in His Downfall* (1971).

Even after death, his wicked sense of humour never deserted him …

But his overwhelming desire to make people laugh from the hereafter inadvertently led to a dispute between his family and the local church diocese after they were told of the proposed wording for his headstone at St Thomas's Church, Winchelsea in East Sussex.

Eventually a compromise was reached. The wording which the church was so reluctant to accept could be written in Gaelic, reflecting the comedian's Irish heritage, but at the same time, masking its true meaning to the majority of people who would visit the graveyard.

The temporary headstone which had marked his grave up until this point was finally replaced with the permanent headstone bearing the inscription:

'Duirt me leat go raibh me breoite!' (I told you I was ill).

THE END

BIBLIOGRAPHY

about1816.wordpress.com
aboutthebeatles.com
aclerkofoxford.blogspot.com
allthathistory.com
allthatsinteresting.com
alphahistory.com
amusingplanet.com
ancient-origins.net
aristocraticfury.substack.com
arthur-conan-doyle.com
astonshaw.co.uk
athleticsweekly.com
atlasobscura.com
autocar.co.uk
bakerstreet.fandom.com
bartitsusociety.com
bbc.com
bbc.co.uk
bloodcancer.org.uk
bmmhs.org
bristolmuseums.org.uk
britannica.com
britishmuseum.org
chippingcampdenonline.org
cnn.com
commonplacefacts.com
cornwallforever.co.uk
countrylife.co.uk
cumbriaguide.co.uk
curiousrambler.com
daily.jstor.org
dailymail.co.uk
dailypost.co.uk
dappledthings.org
dawlishchronicles.blogspot.com
discoveryuk.com
donttakepictures.com
eatsleepliveherefordshire.co.uk
edp24.co.uk
en.wikipedia.org
everything-everywhere.com
exclassics.com
exeter-cathedral.org.uk
exploring-london.com
express.co.uk
facebook.com
felinfach.com
fourfourtwo.com
fveverleigh.com
georgianera.wordpress.com
geriwalton.com
gla.ac.uk
greatbritishcoast.com
greatnorthroad.co.uk
guernseydonkey.com
guinnessworldrecords.com
hauntedpalaceblog.com
his-ill-fated-wives.wixsite.com
historicengland.org.uk
historiclondontours.com
historicmysteres.com
historic-uk.com
historyandimagination.com
history.co.uk
historyextra.com
history.gg
historyguild.org
historyhit.com
history.howstuffworks.com
historynet.com
historyofnothing.wordpress.com
historyofparliament.com
historytheinterestingbits.com
historytoday.com
hoaxes.org
horridhackney.com
hrp.org.uk
independent.co.uk
inews.co.uk
ingliando.net
inostalgia.co.uk
janeaustenslondon.com
lady.co.uk
laughlab.co.uk
londonist.com
londonmuseum.org.uk
manorialcounselltd.co.uk
mcnaught.orpheusweb.co.uk
medieval.eu
medievalists.net

medievaltraveler.net
medium.com
mentalfloss.com
murderpedia.org
museumofhealthcare.blog
myartbroker.com
mymacabreroadtrip.com
mythicalireland.com
nationalpost.com
networkrail.co.uk
news.artnet.com
news.bbc.co.uk
newscientist.com
nms.ac.uk
nowiknow.com
npr.org
oldedinburghclub.org.uk
olivercromwell.org
olympics.com
originalshrewsbury.co.uk
oxfordhistory.org.uk
oxfordvisit.com
pastmedicalhistory.co.uk
peter-moore.co.uk
postalmuseum.org
publicdomainreview.org
raithrovers.net
regencyhistory.net
retrospectjournal.com
riflemantours.co.uk
rigb.org
rmg.co.uk
ryesown.co.uk
sagasofshe.wordpress.com
sal.org.uk
scmp.com
scortonarrow.com
scotsman.com
slate.com
smithsonianmag.com
spartacus-educational.com
stand-and-deliver.org.uk
strandmag.com
telegraph.co.uk
theaviationgeekclub.com
thebritishacademy.ac.uk
thecollector.com
theconversation.com
thecourier.co.uk
theguardian.com
thehistoryoflondon.co.uk
thehistorypress.co.uk
thehistoryreader.com
thesefootballtimes.co
thetudorenthusiast.weebly.com
thetudorials.com
theyorkhistorian.com
theyorkshirejournal.wordpress.com
thisdayinaviation.com
todayifoundout.com
topendsports.com
turbulentisles.com
ukmythology.wordpress.com
ultrarunninghistory.com
utterlyinteresting.com
vauxhallhistory.org
vice.com
visitnorfolk.co.uk
vox.com
voyagerofhistory.wordpress.com
walesonline.co.uk
warfarehistorynetwork.com
warhistoryonline.com
warhistory.org
wbur.org
webhispania.info
westaucklandtownafc.co.uk
westerntelegraph.co.uk
westminster-abbey.org
whitehavenandwesternlakeland.co.uk
windowthroughtime.wordpress.com
worldathletics.org
wrongsideoftheblanket.com

www.ingramcontent.com/pod-product-compliance
Lightning Source LLC
LaVergne TN
LVHW020528100826
845148LV00010B/1388

9781845832605